Authentic Metaphysics in an Age of Unreality

Leo Sweeney, S.J.

with William J. Carroll
and John J. Furlong

Authentic Metaphysics in an Age of Unreality

Second Edition

Wipf & Stock
PUBLISHERS
Eugene, Oregon

Wipf and Stock Publishers
199 W 8th Ave, Suite 3
Eugene, OR 97401

Authentic Metaphysics in an Age of Unreality, Second Edition
By Sweeney, Leo, Carroll, William J., and Furlong, John J.

ISBN 13: 978-1-59752-215-1
ISBN 10: 1-59752-215-5
Publication date 3/7/2007
Previously published by Peter Lang, 1996

Contents

Preface vii

Part I: Introduction

I. Metaphysics a Valid Science? 3
1. Contemporary Opponents of Metaphysics.
2. Broader Description of "Science."
3. "Evidence of a Different Sort."
4. Methodology.
5. Summary and Conclusions.

II. Lessons from Heraclitus and Plato 17
1. An Initial Reaction: Thales.
2. Heraclitus and Radical Existentialism.
3. Plato and Radical Essentialism.
4. Summary and Conclusions.

III. Lessons from Aristotle 41
1. "Diverse Evidences Indicate . . ."
2. Unity.
3. Change/Stability in the Accidental Order.
4. Change/Stability in the Substantial Order.
5. Summary and Conclusions.

Part II: Primacy of Existence

IV. Existence and Essence 73
1. Position of Thomas Aquinas.
2. Two Initial Considerations: What Is a Real Distinction? What Is "Actual Existence"?
3. The Crucial Question. Actual Existence Is Not Efficiency; Actual Existence Other Than Quiddity.
4. The Process.
5. Summary and Conclusions.
6. Act and Potency.

V. Primacy of Existence in Existents 109
1. "Existence Precedes Essence."
2. Actual Existence and Other Perfections.
3. Actual Existence and Autodetermination: Which Components Are Autodetermining? Conclusions.
4. Actual Existence and Amateriality: Materiality; Immateriality.
5. Summary and Conclusions.
6. Actual Existence and God.

VI. Primacy of Existence in Metaphysical Knowledge 141
1. Actual Existence and "Being."
2. The Analogy of Being.
3. Actual Existence and Other Transcendents: As Known Spontaneously, Metaphysically.

4. Actual Existence and Evil.
5. Actual Existence and the Individual: Data from Revelation; The Principle of Individuation.
6. Summary and Conclusions.

VII. Existence and Relations 201
1. The Relational Situation.
2. The Affirmative Reply.
3. The Negative Reply.
4. The Predicaments.
5. Summary and Conclusions.

Part III: Causality

VIII. Efficient Causality 235
1. Six Causal Factors.
2. Some Corollaries.
3. Co-operation with God.
4. The Efficient Cause Proposition.
5. Summary and Conclusions.

IX. Final Causality 267
1. Several Opinions.
2. Finality on the Cognitive Level.
3. Finality on the Noncognitive Level.
4. Chance in the Universe.
5. Summary and Conclusions.
6. Exemplary Causality.

Part IV: Metaphysics as a Science

X. Separation and Knowledge of the Real 321
1. Metaphysics and Separation.
2. Twofold Description of Knowledge.
3. First Description: Intellectual Operations Involved.
4. Second Description of Philosophic Knowledge: Abstraction.
5. Summary and Conclusions.

XI. Recent Developments in Metaphysics, by John J. Furlong 353
1. Whitehead's Cosmology.
2. Empiricism, Positivism, and Beyond.
3. Existentialism and Beyond.
4. Summary.

Appendices

A. Jacques Maritain on Existence/Essence 393
B. How the Meaning of "Being" Is Worked Out 401
C. Aquinas on Separation 405

Indices

Index of Names 411
Index of Topics 417

Preface

Authentic Metaphysics in an Age of Unreality, originally titled *A Metaphysics of Authentic Existentialism,* has resulted from nearly three decades of teaching metaphysics and is so conceived and written as to be both a textbook and a scholarly tradebook. But why the change in title? Because a characteristic of the 1950s and '60s has become even more prominent in the subsequent decades—namely, unreality. What does this noun mean, and why is it applicable especially to our times? Because so much of what is going on now is phony, misleading, deceitful: it is not authentically and actually what it seems and pretends to be and thus is unreal.

An Age of Unreality

As an example, take television, which can on occasion provide worthwhile entertainment and information, but its daily soap operas almost constantly put across false and misleading views of what genuine success for human beings consists in (e.g., sexual license, abortion, divorce), and are interrupted by commercials for products (e.g., detergents, cosmetics, franchise foods, and so on) that promise extravagant and (at best) superficial solutions to life's problems. Or consider the "religious" programs, where, as scandals revealed, ministers used their glamorous preaching to fleece their TV audiences of millions and millions of dollars to finance their own plush life-styles.

To be aware of another instance where appearances are deceiving, visit our contemporary schools, which may have impressive buildings, fine athletic teams, state-of-the-art computer systems but where competence in basic skills and knowledges is often lacking, where use of drugs and alcohol is commonplace, where no moral or religious education is or can be attempted.[1] Or visit our courtrooms, where lawyers and judges often go through the motions of seeking and dispensing justice but instead are giving and accepting—even demanding—payoffs for unjust decisions, as the Greylord and other undercover investigations disclose. Or visit Wall Street or other Boards of Trade, upon whose integrity the financial well-being of America and, for that matter, of much of the Western world depends but which are currently revealed to be places of personal greed and crooked inside trading.

Or inspect our hospitals, where the Hippocratic Oath is a sham when doctors there perform abortions, where even the most promising technological revolutions in the biological sciences have led to consequences quite different from hopeful expectations: the burgeoning research in genetics and biomedicine has underwritten the sexual revolution, which paradoxically has led to fear of intimacy, as well as to chimerical and exotic bioethical problems, some involving questioning the very notion of motherhood itself (surrogacy, in vitro fertilization, frozen embryos, artificial wombs, etc.), and the very definition of death.

Or follow a candidate for a political office (whether in the city, state or national arena) and listen to his promises and then observe how few he implements when elected and how political expediency and hope of reelection rather than genuine wisdom and concern for the common good guide his decisions. Or take a good look at our cities next time you fly over them. From a distance how prosperous they can look with their imposing skylines, smoothly flowing traffic, green parks, row on row of well-kept homes but how tenuous their financial future is, given the default of payments on loans by Third World countries, the national debt itself and unbalanced budget, even the credit card indebtedness of individual families. How safe their streets seem from a distance and yet how few areas there are where one may safely walk because of gang violence and other crimes or which are free of the threat of AIDS, the ubiquitous killer once thought to be the plight of a few but now targeting more and more of the general population.

---

[1] See Allan Bloom, *The Closing of the American Mind: How Higher Education Has Failed Democracy and Impoverished the Souls of Today's Students* (New York: Simon and Schuster, 1987), who finds Friedrich Nietzsche, Sigmund Freud and Martin Heidegger to be responsible for much of the intellectual malaise in our schools and elsewhere.

How secure our country itself may seem in this post–Cold War era, but are we? According to R. C. Longworth, "New World Disorder" (*Chicago Tribune*, November 22, 1992),

> probably never before has the governent of every major nation [including the U.S.A.] been so weak. At no time since the end of World War II have these governments been so fixated on their own domestic woes and so disinclined to work together to solve the world's problems. Yet these problems—from civil war in former Yugoslavia to famine in Somalia to chaos in post-Soviet Russia to battles over world trade—won't go away.

He then added:

> The Cold War ended in dreams of new cooperation, led by the U.S., Europe and Japan, to build a new world order. Few realized that the Cold War itself created cooperation. With no common enemy, the allies began to scratch domestic itches at the expense of larger problems. . . . A result is that this concentration on national navels only makes each government weaker, not stronger.

Such weakness on the international level, plus our inability or unwillingness to see things in our own nation and elsewhere as they really are, puts us in a perilous situation.

What can be done? As a start and of great importance, we must come to see things (events, trends, cultures, individual persons, nations) *as they actually are* and not as they are made to appear to be. We must not be taken in by the pretense, sham, deception in all the areas listed above. Then help, remedies, solutions *based on wisdom, truth and objective values* must be sought and this from many quarters—churches, educational institutions, governments on all levels, civic organizations, communication media, once these have imbibed from sources of such wisdom and truth.

Authentic Metaphysics

One such font is, let me suggest, the contents of this book: authentic metaphysics or, expressed more fully, a metaphysics of authentic existentialism. Why can it help in our age of unreality? Because it results precisely and entirely from taking things as they actually are. Its methodology aims at cutting through deception. It realizes that actual existents, of whatever sort, are the very content-determining causes of our knowledge.[2] It studies existents as they themselves concretely are and act and are acted upon. It deciphers the evidences which such concrete cases give off and thereby discovers that reality is actual existence wherever found. Only what is actual is real and, thereby, true, valuable and worthwhile. Anything else is unreal.

This realization *Authentic Metaphysics in an Age of Unreality* presents to its readers and can thus help dispel the prevailing fog of unreality blanketing so much of our contemporary societies by offering valid and objective views on reality as coterminous with actuality, with what actually is (Chs. I–V). Subsequently it considers God (Ch. V, Sec. 6; Ch. VI, Secs. 2 and 3; Ch. VIII, Sec. 3; Ch. IX, Secs. 2b2 and 3b2); the true, good and beautiful (Ch. VI, Sec. 3); human existents as individual (Ch. VI, Sec. 5); the nature of the family and other relational units (Ch. VII); agents and their goal-tendency and -seeking (Chs. VIII and IX); chance (Ch. IX, Sec. 4) and evil (Ch. VI, Sec. 4); the nature of knowledge as the situation by which the knower becomes and is the known (Ch. X). In all these areas it stands in contrast with other contemporary metaphysics, which provide no valid or lasting responses to the unreality of our era and may even have contributed to its relativism, subjectivism and nihilism—namely, radical existentialism (see Ch. II, Sec. 2; Ch. V, Sec. 1), phenomenology, hermeneutics, deconstructionism (Ch. XI).

How, then, can *Authentic Metaphysics in an Age of Unreality* best be used? As a textbook and also as a scholarly tradebook.

A Textbook and a Tradebook

Because this book is a textbook, it endeavors to be as clear and as pedagogically helpful as is possible with difficult subject matter. Pedagogy suggested the use of history (see Chs. I–III; IV, Sec. 1) as a means of introducing students to philosophical problems and to

---

[2] In this realization it opposes any Kantian position on knowledge, in which the knower constructs what is known by imposing upon sense data the *a priori* forms of Space and Time and the Categories of substance, cause, effect, reality and so on. Accordingly, in Kantian epistemology one does not know existents as they are in themselves and outside the mind—that is, as noumena—but only as they are worked upon by the knower, as phenomena, *as they appear*—in fact, as they are (literally) *made* to appear. Manifestly, Immanuel Kant is an ancestor too, besides those named by Bloom (see note 1 above), of our contemporary intellectual, emotional, religious and moral climate.

a philosophic approach in answering them. Yet one should remember that history here is only a means. The historical sections do not always present a full picture of the philosophers studied. Some elements of their position may be emphasized, others down-played or even passed over in silence (for example, see our remarks on Sartre, Ch. II, n. 10), but references are given to other studies where students may supplement their knowledge.

Pedagogy also advised the length and make-up of the chapter on Aristotle (Ch. III: "Lessons from Aristotle"). His philosophy of nature (with respect, at least, to substance/accidents and matter/form compositions in material things) still seems true. Hence, rather detailed attention is given it in that chapter and those components are not treated as such in any subsequent chapter.

Good pedagogy also demanded that the book should develop organically. Besides the use of history already mentioned, this organic development is achieved by moving from the known to what is unknown. In Parts Two to Four this movement is implemented by the use of frequent examples and concrete cases. These provide the data, the evidence which stimulates teacher and student alike to think philosophically and which eventually ushers them toward both answers and conclusions—in a word, toward a philosophic position. Concrete examples are absolutely necessary, if we are to understand anything as it actually is. Without them, a student may parrot terms, memorize definitions, and repeat conclusions, but he will not have thought or philosophized.

As every teacher has experienced, students vary greatly in talent and the time allotted to metaphysics also varies from college to college. Consequently, not all of the sections in this book need be taken in class. Those paragraphs and sections marked with an asterisk may conveniently be assigned to better students as additional reading or for written reports and discussion.

This book also contains a good deal of material on God—for example, Ch. V, Sec 6: that God exists and the sort of existent He is; Ch. VI, Sec. 2: God and the transcendents of truth, goodness and beauty; Ch. VIII, Sec. 3: God and the analogy of being; Ch. VI, Sec. 3: God as proper cause of existence, with whom creatures co-operate; Ch. IX, Secs. 2b2 and 3b2: God and finality on the cognitive and noncognitive levels; Ch. IX, Sec. 4: God and chance. The result is that it can be used also for a course of philosophy of God (either separate from or together with general metaphysics) and philosophy of religion.

But *Authentic Metaphysics in An Age of Unreality* is also an original and scholarly tradebook which includes discussions, for instance, on autodetermination, which solves the problem of how essence can be real but still be subordinated to existence and of how form helps individuate a material existent (Ch. V, Sec. 3, and Ch. VI, Sec. 5); on existence as amaterial (Ch. V, Sec. 4); on quantity as presential cause of several real relationships and on relations as accidental perfections but not accidental forms (Ch. VII); on the fact that abstraction is not a mental activity, as generally held, but describes the content of our intellectual awarenesses (Ch. X); on other contemporary trends in metaphysics, such as process philosophy, analytic philosophy, hermeneutics and deconstructionism (Ch. XI); on "authentic" existentialism (in which whatever actually exists is real) as confronting the "radical" existentialism (in which "existence" is restricted to human agents while freely choosing) of Sartre, Camus, Marcel, etc. (Ch. II, Sec. 2; Ch. V, Sec. 1).

Some Words of Thanks and Dedication

I am deeply indebted to Henri J. Renard, S.J., who was my first teacher in philosophy, and to Etienne Gilson, who was my last. Thanks are due also to Dr. Anton Pegis, Fathers Joseph Owens, Armand Maurer, and to other faculty members at the Pontifical Institute of Mediaeval Studies and the University of Toronto, as well as to Francis A. Preuss, S.J., of St. Louis University. I must also thank Dr. William J. Carroll for help with the first printing and Dr. John J. Furlong for writing Ch. XI: "Recent Developments in Metaphysics"; Joseph A. Mordente, whose careful reading of the first printing greatly improves the book in its current version; Suzanne Mazurek and Erin Milnes for their computer expertise in preparing the camera-ready copy for the second printing; Carol Szablewski for proofreading and helping with the Indices.

I dedicate this book to those who made sure I look at things as they actually are: my parents (Ellen Theresa [McDowell] and John Michael Sweeney) and to my brothers and sisters (Bernard, Mary, Daniel, Elizabeth, John, Bernice and Paul).

Leo Sweeney, S.J.
December 8, 1992

Part I

Introduction

I

Metaphysics a Valid Science?

In antiquity metaphysics was described by many complimentary terms.[1] It was called a "theology" because it attempted to find and furnish knowledge about God. It was also named an "ontology" inasmuch as the extent of its study was as wide and varied as being itself—indeed, its material object was all beings and its formal object, all beings considered precisely as beings. Moreover, a metaphysician was termed a "philosopher"—literally, one who loved wisdom. In fact, he was "first philosopher," and the addition of the adjective implied that the wisdom to which he aspired was most important because it involved God, the First Cause, and was man's greatest achievement in the merely human order. But what is more, it suggested that his wisdom had a genuine pre-eminence over other philosophical disciplines (such as philosophy of nature, ethics, and others), which received from it some of their basic notions.[2] Actually, too, the term "metaphysics" pointed to the valuable and unique nature of the science. In the phrase, *meta ta physica,* the Greek preposition *meta* means "beyond," and thus "metaphysics" expressed that the science so described was beyond the physical science of cosmology (and, for that matter, all other physical sciences) insofar as it

---

[1] See Jacques Maritain, *An Introduction to Philosophy* (New York: Sheed & Ward, n.d.), p. 17 sq. and p. 102 sq.; Daniel J. Sullivan, *An Introduction to Philosophy* (Milwaukee: Bruce Publishing Co., 1957), p. 1 sq.

[2] For example, ethics deals with marriage, the family, the state, each of which basically is the complex of real relations between the members. Metaphysics properly investigates real relations—what they are, what causes them, whether they are distinct from their causes, and so forth. Hence, metaphysics provides a general theory of relations to the ethician.

treated of God, of being qua being, and of other topics which transcend the merely physical and material.[3]

In the remote past, then, metaphysics was looked upon with great favor, and anyone who endeavored to become a metaphysician was considered to be aiming at a worthwhile goal.

1. Contemporary Opponents of Metaphysics

Currently, though, many hold metaphysics to be of little or no value. True enough, some of these need not be taken seriously, because they themselves are not philosophers and hence probably do not know much about metaphysics. Take as an example H. L. Mencken, the American journalist and satirist, for whom "metaphysics is almost always an attempt to prove the incredible by an appeal to the unintelligible."[4] His judgment can be easily set aside in view of the fact that Mencken himself was no philosopher in any strict sense of the word and marshals no rigorous defense of his position. So too with the novelist and essayist, Aldous Huxley, according to whom "the Other World—the world of metaphysics and religion—can never possibly be as interesting as this world and for an obvious reason. The Other World is an invention of the human fancy and shows the limitations of its creator."[5] The many undergraduates who know little more after a semester of metaphysics than they knew before also fit into this group.[6]

---

[3] See J. Owens, *Doctrine of Being in the Aristotelian Metaphysics* (3rd Ed.) (Toronto: Pontifical Institute of Mediaeval Studies, 1978), pp. 73–74; Anton-Hermann Chroust, "The Origin of 'Metaphysics,'" *Review of Metaphysics*, 14 (June, 1961), 601–16; J. Owens, *An Elementary Christian Metaphysics* (Milwaukee: Bruce Publishing Co., 1963), pp. 1–3.

[4] *Minority Report* (New York: Alfred A. Knopf, Inc. 1956), p. 238. *Ibid.*, p. 56: "The capacity of human beings to bore one another seems to be vastly greater than that of any other animals. Some of their most esteemed inventions have no other apparent purpose, for example, the dinner party of more than two, the epic poem, and the science of metaphysics." Also see *ibid.*, pp. 46, 48, 178, 248.

[5] A. Huxley, *Jesting Pilate* (New York: Harper & Row Publishers, 1926), p. 130.

[6] Take as an example this verdict passed by an anonymous student and reported by Archie J. Bahm, *Philosophy: An Introduction* (New York: John Wiley & Sons, Inc., 1953), p. 1: "The term philosophy [read: metaphysics] conveys to most people a vagueness and uncertainty. . . . It is a collection of

But metaphysics has other opponents who do deserve serious consideration precisely because they themselves are philosophers and argue their case rigorously. One such is the German-born American author, Rudolph Carnap: "The danger lies in the deceptive character of metaphysics; it gives the illusion of knowledge without actually giving any knowledge."[7] Another is the British writer, A. J. Ayer, for whom every metaphysician inevitably and unwittingly writes sheer nonsense:

> It is in fact very rare for a literary artist to produce sentences which have no literal meaning. And where this does occur, the sentences are carefully chosen for their rhythm and balance. If the author writes nonsense, it is because he considers it most suitable for bringing about the effects for which his writing is designed. The metaphysician, on the other hand, does not intend to write nonsense. He lapses into it through being deceived by grammar, or through committing errors of reasoning.[8]

In fact, philosophers such as Carnap and Ayer have established an anti-metaphysical tradition within contemporary philosophy which has grown stronger over the last decades.[9]

Why do such opponents so belittle metaphysics? Primarily because for them it is not a genuine, valid science.[10] And why this?

---

high-flown, meaningless words and phrases on useless subjects." Or this clever comparison: "A metaphysician is like a blind man in a dark room, looking for a black cat—which isn't there" (B. Hagspiel, *Smiles and Chuckles* [Techny, Illinois: Mission Press, 1952], p. 1).

7 R. Carnap, *Philosophy and Logical Syntax* (London: K. Paul Trench Trubner and Co., Ltd., 1935), p. 20. See also W. v. O. Quine, *Word and Object* (Cambridge, Mass.: M.I.T. Press, 1960), Ch. 7 for another and more recent variation of Carnap's position. See Ch. XI *passim* for a more detailed overview of recent developments in metaphysics.

8 A. J. Ayer, *Language, Truth and Logic* (2nd Ed.) (London: V. Gollancz, Ltd., 1951), p. 45.

9 See Richard Rorty, *Philosophy and the Mirror of Nature* (Princeton, N.J.: Princeton University Press, 1979). Rorty attacks not only metaphysics but also epistemology and the very role of philosophy in human culture. For critical reviews of Rorty's position, see Hubert L. Dreyfus, "Holism and Hermeneutics," *The Review of Metaphysics*, 34 (1980), 3–24, and Charles Taylor, "Understanding in Human Science," *The Review of Metaphysics*, 34 (1980), 25–38.

10 See R. G. Collingwood, *An Essay on Metaphysics* (Oxford: Clarendon Press, 1940), pp. 15–16: "The science of pure being [metaphysics] cannot be

Because a genuine science can, they maintain, be based only upon the quantitative, the measurable. Physics, chemistry, experimental psychology, and other empiriological studies[11] are rooted in such evidence and, accordingly, are valid bodies of knowledge. But metaphysics as traditionally conceived obviously is not built upon such evidence and, consequently, cannot be listed as a valid science.[12]

---

called a science in the sense in which an ordinary science is so called . . . [because] the 'science of pure being' has a subject matter which is not a something but a nothing. . . . This is only a roundabout way of saying that there can be no such science. There is not even a quasi-science of pure being; not even a thing which in certain ways resembles an ordinary science and in certain ways differs from it. . . . There is not even a pseudo-science of pure being."

[11] We use "empiriological" here to refer to an area of research (1) which studies material things (hence, the force of the initial syllables in the adjective, "*empirio*logical"), but (2) only as affected by some sort of human activity (hence, the force of the last syllables, "empirio*logical*"). Because of this second factor every empiriological science is constructural.

Contemporary physics is an example of an empiriological science because (1) it is concerned with the structure and activities of material things, (2) but only under laboratory conditions and as mathematically formulated. Although constructural, mathematics or logic is not empiriological science because each lacks the first factor. Although it directly studies actual existents, metaphysics will turn out not to be empiriological because it is not a constructural knowledge.

On constructural knowledge, see Ch. VI, n. 10; Ch. X, Sec. 4. On empiriological knowledge, see Jacques Maritain, *Degrees of Knowledge,* trans. Gerald B. Phelan (New York: Charles Scribner's Sons, 1959), pp. 202–5; Louis de Raeymaeker, "The One Voice of Science and the Many Voices of Philosophy," *Philosophy Today*, 5 (1961), 83–91; Alden L. Fisher, "The Contemporary Status of Scholastic Psychology," *Proceedings of the American Catholic Philosophical Association*, 31 (1957), 144–56; G. P. Klubertanz, S.J., *Introduction to the Philosophy of Being* (2nd Ed.) (New York: Appleton-Century-Crofts, 1963), pp. 290–93; *idem, Philosophy of Human Nature* (New York: Appleton-Century-Crofts, 1953), pp. 388–96.

[12] For example, see Richard von Mises, *Positivism: A Study in Human Understanding* (Cambridge, Mass.: Harvard University Press, 1951), p. 271: "Contemporary metaphysics often claims to provide an indispensable supplement to the present-day stage of the positive sciences. We reply to this that, wherever science shows gaps and a need for further and deeper elucidation, this elucidation cannot be reached in any other way than that of scientific research, and as soon as it is attained, it will form another part of the positive sciences." Earlier: "Our position seems, in any case, to be in opposition to metaphysics: . . . in our rejection of a 'bifurcation' of the world, in which one part is reserved for the positive sciences, and the other for a purely speculative study" (p. 62). Also see Bertrand Russell, *History of Western Philosophical*

Hence, any young man or woman who aims at studying metaphysics is simply wasting time and energy.[13]

What should be our reaction to such opposition? First, let us gladly acknowledge that the various branches of chemistry, physics, and other empiriological disciplines are, in their own way and within their own areas, genuine sciences and are extremely valuable for a progressive understanding and mastery of the material universe. Second, we should be grateful to our opponents for forcing us at the very outset to take nothing for granted and to face the extremely important and difficult question: can metaphysics be as valid a "science" as those empiriological studies? At the very outset one thing is also clear: to answer affirmatively we cannot grant their equation of "science" with "empiriological science." We cannot accept their restriction of science to knowledge based solely on the quantitative and the measurable. Rather, we must work out a more ample notion. We must attempt to elaborate a description of "science" which is broad enough to fit metaphysics as well as mathematical and empiriological fields of knowledge.

Thought (London: George Allen & Unwin. Ltd., 1940), p. 864: "Many questions, formerly obscured by the fog of metaphysics, can be answered with precision, and by objective methods which introduce nothing of the philosopher's temperament except the desire to understand. . . . In the welter of conflicting fanaticisms, one of the few unifying forces is scientific truthfulness, by which I mean the habit of basing our beliefs upon observations and inferences as impersonal . . . as is possible for human beings."

[13] Some of the contemporary authors we have been mentioning do concede a place within the curriculum to metaphysics when understood as "a spirit or method of approaching experience, rather than a body of conclusions about experience" (E. S. Brightman) or as a "general theory of criticism" (C. J. Ducasse) or as "an historical science . . . [whose] business is to find out what absolute presuppositions have actually been made by various persons at various times in doing various pieces of scientific thinking" (R. G. Collingwood, *An Essay on Metaphysics*, p. 60). (The quotations of Brightman and Ducasse are from A. J. Bahm, *Philosophy: An Introduction*, p. 2, where I interpret "philosophy" as synonymous with "metaphysics.")

What these critics reject is a metaphysics which claims to achieve knowledge of God, the human soul, the nature of reality, and so forth. Rorty (*Philosophy and the Mirror of Nature*, Ch. VIII) attempts a synthesis of similar and more recent criticisms.

2. Broader Description of "Science"

How shall we proceed in that elaboration? Let us base it upon the rather evident parallels which such sciences as mathematics, physics and the like have with sports (for example, basketball), skills (typing) and arts (piano-playing) and, accordingly, let us begin with the latter. From our past experience we know how they are acquired, what they are, and how many an individual person can acquire. First of all, we know that they are acquired by practice, by the repetition of definite physical activity: no one becomes a basketball player or a typist or a pianist except through hours of actually playing basketball, typing, or playing Mozart. We also know what they are—genuine acquired abilities by which we can easily, gracefully, enjoyably perform within given areas of physical activities. Finally, we realize how many an individual person can acquire—everything else being equal (that is, provided he has the requisite natural endowments, talents, time and so forth), the number of such abilities he can achieve is in proportion to the different sorts of physical activities he engages in. Recreational activity of a prescribed sort on a basketball court will produce proficiency at playing basketball, but not necessarily proficiency at baseball or football and not at all at swimming. Put more generally and abstractly, there are as many distinct sports, skills, and arts as there are different kinds of diverse areas of physical activities which cause those acquired abilities.

The parallel between such physical abilities and sciences should now be clear. Every body of organized knowledge also is acquired by intellectual activity—by repeated operations of reflecting, reasoning, analyzing, synthesizing, and the like. No one becomes a chemist or a biologist or a physicist except through long hours of actual mental work in a laboratory. Again, such activities are acquired mental abilities by which we can with comparative ease and accuracy cope with problems within given areas of intellectual endeavor. Finally, the number of such intellectual abilities an individual person can acquire is in proportion to the different sorts of intellectual activities he engages in (provided, of course, he has the requisite mental endowments and talents). Solving problems concerning plane and solid figures and allied topics will produce proficiency in geometry, but not necessarily proficiency in biology or sociology or economics. Stated in a more general fashion, there are as many distinct sciences as there are different sorts of, diverse areas of intellectual activities from which those sciences result.

The information gained from juxtaposing fields of knowledge with sports and other physical abilities enables us now to focus much more precisely upon the problem we face as a result of the opposition to metaphysics by many contemporary philosophers. A science is an acquired intellectual ability by which one can easily master problems within a given area of mental endeavor and, second, there are as many different sciences as there are genuinely different areas of intellectual activity, because these latter cause the former. If, then, metaphysics is to be a science at all, it must arise from an area of intellectual activity which furnishes valid evidence, which has a genuine message for the mind, which delivers insights into what material existents are. If it is to be distinct from other sciences, that area of intellectual activity and evidence must be different from all others, that message and those insights must be truly diverse. According to modern opponents of metaphysics, the only area of intellectual activity which furnishes valid evidence to the human knower is the quantitative and the measurable and, hence, metaphysics as traditionally understood cannot be a genuine science, but is rather a mere collection of high-flown, meaningless, valueless constructs. Hence, our question now has become: do the measurable and the quantitative alone provide evidence for an understanding of material things? Or do not material things also offer evidence of an entirely different sort, which can initiate mental activity issuing into a genuine science of metaphysics? I contend that they do and, accordingly, that a valid science of metaphysics is possible. The present book is an attempt to test and work out that contention.

3. "Evidence of a Different Sort"

Before starting that attempt, let us briefly investigate that "evidence of an entirely different sort" which I have just proposed material existents do offer in order to have an initial and general awareness of what to look for.

As we have previously granted, material things can be legitimately studied within laboratory conditions, and valuable empiriological sciences result. As an instance of such study, consider the experiments conducted on dreams at the University of Chicago.[14] Volunteer subjects went to sleep on plain iron cots in the laboratory. Electrodes were pasted to their scalps, to the bony ledges of their eye sockets, to their backs and chests. A tangle of red, blue, green, and yellow wires sprouted from their heads; these wires were connected to machines in the adjoining instrument room. As the subjects slept, a cardiotachometer clicked away their heartbeats. The swinging pens of the electroencephalograph recorded the infinitesimal brain waves, multiplied a millionfold, that pulsed through the varicolored wires. Through these graphs of some four hundred dreams gathered from more than one thousand hours of sleep, those conducting the experiments finally arrived at several conclusions—that everyone dreams twenty to twenty-five percent of the time of sleep (except those who are less than six months old and those who are drunk), that we compress and elide time in our dreams, that our eyeballs move greatly during a dream whereas other bodily members move very little, that the direction of the eye-movement indicates the direction of events in the dream, that dreams of a schizophrenic consist of the images of one object, motionless in midair, and so on.

Such a case certainly illustrates that "material things studied within a laboratory" do constitute one area of evidence which can initiate mental activity culminating in valuable conclusions of an empiriological sort (here belonging to physiology and experimental psychology).

But material things also exist outside the laboratory and are not known only through cardiotachometers and electroencephalographs. Men and women are caught up in the actual events of history. They are immersed in the give-and-take of everyday life in the twentieth century. And what they experience, what they do and suffer can be known through our own direct observation and through their own accounts. As an example, consider an incident that a mother relates concerning her young daughter.

> My daughter was about four years old when she first became aware that numbers were not just new words in her vocabulary nor names of digits, but that they can be useful to express

---

[14] For a description of the experiments, see Robert O'Brien, "Almost Everybody Has Dreams on Every Night," *Life*, May 5, 1958, pp. 121 sq. For more recent developments in dream research, see A. R. Morrison, "A Window on the Sleeping Brain," *Scientific American*, 248 (April, 1983), 94–102.

> quantity. This step, as all parents learn, follows the "so big" stage. One memorable day, F. turned to me to express her love with the help of her newfound knowledge and said, "Mummy, I love you ten times," followed by deep thought and "I love you twenty times." After another short pause, she reached a breathless pinnacle with "I love you six hundred times." A grateful hug and kiss from me produced a tiny frown and more concentrated thought which disappeared in a sigh of relief in her final outburst, "Mummy, I love you outside the line of numbers."[15]

As the last exclamation would seem to indicate, the young girl had achieved the quite significant awareness that some items (here, love) somehow are genuinely immaterial and nonquantitative. She experienced love for her mother, she came to know quantity and number, then by contrast she realized (however momentarily and obscurely) that love under certain circumstances is simply unlike quantity. It cannot be measured by number, it is outside the realm of the strictly material.

How is that incident important to us? It is an indication that human beings are sources for valid knowledge not only when they are within a laboratory but also as they actually live out their daily lives. In the present case an actual event in the life of a child gives an insight into what any human being, by the very fact she or he is human, actually is and can do. In this incident a child goes through a series of perfective changes and yet remains basically human—and, in fact, the same human being she was since her birth four years earlier: she had grown to her present physical size, she had digested her dinner eaten perhaps two hours earlier, yet she now is actually loving her mother, is thinking of that love and her newly gained awareness of numbers, wishes to express her love, and then comes to the further realization that love is outside the sphere of quantity. Such data (one and the same thing changing and yet remaining basically the same) can initiate reflection terminating in the realization that a human person is a genuine unity, which nevertheless is somehow intimately composed of the permanent and the changing; that some of those changes are material (for example, physical growth, digestion of food), others are not (for instance, love for a parent, intellectual awareness of that love as transcending matter); and, therefore, that a human person who is

[15] "Love Without Measure," *This Week Magazine,* March 23, 1958, p. 2.

capable of both material and immaterial activities must himself be somehow both material and immaterial.

True enough, such realizations belong properly to the philosophy of human nature and not to metaphysics, but metaphysics is simply a further development along the same line of reflection.[16] Also such conclusions need much more elaboration to be clear and convincing, but enough has been said to see that they have been derived from evidence issuing from a moment in the actual career of a human existent. Accordingly, they testify to the possibility of philosophy as a genuine science and yet distinct from empiriological sciences, and they suggest that material existents as they actually exist and as known by direct perception can and do provide an area of evidence which can stimulate intellectual activity culminating in a philosophy of nature, and eventually in metaphysics.

4. Methodology

Such, then, is an example of evidence belonging to an entirely different order from that which grounds empiriological research and furnishing the foundation of the present book.

How shall we proceed? Our immediate aim must be to understand as thoroughly as possible that material things as they actually exist and as directly perceived are genuinely an area of unique evidence; simultaneously, we shall see precisely what that evidence is. What messages do material existents, precisely as actual, deliver to an attentive human mind? What insights do they furnish?

Undoubtedly there are many ways of achieving that aim, but the one we shall utilize is a brief excursion into the history of Greek philosophy. In the next chapter we shall watch the reactions of various Hellenic thinkers when confronted by the material universe in all its variety, richness, mystery. The advantage of thus beginning with Heraclitus, Plato, and Aristotle is that they formulated intellectual reactions to the universe without any awareness of the revelation God gave the Hebrews and, thus, we can expect that formulation to be the product of human reason when working upon data from material things. Moreover, they lived long before the appearance and development of empiriological sciences; hence, material existents as known through direct perception were auto-

[16] The difference between philosophy of nature and metaphysics will be explained later. See Ch. X, Secs. 4 and 5.

matically taken as the starting-point for philosophical reflection. Accordingly, here are thinkers of outstanding intelligence who are without divine revelation and are unprejudiced by modern scientific methodology and yet who face the same material universe as we. What messages do the material existents which fill that universe have for their intellects? How far do they accurately interpret that evidence? Where do they err? Profiting by their success and their failures, perhaps we can more easily detect the evidence such actual existents really do give and, thus, eventually build up an adequate metaphysics.

5. Summary and Conclusions

(a) According to an articulate group of contemporary philosophers, metaphysics is of no value because it is not a genuine science. Why so? Because the only sort of evidence which can beget a valid science is that which is somehow measured and quantified. Obviously, metaphysics transcends quantity and measurement; accordingly, it cannot be a genuine science, but is a mere collection of high-flown, insignificant, futile statements.

(b) On the other hand, we refuse to restrict science to knowledge based solely on the quantitative, the measurable. We propose that material existents provide evidence for genuine sciences not only as such existents are viewed under laboratory conditions but also as they are directly perceived in their actual day-by-day conditions. Accordingly, a genuine science of metaphysics is possible and the present book is an effort to make good that proposal.

(c) The notion of science, then, has become broad enough to be applicable to any sort of valid, universal knowledge—the empiriological as well as the philosophical.[17] By comparison with such acquired physical abilities as sports, skills, and arts, a *science* turns out to be *an acquired intellectual ability by which one with ease and accuracy solves problems within a given area of mental activity;* second,

---

[17] One must, therefore, go against the current trend of using "science" as a synonym for "empiriological science." Throughout this book, whenever I contrast chemistry, physics, and the like with metaphysics, I shall speak of the former as "empiriological sciences." Whenever "science" is used without the adjective, it means any sort of acquired intellectual ability and can refer to any kind of knowledge—philosophical, empiriological, theological. Its meaning is the same as the Latin term, *scientia.*

there are as many different sciences as there are genuinely different areas of intellectual activity.[18]

(d) Within this context, then, *metaphysics is that acquired intellectual ability by which one with ease and accuracy knows existents precisely as actually existing through reflection upon material existents in directly perceived situations.*[19]

It is distinct from all other sciences because of its unique area of intellectual endeavor: from empiriological sciences, which deal with material things insofar as they are known within various laboratory conditions and, frequently, under mathematical formulations; from sacred theology, which deals with (among other things) material existents inasmuch as they are known through divine revelation.[20]

---

[18] We can rather easily translate the present statement into more technical language if we realize that the words, "an acquired intellectual ability by which one can . . . ," are basically equal to "an operative habit," whereas the words, "area of mental activity," are roughly equivalent to "formal object." Put more technically, then, a science is an *intellectual operative habit which has its own formal object;* second, there are as many distinct sciences as there are distinct formal objects.

On operative habit, see Henri Renard, S.J., and Martin Vaske, S.J., *Philosophy of Man,* 2nd Ed. (Milwaukee: Bruce Publishing Co., 1956), p. 266 sq.; G. P. Klubertanz, S.J., *Philosophy of Human Nature,* pp. 272 sq., especially p. 295; James E. Royce, S.J., *Man and His Nature* (New York: McGraw-Hill Book Company, 1961), pp. 238 sq.; Maurice R. Holloway, *An Introduction to Natural Theology* (New York: Appleton-Century-Crofts, 1959), pp. 3 sq.

What is meant by "material" and "formal" objects with reference to a science? The two adjectives are equivalent to "indeterminate" and "determinate." That is, actual existents can be studied both by an empiriological scientist and by a metaphysician and, in this sense, both have the same material object—actual existents considered without the definite, precise aspect under which each properly studies such existents. However, the formal object of each is different: "material existents *precisely as actually existent*" expresses the determinate approach of the metaphysician, "material existents *precisely as within the laboratory*" expresses the determinate approach of the scientist. Accordingly, when we speak of the "material object of a science," the adjective does not refer to matter as such, but is equivalent to "indeterminate," while "formal" is equivalent to "determinate." On this meaning of "material" and "formal," see Ch. III, Sec. 4, *ad finem.*

[19] The exact and technical significance of this description will be clarified and justified later. See Ch. VI, Sec. 1; Ch. X, Secs. 3–5.

[20] Metaphysics has had another group of opponents, the Tertullianists, so named after one of its early and prominent leaders, Tertullian (ca. A.D. 160–240). According to them, metaphysics (and, in general, any attempt to arrive through reason at knowledge of God, the human soul, and the nature of real-

Suggested Readings

Augros, Robert M., and George N. Stanciu, *The New Story of Science: Mind and the Universe.* Lake Bluff, Ill.: Regnery Gateway, 1984. An illuminating account of the contrast between the "new" and "old" stories of science.

Ayer, A. J., "The Elimination of Metaphysics," in *Language, Truth and Logic* (2nd Ed.), pp. 33–45. London: Victor Gollancz, Ltd., 1951.

Born, Max, "Physics and Metaphysics," *Scientific Monthly,* 82 (1956), 229–35.

Caldin, E. F., "Science and Christian Apologetic," *Aquinas Papers* 17, pp. 1–12. London: Blackfriars, 1951. On the method of contemporary science.

Chroust, Anton-Hermann, "The Origin of 'Metaphysics,'" *Review of Metaphysics,* 14 (1961), 601–16. On the etymology of "metaphysics."

De Raeymaeker, Louis, "The One Voice of Science and the Many Voices of Philosophy," *Philosophy Today,* 5 (1961), 83–91.

Drennen, D. A., *A Modern Introduction to Metaphysics: Readings from Classical and Contemporary Sources,* pp. 325–26, 328–30. New York: Free Press of Glencoe, 1962. A selected bibliography of writings by linguistic analysts and naturalists.

Gilson, Etienne, *The Unity of Philosophical Experience,* pp. 299–320. New York: Charles Scribner's Sons, 1940. On the nature of metaphysics (after a survey of what happens when nonmetaphysical methods are used to solve metaphysical problems).

———, *Wisdom and Love in Saint Thomas Aquinas,* Aquinas Lecture, 1951. Milwaukee: Marquette University Press, 1951. On the nature of wisdom, metaphysics, philosophy.

Hanson, Norwood Russell, "On the Impossibility of Any Future Metaphysics," *Philosophical Studies,* 40 (1960), 86–96.

Heidegger, Martin, "What Is Metaphysics?" in *Existence and Being,* trans. R. F. C. Hull and Alan Crick, pp. 355–92. Chicago: Henry Regnery Co., 1949.

---

ity) is dangerous and harmful because it counteracts or even destroys one's ability to believe in divine revelation. Faith alone can and does provide all the information needed on such topics. Hence, metaphysics should be avoided.

In the twentieth century this position has few defenders, since faith in divine revelation is not nearly as widespread now as it was in early and medieval Christian eras when this attitude originated and developed. Accordingly, the attempt of philosophy to know God, the nature of man, and so on is welcomed rather than rejected by those who in other times might be Tertullianists. Hence, we shall give no time here to this group. For an excellent study of the Tertullianist position, see E. Gilson, *Reason and Revelation in the Middle Ages* (New York: Charles Scribner's Sons, 1939).

Henle, R. J., *Theory of Knowledge.* Chicago: Loyola University Press, 1983. Ch. 12: "The Multiplicity of Disciplines," pp. 288–336. A helpful discussion (with several readings) on "science" in its multiple meanings, on empiriological and constructural knowledges.

Hocking, W. E., S. N. Lamprecht, and J. H. Randall, Jr., "Metaphysics: Its Function, Consequences and Criteria," *Journal of Philosophy*, 43 (1946), 365–8, 393–412.

Jaki, Stanley L., "Physics and the Ultimate," *Ultimate Reality and Meaning,* 11 (1988), 61–73.

———, "Cosmology and Religion," *Athéisme et Foi,* 25 (1990), 252–65.

Martin, Oliver, "An Examination of Contemporary Naturalism and Materialism," in *Return to Reason,* ed. John Wild, pp. 68–91. Chicago: Henry Regnery Co., 1953. On the inadequacy of materialism.

Miller, Robert G., "Linguistic Analysis and Metaphysics," in *Proceedings of the American Catholic Philosophical Association,* 34 (1960), 80–109.

Owens, Joseph, *An Elementary Christian Metaphysics,* pp. 1–14. Milwaukee: Bruce Publishing Company, 1963. On "metaphysics," its etymology and meaning.

Rorty, R., *Philosophy and the Mirror of Nature,* Princeton, N.J.: Princeton University Press, 1979. A summary and analysis of contemporary objections to philosophy from linguistic analysts, pragmatists, and various European schools. See below, Ch. XI.

Sullivan, J. W. N., *The Limitations of Science,* pp. 125–50. New York: The Viking Press, Inc., 1954. A description of how the nineteenth-century mentality of science has been succeeded by an outlook that admits that there are approaches to reality other than those of the empiriological sciences.

Van Melsen, Andrew Gerard, *Science and Technology,* pp. 9–26. Pittsburgh: Dusquesne University Press, 1961. On the difference between philosophy and physical sciences.

Also see references to D'Espagnat, Jaki, Penrose, Searle and Wallace in "Suggested Readings" of Ch. X below.

II

Lessons from Heraclitus and Plato

By awareness of the position of previous philosophers, our own speculative endeavors are improved and, in fact, can surpass those very predecessors who aided us. "We are," Bernard of Chartres (d. ca. 1125) reminds us, "like dwarfs sitting on the shoulders of giants; we see more things and more far-off ones than they did, not because our sight is better nor because we are taller than they were, but because they raise us up and add to our height by their gigantic loftiness."[1] A similar reminder has been sounded by Paul Tillich, prominent contemporary author, who advises that no one should attempt to philosophize without first making the acquaintance of the early Greek thinkers.

> Can any philosophy ignore some of the fundamental insights of Parmenides, Plato, and Aristotle? I would say no, and if they do, then they ignore elements which belong to the very nature of the task of philosophy. . . . I would say ignoring it [the wisdom achieved by the Greeks], as some people do who think philosophy starts about 1890, is very wrong. . . . Therefore, do not let us forget to sit down first and to learn, both in philosophy and in art.[2]

---

1 Quotation given by John of Salisbury, *Metalogicon*, III, 4 (*PL* 199, col. 900).

2 Paul Tillich, "Art and Ultimate Reality," *Cross Currents*, 10 (1960), p. 13.

But even had Bernard and Tillich not spoken out so strongly, we still would have reason to turn to those Hellenic philosophers by the very nature of the problem we face. Our task is to realize that material things as they actually exist in directly perceived situations are an area of unique evidence and, simultaneously, to discover what that evidence is. How better achieve that realization than by observing the reactions of such intellectual giants as Plato and Aristotle, who were without divine revelation and were unprejudiced by modern scientific methodology and yet faced the same material universe as we?

In understanding and profiting by their reactions to that universe, we must identify ourselves with them as much as possible. In imagination we must turn from our contemporary world with its entertainment media (TV, VCRs, movies, radio), its planes and automobiles, its computers, its nuclear bombs and star wars technology. We must go back past the Civil War, the American and French Revolutions, the Renaissance, the centuries of the Holy Roman Empire, even past the birth of Christ, until the year becomes about 600 B.C. and we find ourselves dressed in cloak and sandals, standing on Grecian soil.

Setting aside the machines men have made during the past centuries, we discover that the material universe then is not basically different from that which confronts us now. Then as now there is the dazzling beauty of the heavens by night, the golden sunshine and blue skies by day. There are turbulent storms with blinding, deafening thunder, driving sheets of hail and rain; the mystery of the earth, rough with hills and mountains, studded with oceans, lakes, and streams. There are innumerable plants, big and small, useful and ornamental. There are animals almost endless in number and kind, in the air or on the land or in the sea. Finally, there is the greatest mystery of all: individual men and women, who walk, sleep, eat, grow, reproduce; who see, hear, become angry, fight; who think, explain, laugh, write poetry, do as they please, sin, suffer. Such is the universe which we would try to understand.

And in 600 B.C. no answers are furnished us by modern empiriological sciences or by divine revelation (there is then, for example, no awareness in Greece of *Genesis,* 1, 1: "In the beginning God created heaven and earth"). We have only the actual universe itself and the innate curiosity and power of our human minds. If these have become dulled under the routine of everyday concerns, we must sharpen and revive them. We must learn to renew the wonder we experienced as children;[3] we must strive for the admiration and astonishment of the artist.[4] We must come to view each situation as if it had never occurred before and might never occur again;[5] we must stare at events transpiring around us.[6] In short, before "the secretive depths and the implacable advance of that infinite host of beings, aspects, events, physical and moral tangles of horror and beauty—of that world, that undecipherable Other—with which Man . . . is faced," we must put on the open attitude and the "feelings of primitive man looking at the all-pervading force of Nature or of the old Ionian philosophers saying that 'all things are full of gods.'"[7] Then, perhaps, we shall understand and

---

3 Gerald Vann, *The Water and the Fire* (New York: Sheed & Ward, 1954), p. 19: "Wonder is one of the faculties most easy to lose. We have it in childhood, undiscriminating, no doubt, but vivid and deep. We all too easily lose it as we grow older and become immersed in our daily concerns; and so, unless we are very careful, not beauty only but life itself passes us by. For inevitably life loses its meaning when it loses its mystery." We must remember that both Plato and Aristotle link philosophy with the sense of wonderment. Plato, *Theaetetus*, 155D: "This sense of wonder is the mark of the philosopher. Philosophy indeed has no other origin." Aristotle, *Metaphysics*, I, Ch. 2, 882b12: "It is owing to their wonder that men both now begin and at first began to philosophize."

4 Gerard Manley Hopkins, *A Hopkins Reader* (London: Oxford University Press, 1953), p. 33: "I have particular periods of admiration for particular things in Nature: for a certain time I am astonished at the beauty of a tree, shape, effect, etc.; then when the passion, so to speak, has subsided, it is consigned to my treasury of explored beauty, and acknowledged with admiration and interest ever after, while something new now takes its place in my enthusiasm."

5 Nan Pendergast, "The Gift of Wonder," *Catholic Digest*, January, 1959, p. 34: "Genius . . . is merely the ability to view each situation as if it had never occurred before."

6 G. K. Chesterton, "A Second Childhood," *Collected Poems of G. K. Chesterton* (London: Cecil Palmer, 1927), p. 70: "When all my days are ending/and I have no song to sing, I think I shall not be too old/To stare at everything;/As I stared once at a nursery door/Or a tall tree and a swing." See also Helen Keller, *Three Days to See* (New York: Doubleday & Company, Inc. 1955), p. 696: "I who am blind can give one hint to those who see: Use your eyes as if tomorrow you would be stricken blind. And the same method can be applied to the other senses. . . . Glory in all the facets of pleasure and beauty which the world reveals to you; make the most of every sense." Also Peter Michelmore, "Blind Runner Coming Through," *Reader's Digest* for July 1990, pp. 128–29.

7 Jacques Maritain, *Creative Intuition in Art and Poetry* (New York: Pantheon Books, Inc., 1953), p. 10.

benefit by the reactions of those Ionian philosophers, the first of whom is Thales (fl. 585 B.C.).[8]

1. An Initial Reaction: Thales

Confronted by the sensible universe, Thales asks, "What are all those things? What is the common stuff which they all share and which makes them real?" His answer: water. All things are, basically, water, and this because of evidence almost too obvious to mention. On the surface of the earth are countless streams, lakes, oceans. Dig a hole beneath the surface and one finds water. Pierce the skin of an animal, cut the bark of a tree, and there comes forth watery liquid. From the heavens fall constant rain, snow, dew. In a word, all things are water.

Thales' contribution to us is evidently not his answer, because his doctrine is what can be called a materialistic monism—that is, an identification of all reality with some material component, the reduction of the whole to one of its physical parts. Every such monism is unsatisfactory because whole areas of the universe are left unexplained—for example, human operations of thinking, of willing, even of sensing are simply not water. He is of great assistance, though, in the sort of question he asks and in the methodology used in answering. The question he proposes is the basic inquiry of metaphysics. What are actual existents? What makes them be real?

---

[8] In our excursion into Greek philosophy, no one should expect a full treatment of Thales and the other Hellenic thinkers. This can be found in such competent histories of philosophy as J. Owens. *A History of Ancient Western Philosophy* (Englewood Cliffs, N.J.: Prentice Hall Inc., 1959) (hereafter referred to as *History*), F. Copleston, S.J., *History of Philosophy,* Vol. 1: *Greece and Rome* (London: Burns, Oates & Washbourne, Ltd., 1951).

Our concern is not to write a history of philosophy but to philosophize, to work out our own philosophical position. Hence, we shall emphasize those factors in each philosopher which are conducive to our philosophical endeavor.

On Thales, see J. Owens, *History*, pp. 6–12: F. Copleston, S.J., *op. cit.*, 22–24; S. Sambursky, *The Physical World of the Greeks*, trans. Merton Dagut (New York: The Macmillan Company, 1955), pp. 5–6, 12; A. H. Armstrong, *An Introduction to Ancient Philosophy* (London: Methuen and Co. Ltd., 1949; reprinted, Totowa, N.J.: Roman and Allanheld [A Helix Book], 1983), pp. 2–5; Eduard Zeller, *Outlines of the History of Greek Philosophy* (New York: Meridian Books, 1955), 42–43; G. S. Kirk, J. E. Raven and M. Schofield, *The Presocratic Philosophers*, 2nd ed. [hereafter: *PS*] (Cambridge University Press, 1983), pp. 76–99.

What does "to be real" mean? And his procedure of arriving at a reply is standard for any genuine metaphysician: he turns to actual existents and observes whatever evidence they may give.

2. Heraclitus and Radical Existentialism

Heraclitus[9] takes up that basic question and, using the same procedure, comes up with an answer which is as true today as it was in the sixth century B.C.

What are actual existents? What makes them real? What is reality? Look at the actual universe, Heraclitus counsels, and there you see a vast panorama of constant change. Spring replaces winter and in turn succumbs to summer, which in time gives way to fall. In the heavens, stars are continually shifting positions, the moon waxes and wanes, the sun steadily moves from east to west.[10] On

---

[9] The proper noun, Heraclitus, as used throughout this book, does not refer so much to Heraclitus himself (fl. ca. 500 B.C.), as to subsequent philosophers who "were referred to as Heracliteans or as having Heraclitizing tendencies. . . . They claimed that there is only flux, with no stability whatsoever, not even such as would allow the fixed meanings of words necessary for the use of ordinary language. Their teaching was summed up in the formula, 'All things are flowing' (*panta rei*)" (J. Owens, *History*, p. 52). Heraclitus himself does not seem to have made that claim. Still for purposes of convenience I shall use his name to designate those subsequent philosophers who did hold that doctrine. On Heraclitus see Kirk, Raven and Schofield, *PS*, ch. VI; W. K. C. Guthrie, *History of Greek Philosophy* [hereafter: *HGP*] (Cambridge University Press, 1962), Vol. I, Ch. 7; Charles H. Kahn, *The Art and Thought of Heraclitus* (Cambridge University Press, 1979), especially "General Introduction," pp. 1–24, "On Reading Heraclitus," pp. 87–95, "Commentary on the Fragments," pp. 96 sqq.

[10] Of course, the motion of the sun from east to west is only apparent, because it is the earth which moves, as we know in modern times. But this movement of the earth, had these Heracliteans known of it, would be but another instance of the constant change they find in the universe. Current theories that the universe is constantly expanding as galaxies of stars recede from one another at enormous speeds would be another and impressive instance. See Robert Jastrow, *God and the Astronomers* (New York/London: W. W. Norton, 1978), chs. 4 and 5 especially; Stephen W. Hawking, *A Brief History of Time: From the Big Bang to Black Holes* (New York: Bantam Books, 1988), ch. 3; Stanley L. Jaki, *God and the Cosmologists* (Washington, D.C.: Regnery Gateway, 1989), ch. 2 especially; for a critique of Hawking's unfortunate excursions outside of astrophysics into philosophy and religion, see *ibid.*, pp. 90–95 and "Evicting the Creator," *Reflections*, VII (Spring, 1988), pp. 1, 20–21.

the earth springs flow into creeks, creeks into rivers, rivers into lakes and oceans, whence moisture is taken up into the atmosphere only to condense into rain, which begins the water-cycle all over again. Falling into the ground, seeds produce plants, which in turn grow, flower, send forth the seeds of new plants to succeed them. Animals (humans included) are born, grow to maturity, decline, and die, but are replaced by offspring they themselves have begotten. And within the life of any man or woman what do we find but a constant shift of psychological moods? Now they're up, now they're down; now they're angry, now they're calm. What is the history of nations and civilizations but a story of development and decline? The currently dominant nation has replaced those which previously were supreme, but it will in time become decadent itself and give way to another, energetic people now on the rise. "In time," we say—time itself is one of the greatest mysteries of all, but this much is true: time itself marches on steadily, inexorably.

The sensible universe is, then, a tremendous complex of unending succession, movement, change. Under pressure of that overwhelming evidence Heraclitus concludes that actual things are real precisely because and insofar as they undergo change. The very heart of their reality is change. Their apparent permanence and self-identity are only deceptive masks, covering up the inner currents of fluency which alone make them real. In short, reality is change. To be real and to be changing are synonymous.

Such is Heraclitus' conclusion. Although others may hesitate to identify reality with change, reflective humans down through the ages have been similarly struck by the ubiquitous and ceaseless flux which the universe involves. One such is the Psalmist, who finds himself crumbling under the attacks of time[11] and for whom all human beings are

> like a dream in the morning, like grass that shoots up—
> In the morning it flourishes and is green, in the evening it is
> mowed down and withers. . . .

---

[11] *Psalm* 30, 10 sqq.:

> Have pity on me, O Lord, for I am in trouble; my eye grows weak
> with grief, my soul and my body.
> For my life is spent in sorrow, my years in groaning.
> My strength has failed through affliction, and my bones have
> wasted away . . .
> I am fully forgotten, as one dead. I am like a broken vessel.

The sum of our years is seventy and, if we are strong, eighty,
And most of them toil and trouble, for they quickly pass and
we vanish.[12]

Another is the author of the *Following of Christ,* who has written a chapter aptly called, "On the Thoughts of Death": "A very little while and all will be over with thee here. . . . Man today is, and tomorrow he is seen no more. . . . When it is morning, think thou wilt not live till evening. And when evening comes, venture not to promise thyself the next morning."[13] Shakespeare is yet another; he has Macbeth, upon hearing of his wife's death, call out:

Tomorrow and tomorrow and tomorrow
Creeps in this petty pace from day to day
To the last syllable of recorded time.
And all our yesterdays have lighted fools
The way to dusty death. Out, out, brief candle;
Life's but a walking shadow, a poor player
That struts and frets his hour upon the stage
And then is heard no more.[14]

The list could be lengthened, but let us move to the contemporary scene, where one finds such radical existentialists as Jean Paul Sartre and his followers almost obsessed with the omnipresence of fluency and change.[15]

---

[12] *Psalm* 89, 5 sqq.

[13] Thomas à Kempis, *Following of Christ,* 1, Ch. 23.

[14] *Macbeth,* Act V, Scene 4.

[15] Who is a "radical existentialist?" According to J. Maritain, *Existence and the Existent* (New York: Pantheon Books, Inc., 1949), p. 3, there are two sorts of existentialism: "There are two fundamentally different ways of interpreting the word existentialism. One way is to affirm the primacy of existence, but as implying and preserving essences or natures and as manifesting the supreme victory of the intellect and intelligibility. This is what I consider to be authentic existentialism. The other way is to affirm the primacy of existence, but as destroying or abolishing essences or natures and as manifesting the supreme defeat of the intellect and of intelligibility. This is what I consider to be apocryphal existentialism, the current kind which 'no longer signifies anything at all.' "

Those whom Maritain calls "apocryphal existentialists," I call "radical existentialists," but the meaning is the same: those for whom there is only existence and no essence or, in terms more readily understood at the present

What are material things? Each is a series of appearances and nothing more, Sartre tells us in his early philosophic *opus magnum, Being and Nothingness:*

> Modern thought has realized considerable progress by reducing the existent to the series of appearances which manifest it. . . . In the first place we certainly thus get rid of that dualism which in the existent opposes interior to exterior. There is no longer an exterior for the existent if one means by that a superficial covering which hides from sight the true nature of the object. And this true nature . . . no longer exists. The appearances which manifest the existent are neither interior nor exterior; they are all equal, they all refer to other appearances, and none of them is privileged. . . . The obvious conclusion is that the dualism of being and appearance is no longer entitled to any legal status within philosophy. . . . Appearance becomes full positivity; its essence is an "appearing" which is no longer opposed to being but on the contrary is the measure of it. For the being of an existent is exactly what it appears.[16]

What Sartre has just explained technically can also be found concretely expressed in this scene from his novel *Nausea.* First he pictures the fluid state of its hero's mind.

> I think of no one any more. I don't even bother looking for words. It flows in me, more or less quickly. I fix nothing, I let it

---

stage of this book, those for whom there is only change and no stability. For them reality is identified with change.

There are various groups within radical existentialism (see J. Collins, *The Existentialists: A Critical Study* [Chicago: Henry Regnery Co., 1952; reprinted, Westport, Conn: Greenwood Press, 1977]). The best examples of the particular brand of radical existentialism I have in mind are Jean Paul Sartre and his followers.

[16] Jean Paul Sartre, *Being and Nothingness: An Essay on Phenomenological Ontology* (New York: Philosophical Library, 1956), p. xlvii sq. (Emphasis mine.) See also Sartre, *Nausea* (New York: New Directions, 1949), p. 130: "I looked anxiously about me: the present, nothing but the present. Furniture light and solid, rooted in its present, a table, a bed, a closet with a mirror—and me. The true nature of the present revealed itself: it was what exists, and all that was not present did not exist. The past did not exist. Not at all. Not in things, not even in my thoughts. . . . Now I knew: things are entirely what they appear to be—and behind them . . . there is nothing."

> go. Through the lack of attaching myself to words, my thoughts remain nebulous most of the time. They sketch vague, pleasant shapes and then are swallowed up. I forget them almost immediately.

He goes on to depict a chance meeting of a man and a woman, which can be looked upon as a picture in miniature of the universe itself, the sum-total of such haphazard, contingent, senseless, fluid events.

> You let events flow past; suddenly you see people pop up who speak and who go away, you plunge into stories without beginning or end: you'd make a terrible witness. But in compensation, one misses nothing. . . . For example, Saturday, about four in the afternoon on the end of the timbered sidewalk of the new station yard a little woman in sky blue was running backwards, laughing, waving a handkerchief. At the same time, a negro in a cream-colored raincoat, yellow shoes and a green hat, turned the corner of the street and whistled. Still going backwards, the woman bumped into him, underneath a lantern which hangs on a paling and which is lit at night. All at once there was the paling smelling strongly of wet wood, this lantern and this little blonde woman in the negro's arms under a sky the colour of fire. . . . Then everything came asunder. There was nothing left but the lantern, the palisade and the sky; it was still rather beautiful. An hour later the lantern was lit, the wind blew, the sky was black; nothing at all was left.[17]

At four o'clock on that Saturday afternoon, then, the lives of two human beings temporarily and accidentally crossed. Two lines of appearances[18] momentarily intersected, and reality then was that temporary, unstable, fleeting intersection. A moment later everything came asunder. The woman, let us say, boarded the train, the man continued walking down the street, each heading for other chance events just as temporary and transient as what had oc-

---

[17] *Ibid.*, p. 15 sqq.

[18] Individual existents are, we must remember, nothing but a series of appearances. See *Being and Nothingness*, p. xlviii (just referred to in note 16): "The being of an existent is exactly what it appears." *Nausea*, p. 131: "Things are entirely what they appear to be—and behind them . . . there is nothing."

curred in the station yard. And reality at this later moment would be these new temporary intersections. Those streams of appearances, together with the crisscrossings between them, are all there is. The actual universe is itself nothing more than the current aggregation of such fluid appearances.

Quite obviously Sartre is as much preoccupied with the fact of change as was Shakespeare, Thomas à Kempis, or even Heraclitus: reality is flux, mobility, fluency.[19] To be real is to be changing, they are identical.

And Sartre does not hesitate to draw forth the inevitable consequences of his (and Heraclitus') position. If the very heart of reality is change, then one can acquire no certain knowledge of God, since individual material existents, constantly moving currents of appearances as they are, provide no stable footing upon which the human mind can stand in an intellectual search for a

---

[19] *Nausea*, p. 171: "And then all of a sudden, there it was, clear as day: existence had suddenly unveiled itself. It had lost the harmless look of an abstract category; it was the very paste of things, this root was kneaded into existence. Or rather the root, the park gates, the bench, the sparse grass, all that had vanished: the diversity of things, their individuality, were only an appearance, a veneer. This veneer had melted, leaving soft, monstrous masses, all in disorder—naked, in a frightful, obscene nakedness." Later: "[This enormous presence] was there, in the garden, toppled down into the trees, all soft, sticky, soiling everything, all thick, a jelly. And I was inside, I with the garden. I was frightened, furious. I thought it was so stupid, so out of place, I hated this ignoble mess. Mounting up, mounting up as high as the sky, spilling over, filling everything with its gelatinous slither. . . ." Also see *ibid.*, p. 180.

See Gabriel Marcel's explanation of Sartre's position: "Thus nausea . . . seems to be bound up in its origin with an experience of fluency . . . insofar as what is fluent slows down and assumes a kind of soft and spurious solidity. The sensation which this suggests is admittedly repellent. . . . 'Gooeyness' is indeed the key word, and it is, for Sartre, gooeyness on an enormous scale: . . . the whole of life is, if not actually gooey, at least tending towards gooeyness. What he has in mind is a certain experience of secretions and mucus in process of formation" (*Philosophy of Existence* [New York: Philosophical Library, 1949], pp. 34–35).

Sartre's position also gives prominence to the self, the human subject. See J. Collins, *The Existentialists: A Critical Study*, pp. 45–63; H. J. Blackham, *Six Existentialist Thinkers* (London: Routledge & Kegan Paul, Ltd., 1961), pp. 110–48: W. Desan, *Tragic Finale* (Cambridge, Mass.: Harvard University Press, 1954). This aspect of his thought I omit here for pedagogical reasons since it is not directly relevant. But see Ch. V below, Sec. 1: "Existence Precedes Essence."

First Cause.[20] Moreover, without God and without stable natures which would ground norms of conduct, there can be no invariable, universal laws—rather, each person is a law to himself as he finds himself now in this, now in that actual situation.[21] Without God, too, there is no divine providence and, hence, the countless chance events constituting reality are totally meaningless and unintelligible. The career of each existent begins and ends in random absurdity: "Every existing thing is born without reason, prolongs itself out of weakness, and dies by chance."[22] What is the resultant psychological state of man? That of anguish, forlornness, nausea. "The existentialists say at once that man *is* anguish."[23] "I am bored. From time to time I yawn so widely that tears roll down my cheeks. It is a profound boredom, profound, the profound heart of existence, the very matter I am made of."[24] "As a result man is forlorn, because neither within him nor without does he find anything to cling to."[25]

---

[20] Jean Paul Sartre, *Existentialism* (New York: Philosophical Library, 1947) p. 60: "Existentialism is nothing else than an attempt to draw all the consequences of a coherent atheistic position."

For Sartre God is a mere concept—that of a *pour soi* which would simultaneously be an *en soi,* that of a self which would be a thing, of a subject-object, of emptiness-fullness, of activity-passivity. Manifestly, such a concept is contradictory and nothing corresponds to it in reality. But the human existent inevitably and inexorably fabricates it because of the absurd, frustrating unrest built into the very nature of consciousness and knowledge. See Sartre, *Being and Nothingness*, especially pp. 617 sqq.

[21] *Existentialism*, p. 18: "Atheistic existentialism . . . states that if God does not exist, there is at least one being in whom existence precedes essence, a being who exists before he can be defined by any concept, and that this being is man. . . . There is no human nature, since there is no God to conceive it. Not only is man what he conceives himself to be, but he is also only what he wills himself to be after this thrust towards existence. Man is nothing else but what he makes of himself. Such is the first principle of existentialism."

[22] *Nausea*, p. 180. Also see *ibid.*, p. 173: "I understood that I had found the key to Existence, the key to my Nausea, to my own life. In fact, all that I could grasp beyond that returns to this fundamental absurdity."

[23] *Existentialism*, p. 21. (Emphasis mine.)

[24] *Nausea*, p. 210.

[25] *Existentialism*, p. 27. Also see Albert Camus, *The Stranger* (New York: Alfred A. Knopf, Inc., 1957), p. 154: "It was as if that great rush of anger had washed me clean, emptied me of hope, and, gazing up at the dark sky spangled with its signs and stars, for the first time, the first, I laid my heart open to the benign indifference of the universe. . . . For all to be accomplished, for me to feel less lonely, all that remained to hope was that on the day of my execution there should be a huge crowd of spectators and that they should

In the face of such a situation, all that an individual human existent can do is to immerse himself totally in the actual moment in which he finds himself. The past is no longer, the future as yet is not, the present alone is. To be sure, the present instant is no sooner here than gone, but there is nothing else to be had.[26]

Those somber consequences caution one to be slow in adopting the Sartrean and Heraclitean identification of reality with change. Actually, abundant evidence exists that things involve not only change but also permanence as well. An individual man or woman does go through a rather constant series of psychological and physical modifications over a period of time, but it is one and the same person who is now angry, now happy, now thinking, now suffering, now speaking. The person himself is the common denominator of the changes, the subject to which they are attributed. Accordingly, no one should say reality is change because existents are also relatively stable.[27]

Nonetheless—and this is one important lesson Heraclitus (and Sartre) teaches—reality does involve change. Real existents do change, and change thus is real, even though reality is not synonymous with change but arises, as we shall see, from an altogether different factor. Accordingly, any metaphysics which claims to be an adequate expression of the actual universe must find room for change as a genuine factor in reality. Second, observing the reac-

---

greet me with howls of execration." Sartre, *Nausea*, p. 180: "[This ignoble mess which is reality] was the World, the naked World suddenly revealing itself, and I choked with rage at this gross, absurd being."

[26] *Nausea*, p. 54: "Something is beginning in order to end: adventure does not let itself be drawn out; it only makes sense when dead. . . . Each instant appears only as part of a sequence. I cling to each instant with all my heart: I know that it is unique, irreplaceable—and yet I would not raise a finger to stop it from being annihilated. This last moment I am spending . . . moment I love passionately, woman I may adore—all is going to end, I know it. Soon I shall leave for another country. I shall never rediscover either this woman or this night. I grasp at each second, trying to suck it dry: nothing happens which I do not seize, which I do not fix forever in myself, nothing, neither the fugitive tenderness of those lovely eyes, nor the noises of the street, nor the false dawn of early morning: and even so the minute passes and I do not hold it back, I like to see it pass."

[27] Moreover, existents not only combine permanence with change but they also are distinct from one another and retain that distinctness and individuality, despite the imaginative picture which Sartre draws (see note 19 above). Your eating nourishes you and not me. My headache afflicts me and not you.

tion of Heraclitus and company establishes that the actual universe does provide evidence of a different sort from that encountered within a laboratory—the fact that material existents as they are immersed in the daily give-and-take of actual situations involve various, frequent, deep-seated changes. This is one message which such beings put across to attentive minds and which can be the germ of a genuine science of philosophy of nature and, eventually, of metaphysics.

3. Plato and Radical Essentialism[28]

Another instructive group for our endeavor to build up a valid metaphysics is headed by Plato (428–348 B.C.). He agrees perfectly with the former group that the sensible universe is indeed shot through with change, flux, fluency. But there the agreements ends. He adds: And for that very reason it is unreal and unimportant. Reality is not change, which is rather the very stuff in which unreality centers. To be real is to be stable, to be permanent, to be immutable. The very heart of reality is stability, of which individual material things are totally bereft. Where, then, is it located? Solely in a realm completely separated from the sensible—that of subsistent Forms or Essences.

What evidence leads Plato and his followers to this conclusion? They start with the fact of intellectual knowledge. Human souls discover that they know with certitude and conviction what Man, Dog, Beauty, Justice, Courage, Circle, and so on are. Such cognition is true and certain because it is stable and immutable. But it could not have come from individual men, dogs, and the like, which are completely unstable and mutable. Hence, the source of my knowledge of man must be, so to speak, the concentrate of humanness,

---

[28] Who is a radical essentialist? As will become clearer later, he is the counterpart of a radical existentialist (see note 15 above). For him there is only essence and no existence or, in more easily intelligible terms, not change but only stability counts. Stability and reality are interchangeable. The sensible universe is unimportant and unreal. Also see note 39 below.

On Plato's essentialism and theory of forms, see David Ross, *Plato's Theory of Ideas* (Oxford: Clarendon Press, 1951); J. Owens, *History*, pp. 189–229. Both authors give frequent references to relevant passages in Plato's own dialogues. Also see W. K. C. Guthrie, *HGP*, vols. 4 and 5.

with which the human soul comes into contact.[29] That is, that source must be the distillation of what makes man be man and be other from everything nonhuman, and this is concentrated in a single, eternal, perfectly invariable item, which can be called "the Form of Man" or "the Essence of Man" or "Man-as-Such" or "Absolute Man" or "Humanity-in-itself" and which alone is genuinely real because it solely is genuinely stable and everlastingly self-identical. And the source of my knowledge of Dog, of Beauty, of Justice, of Courage, and so on would be similar concentrates, similar Forms or Essences. These the sensible universe mirrors, but individual humans, dogs, beautiful things and so on, never actually succeed in truly becoming real because of their mutability and materiality.

Accordingly, anyone desiring to acquire true knowledge must first turn away from that universe and from the actual existents which inhabit it. Then let him enter within himself so that he may mentally ascend and find the realm of the Essences. "How shall we find the way [to certain knowledge, to the Forms]? What method can we devise?" asks Plotinus (A.D. 205–270), one of Plato's most intelligent and influential followers. "How can one see the inconceivable Beauty which stays within . . . and does not come out where the profane may see it?" His answer: "Let him who can, follow and come within and leave outside the sight of his eyes and not turn back to the bodily splendors which he saw before. When he sees the beauty in bodies, he must not run after them. We must know that they are images, traces, shadows, and we must rather hurry away to that which they image."[30] In the next chapter Plotinus continues:

---

[29] For Plato this contact was achieved by the human soul when it existed with those Essences before it became linked with a body. To know now is merely to recall those Essences previously known. See J. Owens, *History*, especially pp. 205–6; W. K. C. Guthrie, *HGP*, III, 249–53, 345–46, 426–28.

For St. Augustine, this contact is achieved by God's illumining the human soul. To know is the result of divine illumination in each intellect. (Incidentally, the very fact that a man knows any truth is sufficient to prove there is a God, for otherwise he would not know that truth.) See E. Gilson, *History of Christian Philosophy* (New York: Random House, Inc., 1955), pp. 74–77; Vernon Bourke, *Augustine's Quest of Wisdom* (Milwaukee: Bruce Publishing Co., 1945), pp. 116 sqq. and 216 sqq.; E. Gilson, *Spirit of Mediaeval Philosophy* (New York: Charles Scribner's Sons, 1940), Ch. XII, pp. 229 sqq.; Eugene TeSelle, *Augustine the Theologian* (New York: Herder and Herder, 1970), pp. 103–7.

[30] *Enneads*, I, 6, 8, 1 sqq. (A. H. Armstrong translation [*Plotinus* (London: George Allen & Unwin, Ltd., 1953)], pp. 136–37). The sentences immediately

> When you know that you have become the perfect work (by turning away from the outside world, by acquiring the requisite virtues), when you are self-gathered in the purity of your own being, nothing now remaining that can shatter that inner unity, nothing from without clinging to the authentic man, . . . now call up all your confidence, move upwards yet a step—you need a guide no longer—strain and see [Beauty and the other Essences].[31]

The Platonist identification of reality with immutability has consequences which are just as inevitable as those flowing from Heraclitus' position, but which are as diametrically opposed as is day to night.

Because reality is coterminous with stability and because the sensible universe is nothing but a complex of change and variation,

---

following the quotation just given are also significant: "If a man runs to the image and wants to seize it as if it was the reality (like a beautiful reflection playing on the water, which some story somewhere, I think, said riddlingly a man wanted to catch and sank down into the stream and disappeared), then this man who clings to beautiful bodies and will not let them go, will, like the man in the story, but in the soul, not in body, sink down into the dark depths where intelligence has no delight, and stay blind in Hades, consorting with shadows there and here." For a more complete English translation of Plotinus' *Enneads* with Greek text, see A. H. Armstrong (trans.), *Plotinus*, 7 Vols. (Cambridge: Harvard University Press, "Loeb Classical Library," 1966–88).

[31] *Ibid.*, I, 6, 9, 15 sqq. Augustine used the same technique and ended in an awareness of God Himself (*Confessions*, Book VII, Chs. 9, 10, and 17): [God having provided for me certain books of the Platonists which were translated from the Greek tongue into Latin] and thus admonished me to return unto myself, I entered into my innermost parts under Thy guidance. . . . I entered in and saw with the eye of my soul (whatever its condition) the Immutable Light, above this same eye of my soul and above my mind. . . . Thus, by a gradual process, from bodies to the soul which senses through the body, and thence to its interior power to which bodily sensation takes messages about exterior things . . . and then further to the reasoning power, to which what is taken by the bodily senses is brought for judgment. And this power, also finding itself mutable in me, lifted itself to its understanding and withdrew the thinking process from the customary level . . . so that it might discover by what light it was besprinkled when it cried out without any hesitation that the immutable is to be preferred to the mutable; that it might know from this the immutable itself. . . . And, in the flash of a trembling glance, it reached up to That Which Is" (*Fathers of the Church* edition, Vol. 21, pp. 176, 180, and 187).

one must look elsewhere for the realm of what is really real.[32] This is not difficult to find, though, for the very fact that a human soul can and does achieve true and certain knowledge of Humanness, of Beauty, of Courage and so on proves without a doubt that such a realm does exist and also indicates what it is. Why so? Such knowledge must have an adequate cause. But this, obviously, cannot be individual humans, beauties, and so on because of their complete mutability, nor can it be the human soul itself, because this too is variable and inconstant. Hence, there exists a realm of what is really real, which is marked by supreme constancy and perfect permanence and which is the cause of our true cognition. For Plato himself, as we have seen, this realm consists of the subsistent Forms or Essences—pure concentrates of Humanness, Beauty, Goodness and the like. For Plotinus it is headed by The One or The Good, Who transcends such essences but from Whom they emanate and Who is absolute immutability and supreme unity.[33] For Augustine the really real is God, Who is the Unchangeable Light, the Eternal Simplicity, Eternal Truth, True Eternity, Subsistent Beauty, and Who contains the ideas of all creatures.[34]

---

32 "Really real" translates Plato's phrase, *to ontôs on*, by which he contrasts the world of Essences with the visible world, which is not genuinely real at all but a mere collection of shadows, images, reflections.

Prescinding from this contrast, we can say that the "really real" is characterized by immutability, permanence, self-identity, intelligibility, truth, and eternity; it will be applied by various authors to whatever has those characteristics—by Plato to the Essences, by Plotinus to the One-Good, by Augustine to the Christian God.

33 For a list of texts from the *Enneads* on The One, see A. H. Armstrong, *Plotinus*, pp. 56–68.

What is the relationship of The One to the Forms? The One transcends the Forms, which are contained within The Intelligence. But the Forms, as well as The Intelligence itself (and, for that matter, all souls), are not really distinct from The One. All such subsequent realities are nothing more than The One deploying Himself on a lower level. See L. Sweeney, S.J., "Basic Principles of Plotinus' Philosophy," in *Divine Infinity in Greek and Medieval Thought* (New York/Bern: Peter Lang Publishing, Inc., 1992), ch. 11, pp. 243–56; *idem*, "Are Plotinus and Albertus Magnus Neoplatonists?" in L. Gerson (ed.), *Graceful Reason: Essays in Ancient and Medieval Philosophy Presented to Joseph Owens* (Toronto: Pontifical Institute of Medieval Studies, 1983), especially pp. 181–91 (forthcoming as ch. 17 in my *Christian Philosophy: Nature, Origin, Developments* [hereafter: *Christian Philosophy*] [New York/Bern: Peter Lang Publishing, Inc., 1994]).

34 See *Confessions*, especially Book VII in its entirety; IX, Ch. 5; X, Ch. 27; XI in its entirety.

From the very fact that a human soul has intellectual knowledge, then, one also can easily know that the Really Real exists and what it is. Since ultimately the Really Real is God,[35] the first consequence of the Platonist position is that one can easily know God—that He is and, to an extent, what He is.

Another consequence of this position is that law is an easily known and ubiquitous factor. Reality as linked with permanence and intelligibility is also coterminous with good order—everything has and should keep its own place and function, the lower subordinated to the higher, the higher ruling the lower. But right order is synonymous with law, which, consequently, is an important and inescapable factor in Plato's view of reality.[36]

Permanence, truth, certitude, easy knowledge of God, law with the good order and intelligible direction it implants—all such provide for the human soul an atmosphere of well-being, of achievement, of peace, so that the normal psychological state of each person is happiness and joy. And if only he perseveres in stripping himself of the material and the mutable and continues to open himself up more and more to what is higher, his efforts will terminate in perfect union with the Supremely Real. This union is, Plotinus assures us, "a kind of seeing, a being out of oneself, a self-surrender, a pressing towards contact, a rest, a sustained thought directed to perfect conformity. . . . This is the life of gods and of divine and blessed men—deliverance from the things of this world, escape in solitude to the Solitary."[37]

Those consequences of the Platonist *Weltanschauung* are as attractive as those of the Heraclitean view were depressing. None-

---

[35] True enough, Plato did not consider the Forms to be gods because at his time a god was an "individual living being, similar to those we know from sensible experience," but necessary and immortal (see E. Gilson, *God and Philosophy* [New Haven, Conn.: Yale University Press, 1941], pp. 27–28), whereas the Forms were not individual living beings at all. The Forms are, though, the philosophical first principles of his universe and were supremely real—much more real than if they had been gods. By Plotinus' time the term "god" had lost its pejorative connotations and The One-Good was equated with God (for example, see V, 1, 11 [*Enneads*, Armstrong's Allen & Unwin Ed., pp. 53–54]).

[36] It is significant that Plato wrote dialogues (*Republic, Statesman, Laws*) dedicated to laws—their nature and content, their application to various classes of men and to states. For Plato, actually, Law is as much an Essence as is Humanness or Courage.

[37] *Enneads*, VI, 9, 11, 35 sq. (Armstrong's Allen & Unwin Ed., p. 160).

theless, their attractiveness should not prompt us personally to identify reality with immutability because of a grave difficulty that such identification entails. By making reality and stability synonymous, one is forced to conclude that individual material things are basically unreal, insignificant, worthless, because such actual existents are undoubtedly immersed in constant and manifold changes.

This conclusion every Platonist is forced to formulate, implicitly or explicitly. Let us take as an example Plotinus, who in the following passage is outlining to a human soul what happened when it separated itself from God and the world of true reality by descending into matter and becoming an individual man.

> Because something else other than the All [= the sum-total of true reality] added itself to you, you became less by the addition, for the addition did not come from real being (you cannot add anything to that), but from that which is not. You have become a particular person by the addition of non-being.

In order to find God and to become truly real again, it must put off that accretion of individuality and uniqueness.

> When you have become a particular person by the addition of non-being, you are not all till you reject the non-being. You will increase yourself then by rejecting the rest, and by that rejection the All is with you. . . . You must not say even about yourself, "I am so much." For by rejecting the "so much," you become all, even though you were all before.[38]

That is to say, when a human soul achieves a measure of independence from The One by putting on unique and distinguishing

---

[38] *Ibid.*, VI, 5, 12, 16 sqq. (Armstrong's Allen & Unwin Ed., p. 152). For purposes of clarity and emphasis, I have changed the tense and mood of the verbs in the last two sentences, which in the original Greek initiate the excerpt rather than terminate it. See Leo Sweeney, "Are Plotinus and Albertus Magnus Neoplatonists?" in Lloyd Gerson (ed.), *Graceful Reason*, pp. 177–91; *idem*, "Mani's Twin and Plotinus: Questions on 'Self'" in Jay Bergman (ed.), *Neoplatonism and Gnosticism* (Albany: State University of New York Press, 1992), pp. 381–424 (forthcoming as ch. 6 in my *Christian Philosophy*); *idem*, "The 'Individual' in Plato, Plotinus and Aristotle," in *The Quest for the Individual: Roots of Western Civilization*, eds. W. J. Carroll *et alii* (New York/Bern: Peter Lang Publishing, Inc., 1990), pp. 35–87 (forthcoming as ch. 5 in my *Christian Philosophy*).

characteristics and by immersing itself in matter to become an individual man, it is to that extent destroying its true reality. Those individual characteristics are a sign of weakness, evil, unreality. Such a soul only becomes truly real and truly itself when it becomes totally identified with The One, Whom it should never have left in the first place. In short, an individual human being, precisely in his individuality, uniqueness, and actual existence is unreal, valueless, unimportant.[39]

The only way to see that such an attitude toward the actual universe is false is to look at a concrete case in which actual existents show themselves to be genuinely significant, valuable, and thereby real in the very actual situations in which they find themselves. One such is the lady, Patricia Markor by name, who thwarted the attempt of a woman to commit suicide by throwing herself in the path of an oncoming train. Let its engineer (David Lundahl) and fireman (Stephen Frankowiak) relate what happened as they pulled into the station at Great Lakes Naval Training Center.

> A woman stepped from the platform and onto the tracks directly in front of us, less than 100 feet away, an apparent suicide. . . . We made an emergency brake application and

---

[39] This negative, pejorative attitude toward individual actual existents is, in fact, so intrinsic a part of radical essentialism that it is a criterion for deciding whether or not an author is an essentialist. Whenever you find someone commenting that actual existence has nothing to do with whether or not a being is real, you are in the presence of a radical essentialist. For example, see Suarez, *Disp. Meta.*, II. Sec. 4: "*Being* as a noun signifies that which has a real essence, prescinding from actual existence." Or J. Kleutgen (a nineteenth-century Suarezian), *La Philosophie scolastique*, Vol. II, p. 89 f: "The *real* is not confused with what is *actual or existing*. . . . When we conceive a being as real, . . . *we leave existence out of consideration*" (quoted by E. Gilson, *Being and Some Philosophers* [2nd Ed., Toronto: Pontifical Institute of Mediaeval Studies, 1952], p. 106) [emphasis mine]. Also see Edmund Husserl, *The Idea of Phenomenology* (The Hague: Martinus Nijhoff, 1964), especially pp. 43–51.

So too, it is a sign of radical essentialism when someone makes possible essences more real than actual ones. For instance, see C. Frick (*Ontologia* [Fribourg: Herder, 1934], pp. 74–79), according to whom the philosophy of nature studies actual essences, but only metaphysics, the queen of natural sciences, studies possible essences. The implication is that essences as actual are immersed in change and, thereby, are less real and intelligible, whereas essences as possible are free from change and the debilitating conditions it inflicts upon essences. When so conceived, possible essences do not seem to differ in any important way from Platonic subsistent Essences.

> blew the whistle, but there just wasn't sufficient distance to stop the train. There was no doubt in our minds that the woman was about to die. But one person didn't agree. [Another woman] leaped out of the crowd [on the platform] and onto the tracks with incredible speed. She grabbed the woman, who resisted the rescue effort. [But she was able to maintain her grasp and dragged her to the side of the tracks just in time.] There she was, still clutching the other woman, holding her against the fence [in safety].[40]

Later in an interview the heroine said: "I felt I had to do something, I just couldn't let her die."

This, I would say, is obviously a case in which an individual human existent is significant, valuable, important, and hence real, precisely when confronted with an actual, never-to-be-repeated challenge. Her courage, her worthwhileness, her value—in a word, her reality—are inseparable from the actual event and the actual changes she experienced then: her awareness of the suicidal person's jumping from the station platform onto the tracks, her seeing and hearing the approaching train, her realization of the extreme danger to herself with (no doubt) resultant fear, her decision to save the other's life, her heroically carrying out that decision, her feeling relief and joy when the ordeal was over. Obviously, to be real here is located in her very actuality, in her individual acts of awareness of danger, of overcoming fear, of decision, of bravely carrying out that decision through her physically rescuing the other person. Moreover, one's knowledge of what courage is arises from this and other actual acts of courageous men or women and not from some subsistent idea of courage. Courage is no separate Essence; it is the content of the concept within our minds which comes from our directly perceiving individual brave acts and attitudes of actual men and women.

To identify reality with stability, therefore, is erroneous. But a great help can be derived from studying radical essentialism, because this position serves as a warning never to downgrade actual existents. These afford a constant source of data, and without them a philosopher has nothing upon which to build.

Nonetheless, actual existents involve more than mere change. True enough, they are permeated with frequent and various modi-

---

[40] *Chicago Sun-Times,* Monday, May 20, 1985, p. 7.

fications, but they also are comparatively stable and permanent. She who now is courageous is the same woman who previously was afraid. Stability is as great a factor in reality as change (and this is another lesson to be learned from the essentialists) but only as it is embedded in actual things (this the essentialists deny). Any thinker who realizes that individual existents are combinations of both change and stability will transcend all previous insights. Aristotle had such a realization, and we shall study his position in the next chapter.

4. Summary and Conclusions

(a) In this chapter our aim was to understand that material existents are the source of evidence precisely as they are directly observed in the actual conditions of their day-by-day existence. The means used to implement this aim has been to step back into the era of early Greek philosophers and observe their reactions when confronted with the sensible universe.

(b) The initial reaction was that of Thales, who taught us the basic question of philosophy and the general methodology for answering it. The question: what are sensible existents, what is the heart of their reality, and what does "to be real" mean? The methodology: turn to the material universe and carefully observe what goes on there.

(c) Heraclitus, together with radical existentialists of today, put across the important point that reality genuinely does involve change (even though we must add that reality is not identical with it because things are relatively stable too). To do justice to the actual world, metaphysics must take change into account.

(d) From Plato and other radical essentialists we learned that stability also must be included as a factor in reality. However, stability is not located in a separate realm of subsistent Essences. Rather, it is incorporated into the very fabric of individual material existents, who combine both change and stability into a single, concrete, actual unity. Far from being insignificant and unintelligible, such actual existents are truly valuable and genuinely knowable—in fact, they are the sole sources of whatever natural knowledge we humans have of courage, beauty, justice, value, and the like. They are the starting-point of metaphysics, its constant center of reference, the arbiter of its conclusions.

Suggested Readings

Armstrong, A. H., *Plotinus*, George Allen & Unwin, Ltd., 1953. A translation of significant texts from Plotinus' *Enneads*, with introduction and notes.

———, trans., *Plotinus: Enneads*, 7 vols. Cambridge, Mass.: Harvard University Press: "Loeb Classical Library," 1966–88.

St. Augustine, *Basic Writings*, ed., Whitney J. Oates. New York: Random House, Inc., 1948.

Bergson, Henri, *The Creative Mind.* New York: Greenwood Publishers, 1968, especially pp. 14–16, 154, 167–68, 173–84, 194–220. Fine example of a contemporary philosopher for whom reality is change.

Blackham, H. J., *Six Existentialist Thinkers.* New York: The Macmillan Company, 1952.

Charlesworth, Max, "The Meaning of Existentialism," *Thomist*, 16 (1953), 472–96.

Collins, James, *The Existentialists: A Critical Study*. Chicago: Henry Regnery Co., 1952; reprinted, Westport, Conn.: Greenwood Press, 1977. A survey, with critique, of modern existentialists.

Copleston, S.J., F. C., *Existentialism and Modern Man.* Oxford: Blackfriars, 1948.

Drennen, D. A., *A Modern Introduction to Metaphysics: Readings from Classical and Contemporary Sources*, pp. 218–53, 327. New York: Free Press of Glencoe, 1962. Excerpts from various radical existentialists; a selected bibliography.

Gilson, Etienne, *God and Philosophy*, pp. 1–37. New Haven, Conn: Yale University Press, 1941. On the answers given by Thales, Heraclitus and Plato to the question, "What does it mean to be real?"; splendid exemplification of how the history of philosophy helps unravel philosophical problems.

———, *Being and Some Philosophers* (2nd Ed.), pp. 1–40, 74–107, 108–53. Toronto: Pontifical Institute of Mediaeval Studies, 1952. A study of how the following conceive reality: Platonists, Medieval and Renaissance essentialists (Avicenna, Suarez and others), and radical existentialists.

Guthrie, W. K. C., *A History of Greek Philosophy.* Cambridge University Press, 1971, 1975 and 1978. Vol. One, Ch. 7 on Heraclitus; Vols. Three and Four on Plato.

Hamilton, Edith, and Huntington Cairns, eds., *The Collected Dialogues of Plato*, "Bollingen Series," Vol. 71. New York: Pantheon Books, 1964.

Husserl, Edmund, *The Idea of Phenomenology.* The Hague: Martinus Nijhoff, 1964. Contemporary exposition of essentialism.

Kirk, G. S., J. E. Raven and M. Schofield, *The Presocratic Philosophers*, 2nd ed. Cambridge University Press, 1983.

Maritain, Jacques, *Existence and the Existent,* trans. L. Galantiere and G. Phelan, pp. 1–19 and 129–53. Garden City, N.Y.: Doubleday & Company, Inc., 1956 (Image Books Edition). On radical and authentic existentialism.

Mounier, Emmanuel, *Existentialist Philosophers.* New York: The Macmillan Company, 1949.

Sweeney, S.J., Leo, "Basic Principles in Plotinus' Philosophy," in *idem, Divine Infinity in Greek and Medieval Thought* [hereafter: *Divine Infinity*] (New York/Bern: Peter Lang Publishing, Inc., 1992), ch. 11, pp. 243–56. On essentialistic factors in Plotinus.

———, "Neo-Platonism," *Collier's Encyclopedia* (New York: P. F. Collier and Son, 1961), Vol. 17, pp. 297–98. An aid to intelligent reading of those radical essentialists who are Neo-Platonists.

———, "Existentialism: Authentic and Unauthentic," *New Scholasticism,* 40 (1965–66), 36–61 (forthcoming as ch. 23 in my *Christian Philosophy: Nature, Origin, Developments* [hereafter: *Christian Philosophy*] [New York/Bern: Peter Lang Publishing, Inc., 1994]). Contrast of the two sorts of existentialists: authentic and radical.

———, "Plotinus' Conception of Neoplatonism," in E. G. Weltin, ed., *Great Events of World History* (New York: Salem Press Inc., 1973), II, 823–29 (forthcoming as ch. 4 of *Christian Philosophy*).

———, "Participation in Plato's Dialogues: *Phaedo, Parmenides, Sophist* and *Timaeus,*" in my *Divine Infinity,* ch. 4, pp. 47–68.

———, "Are Plotinus and Albertus Magnus Neoplatonists?" in *Graceful Reason: Essays in Ancient and Medieval Philosophy Presented to Joseph Owens,* ed. Lloyd Gerson, pp. 177–202. Toronto: Pontifical Institute of Mediaeval Studies, 1983 (forthcoming as ch. 17 in my *Christian Philosophy*).

———, "Plato, Plotinus and Aristotle on the Individual," in *The Quest for the Individual: Roots of Western Civilization,* eds. W. J. Carroll *et alii* (New York/Bern: Peter Lang Publishing, Inc., 1990), pp. 35–87 (forthcoming as ch. 5 in *Christian Philosophy*).

Wahl, Jean, "The Roots of Existentialism," in *Jean Paul Sartre: Philosophy of Existentialism,* ed. Wade Baskin, pp. 3–28. New York: Philosophical Library, 1965, pp. 3–28.

III

Lessons from Aristotle

The preceding chapter has prepared us to understand and to appreciate Aristotle (384–322 B.C.). From Heraclitus we learned that reality involves change, from Plato that it also entails stability. Obviously, the next step is to combine those two insights. This step Aristotle took by realizing that both change and permanence are factors in reality, and this in such a way that they make up the very warp and woof of individual material things.

In this realization he not only utilizes his predecessors but also corrects them. To Heraclitus he points out that actual existents also remain comparatively stable and identical while changing.[1] To Plato he indicates that change too is real because it belongs to the intrinsic constitution of individual things, which are real because genuinely important and valuable. Moreover, stability is not located in any separate realm of Essences, but is within actual things. These are, in fact, combinations of change and stability in such fashion that change and stability are not isolated from one another or from

---

[1] In the final analysis radical existentialists such as Heraclitus or Sartre devaluate individual existents as effectively as do radical essentialists. Even though they concentrate upon them, they reduce them to mere streams of appearances by refusing to see or admit the relative permanence and self-identity they involve. (Sartre, *Nausea,* p. 171: "The diversity of things, their individuality, were only an appearance, a veneer. This veneer had melted, leaving soft, monstrous masses, all in disorder—naked, in a frightful, obscene nakedness.") On the other hand, radical essentialists are guilty of the same refusal and simply ignore individual things by turning away to wherever they locate the really real.

the individual existent itself. Rather, they are the existent, they permeate what he is. An individual is both a changing stability and a succession of stabilized changes. The task of the philosopher is to observe those units of modification and permanence and then to receive and to decipher the evidence they provide.

For Aristotle[2] material things show themselves to involve two different sorts of change and stability. One sort occurs on what he calls the substantial level; the other on the accidental level. For instance, death affects an existent much more radically than does thinking or becoming angry or growing because it changes the very kind of thing the existent is. Death transforms what is living to what is nonliving, whereas the other states are mere transitions within the life-span of the same thing. Accordingly, the former belongs to the substantial level, the latter to the accidental.[3]

---

[2] On Aristotle, see J. Owens, *History*, pp. 281 sqq. The positions we shall ascribe to Aristotle can just as accurately be attributed to most Aristotelians throughout the centuries. In fact, his description of material things as composites of substance/accidents and of matter/form is, in my opinion, as true today as when he first made it. Hence, in this area he also speaks for me and I shall offer no subsequent chapter on those components.

One should note, though, that my approval of Aristotle's hylomorphism does not automatically extend to his other positions in philosophy of nature, some of which (for example, his theory of natural place) have been shown to be inadequate or even inaccurate by contemporary cosmology and science. Much less does it extend to his scientific views, which are now rather generally obsolete. See Andrew G. Van Melsen, *Philosophy of Nature* (Pittsburgh: Duquesne University Press, 1954), Ch. 2: "A Survey of the History of the Study of Nature," especially Sec. 3: "Aristotle" (pp. 38–52), Sec. 4: "The Explanation of Aristotle's Unchallenged Authority During Twenty Centuries" (pp. 52–70), as well as the final two sections (pp. 70–76 and 76–80). Also see James B. Conant, *Science and Common Sense* (New Haven, Conn.: Yale University Press, 1954), pp. 64–67, 154, 167 sq.; Philipp Frank, *Philosophy of Science* (Englewood Cliffs, N.J.: Prentice-Hall, Inc., 1957), pp. 122 sqq. and *passim*; Werner Heisenberg, *Physics and Philosophy: Revolution in Modern Science*, Vol. 19 of *World Perspectives* (New York: Harper & Row, Publishers, 1958), pp. 147–66, especially 159–60; Francis J. Collingwood, *Philosophy of Nature* (Englewood Cliffs, N. J.: Prentice-Hall, Inc., 1961), pp. 286–95 and *passim*; Ernest Nagel, *Structure of Science* (New York: Harcourt, Brace & World, Inc., 1961), pp. 42–46; David Hawkins, *Language of Nature: An Essay in the Philosophy of Science* (San Francisco: W. H. Freeman and Company, 1964), pp. 109–14, 178, 252–54.

[3] The adjectives "substantial" and "accidental" arise from the fact that the former establishes the actual presence of constitutive parts within *substance*

In our attempt to understand Aristotle, then, we shall investigate both sorts. First, however, we must briefly study two rather general propositions that guide Aristotle when observing and interpreting the evidence that material existents afford—namely, that diverse evidences indicate the actual presence within a thing of distinct constitutive parts and, second, that an individual material thing is a genuine unity of special stringency and type. Consequently, this chapter has four main sections:

1. "Diverse evidences indicate. . . ."
2. Unity.
3. Change/Stability in the Accidental Order.
4. Change/Stability in the Substantial Order.

1. "Diverse Evidences Indicate. . . ."

The affirmation, "Diverse evidences indicate the actual presence within of distinct constitutive parts," will be operative in most of the subsequent processes by which an Aristotelian answers the fundamental questions of philosophy. Nonetheless, its truth can be easily and indubitably grasped through several very simple concrete cases.

Let us imagine that we come to a wood where the trees and underbrush are so thick that one cannot directly see what animals are within. Suppose, however, we notice the fresh footprints of a lion on the wet path leading into the trees. Without having directly perceived the lion, we can conclude from the directly observed footprints that there actually is a lion in the woods. If we see also the footprints of a bear, we can similarly assent that a bear is actually within. What guides us to such conclusions? Our realization that diverse evidences (here, the footprints) indicate the actual presence within of what has caused them (here, the animals). This realization we first acquired early in our intellectual life (however implicitly and ineffably) when we observed some or other agent actually causing an effect. For then we became aware not only that this cause is responsible for this effect, but also that every effect comes about because of a cause, and this because of the very natures of an

---

(see Sec. 4 of this chapter), whereas the latter points to the actual presence of *accidents* which perfect the substance but are not parts of the substance (see Sec. 3 of this chapter).

efficient cause and its effect.[4] Accordingly, diverse effects point to diverse causes and thus arises the affirmation: "Diverse evidences (the effects) indicate the actual presence of diverse efficient causes."

But that affirmation, in view of its elaboration and wording, is concerned with extrinsic and efficient causes, whereas the assertion which gives Aristotle the key for unlocking the secrets of material things has to do with "constitutive parts"—that is, with intrinsic causes. In order to establish this assertion, though, we need only to consider another sort of example. Let us suppose that we enter a room and come upon a cake which we have not seen made. What is in it? What are its ingredients? From the fact that it is moist, we can conclude to some sort of liquid (milk, applesauce, etc.) as an ingredient; from its sweetness, to sugar; from its bulk, to flour; from its tangy taste, to citrus-fruit rinds; and so on. What guides us to such conclusions? Our awareness that diverse evidences (here, the moistness, sweetness, etc.) indicate the actual presence within of what causes them (here, the milk, sugar, etc.), and this awareness we first achieved as a child when we watched, say, our mother make a cake by actually combining sugar, flour, milk, spices, and the like. We then realized not only that that cake (that composite, that combination) was those ingredients mixed-and-baked, but also that every composite (in what it is and appears) is its ingredients-as-combined, because such is the nature of ingredients and the resultant composite. In other words, we became aware not merely that those evidences indicated those ingredients, but that external evidences in general indicate internal ingredients, and, even more generally and relevantly, that diverse evidences reveal the actual presence within of diverse constitutive parts.[5]

---

[4] The case here is similar to our awareness that "Every (nonmathematical) whole is bigger than any of its parts." In the presence of a concrete case (which let us represent thus:

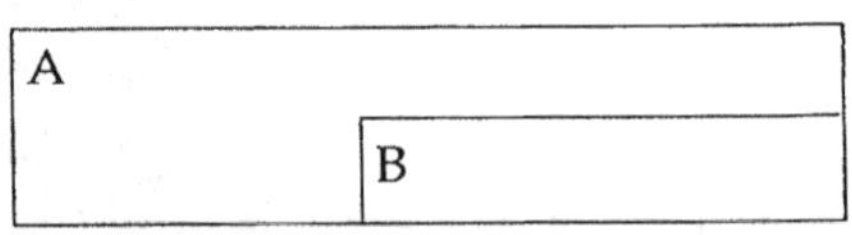

), we immediately become aware not only that this A is bigger than this B but that every A is bigger than every B, and this because of the very natures of A and B. Such a psychological process we shall later describe as "intellective induction through immediate insight" (see Ch. X, Sec. 3). On the efficient cause proposition, see Ch. VIII, Sec. 4b.

[5] Manifestly, this awareness also is similar to our realization concerning the whole-part relationship (see previous note) and will also be later described as an "intellective induction through immediate insight."

Such is the proposition which Aristotle will constantly use in handling the evidences of change/stability, but before outlining those processes we must consider his second general assertion—namely, that an individual material thing is a genuine unity of special stringency and type.

2. Unity

To judge by one of his speeches, Charles de Gaulle, former President of France, was keenly aware of the importance of unity as the essential factor in keeping his country strong and independent. "France has retained her national unity and her national cohesion," he said. "Our salvation depends entirely on maintaining our national unity. I say here with special emphasis that outside this unity, there is no salvation for us."[6]

Aristotle too is convinced that unity is important, but his concern is with the role it plays when a philosopher comes to evaluate the internal make-up of individual things. This role will be clear when we present in detail the process which that evaluation entails, but perhaps a single statement will enable us even now to have an initial appreciation of how significant unity is: "One and the same thing (for example, this man) presents the twofold evidence of change/stability, and, therefore, that thing is made up of two constitutive parts." The parts are not the thing itself, which is truly one, and yet both the thing and its parts are genuinely real because both are actually present. Consequently, although the parts are real, they are not of identically the same nature as the thing itself, because neither part is the thing itself but only one of its real constituents. Accordingly, what the parts are is determined by the sort of unity to be found in the whole which they constitute. If the whole is, say, an army or a basketball team, then its parts are themselves individual men or women. But if the whole is itself an individual man, then his parts are themselves real and yet are not other individuals. As we shall see later, they are that by which the man is human or is mathematical or is angry.

Unity is, then, of supreme importance in our philosophical endeavor; accordingly, we must investigate what it is. When we speak of "one and the same thing," what does *one* mean? If I say that a thing is yellow or round or a cabbage plant, I know what

---

[6] Reported in *St. Louis Globe-Democrat,* Sunday, October 23, 1960, p. 1.

those predicates mean. But when I say, "The thing is one," what is signified? Let us answer by looking at some concrete cases.

If we contrast a set of bricks, cement, and lumber found in a supply-store with another and equal set which makes up a house, what is the difference between the two sets? Not in the number of bricks or sacks of cement, since the amount in each case is equal, but in the fact that the materials in the second case have been so brought together as to fashion a house. The difference is, then, that the first set is in a state of separation and division, whereas the second is in a state of togetherness, of undividedness, of cohesion. In short, the first is a mere aggregation, a pile, a multitude; the second is a unity. The same difference is manifest if we contrast a set of wheels, sparkplugs, upholstery fabric, and other parts found in a store with another set of wheels and sparkplugs and so on which form an automobile, or if we contrast a set of ten students as each eats his evening meal at his own home with another set of ten students actually playing a basketball game in the gymnasium.

According to the present level of consideration, then, unity is a status of togetherness, cohesion, undividedness.

But a more rigorous sort of cohesion exists than that found in a house, machine, or team, as can be readily seen in the constitutive parts of any individual living thing, whether it be a plant or animal or human. If one cuts off a man's arm or a bear's paw or a tree branch, the arm, paw and branch are no longer alive and can no longer perform their previous functions. In short, they no longer are what they were, and in that sense their very natures have changed. Such a change indicates that as parts of the living thing they depend upon the whole in a way totally different from the way in which a soldier depends upon the army or a student upon the football team of which he is a member, for a soldier or a student can leave the army or the team without undergoing such a radical change, without ceasing to be human. The former are dependent intrinsically and entitatively: they were originally produced by the living organism as it grew, they are nourished by it, their injuries are repaired by it, they die if removed from it. The whole also shows itself to be intrinsically and entitatively dependent upon its essential parts. Remove a man's liver or a lion's heart or an oak tree's roots and the entire human being, lion, or tree will die. Such internal and ontic (see note 10, last paragraph) dependence of living parts upon the whole and of a living whole upon its parts points to an inner bond of unity which differs not merely in degree but also in kind from that found in a house or machine or army.

That more stringent unity also is manifested in other ways by living beings. For example, my bodily condition has repercussions upon my psychological state, and vice versa. If I am in good health, I can think clearly; if not, my thought processes are disturbed or perhaps entirely disrupted. If I am struck on the head or take drugs, I may become unconscious. On the other hand, if my mental and emotional state is one of shame, I blush; if of anger, I become flushed, my pulse beats faster, adrenalin flows; if of fear, I grow pale and cold, I tremble; if of constant worry, I develop ulcers. This reciprocal influence of matter upon mind and mind upon matter arises from the intrinsic and entitative reliance of each upon the other, and thereby reveals again the strict unity of the whole which they constitute.

Again, the parts of an automobile and of an army work together for a goal which is extrinsic to themselves—that of the driver or of the commander-in-chief. The parts of a living thing, however, work together directly for a goal which is intrinsic to themselves and to the thing, for by their cooperation they produce, nourish, and conserve themselves and the life of the whole. This cooperation can be clearly seen in the coordinating members of a living existent. Not only does a man consist of such distinct organs as senses, glands, brain, lungs, and heart, each with its own function for the benefit of the whole and (ultimately) of itself (for example, the lungs oxygenate the blood, the heart pumps it), but he also has members whose entire function is to coordinate other parts. For example, the circulatory system brings food and oxygen throughout the body and removes waste products. The endocrine and nervous control systems keep all particular functions balanced, in harmony with each other, and adjusted to the requirements of the whole. All such parts can work together because they are together in a single living organism that entitatively and internally depends upon them and they upon it.

These evidences, together with much more which could be brought forward,[7] clearly indicate that a man, a giraffe, or a rose-

---

[7] See G. P. Klubertanz, S.J., *Philosophy of Human Nature* (New York: Appleton-Century-Crofts, 1953), pp. 15–34, where he furnishes evidence for the essential unity of a living thing and interprets facts from modern physical, chemical, and biological sciences which seem to militate against that unity. One such fact (pp. 22 sqq.) is that the spectrograph of a living thing shows the characteristic spectrum lines of water, carbon, and so forth. In view of that fact a chemist might say that a living thing is (using our terminology) not an intrinsic unity but an accidental unity, a mere collection of chemicals. What

bush enjoy (or even are)[8] a condition of cohesion and togetherness which essentially surpasses that found in a house, an army, or a machine. In short, an individual living thing is a genuine unity of a unique rigor and kind.

In conclusion, then, what have we seen from our examination of concrete cases?

1. Unity is a state or condition of cohesion, togetherness, undividedness.
2. There are at least two kinds of unity:
   (a) that which is found in a house, team, or machine and which is traditionally called "accidental" (*per accidens*) or "extrinsic" unity;
   (b) that which is found in a man, lion, or tree and which is called "essential" (*per se*) or, better, "intrinsic" unity.[9]

---

can be said in reply? Let us grant the fact, yet recall that water in living human skin does not have all the characteristics of water in a relatively pure liquid state and has some alien characteristics (for example, it shares in the living, sentient, rational state of the whole). To cover this situation, the phrase, "virtual presence," is used (which seems to come from the everyday expression meaning "almost but not quite"—"The fog is so heavy that it's virtually raining," "This wine is virtually vinegar"). Water is only virtually present in a living human being—that is, it is present *partially* (with only some of its own characteristics) and as *subordinated to another* (it is part of another and more complex thing, some of whose characteristics it takes on). Water is formally present in, say, this glass or this river—that is, it is present *fully* (with all its own characteristics) and *independently* (it is not an intrinsic part of something else). Thus, because water and other chemicals are only virtually present in a man, he still retains his essential unity.

This notion of virtual presence seems accurately to describe not only how chemicals are present in living things but also how simple elements are present in compounds (for example, how hydrogen and oxygen are present in water) and how the physical counterparts of subatomic particles are present in atoms.

See also James E. Royce, S.J., *Man and His Nature* (New York: McGraw-Hill Book Company, 1961), p. 259 sq.; *idem, Man and Meaning* (New York: McGraw-Hill Book Co., 1969), pp. 229, 236, 253.

[8] The state of cohesion and togetherness to be found in an accidental unity is a mere complex of real relations between its members, and that is what "army," "family," and other collective nouns directly express. But the state of cohesion in an intrinsic unity is more than a mere relationship between its parts. It *is* the entire individual, it *is* his very entity. Unity and entity here are coextensive.

[9] Because of the ambiguity of "essence" (see Ch. IV, Sec. 4 and notes 51–53), we shall generally substitute "intrinsic" for "essential." The other sort of

3. *Accidental unity* is that state of togetherness and cohesion which is comparatively extrinsic and nonentitative[10] because its parts are entitatively independent of the whole.
4. *Intrinsic unity* is that state of cohesion and togetherness which is internal and entitative because its parts entitatively depend upon the whole and work together for an intrinsic goal: to produce and conserve the parts themselves and the whole.

The latter sort of unity Aristotle finds within individual material things[11] and, hence, also finds their constitutive parts to be by

---

unity, though, can conveniently be designated as either "accidental" or "extrinsic."

There is also a third sort of unity—the state of cohesion and undividedness to be found in something which has no parts. This can be called "unity of simplicity" or "absolute unity" and is found in God, in a substantial form, and in various other constitutive parts.

[10]The significance of "entitative" (and its opposite) should be clear from our previous discussion and examples. It is derived from "entity" and points to the connection which unity has with what a being is, with its very entity. In some cases the unity is such that if you separate a part from the whole, you introduce little or no intrinsic change into the part itself (nonentitative). But in other instances if you remove a part from the whole, the unity is so stringent that the part no longer remains specifically what it was (entitative). Also see note 8 above.

Incidentally, "ontic" when used in this section (for example, see above, Sec. 2, prgr. 6) and, for that matter, throughout the entire book, is directly based upon the Greek *on, ontos* ("being," "entity") and is intended simply as synonymous with "entitative." It has none of the connotations of the word as used by various contemporary radical existentialists.

[11] So far our discussion of intrinsic unity has been directed to living things, and this for the reason that such offer more easily perceived data. Still there is evidence of intrinsic unity also on the inanimate level. See Phillipus Selvaggi, S.J., *Cosmologia* (Romae: Apud Aedes Pont. Universitatis Gregorianae, 1959), pp. 264–86; Fredericus Saintonge, S.J., *Summa Cosmologiae* (Montreal: Imprimerie du Messager, 1941), pp. 416–39; Petrus Hoenen, S.J., *Cosmologia* (Romae: Apud Aedes Pont. Universitatis Gregorianae, 1956), pp. 358 sq.; Jaime Echarri, S.J., *Philosophia Entis Sensibilis* (Romae: Herder, 1959), pp. 98 sq.; K. F. Dougherty, *Cosmology* (Peekskill, N.Y.: Graymoor Press, 1952), pp. 125–33; D. Nys, *Cosmology* (Milwaukee: Bruce Publishing Co., 1942), II, 161–264 and 433–40; V. Smith, *Philosophical Physics* (New York: Harper & Row Publishers, 1950), pp. 189–231.

That inanimates do involve intrinsic unity is not as difficult to see as where it is located. Is the water in this glass an intrinsic unit? Or is each molecule of water the unit (and, thus, a glass of water is an accidental unit)? Or is an atom

nature genuinely different from those of a machine or house or army. In the next sections we shall face just what those parts are and how great that difference is.

3. Change/Stability in the Accidental Order

In the example already given (Ch. I, Sec. 3), the young daughter experiences love for her mother. Then she learns what "one," "two," and other numbers mean. Next she tries to express that love in those newly acquired quantitative terms, and then comes the new discovery that love and quantity are incompatible. All those psychological states she goes through while remaining basically human, and, in fact, the same human person who was born some four years earlier, who grew physically, who gradually came to a fuller use of her cognitive powers, who learned to express herself through language, who even earlier that day had spoken and eaten and played. Or take again the instance of Patricia Markor (see Ch. II, Sec. 3). On the very day of her heroic act she awoke and may have read the paper, taken breakfast, planned the day ahead, daydreamed about a vacation as she walked to the station; she saw the woman step onto the tracks, blanched in horror, wondered what to do, struggled with her fear, ignored her pounding heart, cooperated with a sudden surge of strength she experienced within, calculated the speed of the on-coming train, leapt after the woman and pulled her to safety. And all the while she remained human, and, in fact, the same human existent who was born some years ago in a certain place, went to school, graduated, moved away from home, and began a new job a week ago.

What would be Aristotle's reaction to such cases? He would first say that they involve accidental changes, since the modifications undergone, frequent and impressive as they are, do not specifically change either person: each remains a living human being. Next,

---

within the molecule the unit? Or are the various subatomic particles (or, more accurately: the physical counterparts to what empiriological scientists call subatomic particles) the units?

At any rate, no matter where one locates the intrinsic unity, the first portion of its definition as worked out for living things seems applicable to nonliving items: "An intrinsic unity is that state of cohesion and togetherness which is internal and entitative because its parts entitatively depend upon the whole."

such modifications on the accidental level provide a twofold evidence of change and stability: one and the same thing remains specifically and generically what it is and yet acquires new individual perfections (thinking, loving, rescuing). Such evidences are clues to the internal make-up of each person, as the following process makes clear.

> [Directly perceived fact:] In accidental changes one and the same thing
> (a) remains specifically and generically what it is [stability]
> (b) and yet acquires new individual perfections [change];
> But evidence #a is other than evidence #b;
> But diverse evidences indicate the actual presence within of diverse constitutive parts;
> Therefore, such evidences indicate that the thing is actually made up of diverse constitutive parts:
> (a) that by which the thing specifically and generically remains what it is and yet receives individual perfections—"SUBSTANCE";
> (b) that by which the thing, while remaining specifically and generically what it is, is actually modified through a new individual perfection—"an ACCIDENT."

This process[12] indicates both that such parts do actually exist and, to an extent, what they are. It establishes their actual existence because, as we have previously seen (Ch. III, Sec. 1), the relationship between an evidence and a constitutive part is that between an effect and its intrinsic cause. But an effect of an intrinsic cause is present only because what causes it is also present. But accidental changes involve distinct evidences of modification and stability (effects) and, accordingly, reveal that distinct constitutive parts (causes) actually exist within the thing changing.

Second, it also shows what those parts are, and here the force of the fact that a material existent is an intrinsic unity (see Ch. III, Sec. 2) is apparent. An individual man is not a mere accidental unity such as an army or a hockey team, in which the parts are themselves

[12] The propositions which make up this process (and subsequent ones) have been organized into what may look like a syllogism for purposes of clarity and convenience. No one should think, though, that it is strictly a syllogism or involves formal deduction. That process is an intellective induction, as we shall see later (see Ch. X, Sec. 3).

individual men and thereby are intrinsically and entitatively independent of the whole which they help constitute. Rather he is an intrinsic unity, whose parts depend internally and entitatively upon him. Nevertheless, the whole (here, the man) is not any one of its parts, nor is any part the whole. Still both the whole and its parts are real (because actually present). Consequently, there is a difference between what the whole is and what each part is. This difference is difficult to put in words, but perhaps the expressions, "that which" and "that by which," will serve. The whole (the man himself) is *that which* is human, thinking, mathematical, and so forth. Each of its parts is *that by which* he is human, etc. For example, his substance is *that by which* he is human and remains human while receiving various accidental perfections. His mental activity (accident) is *that by which* he is thinking. His operative habit[13] of mathematics (accident) is *that by which* he is a mathematician.

Quite obviously, our knowledge of such parts is more than direct perception. True enough, we directly perceive that this man is accidentally changing, that he is acquiring some new individual perfection while remaining human. This perception we express in judgments, which furnish the starting point of our process. But our awareness of substance and accidents themelves transcends mere perception. We reflect upon that data offered through perception. We intellectually realize that change and stability are diverse evidences, that diverse evidences indicate the actual presence of distinct constituents, and that accordingly an accidentally changing thing is made up of diverse constitutive parts conveniently called substance and accidents. This last stage is an assent of the intellect to which it is forced by evidence: "There actually *is* substance, there actually *are* various accidents." In short, the process terminates in intellectual judgmental knowledge, by which we become aware that such constituents exist and what they are.

Such constitutive parts, then, are known by reflection upon perceived data, and this reflection is a genuinely intellectual operation. We cannot directly perceive substance or accidents. We cannot imagine or picture them. We know them through genuine intellection.[14]

---

[13] See Ch. I, n. 18.

[14] The term "substance" is derived from the Latin *substantia*, which in turn translates the Greek *to hypokeimenon* or *hê hypostasis*, which means "that which lies or stands under." If taken literally, the English, Latin and Greek words all have a spatial connotation, and one must be careful not to conceive substance as lying physically under the accidents as a sort of pincushion or foundation.

Manifestly, such constitutive parts are real in a unique sense and differ both from the whole which they make up and from its integral, physical parts (for example, lungs, arms, and heart). Up to this time we have been calling them "constitutive parts," but that general phrase is awkward, and moreover, is applicable to either an accidental, extrinsic unity (for example, individual soldiers are constitutive parts of an army) or an intrinsic unity. Even when applied to the latter, it fits either integral parts or substance/accidents. Some special term, then, is needed. Sometimes substance and accidents are called "principles" of the thing they constitute, but "principle" can refer also to intramental items, as occurs when one speaks of the premises of a syllogism as its *principles* or law as a *principle* of morality. Hence, that term will not do, for care must be taken to stress the fact that substance and accidents (and other such parts still to be considered) are actual, extramental constituents of things.

Is there any other term which might prove suitable? We have decided on "component." True enough, that word is as general as "constitutive part," because it can be applied to the parts of an accidental unity and to those of an intrinsic unity. But it is a single word, not a phrase, and seems to have few connotations of the merely intramental. In this book, then, "component" will be arbitrarily restricted to express only substance and accidents (and similar parts) and can be defined as follows: *A component is a constitutive part of an intrinsic unity, is known by intellectual consideration of directly perceived data, and is a "that by which."*[15]

The process we have been considering also reveals that the relationship between substance and accidents is one of "potency" to "act." What does this second set of terms mean? Historically, the

---

"Accident" does not so obviously connote the spatial and physical, for it comes from the Latin *accidens*, which translates the Greek *to sumbebêkos*, which is equivalent to "that which befalls or happens"—see Aristotle, *Metaphysics*, V, Ch. 30, 1025a13 sq.

Consequently, one must keep reminding oneself that substance and accidents are not spatial items and are not physically separated from one another. Substance permeates entity and is always to be conceived as a "that by which." Various and numerous accidents also permeate the entity, and each of them is also a "that by which."

[15] One must grant that "that by which" is clumsy, but it seems the best way to describe the function and nature of a component in contrast to the whole ("that which") of which it is a part. Their counterparts in Latin are *id quo* and *id quod*, which are perhaps no less barbarisms.

doctrine of act/potency arose as a reaction against those who claimed that all change (even local motion) is impossible, however apparent it may be in the visible universe.[16] Here is an example of the dialectical way they argued.

> In a change that which changes acquires something new;
> But that which changes either already is or is not;
> But if it already is, then it cannot change because it would already be what it was to have acquired or else it no longer would be what it had been;
> But if it is not, then it cannot change because there would be nothing to change;
> Therefore, change is impossible.

Aristotle replied by elaborating the theory of act/potency. You must distinguish the first minor, he advised, for that which will change from *A* to *B* is actually *A* but, simultaneously, is potentially *B*.[17] Take a man who is now at *A* but will move to *B*. Now he is actually at *A*, but even while there, he potentially is at *B* insofar as his bone-structure and muscles give him ability to walk. His walking is nothing but the progressive actuation of that potentiality.[18]

The notions of "act" and "potency" simply summarize what Aristotle expressed by the two adverbs, "actually" and "potentially." Thus in the previous example of the walking man, "act" is the perfection of his being at this or that place, whereas "potency" is his capacity of having that perfection. More generally, "act" is any such perfection, "potency" is the capacity of receiving a perfection.[19]

If we return now to substance/accidents, we see that these two components are examples of the potency/act relationship. The sub-

---

[16] This group includes Parmenides (fl. ca. 484 B.C.) and Zeno (fl. ca. 465–455 B.C.). See F. Copleston, S.J., *History*, I, pp. 47 sqq., pp. 54 sqq., and especially p. 311; J. Owens, *History*, pp. 56 sqq. and pp. 79 sqq.; G. S. Kirk, J. E. Raven and M. Schofield, *PS*, Chs. VIII and IX; W. K. C. Guthrie, *HGP*, II, 1–80.

[17] See *Metaphysics*, XII, Ch. 2, 1069b15 sq.: "Since that which 'is' has two senses, we must say that everything changes from that which is potentially to that which is actually." Also, *Physics*, III, Ch. 6, 206a14.

[18] Aristotle's justly famous definition of local motion: "The actuation of what exists potentially insofar as it exists potentially" (*Physics*, III, Ch. 1, 201a10–11). While actually changing, then, a thing is actually-potentially.

[19] Expressed in the more technical language of "that by which," an act is "that by which a thing is actually perfected," whereas a potency is "that by which a thing receives a perfection."

stance is that by which a thing receives perfections and an accident is that by which it is perfected. Consequently, substance is as potency to its accidents, which in turn function as acts.[20]

* One final point, and that is to issue a warning. "Substance" and "accident" are both used in everyday life and in technical contexts to convey various meanings. For example, one commonly hears said of a politician, "The substance of his speech last night was easily grasped," where "substance" is equivalent to "the important points." Or, more technically, a theologian will speak of the "divine substance," in which usage the term is the same as "reality" or "being."[21] Or a logician speaks of an individual thing as "first substance" and of the species or genus to which it belongs as "second substance";[22] he even locates substance on the top of his Porphyrean tree as the supreme genus.[23] Our warning is this: a metaphysician's meaning for "substance" differs from all the preceding. He restricts "substance" to a component, to a "that by which." For him substance is "that by which a thing specifically and generically remains what it is and yet receives various individual perfections." Such will be the only meaning which the term has hereafter in this book.

* Similarly, "accident" commonly signifies a chance event ("An automobile accident just occurred on the turnpike"). Or, technically, a logician classifies "white," "standing," "being an American" as accidents rather than as properties (for example, "capable of speech") because the former express concepts of attributes which belong to the subject only contingently.[24] Again our warning is that the meaning "accident" has for a metaphysician is unlike all of those. For him an accident is a component—"that by which a thing, while remaining specifically and generically what it is, is actually modified through a new individual perfection." The term "accident" will be restricted to that meaning hereafter in this book.[25] Let us now move on to the evidences offered by substantial changes.

---

[20] For a further discussion of act/potency, see Sec. 6 below.

[21] For example, Thomas Aquinas, *Summa Theologiae*, I, 13, 2 resp.

[22] Aristotle, *Categories*, Ch. 5, 2a11 sq.

[23] Andrew H. Bachhuber, S.J., *Introduction to Logic* (New York: Appleton-Century-Crofts, 1957), p. 245.

[24] *Ibid.*, p. 243.

[25] The basic difference between "accident" as understood by a logician and by a metaphysician is that for the former an accident is a concept, while for the latter it is a real, extramental component. For a metaphysician the term "accident" embraces what a logician expresses by both "accident" and "prop-

4. Change/Stability in the Substantial Order

In the last section we considered accidental changes—that is, modifications which do not specifically affect the thing. The young daughter experienced love for her mother, learned to count, tried to express her love in those numerical terms, discovered that love transcends quantity. Yet throughout she remained human and actually the same human being she had been.

But material things are subject to other changes which do specifically modify them. For example, the inanimate becomes living when food is assimilated into the human flesh of someone who eats it. The living becomes nonliving when a person dies. Let us consider a concrete case of this latter sort of substantial change—the heroic death of a surgeon, Dr. Andrew Ross, as told by his wife.[26] Her account I reproduce in some detail so as to make clear the difference between the series of accidental changes he went through and the substantial change with which they terminated.

In June of 1951 Dr. Ross was told he had cancer. An operation disclosed that all his abdominal glands were infected and that death was merely a matter of time.

> From then on, there was fear in his eyes. It was a controlled and disciplined fear, probably only visible to those who loved him—but it was there. . . . For all fit and happy people fear death: this terrible step which must be taken alone, and which cuts us off so irrevocably from all those we have known and loved.
>
> However, there were few changes in our life. We both clung to normality. If anything, Andrew worked harder—to accomplish as much as possible in what little time was left to him.

---

erty." The addition of "contingent" and "necessary" to our previous definition brings this out—an accident is "that by which a thing . . . is actually modified through a new individual perfection, which is either contingent [logician's 'accident'] or necessary [logician's 'property']."

[26] Mrs. Andrew Ross, "Death of a Man," *Jubilee*, 6 (September, 1958), 20–23. Her account was occasioned by Lael Wertenbaker, *Death of a Man* (New York: Random House, Inc., 1957), in which the author describes how her husband committed a carefully planned suicide rather than face a slow, painful death from cancer. This justification of suicide Mrs. Ross found depressing and frightening. To counteract its bad influence she wrote a report on her own husband's death.

> He lectured to his students, wrote his medical papers, treated his patients and enjoyed his friends. Toward me and the children, he showed a heightened awareness of the joy of being together and a hunger to lose none of our simple pleasures. The quiet country walks in lanes we knew so well took on an added significance. We looked at beauty with new eyes, because we now knew, as never before, that life was ephemeral. We realized that death gives life its meaning.

Two years and nine months thus passed by until, in the middle of March, new and disquieting symptoms manifested themselves.

> . . . and now the end had begun. Frequently there were depths of weakness so exhausting that it was worse than pain. There was the humiliating loss of speech which made his brilliant brain capable only of an agonized and frustrated gibberish; the useless paralyzed arm, which meant he had to be fed and bathed and dressed; the dragging leg which made movement impossible. . . . These are the times when man's dignity and strength are sublime. His never failed him. Dumb, wasted and worn, he asked for no drugs. . . . He neither asked nor took the easy way, but consciously went on paying his debt, with the greatness of his spirit shining through his ravaged body.

On the first of June, his doctor said that he could not possibly live through the night.

> Once more I sent for our priest to give him the blessings for his last journey. . . . The blessed candles were lit and flickered on either side of his bed in the warm twilight air. His sons, and I, and his sister-in-law, who had nursed him devotedly, knelt around his bed. Kneeling also in the room and stretching all along a wide corridor, were our friends. Together we prayed for his soul, poised in flight, between this world and the next. . . .
>
> He did not die that night, and early the following morning, for three precious minutes, he regained consciousness. Once again his dear blue eyes were alight with love and peace and memory, and God granted him three syllables to bid me goodbye. A moment later he closed his eyes, and a cuckoo, on a tree beneath his window, began his heartless calling. The sun was shining into the room—it was warm with the prom-

ise of a glorious day. Very soon we folded his pale hands reverently upon his breast. This was the death of a man.

What would be Aristotle's reaction to such a case? First, that the long series of accidental changes (Dr. Ross feared, lectured, wrote, treated patients, conversed with friends, loved his wife and sons, suffered, courageously refused drugs, and so forth) finally terminated in a change which substantially modified him: what was human and living became nonhuman and nonliving—a mass of pure chemicals. Second, that substantial modification provides a twofold evidence of change and stability. Accidental modifications combine change (the loss and acquirement of individual perfections—the doctor's fear replaced his previous carefree attitude, his illness excluded his former good health) with stability (the substantial continuity—the doctor feared death and yet remained human). So too a substantial modification combines change (the loss and acquirement of specific perfection—here, the living becomes nonliving) with stability, as illustrated by the "corporeal" continuity which endures through the modification. For death is not an annihilation. What was living remains somehow the same after death, as indicated by the fact that it retains temporarily at least (that is, until subsequent substantial changes or outside interference) the same appearances—the same shape, weight, color.[27] The amount, kind, and location of the pure chemicals which result after death are determined by the amount, kind, and location of virtual chemicals before death.[28] Finally, just as the diverse evidences of change/stability in accidental modifications indicate the actual pres-

---

[27] Our respect for the dead is a witness to this continuity, for if the body of a loved one was not somehow the same before and after death, we might just as well wake and bury the corpse of a stranger. In what sense is the body the same? Not specifically (since death is a substantial change), but generically or virtually (this last adverb arises from the notion of "virtual presence" [see note 7 above], for death can be looked upon as a change in which what was virtually present becomes formally present).

For additional information on substantial change (for example, that it is instantaneous, takes place through accidental changes and material dispositions, and so forth) see G. P. Klubertanz, S.J., *Philosophy of Human Nature*, pp. 404–7.

[28] By the substantial change the chemicals which were virtually present in the living thing now become formally present (see note 7 above). I call chemicals which are virtually present "virtual chemicals" and those which are formally present "pure chemicals." A chemist's terminology would be "bound" and "free" chemicals.

ence within of substance/accidents, so too the diverse evidences of change/stability in substantial modifications indicate the actual presence within the substance of two additional components. Accordingly, prior to substantial change the very substance is itself composed of two constitutive parts, for otherwise substantial change would be impossible.

The following process establishes and clarifies this composition.

> [Directly perceived fact:] A substantial change in a thing involves
> (a) the loss and acquirement of specific perfection [change]
> (b) together with corporeal continuity [stability];
> But evidence #a is other than evidence #b;
> But diverse evidences indicate the actual presence within of diverse components;
> Therefore, such evidences indicate that on the substantial level a material thing is actually made up of two real and diverse components:
> (a) that by which a thing is of such and such a specific nature and, hence, has its own distinctive characteristics—"SUBSTANTIAL FORM";
> (b) that by which a material thing receives a substantial form and yet which is capable, through subsequent substantial change, of receiving other substantial forms—"PRIME MATTER."

That process indicates both that such components do actually exist, and, to a degree, what they are (as the previous process concerning accidental modifications had done for substance/accidents [see Ch. III, Sec. 3], and what we say in the next paragraphs will be an adaptation of what we previously remarked with respect to that former process).

This process establishes their actual presence because the relationship between an evidence and a component is that between an effect and its intrinsic cause. But an effect of an intrinsic cause is present only because what causes it is also present. But substantial modifications involve distinct evidences of change and stability (effects); therefore, they reveal that distinct components (causes) actually exist within the thing changing.

It also shows, to an extent, what those components are, and once again the force of the fact that a material thing is an intrinsic unity is apparent. An individual man is not a mere accidental or extrinsic unity such as is an army or a football team, in which the parts are themselves individual men, and thereby, are intrinsically and entitatively independent of the whole which they help constitute. Rather he is an intrinsic unity, whose parts depend internally and entitatively upon him. Nevertheless, the whole (here, the man) is not any one of its parts nor is any part the whole. Still both the whole and its parts are real (because actually present). Accordingly, there is a difference between the reality of the whole and of the parts, between what the whole is and what each part is. This difference can again be expressed in terms of "that which" and "that by which." The whole (the man himself) is *that which* is human. His substantial form is *that by which* he is human (and, thus, is specifically like other humans and unlike dogs, petunias, hydrogen). His prime matter is *that by which* he has received his substantial form and, ultimately, is this man.[29]

Once again, our knowledge of such components is more than direct perception. True enough, we directly perceive situations in which this or that sort of substantial change occurs. This perception we express in judgments, which furnish the starting point of our process. But our awareness of primary matter and substantial form themselves transcends mere perception. We reflect upon the data offered through perception. We intellectually realize that the loss and acquirement of specific perfection and corporeal continuity are diverse evidences, that diverse evidences indicate the actual presence of the diverse components causing them, and that consequently a thing which is capable of substantial change is made up of the diverse components called prime matter and substantial form. This last stage is an assent of the intellect to which it is forced by the evidence of substantial modifications: "There actually *is* substantial form, there actually *is* primary matter." In brief, the process terminates in intellectual judgmental knowledge, by which we become aware that such components exist and what they are.

Such constitutive parts, then, are known by reflection upon perceived data, and this reflection is a genuinely intellectual operation. We cannot directly perceive prime matter and substantial form. We cannot picture or imagine them. We know matter and form through genuine intellection.

The process we are currently considering also indicates that the relation between prime matter and substantial form is one of po-

---

[29] On prime matter as the ultimate source of substantial individuation, see Ch. VI, Sec. 5b.

tency to act. An act is a perfection and potency is the capacity of receiving a perfection. But prime matter is such a capacity and substantial form is a perfection, for our process ends in our affirming that the former is "that by which a material thing receives a substantial form and yet which is capable, through subsequent substantial change, of receiving other substantial forms," and that the latter is "that by which a thing is of such and such a specific nature and, accordingly, has its own distinctive characteristics and activities." Therefore, prime matter and substantial form are related to one another as potency and act. In fact, prime matter is *pure* potency, because the adjective means "nothing but." Prime matter is *nothing but* a recipient and a capacity. Although it is real because it actually exists within a material existent, still, of itself, it has no act whatsoever.[30] Its sole function within the thing of which it is a constitutive part is to receive, to limit, to individuate.

* A final (and important) point is to investigate the force of the phrases "prime matter" and "substantial form." Why call the one component "matter," and, in fact, "prime matter"? What is the force of the adjective? Then, too, why call the other "form," and also, "substantial form"? Again, what is the significance of the adjective?

* First of all, "material" can be used in opposition to "immaterial." When contrasted with intellection, freedom, courage, value, and the like, such things as these humans, these animals, these plants, and these chemicals all have at least one common trait: each has parts outside of parts, each is actually extended, is directly in place. This common characteristic has come to be expressed by the term "material," which therefore means simply "that which has parts outside of parts, is actually extended, is directly in place." Of what can that term be directly predicated? Only of that which itself has parts outside of parts—thus of humans, animals, plants, and minerals. Is it directly predicable of components? No, because none of them (whether they be prime matter, substantial form, or various accidents) is a *that which* but rather a *that by which*. None of

---

[30] Prime matter is thus unlike substance, which is potency with respect to accidents and yet is itself a composite of act/potency—that is, of substantial form/prime matter. Accordingly, substance is not pure potency but of itself involves an act (substantial form).

One way to establish that prime matter is pure potency is to rely on the fact that there is only one substantial form in each thing, and this because an individual thing is an intrinsic unity. His single substantial form is that by which this man is corporeal, living, sentient, and rational. For prime matter to have an act or form of its own would disrupt the stringent unity each human is.

them is itself actually extended, has parts outside of parts, is immediately in place. Therefore, each one is in itself not material, which is the same as saying that each is, in its own way, immaterial. And this latter adjective then points simply to the fact that of itself each is without parts and is not actually extended.[31] Thus a human soul, a canine soul, and prime matter are not themselves material. What, then, does the noun mean in the phrase "prime matter"? Quite obviously, it does not have reference directly to actual extension, to parts outside of parts, since prime matter and substantial form are themselves, in this frame of reference, both non-material.

* But what, positively, does the noun signify? In everyday life "material" is also used in another way and here it is in contrast with "formal." For instance, gabardine, silk, wool, and the like are the *material* from which suits are made. Bricks, cement, lumber, and glass are the *materials* going into the construction of a new house. Wood or marble or bronze is the *material* for a statue. Words and rhythm are the *materials* of a poem. But those artifacts do not consist just of the materials from which they are made. Gabardine and the other cloths become a suit only if they are cut according to a definite pattern. Bricks, cement, lumber, and the like become a house only when assembled and set up according to a definite plan and shape. Wood or marble is a statue only when a definite figure is carved or chiseled in it. Words and rhythm become a poem only when organized in a definite structure. If such things as cloth, bricks, marble, and words are the *materials* of the artifacts, then the pattern, plan and shape, figure and structure are their "forms." In such examples "matter" is that which can receive some or other

---

[31] Of course, each of the various components is immaterial in its own way. Some (for example, the human soul) are intrinsically independent of matter and the term "spiritual" is used to describe this status. Others (for example, a canine soul) are intrinsically dependent on matter, and "barely immaterial" or some such expression can be used for their status. Prime matter is still more intimately linked with materiality, for quantity, although a property of the composite, flows more directly from prime matter than from substantial form (see Ch. VI, Sec. 5b). Still prime matter of itself is not actually extended, and thus it too is immaterial in its own way (see Ch. V, Sec. 4).

All the components can be classified as "material" only through extrinsic denomination (see Ch. IV, n. 35, below)—that is, they are the constitutive parts of a thing which is itself actually extended and to which "material" is directly and properly applied. Of course, this classification too will vary in accordance with the varying function each component has within the thing and with the varying degrees of dependence each has upon matter.

pattern, shape, figure, structure. It is that which is of itself without determination but which is determinable in various ways by the introduction of diverse formal factors—for example, a piece of suitably large cloth can become a suit or a dress or a tent, the difference arising from the pattern used. It is that which can be perfected in this or that manner by submitting to this or that determining element. More generally, then, "matter" is simply *that which receives, that which is perfected, that which is determinable,* whereas "form" is *that which is received, that which perfects, that which determines.*

* Such is the meaning which the noun has in the phrase "prime matter." Within the substance, the component which has substantial form as its counterpart is said to be "matter" not because it is itself extended or has parts outside of parts, but because it receives that form and thereby is perfected and determined. On the other hand, the component within the substance which has prime matter as its partner is called "form" because it is received by prime matter, which it thereby perfects and determines.[32]

* But why "*prime* matter" and "*substantial* form"? What is the force of the adjectives? They have traditionally been considered to be at least useful because there are two sets of recipients, as well as two sets of received perfections. This man, say, consists of a component (prime matter) which receives the specific perfection (substantial form) and of a component (substance) which receives individual perfections (accidents). If one were perfectly consistent, the recipients of specific perfections and of individual perfections would be both called "matter" because they are recipients, and then termed "first" or "second" matter to indicate that each receives different perfections: "first" or "prime" matter receives the more basic, ontologically prior, specific perfection; "second" matter receives the

---

[32] This general description of matter and form will have to be refined a bit later on. First of all, determination will turn out to be of two sorts—"to limit a perfection" and "to confer a perfection." (See Ch. V, Sec. 3, on auto-determination.) As used in connection with form, the term signifies the conferment of perfection. Also, form in a strict sense will be seen to be an intrinsic, static, and quidditative perfection in order to contrast it with real relations, operations, and the act of existing; these latter are perfections but are not forms. Finally, matter/form are not synonymous with potency/act but, rather, are potency/act *within the essence.*

These refinements will be made clearer later on, but for the present time and purposes the general description of matter and form is sufficiently accurate and detailed.

less fundamental, ontologically posterior, individual perfections.[33] But language is seldom consistent; hence philosophers commonly designate the recipient of substantial form as "prime matter" while calling the recipient of accidents "substance." We shall abide by this common practice.

* The case is somewhat similar with respect to "substantial form." As we have just remarked, there are two sets of received perfections—the specific and the individual. If one were completely consistent, both those perfections would be called "form" because they are both perfections received by potencies. Then, if we were to keep in line with "first" and "second" matter, the specific perfection could be designated as "first form" and an individual perfection as "second form." But the former perfection has come to be called "substantial form" and the latter "accidental form," or simply "accident." We shall again abide by this common practice and use "substantial form" and "accident" to designate the specific perfection and an individual perfection.[34]

* The preceding analysis has been rather tedious, but it is important in this way. It enables us to realize that the noun in the phrase "prime matter" does not imply that the component to which it is applied is itself actually extended or has parts outside of parts. Rather, it simply indicates that that component is a recipient—the recipient of a specific perfection, which perfects and determines it. This realization is an important factor in gaining an accurate understanding of that component, as well as of the others.

5. Summary and Conclusions

(a) In Chapter III our goal has been to observe and then to profit by Aristotle's reaction to the sensible universe. This Greek philosopher had himself profited by observing his predecessors. From Heraclitus he learned that change is a factor in reality because real things change. From Plato he became aware that reality also involved stability, but maintained that this stability is not located in

---

[33] In this interpretation, "second matter" is the same as substance. In actual use, though, the phrase has come to be restricted to the realm of artifacts. For example, a block of marble is "second matter" with respect to the statue it can become: it can receive and be perfected by various figures or shapes.

[34] I shall use "accident" rather than "accidental form" because, as will be clear later, not every accident is a form. See Ch. VII, Sec. 3, on relations.

some separate realm of subsistent Essences but in actual things. Here is a clear token of Aristotle's genius: his realization that actual things are neither total change nor total permanence but rather combine the two. An individual thing is a changing stability and stabilized change, and this on two levels—on the substantial or on the accidental level, depending upon whether or not the modifications specifically affect what the existent is.

(b) In exploiting this double evidence of change/stability on the two levels, Aristotle relies on two important insights gained from the actual world in which we live.

1. First of all, *diverse evidences indicate the actual presence within of diverse constitutive parts,* since the latter are the intrinsic cause of the former. Accordingly, change and stability on the two levels point to two sets of distinct, actually present constitutive parts, for otherwise such evidences would themselves be absent: effects (here, change and stability) are present only because their intrinsic causes (here, diverse constitutive parts) are present.

2. Second, a material existent involves intrinsic (*per se*) unity—*a state of cohesion, togetherness, undividedness which is internal and entitative because its parts entitatively depend upon the whole.*[35] The result of this unity is that the constitutive parts of which we have been speaking are real in a different way from that of the whole which they help make up. This difference let us express by the phrases *that which* and *that by which*. The whole (this man) is *that which* is human or mathematical; his constitutive parts are each *that by which* he is human or mathematical. For purposes of convenience and clarity, let us call such parts "components"; hereafter that term will have the following meaning. *A component is a constitutive part of an intrinsic unity, is known by intellectual consideration of directly perceived data, and is a "that by which."*

(c) So far four such components have been uncovered in material existents. The first set has been named "substance" and "accidents" and is indicated by the accidental modifications which things undergo and which involve the twofold evidence of change (the loss and acquirement of individual perfections) and stability (substantial or specific/generic continuity).

---

[35] This description would seem to fit both the living and the nonliving. For the living, though, one can also add the clause, "and because the parts work together for an intrinsic goal." On intrinsic (*per se*) unity on the inanimate level, see n. 11 above.

1. This evidence reveals not only that such components actually exist but also, to an extent, what they are. *Substance is that by which a material thing specifically and generically remains what it is and yet receives various individual perfections. An accident is that by which the thing, while remaining specifically and generically what it is, is actually modified through a new individual perfection.* As those descriptions readily indicate, a substance and an accident are each a *that by which.*

2. Although they are known by reflection upon perceived data, this reflection is a genuinely intellectual operation, which terminates in intellectual judgmental knowledge. They themselves cannot be directly perceived or imagined or pictured, but are known by genuine intellection.

3. Finally, substance and accidents are related to one another as potency to act because the role of substance is to receive accidents, which simultaneously perfect it.

(d) The second set of components is named "prime matter" and "substantial form" and is known to exist within an individual thing because of the substantial modifications which such things undergo and which involve the twofold evidence of change (the loss and acquirement of specific perfection) and stability (corporeal continuity).

1. This evidence reveals not only that such components actually exist but also, to a degree, what they are. *Prime matter is that by which a material thing receives a substantial form and yet which is capable, through subsequent substantial change, of receiving other substantial forms. A substantial form is that by which a thing is of such and such a specific nature and, hence, has its own distinctive characteristics and activities.* According to those descriptions, prime matter and substantial form are each a *that by which.*

2. Although the starting-point of the process by which they are known is directly perceived data, those components themselves are known by reflection upon that data and this reflection is a genuinely intellectual operation, terminating in intellectual judgments. They themselves cannot be directly perceived or imagined or pictured but are known by genuine intellection.

3. Again, prime matter and substantial form are to one another as potency to act inasmuch as the former receives and limits the latter, which simultaneously specifies and thereby perfects it. In fact, prime matter is pure potency, because it is *nothing but* potency. Without any act or form of its own, it itself is nothing but a recipient, a capacity, a limit, although it is real because it actually exists within the substance.

4. Finally, the noun in the phrase "prime matter" does not entail that the component of which it is predicated is itself actually extended, has parts outside of parts, or is directly in place. Like other components, prime matter itself is free of those characteristics, which are applied to it only through extrinsic denomination. Rather, the noun "matter" signifies simply that the component of which it is predicated is a recipient—the recipient of a specific perfection, which perfects and determines it and which for that reason is designated as "substantial form."[36]

(e) Are those four the only components to be found within a material thing? To answer, one must ask another question: does a material thing furnish any evidence over and above change and stability on the accidental and the substantial levels? If not, then such are the only components. If it does, then it also contains whatever component is manifesting itself through that additional evidence.

Aristotle's answer to this second question would be negative: a sensible thing offers the two evidences of change and stability on the two levels and nothing more. One must wait some fourteen centuries for a different answer, and then it is given by a Catholic priest and Dominican theologian. The most important clue that a sensible thing gives to its internal make-up, Thomas Aquinas (1225–1274) replies, is not that it changes accidentally and substantially but that *it does actually exist,* that it is an *actual existent.* Since a diverse evidence indicates the actual presence within of a diverse component, a sensible thing involves not only substance/accidents and prime matter/substantial form but also a new and different component—namely, *that by which* a thing actually exists and which can be called "the act of existing" or simply "existence."

---

[36] Up to this time the components have been exemplified only with respect to living existents. What of the nonliving? Wherever one finds intrinsic units on the inanimate level, there one also finds substance/accidents and prime matter/substantial form, which can be described as follows. With respect to, say, hydrogen, "substance" would be "that by which this unit is and remains hydrogen and yet receives various individual perfections" (such as weight, transparency, and so forth). "Accident" would be "that by which this unit, while remaining hydrogen, is actually modified by some or other such individual perfection." "Substantial form" would be "that by which this unit is hydrogen (rather than oxygen or any of the other elements)." "Prime matter" would be "that by which this unit has received the substantial form of hydrogen but which is capable, through subsequent substantial change, of receiving other substantial forms (for example, that of water)."

This component is the heart of the existent's reality, the ultimate source of all its perfections. To the metaphysician it contributes the formal object of his science, for he studies beings as being, which is simply another way of saying that he studies existents precisely *as existent*, existents in the very exercise of their acts of existing.

By making this reply, Aquinas stepped from a philosophy of nature up to the distinct and higher level of metaphysics.[37]

Suggested Readings

Adler, Mortimer J., *Aristotle for Everybody: Difficult Thought Made Easy.* New York: MacMillan Publishing Co., 1978.

Aristotle, *Basic Works,* ed. Richard McKeon, pp. 230–36, 253–57, 745–47. New York: Random House, Inc., 1941. On change.

De Raeymaeker, Louis, *The Philosophy of Being,* trans. E. H. Ziegelmeyer, S.J., pp. 170–81. St. Louis: B. Herder Book Co., 1954. On substance and accidents as underlying accidental change.

Gerrity, Brother Benignus, *Nature, Knowledge, and God,* pp. 63–82, 102–44. Milwaukee: Bruce Publishing Co., 1947. On matter and form, substance and accidents.

Gilson, Etienne, *Being and Some Philosophers* (2nd ed.), pp. 41–73. Toronto: Pontifical Institute of Mediaeval Studies, 1952. A study of how Aristotelians conceive reality.

Guthrie, W. K. C., *A History of Greek Philosophy—Aristotle: An Encounter,* Vol. 6. Cambridge University Press, 1981.

Hawkins, D. J. B., "Change, Potency, and Act," in *Being and Becoming,* pp. 97–109. New York: Sheed & Ward, 1954.

———, "Substance," *ibid.*, pp. 110–23.

Jastrow, Robert, *The Enchanted Loom: The Mind in the Universe.* New York: Simon & Schuster, 1981.

[37] Since Aristotle does not seem to have been aware of the act of existing, does that absence mean that he had no metaphysics? No, Aristotle did have a science of being as being, but it was concerned with the First Movers, who alone are being in a strict sense and are fully real, and it dealt with the sensible universe only in reference to them. See J. Owens, *History*, pp. 322 sqq.; *idem, Doctrine of Being,* Ch. XIX, pp. 455–73; for a survey of interpretations prior to Owens' see *ibid.*, Ch. I, pp. 1–68; for a survey of reactions to Owens' own interpretation, see *ibid.*, pp. xiii–xxvii. Also see Henry B. Veatch, *Aristotle: A Contemporary Appreciation* (Bloomington: Indiana University Press, 1974), Ch. V, pp. 128–61; W. K. C. Guthrie, *A History of Greek Philosophy—Aristotle: An Encounter*, Vol. 6 (Cambridge: University Press, 1981).

On Aristotle's unawareness of the act of existing, see Edward Stevens, "The Perfection of Being in Aristotle," *Modern Schoolman*, 41 (March, 1964), 227–49.

McMullin, Ernan, ed., *The Concept of Matter.* Notre Dame: University of Notre Dame Press, 1963. This volume contains valuable articles on "matter" in the Greeks, medievals, moderns, and contemporaries (both philosophers and empiriological scientists). The following are most relevant: Ernan McMullin, "Introduction: The Concept of Matter," pp. 1–41; John J. Fitzgerald, "'Matter' in Nature and the Knowledge of Nature: Aristotle and the Aristotelian Tradition," pp. 79–98; Joseph Owens, "Matter and Predication in Aristotle," pp. 99–121; Norbert Luyten, O.P., "Matter as Potency," pp. 122–41; Ernan McMullin, "Matter as a Principle," pp. 169–213; Milton Frisk, "Primary Matter and Unqualified Change," pp. 214–41; Harry A. Nielsen, "The Referent of 'Primary Matter,'" pp. 244–54; Ernan McMullin, "Four Senses of 'Potency,'" pp. 295–318.

Owens, Joseph, *The Doctrine of Being in the Aristotelian Metaphysics.* 3rd ed. Toronto: Pontifical Institute of Mediaeval Studies, 1978.

———, *Aristotle: The Collected Papers of Joseph Owens,* ed. John R. Catan. Albany: SUNY Press, 1981. Chs. 1, 6, 10 and 11.

Stevens, Edward, "The Perfection of Being in Aristotle," *The Modern Schoolman,* 41 (March, 1964), 227–50.

Sweeney, S.J., Leo, "Aristotle's Infinity of Quantity," in *idem, Divine Infinity in Greek and Medieval Thought* (New York/Bern: Peter Lang Publishing, Inc., 1992), ch. 8, pp. 143–66.

Van Melsen, Andrew Gerard, *The Philosophy of Nature,* pp. 39–48 and 103–23. Pittsburgh: Duquesne University Press, 1953. On matter and form; on difficulties concerning substantial change.

Van Roo, S.J., William A., "Matter as a Principle of Being," *The Modern Schoolman,* 18 (1940), 1–5.

Veatch, Henry, "Aristotelianism," in *A History of Philosophical Systems,* ed. V. Ferm, pp. 106–17. New York: The Philosophical Library, 1950.

———, *Aristotle: A Contemporary Appreciation.* Bloomington: Indiana University Press, 1974.

Wild, John, *Introduction to Realistic Philosophy,* pp. 277–95 and 320–30. New York: Harper & Row, Publishers, 1948. On change; on matter and form; on substance and accidents.

Part II

Primacy of Existence

IV

Existence and Essence

There are some who look on the Middle Ages as intellectually barren, on the Catholic Church as a hindrance to original research, on sacred theology as inimical to progress in philosophy. How amazing and even disconcerting it must be for them to discover that the one who transcended Aristotle by making a most significant contribution to philosophy is a thirteenth-century Catholic theologian. For Thomas Aquinas did just that by realizing that actual existents involve a component heretofore overlooked, which is totally different from essence and which he named *esse* or "act of existing."[1]

---

[1] As an evaluation of Aquinas' contribution to metaphysics, see Etienne Gilson, *Elements of Christian Philosophy* (New York: Doubleday & Company, Inc., 1960), p. 278: "The doctrine of Thomas Aquinas has this superiority over the others: that its principles are, in a sense, the same as those of apparently different and sometimes opposed philosophies—with this difference only, that in Thomism these principles are taken in the fullness of their meaning. This accounts for the privilege of Thomism to be open to all truth and to provide a place even for truths that its author could not explicitly foresee. All that is true in any other philosophy can be justified by the principles of Thomas Aquinas, and there is no other philosophy that it is possible to profess without having to ignore, or reject, some conclusions that are true in the light of these principles. Speaking in a more familiar way, one can be a Thomist without losing the truth of any other philosophy, whereas one cannot subscribe to any other philosophy without losing some of the truth available to the disciple of Thomas Aquinas." One must remember that Gilson wrote those glowing words only after forty years of studying ancient, medieval, modern, and contemporary philosophers.

1. Position of Thomas Aquinas

When and under what circumstances did Aquinas achieve that realization? This question is important historically, since he originated the doctrine of *esse* as a component over and above essence, and it would be interesting and valuable to know how and why he first became aware of that doctrine. It is also important doctrinally, because understanding how he achieved that awareness may help us attain it too. But the question is rather difficult to answer. True enough, even in his early writings[2] he frequently affirms that *esse* is different from essence[3] and occasionally states explicitly that the difference is real and not just conceptual.[4] But in those same treatises we also encounter two difficulties, the first of which is that most frequently he is content to make those affirmations and statements in strictly theological contexts without offering any proof for that difference. The real distinction is presupposed as already established and is merely used to illustrate some point of divine revelation. Take as an instance the following text, where the point at issue is the Scriptural description of God as "He Who Is" (*Exodus*, 3, 14). Is that the best possible description for Him? Thomas answers affirmatively and for this reason.

> In every thing which is, there is a quiddity to consider (that by which the thing subsists in a determinate nature) and also an act of existing (that by which it is said to actually be). Now the

---

[2] His early writings are those written ca. 1254–1260. These include his *Commentary on Lombard's Sentences, On Being and Essence, Disputed Question on Truth, Exposition of Boethius' Treatise "On the Trinity," Exposition of Boethius' "De Hebdomadibus,"* and *Quodlibetal Questions* VII–XI. On the chronology of Thomas' works, see I. Eschmann, "A Catalogue of St. Thomas' Works," in E. Gilson, *Christian Philosophy of St. Thomas Aquinas* (New York: Random House Inc., 1956), pp. 381–437; James Weisheipl, O.P., *Friar Thomas D'Aquino: His Life, Thought and Work* (Garden City, N.Y.: Doubleday, 1974), pp. 53–92.

[3] This affirmation he makes approximately thirty-five times. For a list of texts, see L. Sweeney, S.J., "Existence/Essence in Thomas Aquinas' Early Writings," *Proceedings of the American Catholic Philosophical Association*, 37 (1963), 103–5.

[4] See *In de Hebdomadibus*, Lect. 2, #32 (Marietti Ed., II, 398), *De Veritate*, 27, 1 and 8 (Marietti Ed., p. 513b); *In I Sent.*, 19, 2, 2 sol. (Mandonnet Ed., pp. 470–71); *Quodl.*, IX, 4, 1 resp. (Marietti Ed., p. 185b); *In II Sent.*, 16, 1, 2 ad 5 (Mandonnet Ed., p. 419). For a study of these texts, see L. Sweeney, S.J., *op. cit.*, pp. 128–29.

> term "thing" arises from the quiddity, as Avicenna teaches in his *Metaphysics,* whereas the expression "he who is" or "being" arises from the act of existing. Since *in every creature essence is other than existence,* a creature is properly named from its quiddity (for example, "man" from humanity) and not from the act of existing. But God's very existence is His quiddity and, consequently, the expression which properly describes Him and is His own unique name is that taken from existence [namely, "He Who Is"].[5]

Manifestly, Aquinas takes the fact for granted that *esse* is a component actually present within all creatures and other than essence. He makes no attempt to establish that otherness.

* The second difficulty is that the proofs he does provide in those early treatises are not entirely helpful. Two of them are theological rather than philosophical, for they obviously move from God to creatures.[6] A third sort (the genus-argument) aims at establishing the difference between essence and *esse* by pointing to the fact that things agree in belonging to the same genus or species but differ insofar as they have *esse*.[7] It is so complex and awkward as to be ineffectual.[8] The final sort centers upon studying the concept of

---

[5] *In I Sent.*, 8, 1 sol. (Mandonnet Ed., p. 195).

[6] The first of these can, in fact, be called a "God to creatures" argument (or, more exactly, "God to angels," because the creatures in question are angels); it moves in this fashion: in God alone essence is *esse;* but an angel is not God: therefore, an angelic essence is not *esse,* which however it receives from God. For a study of the five texts in which it occurs, see L. Sweeney, S.J., *op. cit.*, pp. 112–20 and 130.

The second of these theological arguments is based on participation and can be stated as follows: God is subsistent *esse* and thus is Being essentially; but a creature is not God; therefore, a creature is not *esse* and is a being only through participation. For a study of the four relevant texts, see L. Sweeney, S.J., *op. cit.*, pp. 120–26 and 131.

[7] Thomas uses this line of inference in at least six passages. See L. Sweeney, S.J., *op. cit.*, pp. 109–12 and 130.

[8] Here is the structure of that argument drawn from the texts referred to in note 7:

> Genus and species express what things are;
> But what things are is that which they have in common;
> Therefore, things have in common the fact that they belong to such and such a species and genus: this man and that man agree in the fact that each is a man; this man and that dog agree in the fact that each is an animal;

essence rather than upon existence and, besides, needs to be supplemented on two important points in order to be conclusive. Consider the version of it which Aquinas gives in *On Being and Essence.*[9] He is discussing whether separate substances such as angels [note the theological context] and human souls are completely simple. He answers negatively, for the reason that they are composed of potency and act. The key-lines then occur.

> Whatever does not belong to the notion of essence or quiddity comes from without and enters into composition with the essence, for no essence is intelligible without its essential parts. Now, every essence or quiddity can be understood without anything being known of its existing. I can know what a man or a phoenix is and still be ignorant whether it exists in reality. From this it is clear that *esse* is other than the essence or quiddity, unless, perhaps, there is a being whose quiddity is its very *esse.*[10]

* Why does that argument seem inconclusive if taken by itself? First of all, the mere fact that we can know what a man is and yet be ignorant of whether or not he exists need not establish existence to be other than essence, as this parallel makes clear. I can know what "man" is without an awareness of "this man." Yet *in this man* what

---

But the whatness which things entail has *esse* only in individuals;
But individuals are different, unique;
Therefore, the whatness which things entail also involves difference and uniqueness, and this through *esse;*
Therefore, the whatness which things entail is that in which they both agree and differ, is that which is at once common and unique: *common* insofar as it is generic and specific (that is, ultimately it is the basis for intelligibilities predicable of all), but *unique* insofar as it is individual and has *esse;*
But what accounts for agreement is other than what accounts for difference.
Therefore, the fact that things are individual and have *esse* and yet also belong to a genus and species indicates that in them *esse* is other than whatness.

[9] Besides *On Being and Essence,* the essence-argumentation is to be found in the following: *In I Sent.*, 8, *Expositio Primae Partis Textus* (p. 209); *ibid.*, 8, 4, 2 sol. (p. 222); *In II Sent.*, 1, 1, 1 sol. (pp. 12–13); *ibid.*, 3, 1, 1 sol. (pp. 87–88); *De Ver.*, 10, 12 resp. (p. 220b). For an exegesis, see L. Sweeney, S.J., *op. cit.*, pp. 105–9 and 129–30.

[10] *De Ente et Essentia*, c. 4 (Roland-Gosselin Latin Ed., p. 34, lines 4–16; Maurer translation, pp. 45–46).

"man" signifies is not really different from what "this man" expresses. They are really identical.[11] They differ only mentally insofar as "man" signifies indeterminately what "this man" expresses determinately. So too I can know what a man is without an awareness of whether he exists. But *in this existing man* (and the question concerns whether the act of existing and the actual individual essence in this existing man are really distinct), perhaps what "man" signifies is no more really different from what "this man as existing" expresses than are "man" and "this man" in our first example. Perhaps they differ merely mentally as the indeterminate and the determinate. At least, if this man and his existence are really distinct, that distinction is not established by the present line of reasoning unless this contrast is added to it: the relationship between an essence as specific and as individual is that of act and potency, whereas the relationship between essence and *esse* is that of potency and act.[12] The result of this addition is that essence/*esse* are not equivalent in this text to essence-as-specific/essence-as-individual and, thus, are perhaps more than merely mentally distinct.

* The second reason why Thomas' fourth approach is not convincing by itself has, I would suggest, been clearly seen by all Suarezians. Let us grant, they would say, that essence can be under-

---

[11] On this point see J. Owens, *St. Thomas and the Future of Metaphysics* (Milwaukee: Marquette University Press, 1957), p. 81, note 35: "When abstracted without precision, the essence is predicated of the individual thing and so is identical with it"; *idem*, "Thomistic Common Nature and Platonic Idea," *Mediaeval Studies* 21 (1959), 222: "According to the metaphysical procedure followed in the *De Ente et Essentia*, the Thomistic distinction between essence and being is reached from the way in which predication shows that a sensible nature is . . . wholly identified in reality with the changeable individual in which it is found."

[12] Thomas draws this contrast at least by implication. The first relationship is established by this line of reasoning: what is received and the recipient (*receptum/recipiens*) are to one another as act and potency (*De Ente*, c. 4 [Roland-Gosselin Ed., p. 35, lines 10–21; Maurer translation, p. 47]); but in material things specific essence is *received* in signate matter, whence it becomes individuated (*ibid.*, c. 5, p. 42, line 7 sq.; Maurer translation, p. 54); hence, essence-as-specific and essence-as-individual are related to one another as act to potency.

On the second relationship, see *De Ente*, c. 4 (Maurer translation, p. 47): "The quiddity itself, then, or the form which is the intelligence must be potential with respect to the existence which it receives from God, and that existence is received as an act. Potency and act are thus found in the intelligences" (Latin text in Roland-Gosselin Ed., p. 35, lines 21–24). See L. Sweeney, S.J., *op. cit.*, p. 107 and notes 16 and 17, pp. 129–30.

stood without anything being known of its existence. Again, let us grant that essence-as-known is different from essence-as-existing. But in what does that difference consist? In its relationship to God as efficient cause: an essence-as-existing God has actualized by willing it to be. But that actualization is not intrinsic to the essence. It does not arise from a component actually present within the existent. It is merely the effect of God's efficiency; it is the extrinsic state of an essence as efficiently posited by God in the actual universe.[13]

* Whether the essentialist's interpretation of essence-as-existing is true, is open to question. But the cogency of their attack on Thomas' text seems beyond question, unless it is complemented by the important realization that *esse* is an intrinsic and perfective factor within existents.[14] As such a factor, *esse* is more than essence situated within a framework of efficiency, and thus may be really other than essence.

His endeavors to establish the real distinction are not completely successful in his early writings.[15] He does succeed, though, in subsequent treatises.[16] Setting aside reflection upon the concept of es-

---

[13] This interpretation of *esse* as nothing more than efficient cause was made long before Francis Suarez by Thomas' own contemporaries. See L. Sweeney, S.J., *op. cit.*, p. 108, n. 19. On Suarez see F. Copleston, *History of Philosophy* (London: Burns, Oates and Washbourne, 1953), Vol. III, Ch. 22; Norman J. Wells (trans.), *Francis Suarez: On the Essence of Finite Being as Such, On the Existence of That Essence and Their Distinction* (Milwaukee: Marquette University Press, 1983), "Introduction," especially pp. 6–22 and *passim* in Suarez's own treatise.

[14] On *esse* as an intrinsic factor in existents, see *In II Sent.*, 1, 1, 4 sol.: "Existence is more intrinsic to a thing than that which determines and limits existence" (Latin text in Mandonnet Ed., p. 26). On *esse* as a perfection, see *De Ente*, c. 5 (Maurer translation, p. 51): "Similarly, although God is simply the act of existing, it is not necessary that He lack the other perfections or excellences. On the contrary, He possesses all perfections of all genera of beings; so He is said to be unqualifiedly perfect. . . . But He possesses these perfections in a more excellent way than other things, for in Him they are one, while in other things they are diversified. The reason for this is that all these perfections are His according to His simple act of existing. . . . In the same way, God possesses all perfections in His very act of existing" (Latin text in Roland-Gosselin Ed., p. 38, l. 12 sq.). This can be drawn from that text: God is *esse* and, for that very reason, is all-perfect; therefore, *esse* (in God, as well as in creatures) is itself a perfection. See L. Sweeney, S.J., *op. cit.*, pp. 106–9.

[15] One should remember that the question is not whether he holds that existence really differs from essence (he explicitly asserts that he does—see texts cited above, note 4), but whether he adequately *proves* it.

[16] These would embrace what he wrote both in his Middle (ca. 1260–1267) and Late (ca. 1267 sqq.) periods.

sence as an approach to the real distinction, he turns instead to *actual existents themselves*. There he concentrates upon the fact that they do actually exist and upon what that fact does to those existents: it contributes all their perfections to them. The result is that *esse*, the component to which that fact leads and of which it is the evidence, is clearly seen to be a perfection and act within the existent and really other than what the existent is. In fact, it is the perfection *par excellence*, the actuation of all other acts, as the following paraphrased texts show.

When is the perfection of being a man or that of being fire actually achieved? When it exists in dry wood [to restrict ourselves to the latter example], or in the hands of the man holding a piece of flint, or in his mind as he thinks about starting a fire? No, fire is *fire* only when it actually exists. This fact shows that the act of existence is the actuality of all actuations and the perfection of all perfections.[17] Again: everything is perfect because of and according to its existence. For example, wisdom would be no perfection for a man unless because of it he *actually is* wise. And the same holds true for all other perfections. Accordingly, the manner in which a thing exists also determines the degree of its perfections.[18] Again, you actually do not have goodness or humans unless they actually exist. Hence, existence is the actuality of every form and nature.[19] Again, absolutely nothing has actuality except inasmuch as it exists. Hence, the act of existing is the actuality of all things, even of forms. Accordingly, existence for a horse, a man, or anything whatsoever is its actuation and perfection.[20]

---

[17] *De Potentia*, q. 7, a. 2 ad 9 (Marietti Ed., p. 192). The Latin reads: "Quaelibet autem forma signata non intelligitur in actu nisi per hoc quod esse ponitur. Nam humanitas vel igneitas potest considerari ut in potentia materiae existens, vel ut in virtute agentis, aut etiam ut in intellectu: sed hoc quod habet *esse*, efficitur existens. Unde patet quod hoc quod dico *esse* est actualitas omnium actuum, et propter hoc est perfectio omnium perfectionum."

[18] *Summa Contra Gentiles*, I, c. 28 (Leonine Manual Ed., p. 29d). The Latin: "Omnis enim nobilitas cuiuscumque rei est sibi secundum suum esse: nulla enim nobilitas esset homini ex sua sapientia nisi per eam sapiens esset, et sic de aliis. Sic ergo secundum modum quo res habet esse est suus modus in nobilitate."

[19] *Summa Theologiae*, I, 3, 4 resp. (Leonine Manual Ed., p. 17b). The Latin: "Esse est actualitas omnis formae vel naturae: non enim bonitas vel humanitas significatur in actu nisi prout significamus eam *esse*."

[20] *Ibid.*, I, 4, 1 ad 3 (p. 21d). The Latin: "Ipsum esse est perfectissimum omnium: comparatur enim ad omnia ut actus. Nihil enim habet actualitatem nisi inquantum est; unde ipsum esse est actualitas omnium rerum et etiam ipsarum formarum. Unde non comparatur ad alia sicut recipiens ad receptum;

When he came to write the *Summa Contra Gentiles* and other late treatises, then, Aquinas was not only aware that the act of existence is really distinct from essence (this awareness he seems to have had from the first moment he took up his pen),[21] but he also realized that the way in which to establish their real distinction is to turn to the actual universe. Contemplate the myriad existents it contains: the actually existing horses and fires, the women and men who actually are wise and good and virtuous. There one discovers both what actual existence is and that the fact things actually exist is an evidence different from what they are. The consequence is that the real otherness of the act of existing from essence, as well as its primacy in the existent, opens up before him.[22]

We may add that this interpretation of the genesis of Thomas' position on the real distinction does not deny that Thomas may first have elaborated his notion of the act of existing while engaged in theological meditation upon *Exodus* 3, 14 and other Scriptural texts,[23] but it suggests that he simultaneously had his finger on the pulse of the actual world. This it was which had initially conveyed (and was still conveying) to him the everyday notions of existence, actuality, and the like, now being examined under the light of the Scriptural text. Under that illumination they would be transformed, sublimated and deepened both with regard to God and to creatures. Nonetheless, it was they which would be transformed. They had first to be in his mind in order to undergo that change. Without them there was nothing to work upon.[24]

---

sed magis sicut receptum ad recipiens. Cum enim dico esse hominis vel equi vel cuiuscumque alterius, ipsum esse consideratur ut formale et receptum."

[21] See above, n. 4.

[22] Thomas' concern to ground his metaphysics of *esse* upon direct contact with actual existents is matched by a similar concern in psychology, where important doctrines are established through observation of human existents in actual cognitive and appetitive situations. For instance, *S.T.*, I, 76, 1 resp. (p. 358c): man's intellective soul is the form of his body because "intellection is an operation of this man: everyone *experiences* that he it is who intellectually knows (*experitur enim unusquisque seipsum esse qui intelligit*). . . . One and the same man *perceives* that he knows both through intellection and through sensation (*ipse idem homo est qui percipit se et intelligere et sentire*)." Among numberless other instances which could be given, see *ibid.*, I, 84, 7 resp. (p. 414c): ". . . Videmus . . . experiri potest"; *Expositio in Librum de Causis*, Prop. 10 (Saffrey Ed., p. 70, l. 19 sq.): ". . . etiam experimento in nobis percipimus: videmus. . . ."

[23] This is E. Gilson's position. For example, see his *Elements of Christian Philosophy*, pp. 124–33.

[24] See L. Sweeney, S.J., *op. cit.*, pp. 113–14 and note 28.

This interpretation also implies that although a theologian originated the notion of *esse* as the actualizing component within creatures, still that doctrine does not belong of its very nature to theology. It is not a strict mystery, transcending the grasp of human reason. That is to say, the illumination which Thomas experienced while reflecting upon *Exodus* 3, 14 did not superimpose any intelligible content upon the data already gained from material existents through direct experience. Rather, its function was to enable him to see *what actually was already contained within that data* but heretofore overlooked by previous thinkers. And Thomas' role with reference to subsequent students can be conceived somewhat on a parallel—having discovered the nature and primacy of *esse,* he now can point out to us what to look for within the data delivered by the actual world.[25]

Finally, this interpretation suggests how we should now proceed in our own philosophical endeavors: concentrate upon the material universe and so observe the actual men and women, animals, flowers, and nonliving stuff it contains. From them comes our everyday knowledge of existence, actuality, perfection, limitation, imperfection, deficiency, and the like. Directly perceived, they put across the message that they do actually exist and what they are. And the question now confronting us concerns them in their day-by-day actual situations: does the fact *that* they do actually exist furnish an evidence different from *what* they are? Apparently the only philosophical way of determining whether the answer is yes or no is by looking at them long and hard.[26] This project we shall undertake next.

2. Two Initial Considerations

Our survey of Thomas' endeavors to establish the real distinction has focused attention on how precisely to put the question.

---

[25] His function with reference to philosophy is, then, just that: to indicate evidence we might otherwise miss. But we formulate and assent to conclusions only if we see that evidence and if it warrants them. In general, a Thomistic philosopher is one who finds that the evidence adduced by Thomas for his stand on existence and other matters is still genuine and valid, and who then elaborates the same conclusions. If he should accept that position simply because it is Thomas', he may be a Thomist, but he is no philosopher.

[26] For our earlier recommendations of turning to actual existents and of sharpening our awareness of them, see Ch. II, the texts quoted in notes 3–7 and the corresponding paragraph.

What must be asked is: Is the fact that this man *actually exists* genuinely different from the fact that he is *this man*? If so, the first fact reveals a component actually present within, which can be called "act of existing" because of its function and which is other than his quiddity or essence (that by which he is what he is—this man). Why so? Because diverse evidences indicate the actual presence of diverse components (see Ch. III, Sec. 1). Consequently, the act of existing in this human existent is really distinct from his quiddity; thus, their real distinction is a mere corollary of one's affirmative answer to that initial question.

Obviously, one's energy must be expended especially upon that question.

But first let us briefly discuss two preliminary points: first, what a real distinction precisely entails; second, what "actual existence" signifies when one asserts, for example, "Someone actually is downstairs" or "That kind of fruit tree actually does exist."

(a) What Is a Real Distinction?

What a distinction, in general, is and what a real distinction is can both be answered by looking at the following statements.

1. "'Garment' and 'clothing' are synonymous and, hence, are distinct from one another only in spelling."
2. "Ralph Nader is distinct from comedian Bill Cosby."
3. "Nader's substantial form is distinct from his prime matter."

As can easily be gathered from those examples, "to be distinct from" means "to be other than" or "not to be identical with." Distinction, then, is some sort of otherness, some kind of absence of identity. If that condition arises because of my mental activity, it is merely a *mental* distinction.[27] But if it reflects the actual items in question themselves, it is a *real* distinction. Independently of my knowing them, Ralph Nader actually is other than Bill Cosby, his substantial form actually is other than his primary matter.

Notice that Statements 2 and 3 indicate there are at least two sorts of real otherness and nonidentity—that between two indi-

---

[27] As an example consider Statement 1, where "garment" is other than "clothing" only in spelling—when I predicate them both of this coat, they have one and the same meaning.

For more information on various sorts of mental distinction, see Ch. V, n. 29; Ch. VI, notes 39 and 42.

vidual men and that between components within one and the same man. For clarity and convenience we need two adjectives to differentiate them. Let us arbitrarily call the first "a real *major* distinction" and the second "a real *minor* distinction."[28]

How do we know that the first sort is present? By such obvious signs as physical separation (for example, Mr. Nader is here, Mr. Cosby is there) and so on. And the second? By diverse evidences within one and the same intrinsic unit. For example, in the accidental order change (loss and acquirement of various individual perfections) is really other than stability (specific continuity), and hence accidents are really distinct from substance. In the substantial order change (loss and acquirement of specific perfection) is really other than stability (corporeal continuity), and therefore substantial form is really distinct from prime matter.

Manifestly, when we ask whether in this man the act of existing is really distinct from his essence, the question concerns a real minor distinction because it involves components within the same intrinsic unity. And how will we know whether they are so distinct? Not because they are separated or separable (such is the criterion for a real major distinction), but because there are diverse evidences within one and the same existent—that is, the fact that he *actually exists* is not the same as the fact that he is *this man*. Such is the criterion and, apparently, the sole criterion, and this emphasizes again what we said at the outset of this section—energy must primarily be spent upon determining whether or not the fact *that* actual things exist is genuinely different from *what* they are. And that determination demands, as we also have already said before, that we look long and hard at actual existents, a requirement which leads to the next point on the signification of "actual existence."

(b) What Is "Actual Existence"?

In his famous discussion of time St. Augustine remarks: "What is time? If no one asks me, I know; but if I want to explain it to a questioner, I do not know."[29] What he says concerning time fits also the situation of anyone trying to express what "actual exist-

---

[28] One should guard against thinking that the second adjective in the phrase "real minor distinction" transforms the distinction into a mental one. It does not: one component which is distinct from another according to a real but minor distinction is actually not the other. The adjective "minor" states that the distinction is real but is not the same sort as a real major distinction.

[29] *Confessions*, XI, Ch. 14 (Bourke trans., p. 343).

ence" means. Everyone understands immediately and easily what it is—"That type of fruit tree actually does exist," "There actually is a city called Paris," "Someone actually is downstairs now." But putting our meaning into words is another and difficult matter.

Recently, though, a young lady did put it in picturesque words and succeeded rather well. In the following report she is describing what she experienced when confronted with the fact that she had been an illegitimate child.

> I remember walking that day under the elevated tracks in a slum area, feeling the thought, "I am an illegitimate child." I recall the sweat pouring forth in my anguish in trying to accept that fact. Then I understood what it must feel like to accept, "I am a Negro in the midst of privileged whites," or "I am blind in the midst of people who see." Later on that night I woke up and it came to me this way, "I accept the fact that I am an illegitimate child." But "I am not a child anymore." So it is, "I am illegitimate." That is not so either: "I was born illegitimate." Then what is left? What is left is this, "*I Am*." This act of contact and acceptance with "I am," once gotten hold of, gave me (what I think was for me the first time) the experience "Since *I Am*, I have the right to be."
>
> What is this experience like? It is a primary feeling—it feels like receiving the deed to my house. It is the experience of my own aliveness, not caring whether it turns out to be an ion or just a wave. It is like, when a very young child, I once reached the core of a peach and cracked the pit, not knowing what I would find and then feeling the wonder of finding the inner seed, good to eat in its bitter sweetness. . . . It is like a sailboat in the harbor being given an anchor so that, being made out of earthly things, it can by means of its anchor get in touch again with the earth, the ground from which its wood grew; it can lift its anchor to sail, but always at times it can cast its anchor to weather the storm or rest a little. . . . It is my saying to Descartes, "*I Am, therefore* I think, I feel, I do."
>
> It is like an axiom in geometry—never experiencing it would be like going through a geometry course not knowing the first axiom. It is like going into my very own Garden of Eden where I am beyond good and evil and all other human concepts. It is like the experience of the poets of the intuitive world, the mystics, except that instead of the pure feeling of and union with God it is the finding of and the union with my

> own being. It is like owning Cinderella's shoe and looking all over the world for the foot it will fit and realizing all of a sudden that one's own foot is the only one it will fit. It is a "Matter of Fact" in the etymological sense of the expression. It is like a globe before the mountains and oceans and continents have been drawn on it. It is like a child in grammar finding the *subject* of the verb in a sentence—in this case the subject being one's own life span. It is ceasing to feel like a theory toward one's self. . . .[30]

Obviously, her experience consisted in part of cutting away from existence what is nonessential ("I am an illegitimate child . . . I am illegitimate or, rather, I was born illegitimate. . . . I *Am*"). It culminated in a vivid awareness of what actual existence is like—the deed to one's house, one's own aliveness, the inner seed of a peach, the anchor of a sailboat, the first axiom in geometry, Cinderella's shoe, the subject of a sentence, and so on. Those figures of speech pointed to what it is: the absolutely basic fact which gives her being and courage in be-ing ("Since *I Am,* I have *the right to be*") and which grounds her thinking, feeling, and other activities ("*I Am, therefore* I think, I feel, I do").

To supplement her account, let us attempt a less imaginative explanation by reflecting upon the existential judgment, "Someone actually is downstairs now." As a first step we should reduce that judgment to simply, "Someone actually is," thereby eliminating the spatial and the temporal from the notion of actual existence. Actually to exist is not the same as to be in space and time because some items which actually exist (for example, our activities of intellection and free choice, our human souls themselves) transcend the here and now, and also because actual existence reveals itself to be as free of space and time as of illegitimacy or any other such factors. What, then, is the meaning of the statement, "Someone actually is?" Negatively, that the person in question is not the result of our imagination or fantasy or daydreams. Positively, that he actually is present rather than absent,[31] he actually is outside nothingness, he possesses the status of be-ing rather than that of not be-ing.

---

[30] See R. May *et al.* (eds.), *Existence: A New Dimension in Psychiatry and Psychology* (New York: Basic Books, Inc., 1958 [Reprint. New York: Touchstone Books, 1967]), p. 43.

[31] Remember, though, that *presence* should not be equated with *presence in space and time.*

Admittedly, all such descriptions are inadequate, but they will suffice if they are constantly supplemented by our immediate experience of others and especially of ourselves as actually being present outside nothingness and confronted with nonselves.[32]

3. The Crucial Question

Let us now ask: Is the fact that something *actually exists* really different from the fact that it is *something*? Are there any indications that such is the case?

I would say yes, and this unhesitatingly and certainly. Let us develop and substantiate that affirmative answer in two stages, the first of which (actual existence cannot be mere efficiency) is preparatory for the second (actual existence is other than an existent's quiddity).

(a) Actual Existence Is Not Efficiency

First of all, then, what does the adjective "real" mean? It means simply this: "that which has value, worth, perfection."[33] Most philosophers would agree with that answer, but disagreement begins in deciding what factor ultimately causes value, worth and perfection. Is it the fact that something is material and quantitative, as positivists and other materialists claim? Or is it immutability, as Platonists maintain? Or is it absolute change, as Heraclitus and

---

[32] Note C. S. Peirce's description: ". . . the being of an individual thing of fact, the being which consists in the object's crowding out a place for itself in the universe, so to speak, and reacting by brute force of fact, against all other things. I call that existence" (*Collected Papers of Charles Sanders Peirce*, ed. Arthur Burks, Charles Hartshorne, and Paul Weiss [Cambridge, Mass.: Harvard University Press, 1931–1958], I. 19); Also see G. E. Moore, *Some Main Problems of Philosophy* (London: George Allen and Unwin, Ltd., 1953 [Reprint. Atlantic Highlands, N.J.: Humanities Press, "Muirhead Library of Philosophy," 1978]), pp. 225–26; K. E. M. Baier, "Existence," *Proceedings of the Aristotelian Society*, 61 (1961), pp. 19–30.

[33] Value, worth, and perfection can be of least three sorts: *arbitrary* (exemplified by paper money: the government arbitrarily declares this piece of green paper to be worth one dollar, this piece ten dollars, and so on); *subjective* (for example, the special value which a watch acquires in my eyes because given to me by my brother); and *objective* (the worth which is embedded in the object itself, which in fact *is* the object). Throughout Section 3 we will speak of value, worth, and perfection in the objective sense.

Sartre answer?[34] No, I would reply, it is actual existence. By the very fact that something actually exists it achieves perfection and value and significance. To realize the difference actual existence makes, one need only reflect on the contrast between what is merely possible and what is actual—the mere thought of a thick steak in contrast to the piping hot, juicy steak actually on the platter set before us; the mere thought of a cold bottle of beer in contrast to the one actually stored in the refrigerator; the mere thought of one hundred dollars in contrast with the one hundred dollars actually in one's pocket; the mere thought of a perfect friend and companion contrasted with the one we actually may have found. That list could be continued indefinitely, but enough has been said to make clear that the difference between the items contrasted is not in *what* they are: a hundred dollars when actual contains not one dollar more than when merely thought of; a bottle of beer, whether in my mind or actually in our icebox, contains the same ingredients. The difference resides in actual existence, in the fact that what was once only a thought now actually does exist. And this transition from the merely possible to the actual is simultaneously a transition from the nonperfect to the perfect, from what is without value and worth to what is valuable and worthwhile. Because it does contribute perfection, value and worth to existents, then, actual existence is the factor which makes them real. Despite what radical essentialists may say, it does not nullify but literally *realifies* them. It does not detract from, but adds to, them. It does not lessen but enhances them.[35]

---

[34] For Sartre fluency or change is what is real (see Ch. II, Sec. 2). Paradoxically and perversely, though, it is a reality linked with nonreality, a value equivalent to no-value, beings pregnant with nothingness and annihilation. But such is all that existents within his universe are and have, and hence the forlornness and nausea caused within them.

[35] This position is in direct opposition to that of the radical essentialists. For them, to be real is to be *immutable*. But strict immutability is found solely in the realm of the possibles. Hence, the possibles alone are truly real, and actuality as such is synonymous with unreality. Accordingly, the transition from the state of possibility to that of actuality is a going from the real to the unreal, from the perfect to the imperfect, from being to nonbeing, since by that transition immutable essences are immersed in a world of flux and instability. If one insists, "Surely some positive difference must exist between an essence as possible and as actual," the answer is that the difference is no intrinsic change within the essence for the better (in fact, the essence as actual is less real than when possible), but is merely the addition of the notion of efficient causality. An actual essence is simply an-essence-as-efficiently-produced. In such an interpretation, evidently, actual existence

From the fact that actual existence is what makes an existent be real, it follows that actual existence is necessarily intrinsic to that existent.[36] Why so? Because it helps to constitute him, to set him up, to account for him; as the source of his reality, actual existence is also the source of his perfection, value, and worth. But an existent is nothing more than perfection, value, and worth concretized and realized. He is what constitutes him, and his constituents are identical with him. Hence, as a constituent actual existence is a factor intrinsic to him.

The result is that his state of actuality is not explicable simply through efficient causality, as the essentialists would have it. Actuality is not merely a possible essence in relationship to God or some

---

looked at positively is the essence and is identified with the essence. Viewed of and in itself, it is nothing, it is unreality and nonbeing.

On the other hand, if to be real is to be actual, then actual existents alone are truly real, and possibles are on the side of unreality and nonbeing. The passage from possibles to actuals is, then, a going from nonbeing to being, from the valueless to the valuable, from the unreal to the real. Consequently, actuality is a positive factor in existents, which is over and above efficiency and which will eventually show itself to be other than what the existent is. In summary, one can say that one's acceptance or rejection of the real distinction between existence and essence is consequent upon his acceptance or rejection of actuality as the heart of reality.

Let us return for a moment to the last clause of the initial sentence of the previous paragraph ("possibles are on the side of unreality and nonbeing") and ask: Are possible essences real in no way? Inasmuch as they are capable of actualization, they are real but through extrinsic denomination. What is "extrinsic denomination"? It is the application of a predicate to a subject which does not itself contain what the predicate signifies but which does have some relationship to that signification. Thus, one says, "The wind is cold" not because coldness as such is in the wind but because the wind *causes me* to be cold. So, too, an essence as possible is real through extrinsic denomination insofar as it will be real when/if actualized. On the possibles, see below, Ch. VI, prgrs. corresponding to notes 11–15. Many other examples of extrinsic denomination will be given in later chapters.

[36] Something can be intrinsic because it is physically contained by another. For example, the penny within my pocket is intrinsic to the pocket. Or something can be intrinsic because it is identical with or a constituent of another. For instance, lungs are intrinsic to the human body also because they are integral parts of it.

It is especially in the latter sense that actual existence is intrinsic to the existent, because it is a constitutive factor of the existent as the inner source of his reality. In this sense an efficient cause is extrinsic to the existent it produces because it is really other than its product.

other agent. True, efficient causes are required, but they always remain other than, and in that sense are extrinsic to their effects. But the fact that this man actually exists is an internal factor which conditions everything about him. It permeates and realifies every fiber of his being. Actuality is, then, an intrinsic condition of each existent and amounts to a good deal more than setting an essence into a context of efficiency. It is the existent himself viewed in the light of what internally perfects, ennobles, constitutes, and realifies him.

(b) Actual Existence Other Than Quiddity

What precedes has prepared us for the next stage. Having shown actual existence to be intrinsic to the existent, how can we now indicate that it is really other than his essence, which obviously is also an intrinsic factor in him? How point out that the fact Paul actually exists is genuinely different from the fact that he is Paul?

The first indication is an immediate sequel of the fact just discussed—that actual existence causes an existent to be real. If the function of actual existence within an existent is to realify, then his quiddity (the other intrinsic factor) is what is realified. If the former perfects, then the latter is perfected.[37]

But that which realifies and perfects cannot simultaneously be that which is realified and perfected;

Therefore, *that* things actually exist is genuinely different from *what* they are.

The second indication is a reflection upon another facet of the actual universe. The extremely numerous and varied existents within our universe have one thing in common: the fact that they do actually exist. I can correctly say of this man, this giraffe, this

---

[37] This relationship between actual existence and the quiddity has important consequences. The fact that actuality perfects what an existent is does not deny that his whatness may itself entail perfections, but they are perfections subordinated to and dependent upon actual existence. Provided this man actually is, then he is *this man* and almost anything can happen. He can become wise and just and skilled. But there is wisdom, there is justice, there is skill only if there are wise, just, and skilled humans actually existing.

Expressed somewhat differently: it is important that Shakespeare was Shakespeare, that Toscanini was Toscanini, that Einstein was Einstein, that Martin Luther King was Martin Luther King. But in order that Shakespeare should have been *Shakespeare*, he first had to *be* (and the same, obviously, for Toscanini, Einstein, King). All the perfections expressed by "Shakespeare" depend upon the fact that Shakespeare actually existed.

heliotrope, this piece of cobalt, the sun of our solar system that each actually is. But each is unique in *what* it is: this man is not this giraffe or the sun—in fact, this man is not that man. They are alike in *that* they are, they differ in *what* they are.[38]

But what is common cannot simultaneously be what is unique;

Therefore, *that* things actually exist is genuinely different from *what* they are.

Other indications of a similar nature could be given, but let us conclude this section by turning to examples of the intuition Maritain describes as "metaphysical" (see Appendix A). For the French author that unique, immediate, sudden awareness is an insight into *being*[39] and terminates especially in an awareness of the act of existing.[40] But the intuitions communicated to me by acquaintances seem rather to be a vivid, enduring awareness that they actually exist and that this fact is of prime importance, affecting them profoundly.[41] Thus, this awareness is a stone which kills two birds because it points to the fact that actual existence is a factor of importance and perfection within the existent, and thus also implies its otherness from what the existent is. Here are some samples.

---

[38] This relationship too (between actuality and what an existent is) has significant consequences. The fact that actual existence is a perfection common to all existents indicates that it is independent of any one of them: in order to have actuality one must have some whatness or other, but not *this* one. Otherwise, actuality would be confined to this one existent. Accordingly, although any "thisness" is absolutely dependent on existence, the latter is dependent on the former only relatively and with qualification.

One should remember that the fact something actually exists has already been shown to have two characteristics. It is an intrinsic, constitutive factor of the existent, and thus is not merely a relationship to efficient causes (see Sec. 3a of this chapter). Second, it is not the same as being in space or time, or, even more generally, as being material (see Sec. 2b of this chapter). Without those two characteristics somehow established, the current indication that actual existence is other than any essence lacks force.

[39] This point he stresses in *Preface to Metaphysics* (New York: Sheed & Ward, 1948). See Appendix A.

[40] This he stresses in *Existence and the Existent* (New York: Pantheon Books, Inc., 1948). See Appendix A; Leo Sweeney, S.J., "Christian Existentialism of Jacques Maritain" in J.-L. Allard (ed.), *Jacques Maritain: A Philosopher in the World* (Ottawa: University Press, 1985), pp. 31–41.

[41] Raissa Maritain's intuition (reported by Jacques Maritain, *Preface*, p. 48) seems to have been of the same sort, since it contains an explicit awareness of existence: "I have often experienced in a sudden intuition . . . the profound first principle which makes me exist outside nonentity." Such too is the experience of the young woman reported above (Sec. 2b).

> It has been so long ago, but this is the way it seems to have happened. I was lying in bed waiting for sleep to come when it seemed as though the rest of the created universe had faded into nothingness and that one lone being existed in that void or vacuum and that I was that being. I was intensely conscious of myself, of the fact that I had a body, and of my distinctness from all other things.

Again:

> One evening when I was a senior in high school, I was walking down a long corridor of school at the end of which a window allowed entrance to the rays of the near-setting sun. Between myself and the window, I discerned the silhouettes of my school friends among the long shadows. The difference between the force of my being and theirs, between my knowledge of my own being and theirs at once struck me. I seemed cut off from and yet existing with other things.

Again:

> Two weeks following my first year in college . . . I recall sitting on a hill on a farm where I had spent my memory-filled childhood years and watching a small group of children playing in the yard of a nearby farm down a long, declining slope about a third of a mile away. At some intervals their voices would come through just as clearly as if they were a few feet from me and just as suddenly I could see them playing as before but their happy, carefree, childish voices would not carry to the spot where I was sitting. . . . I clearly recall how I felt at the time. Perhaps this awareness was predominantly unconscious, perhaps not, but I had some vague, yet definite awareness that "I now existed—objectively."

Again:

> There were two windows in my bedroom. My bed was in such a position that I could look out both of them without getting up. I woke up once in the middle of the night and sat up in bed. Somehow the night and the stars shot a message into me. I felt a real surge of joy in just being (although I don't think the word being occurred to me at all).

Finally:

> The evening before, the priest at a parish mission service had given a sermon on heaven and hell and had stressed their eternity by some such example as the following. Say a man walks for a million years down a road which has no end—he would cover a long distance and yet actually he would be no closer to the end of that road now than at the beginning of the world, for the road has no end. So too a soul after death lives for a million years, yet that soul then is no closer to annihilation than at the beginning, for it is eternal. . . . The next morning during class (sun streaming through windows of the second-floor sophomore classroom) I was suddenly struck by what it meant for me to exist for all eternity and that this unique person would be forever. This realization has never left me.[42]

Such, then, are some instances of intuitions which have actually occurred. As we have already mentioned, Maritain interprets such experiences as insights into being as being and into the act of existing itself. I would rather describe them as insights into actual existence as a fact and evidence—the people involved vividly and suddenly become aware that they actually do exist and how supremely important that fact is. Existence as a fact and evidence is, of course, nothing but existence-as-a-component-manifesting-itself and will readily disclose its message when one reflects (for instance) in metaphysics class upon the fact that diverse evidences

---

[42] Frequent examples of similar intuitions occur in literature. For instance, see F. Mauriac, *Questions of Precedence* (New York: Farrar, Straus & Co., Inc., 1959), p. 46: "Was I 5 or 10 years old when I used to stand for hours in front of the looking-glass . . . amazed at the thought that I really existed. . . ." Edgar Allan Poe, *The Pit and Pendulum* (New York: Modern Library, Inc., 1938), pp. 246 sq.: "Very suddenly there came back to my soul motion and sound—the tumultuous motion of the heart, and, in my ears, the sound of its beating. Then a pause in which all is blank. Then again sound, and motion, and touch—a tingling sensation pervading my frame. Then the mere consciousness of existence, without thought—a condition which lasted long. Then, very suddenly, thought and shuddering horror. . . . In the return to life from the swoon there are two stages: first, that of the sense of mental or spiritual; secondly, that of the sense of physical existence." Fyodor Dostoievsky, *The Idiot* (New York: The Macmillan Company, 1932), p. 224: "Those moments were only an extraordinary quickening of self-consciousness . . . and at the same time of the direct sensation of existence in the most intense degree."

indicate the actual presence within of components and upon other relevant matters. But some such reflection (however rapid and implicit) seems required, for otherwise the intuition will remain a never-to-be-forgotten psychological experience without formally and explicitly introducing one into metaphysics itself.

Moreover, Maritain makes such intuitions absolutely indispensable for metaphysics—if someone has never had one, he cannot possibly be a metaphysician.[43] I would agree that some sort of personal awareness of the supreme importance of actual existence is absolutely necessary, but I would say intuition is only one way of gaining that awareness. It can also be achieved by making the reflections suggested in the two previous stages (see above, #a and #b).

Summary. Such, then, are considerations designed to show that the fact something actually exists is an evidence really different from the fact that it is something.

First, realize that actual existence is an intrinsic condition of every existent because it is a source of his reality and perfection and, next, that it is other than what he is because the former is what perfects and is common, the latter is what is perfected and is unique.

Second, utilize metaphysical intuitions, which also can underwrite those same two points.

What is the import of this new and different evidence? It reveals the actual presence of a new and different component—that by which an existent actually exists. This revelation will be clear when we formulate the basic process in the next section.

4. The Process

[Directly perceived fact:] An actual material existent
(a) not only is *what* it is (Paul is this man)
(b) but also *actually exists* (Paul is);
But evidence #a is other than evidence #b (See Sec. 3);
But diverse evidences indicate the actual presence within of diverse components;
Therefore, such evidences indicate that an existent is actually made up of two real and distinct components:

---

[43] See J. Maritain, *Degrees of Knowledge* (London: Geoffrey Bles, 1959), p. 215. Also see Appendix A.

(a) that by which it is *what* it is—"ESSENCE" (that is, the composite of substance [prime matter/substantial form] and accidents);
(b) that by which it *actually exists*—the "ACT OF EXISTING" or simply "EXISTENCE."

This process indicates both that such components actually do exist and, to a degree, what they are (as the previous processes concerning accidental modifications had done for substance/accidents [see Ch. III, Sec. 3] and substantial modifications for matter/form [see Ch. III, Sec. 4], what we say in the next paragraphs will parallel what we previously remarked with respect to the former processes).

This process establishes their actual presence because the relationship between an evidence and a component is that between an effect and its intrinsic cause. But an effect of an intrinsic cause is present only because what causes it is also present. But the fact that a material existent does exist and the fact that it is this existent are genuinely different evidences (effects) and hence indicate the really distinct components actually present within (causes).

It also shows, to an extent, what those components are, and once again the force of the fact that a material thing is an intrinsic unity is apparent. As we have often remarked before, an individual man is not a mere accidental unity such as in an army or a soccer team, in which the parts are themselves individual men and, thereby, are intrinsically and entitatively independent of the whole which they help constitute. Rather he is an intrinsic or *per se* unity, whose parts depend internally and entitatively upon him. Nevertheless, the whole (here, the man) is not any one of its parts, nor is any part the whole. Still both the whole and its parts are real (because actually present). Consequently, there is a difference between the reality of the whole and of the parts, between what the whole is and what each part is. Let us again express this difference in terms of "that which" and "that by which." The whole (the man himself) is *that which* exists. His act of existing is *that by which* he actually exists. His essence is *that by which* he exists as this individual man.[44]

Once again, our knowledge of such components is more than direct perception. True, we directly perceive that we ourselves and

[44] The stringent unity to be found in a man (or, for that matter, in any *unum per se*) indicates there to be only one act of existing within him. One and the same act actualizes the substance and accidents which constitute the individual essence. No accident, then, has its own act of existing; each is

other material existents do exist, and, within limits, what we and they are. This perception we express in judgments, which furnish the starting point of our process.[45] But our awareness of existence and essence precisely as components transcends mere perception. We reflect upon the data offered through perception. We intellectually realize that the fact this man actually exists offers an evidence really different from the fact that he is this man (see Sec. 3), that diverse evidences indicate the actual presence of diverse components causing them, and that consequently this human existent, as well as any other material existent, is made up of diverse components called "act of existing" and "essence." This last stage is an assent of the intellect to which it is forced by that twofold evidence: "In this human existent there actually is an act of existing, which is really other than his essence."[46] In brief, the process terminates in intellectual judgmental knowledge, by which we become aware that such components exist and what they are.

Existence as a component, then, is known by reflection upon perceived data, and this reflection is a genuinely intellectual operation. We cannot directly perceive it. We cannot picture or imagine it. We know it through genuine intellection—through intellective induction by reflection (see Ch. X below, paragraphs corresponding to notes 25–28).

The process we are currently considering also indicates that the relation between essence and existence is one of potency to act. The function of an act is to confer a perfection, to actuate, whereas that of a potency is to limit a perfection, to be actuated, to be perfected.

---

existentialized by the single act existentializing the whole. In short, there is no *esse accidentale*. In itself, the act of existing is neither accidental nor substantial. These adjectives can be applied to it only through extrinsic denomination (see n. 35 above)—one and the same existence can be called "substantial" insofar as it is actualizing the substance and "accidental" insofar as it is actualizing the accidents (of course, through the substance in which they inhere).

See James A. Albertson, "*Esse* of Accidents According to St. Thomas," *The Modern Schoolman*, 30 (1953), 265–78.

[45] On existential judgments, see E. Gilson, *Being and Some Philosophers* (Toronto: Pontifical Institute of Mediaeval Studies, 1952), especially Ch. 6, pp. 190–215; Robert J. Henle, S.J., *Method in Metaphysics* (Milwaukee: Marquette University Press, 1951); *idem*, "Existentialism and the Judgment," *Proceedings of American Catholic Philosophical Association*, 21 (1946), 40–53; *idem*, *Theory of Knowledge* (Chicago: Loyola University Press, 1983), pp. 57–59 and 160–63.

[46] This distinction between existence and essence is, of course, a real *minor* one. See Sec. 2a above.

But existence as a component confers the perfection of actuality—it is that by which an existent transcends nothingness and nonbeing, and thus *is* and *is real*, and, thereafter, is in a position to achieve further perfections through subsequent activity. On the other hand, essence is that within an existent which is actualized and perfected by existence, which it simultaneously limits by confining it to this existent (for example, for one to be this man means automatically that he cannot be that man). Accordingly, existence and essence are related to one another as act to potency.

* In fact, existence is pure act in the sense that insofar as it is itself concerned, it is nothing but act.[47] Its sole function is to actuate by actualizing, and, literally, realifying. Of itself it involves no potency. It is in no way perfected by essence. "But," someone may object, "the essence of, say, this human existent involves, besides prime matter, a human soul, intellect, will, other operative powers, and various other accidents. Surely, therefore, his essence involves perfections of its own, which it confers upon existence." No, I would answer, for the reason that his essence has those very perfections only because it *is* and *is real*, and thus only because and inasmuch as it is actuated by the act of existing.[48] The sole *rapport* which existence has to any essence is that of what perfects to what is perfected, of what actuates to what is actuated.

* "But," comes the rejoinder, "compare this man today on his twenty-fifth birthday with what he was twenty years ago. Today he is much more perfect physically, intellectually, and morally than he was as a five-year-old child. Surely, his act of existing twenty years ago was in potency to what he is today; it was per-

---

[47] The adjective, "pure," can also mean "subsistent." Only God is pure act in this sense, because He alone *is* existence and actuality. His very essence is existence. Existence in all other existents is received and limited by an essence which is a distinct component. Thus, existence in such existents is not subsistent, although it is a pure act inasmuch as of itself it is *nothing but* actuation.

[48] But is it not also true that in material existents one never finds an act of existence except with an essence? Accordingly, essence would seem equally important as existence. No, I would answer, and for this reason. Consider this individual human being. Existence is absolutely necessary for this individual human essence: it could not be this essence unless it *is*. But this individual human essence is not absolutely necessary for existence—otherwise, one could have the act of existing only when actualizing this human existent, with the result he would be the sole actual existent. But one finds many existents, each with an act of existing. Therefore, existence is absolutely necessary for this essence, but this essence is not absolutely necessary for existence.

fected by his development. If so, it does involve potency and cannot be pure act." Again, no: his essence is that by which he then was in potency to those future perfections. His essence it is which was directly perfected by that gradual growth in physical and other areas. No internal change took place in his act of existence, which now at his twenty-fifth birthday simply is actualizing what it would have actualized at his fifth birthday *had his essence then been such as it is now.*[49] In short, perfective changes occur immediately only within the essence, which goes from less to more perfect, whereas the function of existence, at no matter what stage of development the existent finds himself, is simply to actuate by actualizing. It is, then, pure act.[50]

* Next let us briefly examine the names given those two components. First, concerning "essence": what is the force of that noun? Why use it to designate the component by which an existent is what it is? What does it signify?

* To begin with, whenever the human mind comes upon some unknown thing (whether it be an object just appearing on the horizon or an abstract painting or a spaceship seen for the first time), it automatically asks, "What is it?" Then an answer comes (sooner or later, depending upon our previous experiences and knowledge), which might run like this if the item in question is a spaceship: "It is something [here the answer arises from what the object is intrinsically] which is dazzlingly bright and moves fast

---

[49] Perhaps an example will help clarify the relation which the act of existing has to the essence it is actualizing. Suppose that we compress a metal spring and put it in a pasteboard box of such a sort that the cover of the box extends down over the sides and thus can be raised gradually. Let us raise the cover one inch. That raising of the cover allows the spring to expand now to where it would have been at the very beginning if the cover then had been where it is now. The change directly occurs in the position of the box-cover, but any change there determines the extent of expansion of the spring.

The act of existing is like the compressed spring, the essence it actualizes is like the box. Essence confines and limits existence to whatever size it is at any stage in its development. As an essence gradually "grows," as it is perfected by accidental changes, it allows existence gradually to expand to where it would previously have been if the essence itself had then been that perfect. Existence gradually actualizes what it would have actualized earlier had the essence then been what it is now. Of course, if existence is in no way confined by an essence distinct from itself, it is unlimited, and thus is infinitely perfect. God is such an existent. He is existence; He is a spring uncontained in any box whatsoever; He is pure actuality because He is subsistent existence. (See note 47.)

[50] For additional information on act/potency, see Sec. 6 of this chapter.

[here the answer is from external appearances], which is made of such-and-such metals [here the answer is in terms of the material from which it is made], which is used for military purposes and for scientific research [here the answer is in terms of its final causes], and so on." The answer which the human mind elaborates expresses *what* the object is. Our intellect now knows what it is, now is aware of its whatness. And the term used to signify that awareness is "quiddity" ("whatness") or "essence."[51]

* Two points should emerge clearly from this analysis. First, there are many different ways of answering what a thing is, depending upon our approach, our level of knowledge, and the intricacy of the thing itself. Consequently, the awareness which "quiddity" or "essence" expresses, and thus the meanings it assumes, can themselves be multiple and varied. Second, one can ask, "What is it?" of any sort of item—of *per se* (intrinsic) unities (for example, "What is a man? a whooping crane? a mammal?"), of accidental unities ("What is an IBM computer? a lunar-ship? a family"), of integral parts of a *per se* unity ("What are the lungs? the liver? the heart?"), of components ("What is prime matter? an accident? the act of existing?"), of intramental items ("What is an irrational number? a surd? a logical species and genus?"). Since "essence" signifies simply the content of the awareness we have of what such items are, it can be applied to all of them. In this sense, then, each of them has an essence. Each has something which initiates that awareness and is signified by that term.

* Let us restrict ourselves to what essence means with respect to a *per se* unit, such as this man. If we inquire what he is, we can give (a) a spontaneous, nonphilosophical reply or (b) a technical, philosophical reply. In the first way of answering we look upon him as a whole, in his entirety; in the second way we consider the components which constitute him. In the first way our knowledge becomes more and more determinate. For example, if I enter a room and unexpectedly come upon something under a sheet of canvas (let us say it will turn out to be a man who is bleeding), my first cognitive reaction is, "There's something or other underneath the sheet." Then as I continue to observe: ". . . which is alive . . . sentient

[51] For reasons of clarity and convenience, I am using quiddity and essence as synonymous. Other authors distinguish between them. For example, G. P. Klubertanz, S.J., *Philosophy of Being*, p. 112, n. 23: "'Essence' implies that we are considering what a thing is as a principle of its being. 'Quiddity' implies rather an absolute consideration of what it is, as a pure intelligibility."

. . . rational." Such is essence when used in its nontechnical, everyday sense. The essence of a man is to be something which is living, sentient, and rational. In this usage it signifies the man as a whole and is in no way contrasted with the act of existing.[52]

* When taken in the other way (b), though, "essence" is a component, although here it can have at least two meanings. For a philosopher of nature, "essence" is the same as "substance." Thus, the essence of this man consists of his substantial form and prime matter. His accidents are outside his essence.[53] But for a metaphysician "essence" includes both substance and accidents: it is everything in an existent except his act of existing. Unless otherwise stated, such is the meaning "essence" has in this book.[54]

---

[52] The meaning a logician and an epistemologist give to "essence" is similar to (and arises from) that which it has in the spontaneous, nonphilosophical approach. For example, according to logic and epistemology, "rational animal" (specific essence) can be predicated of the whole (for example, "John is a rational animal"), and thus must signify the whole. Again, "animal" (generic essence) and "rational animal" differ from one another only as the less determinate differs from the more determinate.

The upshot of this similarity is that essence for them is not a constitutive part or component of a thing but rather *is the thing itself*. Whenever one discusses whether existence is really distinct from essence, one should remember that the latter word is not taken in its logical and epistemological sense.

[53] Thus when we describe substance and accident on the level of philosophy of nature, "essential" and "nonessential" are roughly equivalent to "specific-generic" and "individual." Hence, to say substance is "that by which a thing essentially remains what it is and yet receives various nonessential perfections" is the same as saying substance is "that by which a thing specifically and generically remains what it is and yet receives various individual perfections." (A similar substitution can be made in the description of "accident"—see Ch. III, Sec. 5c.)

[54] The different meaning "essence" has for a philosopher of nature and for a metaphysician arises from the different aim each has. The former is primarily interested in *natures* and in individuals only insofar as they share in, and thus manifest, this or that kind of nature. But the latter is primarily concerned with all actuals precisely as actual. Now that which is actual is each individual existent, and his status of actuality embraces whatever is actually existing in him—accidents as well as substance. Hence, "essence" for a metaphysician signifies substance and accidents, whereas the same term for a philosopher of nature bypasses accidents.

The following technical definitions attempt to emphasize this difference in meaning. Essence for a philosopher of nature is "that by which this existent is what he is as a member of such-and-such a species." Essence for a metaphysician is "that by which this existent precisely as an existent is what he is."

* Next, what about "act of existing?" What is the force of that phrase? Plainly, it describes the function of this component which actuates a thing by causing it actually to exist. A substantial form actuates by specifying, an accident by conferring individual perfections, but the component we call "act of existing" actuates by actualizing and existentializing. It is the actuation which makes a thing be actually present outside nothingness and be a *being,* a term which means simply "that which actually exists."[55]

5. Summary and Conclusions

(a) From Chapter IV it is clear that discussion of the real distinction between existence and essence should begin with this crucial inquiry: Is the fact that something *actually exists* a really different evidence from the fact that it is *something*? If so, then the first fact points to an actually present component which is really other than essence, and, obviously, their real distinction follows as an immediate corollary.

(b) Is the fact, then, that this man *actually exists* a really different evidence from the fact that he is *this man*? Yes, for a reason which involves two stages of reflection.

1. *Actual existence is not explicable merely by an appeal to efficient causality,* as the following consideration makes clear:

> That which intrinsically makes an existent real is that which contributes objective worth, value, perfection to it;
> But actual existence makes that contribution:
> Therefore, actual existence literally *realifies* the existent and all its parts;
> But whatever thus realifies an existent and all his parts is intrinsic to him;
> Therefore, actual existence is intrinsic to the existent: it permeates him as that which actualizes and realifies him;
> But efficient causality is other than its effect (the existent), and in this sense remains extrinsic to the existent;
> Therefore, actual existence cannot be identical with efficient causality: it is not merely the existent-as-efficiently-caused, it is more than an essence set within a context of efficiency.

---

[55] For more information on "being," see Ch. VI, Secs. 1 and 2; also see Appendix B.

2. *Actual existence is really different from the other intrinsic factor in the existent—namely, from what he is*, as these two arguments show:

> Actual existence realifies and perfects, his quiddity is realified and perfected;
> But that which realifies and perfects cannot simultaneously be that which is realified and perfected;
> Therefore, *that* things actually exist is genuinely different from *what* they are.
>
> Actual existence is a factor common to all existents; what each is, is unique;
> But what is common cannot simultaneously be what is unique;
> Therefore, *that* things actually exist is genuinely different from *what* they are.

(c) Accordingly, the fact that an existent *actually exists* is an intrinsic factor in him and is a really different evidence from the fact that he is *this existent*. Hence, it points to a hitherto overlooked component, which can be called "act of existing" in view of its function.

(d) In virtue of the process used in arriving at this component, we know both that it is actually present within an existent and also what it is.

The *"act of existing"* is *"that by which an existent actually exists."* It is the actuation by which a thing is actually present outside nothingness and nonbeing and is no longer imaginary, fictional, or merely possible. *"Essence"* is the counterpart of the act of existing, from which it is distinct by a real minor distinction. As understood by a metaphysician, it encompasses everything in an existent except the act of existing. It is *"that by which an existent is what it is."*

Although what the process has as its starting-point and constant center of reference is actually perceived data (especially important are existential judgments), still those components themselves are known by reflection upon that data, and this reflection is a genuinely intellectual operation, terminating in intellectual judgments. Those components cannot be directly perceived or imagined or pictured but are known by genuine intellection.

The relation between existence and essence is that of act to potency inasmuch as the function of the former is to actuate by actualizing and realifying the latter, which simultaneously receives and limits the former. In fact, existence is *pure* act insofar as in itself it is *nothing but* act, *nothing but* actuation. Of itself it involves no potency; it is in no way perfected by essence. Its sole task is to actuate by actualizing.

* 6. Act and Potency

The last point provides an occasion of clarifying our position on act/potency. According to some prominent philosophers, this doctrine comes at the very beginning of metaphysics and then is used to establish subsequent doctrines. For example, Henri J. Renard, S.J., first works out the "general aspects of this theory [of act and potency]"[56] in a chapter which culminates in three sets of important conclusions.

> [First:] All beings subject to change must be composed . . . of act and potency. . . . A pure act is not subject to change, for it has no potency, but is all perfection. . . . Act and potency adequately encompass being, for whatever exists is either pure act or a composition of act and potency.[57]
>
> [Second:] Every finite, limited perfection requires an intrinsic potential principle, which limits it and to which the act is proportioned. Consequently, by way of immediate deduction an act existing without a limiting potency must be infinite in its own order, and necessarily unique in that order. Wherever beings are found to be many and limited, they must be composed of two principles: one we call the actual, the other the potential and limiting principle.[58]
>
> [Third:] Adequately distinct concepts of realities indicate always a real distinction between these realities, even though they be united to form an essence, or a being that is strictly one [and, hence, act and potency are really distinct].[59]

Renard next applies those general propositions to the three "orders of existence, of essence, and of activity"[60] and thereby proves that a

---

[56] Henri J. Renard, S.J., *Philosophy of Being*, 2nd ed. (Milwaukee: The Bruce Publishing Co., 1946), p. 17.

[57] *Ibid.*, p. 25.

[58] *Ibid.*, p. 37.

[59] *Ibid.*, p. 44.

[60] *Ibid.*, p. 45.

material existent consists of three sets of constitutive parts—existence/essence, substantial form/primary matter and accidents/substance.[61]

Despite the attractive clarity of this approach, we have preferred to proceed differently. First we established that such components actually do exist within an actual thing and what their natures and functions are[62]—accidents confer individual perfections upon the substance, which simultaneously receives and limits them; substantial form specifies prime matter, which at the same time limits it as the ultimate principle of its substantial individuation; existence actualizes and realifies the essence, which simultaneously confines and limits it. Quite obviously, accidents, substantial form, and existence have a similar function—they confer perfections. Their counterparts (substance, prime matter, and essence) also have a similar function—they limit those perfections. How can we describe those common functions more conveniently and accurately than by utilizing Aristotle's notions of act/potency?[63] Accidents, substantial form and existence are acts; substance, prime matter, and essence are potencies. This description was made after the process establishing each set of components had been completed.

Hence, our approach is almost the reverse of such metaphysicians as Renard. For them the doctrine of act/potency comes at the very beginning of metaphysics and is an instrument for proving that an existent is made up of various components. For us it comes only after the components have themselves been uncovered and merely summarizes their roles in relation to one another. For them the doctrine is a principle and starting-point, for us it is a corollary and sequel.

In our approach general propositions concerning act and potency can also be formulated, but this occurs only at the very end of the process, after we know that various components are actually present within the existent and after we realize that their reciprocal functions of conferring and limiting a perfection are aptly expressed by the notions of act and potency. Then we can inspect the various components now depicted as acts and potencies and draw up

---

[61] *Ibid.*, pp. 46–77.

[62] This we did by relying upon the diverse evidences an individual material existent provides—change/stability on the accidental level, change/stability on the substantial level, the fact that something actually exists/the fact that it is something.

[63] On Aristotle's doctrine, see Ch. III, Sec. 3.

whatever summary statements they suggest. As an example, consider the following.

(a) All the various acts and potencies are real, since various evidences have indicated them to be actually present within an existent.

(b) They are also really (and minorly) distinct from one another, as is clear from the fact that the evidences which manifest them are genuinely different.

(c) They are components. This important fact entails several consequences. First, because they are components, acts and potencies are dependent upon one another and are ordered to one another.[64] Second, an act or a potency cannot exist without its counter component, although there are exceptions to this statement—after death the human soul exists without prime matter; some operative powers can be without actually acting.[65] The third consequence concerns the role acts and potencies have toward one another in one and the same order and with reference to one and the same perfection. The function of act is to confer that perfection, that of potency to receive and limit it. Within such a context, then, act of itself says only perfection, whereas potency of itself says only capacity and limitation.[66] Finally, because they are components, acts and poten-

---

[64] Although acts and potencies are *mutually* dependent, they are not *equally so*. An accident is more dependent upon substance than substance is upon the accident. Prime matter depends more upon substantial form than substantial form does upon matter. This essence is more dependent upon the act of existing than the act of existing is upon this essence. For a clarification of this point, see n. 48 above and also Ch. V, Sec. 3.

[65] For instance, when we close our eyes, we no longer see and yet retain our power to see.

[66] The phrases, "in one and the same order and with reference to one and the same perfection" and "within such a context," are important for an accurate understanding of this consequence, as the following point reveals. Although accidents, substantial form and existence are all acts, still only existence is pure act because it alone is *nothing but* act and perfection. The perfections which the other two confer are not absolute ones. From one point of view, they are themselves limited. For example, a dog's substantial form is *of itself* without the perfection of a man's substantial form. The limitation which prime matter works upon it is that it substantially be *this* canine soul and not that it be canine rather than human. This latter restriction issues immediately from itself. Hence, a substantial form is an act which says only perfection, but merely in a certain order, merely with reference to the limitation issuing from prime matter: the form does not immediately individuate itself. Hence it involves only perfection, but merely within a curtailed context.

cies are simultaneously known within the existent because they are indicated by evidences within one and the same thing. But this is also true: an existent is known through its acts—I can know what sort of thing this or that existent is only through its operations, and, even more radically, only if it actually exists. Moreover, within an existent a potency is known and described through its act—for example, substance is "that by which a material thing . . . *receives various individual perfections*," or prime matter is "that by which a material thing *receives a substantial form* and yet which is capable . . . of *receiving other substantial forms*."[67] In fact, all potencies can be classified as operative or entitative precisely because of the acts to which they are ordered. They are operative if the acts are either operations or the direct results of operations (that is, operative dispositions and habits). They are entitative if the acts directly pertain to the thing's entity.[68]

In summary: although an act of itself says only perfection, still not every act is *pure* act (*nothing but* act or perfection), because some acts, while unlimited in one order, are limited of themselves in another order. Only the act of existing is pure act, because actual existence transcends all limitations; it is perfection and nothing but perfection in every order; it is in no way restricted of itself to individuals within the same species or even to any species whatsoever; it is a perfection common to absolutely all existents—to creatures and to their Creator.

Incidentally, by a parallel reflection one can easily see that not every potency but only prime matter is pure potency. Although other potencies (substance, essence) *are* potencies with reference to the acts they receive and limit, from another point of view they are more than mere recipients, more than absolute limitations. Intrinsically they also involve acts of their own (substance = prime matter/*substantial form;* essence = substance/*accidents*).

One should remember, also, that although within a certain context an act of itself says only perfection, still some acts (namely, existence and substantial form) mediately limit themselves. So too, although a potency itself says only limitation, still substance mediately perfects itself. See Ch. V, Sec. 3.

[67] See Ch. III, "Summary and Conclusions," #c1 and #d1.

[68] In line with this classification, operative potencies are all faculties (for example, intellect, will, external and internal senses) and operative powers (the vegetative powers of nutrition, growth, and reproduction). All other potencies (prime matter, substance, essence) are entitative.

The classification of potencies into natural and supernatural (or, more traditionally, obediential) is made on a similar policy. A potency is natural if the act to which it is ordered is on the natural plane (for example, substance with reference to various accidents, the human soul with respect to intellect and will). It is supernatural if the act to which it is ordered is supernatural (for example, the human soul with reference to sanctifying grace, the intellect with reference to faith, the will with respect to charity). See Ch. IX, n. 53.

Here, then, is the procedure followed with respect to act/potency. First, we realized that accidents/substance, substantial form/prime matter, and existence/essence actually make up an individual existent and that the function of accidents, substantial form, and existence is to confer perfections, whereas that of substance, prime matter, and essence is to limit them. In the light of those functions we next described these components as related to one another as act and potency. Only then did we formulate general propositions concerning acts and potencies, and these are based on reflection upon actual components previously verified.

But let us return to our consideration of the act of existing and now especially in the primacy it has both in reality and in metaphysics.

Suggested Readings

Anderson, James F., *Metaphysics of St. Thomas Aquinas.* Chicago: Henry Regnery Co., 1953. A selection of quotations on metaphysics from the writings of St. Thomas.

Aquinas, Thomas, *On Being and Essence,* trans. Armand A. Maurer. Toronto: Pontifical Institute of Mediaeval Studies, 1949.

Bourke, Vernon J., *The Pocket Aquinas.* New York: Washington Square Press Pocket Books, Inc., 1960. Excerpts from thirty-two of Aquinas' writings.

Clarke, S.J., W. Norris, "The Limitation of Act by Potency: Aristotelianism or Neo-Platonism?" *New Scholasticism,* 26 (April, 1952), 167–94. A controversial interpretation of act and potency in Aquinas.

———, "What Is Really Real?" in *Progress in Philosophy,* ed. James A. McWilliams, S.J., pp. 61–90. Milwaukee: Bruce Publishing Co., 1955. On various meanings of "real" and "being"; on the "possibles."

De Raeymaeker, Louis, *The Philosophy of Being,* trans. E. H. Ziegelmeyer, S.J., pp. 115–55. St. Louis: B. Herder Book Co., 1954. A history of the real distinction between the act of existence and essence.

Eslick, Leonard J., "The Real Distinction," *The Modern Schoolman,* 38 (1961), 149–60.

Gallagher, Donald A., "Contemporary Thomism," in *A History of Philosophical Systems,* ed. V. Ferm, pp. 454–70. New York: The Philosophical Library, 1950.

Kovach, Francis J., *Scholastic Challenges to Some Mediaeval and Modern Ideas.* Stillwater, Okla.: Western Publications, 1987. Essay 3: "St. Thomas Aquinas: Limitation of Potency by Act. A Textual and Doctrinal Analysis," pp. 43–66.

Maurer, Armand A., "Revived Aristotelianism and Thomistic Philosophy," in *A History of Philosophical Systems,* ed. V. Ferm, pp. 197–211. New York: The Philosophical Library, 1950.

———, "Form and Essence in the Philosophy of St. Thomas," *Mediaeval Studies,* 13 (1951), 174–76.

Owens, Joseph, "Unity and Essence in St. Thomas Aquinas," *Mediaeval Studies,* 23 (1961), 240–59.

———, *An Interpretation of Existence.* Milwaukee: Bruce Publishing Co., 1968.

Phelan, Gerald B., "The Existentialism of St. Thomas," *Proceedings of American Catholic Philosophical Association,* 21 (1946), 25–40.

Pieper, Josef, *Guide to Thomas Aquinas,* trans. Richard and Clara Winston. New York: Pantheon Books, Inc., 1962. Aimed at helping a student to read Aquinas intelligently.

Sweeney, S.J., Leo, "Scholasticism," *Collier's Encyclopedia* (New York: P. F. Collier and Son, 1961), XX, 487–89 (forthcoming as ch. 12 in *Christian Philosophy: Nature, Origin, Developments* [hereafter: *Christian Philosophy*] [New York/Bern: Peter Lang Publishing, Inc., 1994]).

———, "Existence/Essence in Thomas Aquinas' Early Writings," *Proceedings of the American Catholic Philosophical Association,* 37 (1963), 97–131 (forthcoming as ch. 20 in *Christian Philosophy*).

———, "The Mystery of Existence," *The Modern Schoolman,* 44 (1966–67), 57–73 (forthcoming as ch. 21 in *Christian Philosophy*).

———, "Aquinas or Philosophers of Subjectivity?" *The Modern Schoolman,* 47 (1970–71), 101–24.

Van Roo, S.J., William, "Act and Potency," *The Modern Schoolman,* 18 (1940–41), 1–5.

Walton, W. M., "Being, Essence, and Existence for St. Thomas Aquinas," *Review of Metaphysics,* 3 (1950), 339–65.

Wippel, John F., *Metaphysical Themes in Thomas Aquinas* (Washington, D.C.: The Catholic University of America Press, 1984), Chs. 5 and 6.

V

Primacy of Existence in Existents

The importance of actual existence has been frequently emphasized by G. K. Chesterton, but nowhere better, perhaps, than in this paragraph.

> There is at the back of all our lives an abyss of light, more blinding and unfathomable than any abyss of darkness; and it is the abyss of actuality, of existence, of the fact that things truly are, and that we ourselves are incredibly and sometimes almost incredulously real. It is the fundamental fact of being, as against not being; it is unthinkable, yet we cannot unthink it, though we may sometimes be unthinking about it; unthinking and especially unthanking. For he who has realized this reality knows that it does outweigh, literally to infinity, all lesser regrets or arguments for negation, and that under all our grumblings there is a subconscious substance of gratitude.[1]

Actual existence is, then, that which perfects an existent and is the factor he has in common with all, whereas his quiddity is that which is perfected and is unique. As we have previously seen (Ch. IV, Sec. 3b), that which perfects and is common cannot be identified with that which is perfected and is unique. Therefore, actual existence is an evidence genuinely different from what an existent is, and thus points to a new component, conveniently called "act of existing" in view of its function and really distinct from the essence it actualizes.

---

[1] G. K. Chesterton, *Chaucer* (New York: Pellegrini and Cudahy, n.d.), p. 33.

The previous chapter has aimed at establishing the real distinction between existence and essence. In the present chapter we shall endeavor to explicate what was already implied in the real distinction—the act of existing has primacy over essence. After first outlining what such a primacy entails, we shall next indicate the reasons why the act of existing enjoys such a status: (a) it is the source of all other perfections, (b) it is autodetermining, and (c) it is amaterial.

1. "Existence Precedes Essence"

If we ascribe primacy to the act of existing what does this primacy entail? If we consult a dictionary, primacy is defined as, "State of being first in time, order, rank, etc."[2] Let us omit the reference to time, for actual existence is not temporally prior to essence. This definition is then adequate as a starting-point, since primacy for actual existence does point to the first-rank position it occupies in importance because of its nature and function. As we have already seen, an essence is potency in the order of being and even in its own order is always a combination of potency/act,[3] whereas actual existence is pure act in any existent whatsoever.[4] Of itself it says *nothing but* actuation and perfection. It receives no perfection from any essence. Its sole function is to perfect, to actualize, to realify. Moreover, any essence whatsoever absolutely depends upon the act of existing actualizing it, since this latter is absolutely necessary for that essence. Yet no one essence is absolutely necessary in order to have an act of existing. For example, consider this individual human person. Existence is absolutely necessary for this individual human essence: it could not be this essence unless it *is*. Even in its very "thisness" it depends upon actual existence. But this individual human essence is not absolutely necessary for existence—otherwise, one could have the act of existing only when actualizing this human existent, with the result he or she would be the sole actual existent. But one finds many existents, each with an act of existing. Therefore, existence is absolutely necessary for this essence, but this essence is not absolutely necessary for existence.

---

[2] *Webster's New Collegiate Dictionary* (New York: Simon & Schuster, 1980), p. 1128.

[3] That essence does itself combine potency with act should be clear from the fact that it involves not only prime matter but also substantial form and accidents. See Ch. IV, Secs. 4 and 6.

[4] See Ch. IV, notes 47–49.

Primacy for the act of existing, then, emphasizes the pre-eminent place it occupies because of its nature and function. This pre-eminence can be well expressed by a statement used by radical existentialists, provided it is correctly interpreted—"Existence precedes essence." What does such an existentialist as Sartre intend by it?

In him it can have at least two meanings, which are quite different but closely related. First of all, existence precedes essence by abolishing and destroying it. This destruction arises from the fact that every existent is nothing more than a mere stream or series of appearances. This identification of existence and reality with total fluency automatically entails that no existent can have any stable nature or essence.[5] Nor does he have one even in the mind of God, and this for an obvious reason: "There is no human nature, since there is no God to conceive it."[6]

In its second signification the statement is entirely restricted to humans.

> If God does not exist, there is at least one being in whom existence precedes essence, a being who exists before he can be defined by any concept, and . . . this being is man, or, as Heidegger says, human reality. What is meant here by saying that existence precedes essence? It means that, first of all, man exists, turns up, appears on the scene, and, only afterwards, defines himself. If man, as the existentialist conceives him, is indefinable, it is because at first he is nothing. Only afterward will he be something, and he himself will have made what he will be. Thus, there is no human nature, since there is no God to conceive it. Not only is man what he conceives himself to be, but he is also only what he wills himself to be after this thrust toward existence.[7]

What is Sartre saying? An individual man first appears on the scene, turns up, begins to exist and only then defines himself, changes from nothing to something, chooses what he wants himself to be,[8] hurls himself toward a future,[9] plans himself,[10] fashions

---

[5] See Ch. II, Sec. 2.

[6] *Existentialism*, p. 18.

[7] *Ibid.*

[8] *Ibid.*, p. 20.

[9] *Ibid.*, p. 19.

[10] *Ibid.*

his image of man as he thinks he (and all others) ought to be.[11] His prior existence (appearance on the scene, turning up, actual presence in the absurd universe) allows him to determine, fashion, plan himself, his image, his future—in a word, his "essence." At first sight existence precedes essence here by causing and preserving it rather than by destroying it.

But the essence which a man attempts to build up for himself must be deceptive and illusory if Sartre's view here is to be consistent with his identification of reality with fluency and appearances.

> By reducing the existent to the series of appearances which manifest it . . . we certainly thus get rid of that dualism which in the existent opposes interior to exterior. There is no longer an exterior for the existent if one means by that a superficial covering which hides from sight the true nature of the object. And this true nature . . . no longer exists. . . . For the being of an existent is exactly what it appears.[12]

> Things are entirely what they appear to be—and behind them . . . there is nothing.[13]

> The diversity of things, their individuality, were only appearance, a veneer. This veneer had melted, leaving soft, monstrous masses, all in disorder.[14]

If indeed reality is absolute flux and mere appearances, then man can no more have achieved any sort of permanency (and, hence, genuine nature) for himself at the end of his career than he had at its beginning. The result: here again existence precedes essence or nature by destroying it.

But however one interprets Sartre,[15] the precedence of existence over essence is quite clear in the authentically existentialist approach we have been making. It entails both that existents have genuine essences or natures and that these are subordinated to the acts of existing actualizing them.

First of all, then, each material existent has an essence—that by which it is this man or this dog or this maple tree. True, each has an

---

[11] *Ibid.*, pp. 20–22.

[12] *Being and Nothingness*, p. xlvii.

[13] *Nausea*, p. 131.

[14] *Ibid.*, p. 171.

[15] For interpretations of Sartre, see James Collins, *The Existentialists: A Critical Study*, pp. 60 sqq.; J. Maritain, *Existence and the Existent*, pp. 3 sq.

essence ultimately because there is a God:[16] God sees Himself imitable in endlessly varied ways, and each creature is one of those ways, actualized and literally realized under God's free creative choice. But one need not assent to the existence of God in order to know that material existents have essences. Let him only observe himself and other existents. There he sees that an individual man is not absolute change or a mere series of appearances, but rather intimately combines change with stability. I who write these lines am basically the same person who some weeks ago wrote Chapter I and who many years ago learned to write in a Nebraskan schoolroom. You who are reading these lines are fundamentally the person who read Chapter I at an earlier time and who learned to read some years previously under circumstances proper to you. Each existent, then, combines accidental changes with specific stability, and this unique combination is his essence. Within each essence substance is the principle of specific continuity, as we have seen, and accidents account for the existent's development along physical, emotional, intellectual, cultural and religious lines.

Each material existent, then, has a genuine essence because he is not pure flux but rather unites fluency to permanency within the confines of a single subject. His essence is not discovered in any separate realm of Essences (as Plato would have it) but as concretized in an actual existent. His essence is not static but dynamic and progressive, because within itself it involves accidental changes. Yet those changes do not destroy it (as Sartre would have it) because it also involves substantial stability.[17] Such is the sort of essence

---

[16] One can ground each existent in God even more precisely, but this grounding differs from philosopher to philosopher. According to Descartes (who had been anticipated in this by Abelard and Ockham), essences are what they are ultimately because God wills them to be such and such. A man is a rational animal and is thereby other than a canine animal or any other animal because of the divine will; 2 + 2 = 4 because God so wills it. According to Leibniz and his brand of essentialists, essences are what they are entirely because of themselves and, thus, are ultimately independent of God.

A far better answer is that essences are what they are because God is what He is. In a universe where reality is actuality, God is subsistent actuality. He sees Himself imitable in infinitely varied ways, and each of those ways is a creature, which will actually exist if God freely creates it. In this interpretation divine will and intellect are themselves rooted in divine being.

[17] Even a substantial change does not annihilate the essence, because death entails not only change (the loss and acquirement of specific perfections) but also a corporeal continuity. This latter is indicated by the fact that what was living and is now nonliving retains temporarily the same shape, weight and

each material thing has—a concretized, intimate fusion of change and stability, of accidents and substance.

But in any material existent its essence is also actualized by an act of existing which is other than itself (see Ch. IV, Secs. 3 and 4) and to which it is subordinated. Why the subordination? Because, as we have seen at the beginning of this section, it completely depends upon the act of existing existentializing it, since it has absolute need of it. Yet it is not absolutely necessary in order to have an act of existing. For instance, consider this dog. Existence is absolutely necessary for this particular canine essence: it could not be this essence unless it is. Even in its very individuality and particularity it depends upon actual existence. But this individual canine essence is not absolutely necessary for existence—otherwise, one could have the act of existing only when actualizing this canine existent, with the result that this dog would be the sole actual existent. But one finds many existents, each with an act of existing. Therefore, existence is absolutely necessary for *this* essence, but *this* essence is not absolutely necessary in order to have an act of existing. Thus, any essence is subordinated to the act of existing actualizing it.

Such, then, is the force of "Existence precedes essence" when interpreted within an authentically existentialist context. The nouns in the statement refer to components within one and the same existent—*existence* to the act by which this man actually exists, *essence* to the concretized, unique combination of change/stability by which he actually exists as this man. Each component has its own function—the act of existing actualizes and realifies the essence, which simultaneously limits it by specifying-individuating-individualizing it (see note 18). Of these two components actual existence is the more important, for in any existent the essence absolutely depends in its very uniqueness and "thisness" upon the act of existing: it could neither be this essence nor perform its proper function unless it is. But no one essence is absolutely necessary for the act of existing—it is discovered actualizing this human essence, that human essence, this canine essence, and so on. In brief, it is a perfection common to all existents and in this lies its precedence. Yet this precedence does not destroy but rather establishes and preserves the essence. As actualized and realified by the

---

other appearances, and by the fact that the amount, kind and location of the pure chemicals resulting after death are determined by the amount, kind and location of the virtual chemicals before death. The component underlying and causing such continuity is prime matter. See Ch. III, Sec. 4.

act of existing, an essence not only *is* but also *is itself,* and thus can and does perform its own task of specifying-individuating-individualizing the existent.[18] Although (and because) subordinated to actual existence, an actualized essence is genuinely real and makes a unique contribution to the existent of which it is a part.

Authentic existentialism, then, affirms "the primacy of existence, but as implying and preserving essences or natures and as manifesting the supreme victory of the intellect and of intelligibility."[19] It finds place for both actual existence and essence; the former is prior in nature and function to the latter, but in such a way that its priority safeguards and enhances the latter.

Let us now investigate in more detail at least three reasons why the act of existing enjoys such pre-eminent rank—it is the source of all other perfections, it is autodetermining, and it is amaterial.

2. Actual Existence and Other Perfections

In discovering whether all other perfections in an existent are ultimately grounded in its act of existing, one must first uncover what a perfection is. We commonly speak of a day or a flower or a picnic or a gentleman or a house as *perfect,* but what is meant? Let us concentrate upon a house which is actually being built. When can we describe it as "perfect"? When it is completely finished—when the last nail has been hammered, the final coat of paint and varnish applied, and so on.[20] Then *it has everything which it should have in order to be a house.*

---

[18] As we shall see in Sec. 3, "Autodetermination," the act of existing limits itself, but this it can do only mediately, only through the essence it actualizes. Anyone who would reduce essence to a mere limit or negation so as to stress the primacy of the act of existing would thereby seem also to eliminate one of the prerequisites of that very primacy.

Incidentally, in the phrase, "specifying-individuating-individualizing," used to describe how essence limits existence, "specifying" refers to the function of substantial form within essence, substantially "individuating" refers to that of prime matter, "individualizing" refers to that of accidents.

[19] J. Maritain, *Existence and the Existent,* p. 3. This interpretation of authentic existentialism is not accepted by everyone—for example, see John Wild, "Christian Rationalism (Aquinas, Gilson, Maritain)," in *Christianity and Existentialism* (Chicago: Northwestern University Press, 1963), pp. 40–65.

[20] The English adjective "perfect" is derived from *perfectum,* the perfect passive participle of the Latin verb, *perficio* (to make, to complete) and means literally "that which has been completed, finished."

If we now turn from the adjective "perfect" and ask what the noun "perfection" signifies, the answer should be clear. A perfection is *that which an item ought to possess in view of what it is.* It is *a possession due to an existent.*

Perfections show themselves to belong to at least three classes. Some possessions are due to a material existent precisely *as material*—for example, this man's weight and size, his vegetative and sentient powers, all of which are intrinsically dependent upon his material status. But his intellect and will, together with the operations they elicit and the operative habits which reside in them, are intrinsically independent of matter. Thus, intellection, freedom, wisdom and the like are possessions due to the spiritual side of his nature[21] and hence are perfections of a different sort. Still a third group of possessions are those which are due to a material existent precisely *as existent*—existence itself, as well as unity, truth, goodness and beauty, which are consequent upon being.

Accordingly, perfections are of three kinds:

(a) those whose very perfection contains some potentiality or limitation and, hence, imperfection because they intrinsically depend upon his material status—these let us call "mixed";

(b) those which of themselves contain no such limitation and imperfection because they only extrinsically depend upon his material status and thus are spiritual—these let us call "pure" or "unmixed";[22]

(c) those which of themselves entail no limitation or restriction whatsoever because they are present in a material existent solely *as existent* and thus are present in each and every existent—these let us call "transcendent" (see below, Ch. VI, Sec. 3).

One final point needs clarification before we investigate the act of existing and its relationship to other perfections. It can be stated in this manner: is perfection synonymous with act? Obviously not, because all the components of a material existent (both acts and potencies) are perfections: they are what it ought to have in order to be either material or an existent. This holds true even with respect to prime matter, which, say, this dog must have if he is to be dog and this dog.[23]

---

[21] On the meaning of "spiritual," see Ch. V, Sec. 4.

[22] What we here call "pure perfections," M. R. Holloway calls "perfections proper to a being" (*Introduction to Natural Theology*, pp. 122, 132). See his entire discussion, pp. 119–24, 132.

[23] These statements can be made with reference to prime matter: (1) It is pure potency because of itself it is nothing but a recipient; it has no act of

Hence, perfection is not identical with act. Rather, some perfections are potencies (that is, possessions [substance, prime matter, essence] by which an existent receives other perfections). Some are acts (that is, possessions [accidents, substantial form, act of existing] which an existent receives in and by his potencies).[24]

Having discussed what a perfection is and what the various kinds of perfections are, we are now prepared to ask explicitly what sort of perfection the act of existing is and how all other perfections are rooted in it.

These questions are easy to answer in the light of what has gone before. First of all, the act of existence is a perfection, since it is what any and every existent must have if he or she is to exist. It is a pure perfection, since of itself it contains no limitation and imperfection—it is limited only by the essence it actualizes; it is intrinsically independent of matter.[25] Moreover, it is the only component which even *as a component* is pure perfection and a pure act. Of itself it is completely free from potency and says nothing but actuation, whereas all other components in an existent are in potency to it (see Ch. IV, Sec. 4).

But why is it the source of all other perfections? Because it is the ultimate reason why an individual thing has those other perfections, as the following argumentation shows.

> A perfection is a possession due to an individual man:
> But he has nothing unless he exists;
> But that by which he exists is his act of existing;
> Therefore, his act of existing is fundamentally that by which he has whatever he does have;
> Therefore, his act of existing is the ultimate source of all other possessions or perfections.

* Let us apply this to the other components, one by one.

---

itself. (2) Yet it is a perfection because it is a possession which a material existent ought to have. (3) But it is a "mixed" perfection because even though it is a perfection, its very nature is to be a potency and a limitation.

[24] Manifestly, the classification here of perfections as potencies and acts is not identical with the previous one of perfections as mixed, pure and transcendent. Some potencies entail pure perfections (for example, the operative powers of intellect and will), whereas some acts are mixed perfections (for example, such accidents as quantity and various qualities, substantial forms). Two classifications are made from different points of view.

[25] See Ch. V, Sec. 4.

The function of prime matter in an existent is to limit by individuating;
But this function it can perform only if it actually *is;*
But that by which it actually *is* is the act of existing;
Therefore, that by which prime matter is enabled to substantially individuate is, ultimately, the act of existing;
Therefore, this latter is the ultimate source of prime matter in itself and in its functioning.

The task which a substantial form performs in an existent is to specify—for example, a human soul makes the composite be human rather than canine or equine or geraniaceous or aqueous;
But this task the substantial form can perform only if it actually *is;*
But that by which it actually *is* is the act of existing;
Therefore, that by which a substantial form is enabled to specify is, in the last analysis, the act of existing;
Therefore, this latter is the ultimate source of substantial form in itself and in its functioning.

The function which accidents carry out is to confer individual perfections—for instance, a man's operative habits are that by which he is wise, prudent, temperate, modest, courageous, generous, mathematical, musical, philosophical, and the like; his operations are that by which he is actually thinking, analyzing, reasoning, remembering, loving, freely choosing, and so on;
But this function accidents can carry out only if they actually *are;*
But that by which accidents actually *are* is the act of existing;
Therefore, that by which accidents are enabled to confer individual perfections is the act of existing;
Therefore, this latter is the ultimate source of accidents in themselves and as carrying out their functions.

This entire section on existence and other perfections comes down to this: no component can be itself or exercise its own intrinsic sort of causality unless it is. Therefore, by causing every other component to *be,* the act of existing is the ultimate source of all the other components and of the perfections which they are.

Why, then, is that act the source of all perfections? Because it is the ultimate source of all actuality and thereby, of all reality, for to be real is to be actual. And the fact that it is the source of all perfections reveals the primacy it enjoys within an existent.

3. Actual Existence and Autodetermination

Another revelation of that primacy comes from the additional fact that the act of existence is autodetermining. What does this self-determination involve?

The term is commonly used when colonies seek to become independent nations. Those colonies about to be released from the status of colony find themselves in the process of what is called self-determination. That is to say, various avenues are open to them. They can remain within the economic and cultural orbit of the mother country (as happens, for example, when a British colony [such as Canada] becomes a member of the British Commonwealth), they can gradually achieve complete autonomy, they can immediately sever all relations with the mother country, and so on. Of those different alternatives they freely decide upon one. In this free choice lies their self-determination—they themselves decide what sort of nation they will be.

In metaphysics, the term does not have reference to the free decision of a nation or even of an individual human person.[26] Rather, it refers to the components within an individual material existent, and, more precisely, to the relationships which they have to one another as intrinsic causes of that existent.

In understanding this point, one must first realize that the verb "determine" can have at least two distinct but complementary meanings even in everyday situations. It can signify "to confer a perfection" as when we say, "Using milk rather than Scotch determines the kind of drink we make." It can also signify "to limit a

---

[26] E. Gilson seems first to have used "autodetermination" in our sense. See *Le Thomisme: Introduction à la philosophie de saint Thomas d'Aquinas*, 5th edition (Paris: J. Vrin, 1948), p. 54: "Chaque essence est posée par un acte d'exister qu'elle n'est pas et qui l'inclut comme son *autodétermination*." Also see *idem*, *Christian Philosophy of St. Thomas Aquinas* (New York: Random House, Inc., 1956), p. 36.

Aquinas himself occasionally uses *determinare* in the twofold sense of conferring and limiting a perfection. On *determinatio* as conferment of perfection, see *In I Sent.*, d. 24, q. 1, a. 1 ad 3 (Mandonnet Ed., p. 577); *S.T.*, I, 44, 2 resp.; *ibid.*, I, 119, 2 resp. On *determinatio* as limit of a perfection, see *ibid.*, I, 80, 1 resp.: *ibid.*, 84, 2 resp.; *S.C.G.*, III, c. 66.

perfection," as when we say, "The size of the glass determines the amount we drink."

If we apply this information to components, it is evident that the various acts within an existent determine by conferring perfections (let us refer to this meaning of "determine" as #1). For example, a man's accidents of mathematics and music determine him to be mathematical and musical, his substantial form determines him to be human rather than canine, his act of existing determines him to be existent rather than nonexistent. But his potencies determine by limiting perfections (let us refer to this meaning of "determine" as #2). For example, his intellectual ability and acumen determine how much mathematics he can achieve, prime matter determines him to be this man by ultimately individuating his substantial form (see above, note 18, second paragraph), his essence determines him to be this existent by specifying-individuating-individualizing the act of existing actualizing him.

But what would *self*-determination mean? That an act would not only confer a perfection (and thus, as we would expect, determine the existent in sense #1 of the term), but would also limit itself through its partner-component (and thus determine itself in sense #2 of the term). Likewise, a potency would not only limit a perfection (and thereby, as one would expect, determine that perfection in sense #2 of the term), but would also perfect itself through that act (and thus determine itself in sense #1 of the term).

What decides whether a component, be it an act or a potency, actually is autodetermining? *The fact that the intrinsic causality it exercises upon its partner-component within the existent* (conferring or limiting a perfection) *is of such a nature that the latter relies absolutely upon the former in order to exercise its own intrinsic causality* (limiting or conferring a perfection).[27] If such is the case, if the former necessarily helps the latter in carrying out its own causality, if the former in the function it uniquely performs is absolutely necessary for the latter's function, then the former determines itself through the lat-

---

[27] A somewhat similar relationship exists between the principal and instrumental efficient causes. Take the case of a teacher using a piece of red chalk to write a meaningful word on the blackboard. The proper effect of the chalk is that word as *red*. This it can cause, however, only insofar as it is moved by the writer. Hence, the chalk depends upon the principal cause in order to exercise its own proper causality. Because of this dependence, then, the writer also has produced the redness in the effect, although only through the instrument. On intrinsic causality, see Ch. VIII, prgrs. corresponding to notes 2–5.

ter. If the former is an act, it limits itself through the potency it actuates ("determine" in sense #2). If a potency, it perfects itself through the act it receives ("determine" in sense #1).

(a) Which Components Are Autodetermining?

Which components are self-determining? This we can answer rather easily if we examine the intrinsic causality which various acts and potencies reciprocally exercise. Let us begin with prime matter and substantial form.

* Is, then, prime matter self-determining? Does the prime matter of (say) this man specify itself through his human soul? Does it even mediately humanize itself? It does if each proposition of the following line of argumentation turns out to be true.

> Substantial form determines [sense #1] prime matter by specifying it;
> But substantial form is specifically such and such only because it is individuated, because it is in this individual, because it is this individual substantial form—for example, a human soul is human only because it is *this* human soul;
> But prime matter is ultimately that by which the substantial form is individuated, that by which it becomes *this* form;
> Therefore, prime matter is mediately self-specifying through the substantial form, and thus is autodetermining [sense #1].

Is, then, prime matter mediately self-determining? Obviously not, for the second proposition of the argument is false. No substantial form is specifically such-and-such because of the individuation it receives from prime matter, for if this were the case, the substantial form could be found only in this individual. The species would be confined to him alone. Rather, the substantial form is what it is specifically *from itself*, from its own nature. A human soul is human rather than canine proximately because its very nature is to be human. Accordingly, the substantial individuation which prime matter exercises upon a human soul does not make that soul be human or contribute directly to the humanization which the latter carries out in the existent. The result is that prime matter is not self-specifying, even through the substantial form it receives and limits.

* But is substantial form autodetermining? Does it mediately individuate itself? Once again, it does if each proposition of the following argument is true.

Prime matter determines [sense #2] substantial form by receiving and individuating it;
But prime matter can receive and individuate the substantial form only if it is in an existent which is specifically such-and-such;
But that by which an existent is specifically such-and-such is the substantial form;
Therefore, the substantial form is mediately self-individuating through prime matter, and thus is self-determining [sense #2].

Is, then, substantial form mediately self-determining? Yes, since the crucial second proposition of the argument is true. That is to say, prime matter is the basic cause of substantial individuation, because quantity, although a property of the composite and not of either form or matter taken alone, flows more directly in the composite from prime matter than from substantial form because it is a generic rather than a specific property of material things.[28] But prime matter cannot *by itself* be the more immediate source of quantity because of itself it is only pure potency. Quantity can issue from it only when it is informed, only inasmuch as it is a component within an existent which is material, which is of such a nature as to be extended, as to have physical parts outside of parts. But an existent has such a nature only insofar as it is also aqueous or geraniaceous or canine or human, for we never find any existent which is *only* material, which is without some or other specific perfection. In brief, what makes a nature to be specifically such-and-such also helps make it to be material, because the specific perfection is built upon the generic and carries it along.[29] But that

---

[28] On individuation, see Ch. VI, Sec. 5b. Why is quantity not a specific property? Because nothing exists simply as body, but always as such-and-such a body—aqueous body, living body, canine body, human body, and so forth. Therefore, quantity is not a specific property, and hence its more direct source within the composite is not the substantial form, from which specific properties more immediately flow. That source is, then, the other component within the substance—namely, prime matter.

[29] In an actual thing the specific perfection is not really distinct from the generic. For example, a man's rationality is fundamentally identical with his animality. In fact, his rationality permeates his entire sentient, living, chemical and material constitution. That is to say, his nature as rational is not really other than his nature as sentient, as living, and as material. True enough, the properties which flow from that single nature as rational (intellect, will) are really distinct from those issuing from that nature as sentient (internal and

by which an existent is specifically such-and-such is the substantial form. Hence the substantial form, in carrying out its own function of specifying the existent, also enables prime matter to carry out its function of substantial individuation. Accordingly, through prime matter the substantial form individuates itself, and thus is self-determining (sense #2).[30]

* Let us now turn to substance and accidents. First of all, is substance self-determining? Is it self-accidentalizing? Does it through accidents confer individual perfections upon itself? It does if all the propositions of the following process are true.

> Accidents determine [sense #1] by bestowing individual perfections upon substance—for example, a man's intellect is

---

external sense faculties), as living (vegetative operative powers), and as material (quantity). Also, his substance is made up of two really distinct components (prime matter, substantial form), which provide an objective basis for the mental distinction between rationality and animality and the other essential perfections. But the fact remains that those essential perfections are only mentally distinct (described by some as: *distinctio mentalis ratiocinati maior seu cum fundamento perfecto in re*). Why so? Because an individual man is an *unum per se*, as indicated by the fact that all those various operative powers cooperate together for the intrinsic good of themselves and of the whole. And, second, because "rational" and other terms expressing those essential perfections simply describe one and the same whole in a more or less determinate way.

[30] If the substantial form, indeed, is self-individuating, this fact may throw some light on the centuries-old problem of how prime matter can individuate a human soul (or, for that matter, any substantial form). How can individuality (with its connotations of uniqueness, autonomy, and perfection) be rooted in the component which is of itself only pure potency?

Various answers have been offered. Some distinguish individuality from individuation as the positive from the negative: "Individuality is the sum total of positive perfections pertaining to this individual as this individual. Individuation is the quasi-negative, limiting principle; individuality is the correlative, positive perfection (George P. Klubertanz, *Introduction to Philosophy of Being*, p. 106, n. 15). For others, "the original and individual differences of each concrete being . . . are made possible by its matter [but] they proceed from its form, which alone gives actuality" (Etienne Gilson, *Spirit of Mediaeval Philosophy* [New York: Charles Scribner's Sons, 1940], p. 466, n. 7).

The answer which autodetermination offers need not detract from the above solutions; instead, it complements them. Prime matter does substantially individuate the human soul insofar as it is the more direct source of quantity (and of materiality). But it can be this source only through the influence of the soul, which thereby individuates itself through prime matter. Hence, individuation and individuality arise indirectly from the soul itself.

that by which he is capable of intellection, his will is that by which he is capable of free choice, his external senses are each that by which he is able to see or hear or taste and so on; his operative habit of mathematics is that by which he is capable of coping easily with problems concerning discrete and continuous quantity; his act of reasoning is that by which he actually goes from premises to a conclusion;

But accidents can bestow individual perfections only if they inhere in a substance and only because they are caused somehow by the substance;

But, as we have just intimated, substance is that in which accidents inhere and that by which they are caused;

Therefore, a substance confers individual perfections upon itself through its accidents, and thus is mediately self-determining [sense #1].

Is, then, substance indirectly autodetermining? The answer is affirmative because the crucial second proposition is true. The accidents mentioned in the first proposition (operative powers, operative habits, operations), as well as all other accidents, can confer individual perfections only by inhering in the substance which they perfect and through which they are existentialized—the substance is the channel through which the act of existing actualizing the substance also reaches the accidents.[31] Moreover, the substance causes its own accidents. It is what might be called the "emanative" cause of all its properties (for example, quantity, faculties, operative powers, and so on), which automatically and naturally flow ("emanate") from it once it has itself been efficiently caused.[32] It efficiently causes others through its operative powers. For example, through its will it is the efficient cause of its free choices. Through its intellect it efficiently causes operations of reflecting and reasoning, which in turn produce various operative habits. Accordingly, by receiving and causing the very accidents which are individually perfecting it, the substance simultaneously is accidentally perfecting itself, and thus is mediately self-determining (sense #1) through those accidents.

---

[31] See Ch. IV, n. 44.

[32] On this causality see Michael Montague, S.J., "Active Causality," in *Proceedings of the Twenty-Third Annual Convention of the Jesuit Philosophical Association* (Woodstock, Md.: Woodstock College Press, 1961), pp. 37–65. Also see Henri J. Renard, S.J., *Philosophy of Man*, 2nd ed. (Milwaukee: Bruce Publishing Co., 1956), pp. 84–87.

* What about the accidents themselves? Are they autodetermining? First of all, some distinctions must be made before we formulate the argument. As we have seen in the previous paragraph, substance not only receives accidents but also causes them. Its efficient and emanative causal relationship to accidents will not be taken into consideration when we discuss whether accidents are self-determining, because autodetermination involves intrinsic causality. Also, by receiving accidents, substance determines them in sense #2 of the verb: it limits them. Hence, in inquiring whether accidents determine themselves, we are taking the verb in the same sense: do they receive and ground themselves through the substance, and thus mediately limit and determine themselves?

* Second, the substance directly receives accidents which are properties, but only indirectly receives those which are not properties, since these it receives through the former. (For instance, operative powers [properties] inhere in the substance itself, whereas the operations and resultant operative habits which the substance produces through those powers reside directly in the latter and in the substance only through them). Accordingly, the question of self-determination with respect to accidents can be twofold, depending upon whether we are considering those which are properties or those which are not.

* Because there are two kinds of accidents and because the relationship which substance has to each is somewhat different, we should not discuss the question of autodetermination with reference to accidents in general, but rather with reference to each of the two kinds. In order to simplify matters, though, let us restrict ourselves to properties.[33] Our question now is: are those accidents which are properties self-determining? Are they mediately responsible for their own reception and limitation?

* Once again, they are if the propositions of the following argument are true.

> Substance determines [sense #2] accidents[34] by receiving them;
> But substance can receive accidents only because it has the individual perfections which accidents confer and are;

---

[33] Besides, it is sufficient to inquire concerning properties, for if they do not receive and thereby ground themselves, *a fortiori* those accidents which are not properties will not either.

[34] Throughout this process and the rest of the paragraph, "accident" stands for "those accidents which are properties."

> But accidents are each that by which a substance is individually perfected;
> Therefore, accidents receive and limit themselves through the substance, and hence are mediately autodetermining [sense #1].

In the light of that process, are accidents mediately self-determining? The answer is negative, because the second proposition is incorrect. The reason why substance can and does receive accidents is located in the very nature of the substance itself—in itself it is a potency to such accidental perfections and needs to be complemented by them.[35] Consequently, the individual perfections which accidents confer upon the substance are not the source of its receptivity and potentiality. Therefore, they are not even mediately responsible for their own reception and limitation. They are not self-determining.

Let us now turn to essence and existence, beginning with essence. Is the essence of this man self-determining? Does it actualize itself through the act of existing it is limiting? Once again, it does if the following propositions are true.

> The act of existing determines [sense #1] this essence by actualizing, realifying, existentializing it, and this task it performs because it is what it is—namely, actual existence;
> But the act of existing is what it is (that is, is actual, real and existence) only because it is received and limited by this essence, only because it is *this* act of existing;
> But this essence is that by which the act of existing is *this* act of existing;
> Therefore, this essence actualizes itself through the act of existing, and thus is mediately autodetermining.

Is, then, this essence self-determining? Evidently not, because the second proposition is inaccurate, as will be clear if we refer to what we said some paragraphs back concerning substantial form/prime matter. A substantial form is not specifically such-and-such because of the individuation it receives from prime matter, for if this

[35] The very nature of the substance also accounts for its causality with respect to accidents. For instance, intellect and will emanate from the human soul because by nature it is human. Sense faculties flow from the sentient composite because its very nature is to be sentient.

were the case, the substantial form could be found only in this individual. The species would be confined to him alone. Rather, the substantial form is what it specifically is *from itself,* from its own nature. A human soul is human rather than canine proximately because its very nature is to be human. Likewise, the act of existing is not what it is (the actualizing, realifying, existentializing principle) because it is actualizing this essence—otherwise, it could be found only in this one existent, who alone would be actual and existing. Rather, the act of existing is what it is *from itself,* from its own nature. Accordingly, the limitation which this essence carries out within the existent does not actualize and existentialize the act of existing. Hence, this essence is not self-actualizing, even through the act of existence it specifies-individuates-individualizes.[36] In a word, it is not mediately self-determining.

Finally, what of the act of existing? In this existent is it autodetermining? Does it mediately cause its own limitation? Does it indirectly specify-individuate-individualize itself through this essence? Once again, it does if each proposition in the following line of argumentation is true.

> This essence determines [sense #2] the act of existing by receiving it, by specifying-individuating-individualizing it, by limiting it;
> But this essence can receive, specify-individuate-individualize, limit only if it actually exists;
> But the act of existing is that by which this essence actually exists;
> Therefore, the act of existing specifies-individuates-individualizes and limits itself through this essence and, thus, is mediately self-determining [sense #2].

In the light of this argument, is actual existence autodetermining? Clearly yes, because the crucial second proposition is true. The essence in, say, this man can carry out its own unique causality of specifying-individuating-individualizing him only if it actually ex-

[36] One must remember that the essence of any material existent is always this essence or that essence and never essence simply. If this latter were the case, such an essence might conceivably be autodetermining as self-actualizing. But actually, one never comes upon essence simply (which is an abstraction) but only this human essence, that human essence, this canine essence, and so on. On "specifies-individuates-individualizes," see n. 18 above.

ists. The act of existing which it is receiving and limiting is absolutely necessary for it: it could neither be this essence nor perform its own causal function unless it *is*. Consequently, the act of existing specifies-individuates-individualizes and limits itself through whatever essence it actualizes, and hence is mediately autodetermining (sense #2).[37]

(b) Conclusions

If we look back on those previous paragraphs, these points should be clear—when autodetermination occurs, what it is, which components do determine themselves, why the autodetermination of other components is rooted in the act of existing and, lastly, why the fact that the act of existing is mediately determining reveals the primacy it enjoys in an existent.

1. Autodetermination occurs whenever *the causal function of a component is absolutely necessary for that of its partner-component*. If so, this latter can carry out its own intrinsic causality within an existent only insofar as it is genuinely influenced by the former. By the necessary influence it exerts, then, the former determines itself through the latter.

2. Accordingly, *autodetermination is the self-limiting or self-perfecting property of a component whose causal influence necessarily permeates also that of its partner-component*. If an act, that component limits itself through the potency it actuates. If a potency, that component actuates itself through the act it receives and limits.

3. The components which are autodetermining are three—*substance, substantial form*, and *the act of existing*. The first is a potency, the last two are acts. Substance is self-determining (sense #1) inasmuch as it individually perfects itself through the accidents which it receives and causes (either emanatively or efficiently). A substantial form is self-determining (sense #2) insofar as it substantially individuates itself through prime matter, which it informs and thereby allows to be the more direct cause of quantity. The act of existing is self-determining (sense #2) because it specifies-individuates-individualizes itself through whatever essence it actualizes.

4. The self-determination which characterizes the first two components is rooted in the act of existing, because a substance can

---

[37] For another approach to autodetermination, see Maurice R. Holloway, "Towards the Fullness of Being," *Proceedings of the Twenty-fourth Annual Convention of the Jesuit Philosophical Association* (Woodstock, Md.: Woodstock College Press, 1962), pp. 6–37.

receive and cause accidents (and thereby be the means by which accidents come to be existentialized) only if it actually exists. Likewise, a substantial form can inform and specify prime matter only if both these substantial components actually exist. Accordingly, the self-perfection and the self-individuation which, respectively, a substance and a substantial form achieve, rest on the act of existing.

5. Finally, the self-essentialization which the act of existing mediately achieves in each existent reveals the primacy this component enjoys. For actual existence in this man or woman specifies-individuates-individualizes itself through this human essence by actualizing it. Actualization is absolutely necessary for this essence, for it can be this essence and can carry out its own causal function of specification-individuation-individualization only if it *is*. Even in its uniqueness and particularity it absolutely depends upon the act of existing, which, however, is relatively independent of it: in order to have an act of existing, there must be some essence or other, but it need not be this essence. Consequently, in any existent the essence is subordinated to the act of existing which is actualizing it and which is thereby shown to have primacy in the existent. Because of its nature and function, it is pre-eminent in rank and importance.

4. Actual Existence and Amateriality

Another indication that the act of existence has primacy is its unique independence of matter even in a material existent.

In order to understand how extraordinary this independence is, let us contrast it with the immateriality to be found in other components. But this contrast requires that we first discuss what materiality is, since immateriality is its negation and anything negative can be understood only in light of what is negated.

(a) Materiality

What, then, is meant when we say that something is material? We mean that it is of such a nature as to have extended parts outside of parts, as to be actually extended, as to be directly in place, and so on. This meaning becomes clear when humans, animals, plants, and chemicals are juxtaposed to such items as intellection, freedom, unselfishness, love, value, and the like. The former all have at least this one common trait: each is of such a nature as to have parts outside of parts, as to be actually extended and directly in place. That common characteristic has come to be expressed by the term "material," which therefore means simply "that which is of such a nature as to have parts outside of parts, as to be actually extended and directly in place, and the like."[38]

* Of what can that term be predicated? Obviously, of all humans, animals, plants, and chemicals, each of which receives the predication as *that which* is material.

* But each material existent is made up of two components:

(a) *essence*—that by which that-which-is-material is precisely what it is (namely, material);

(b) and *act of existing*—that by which that-which-is-material actually exists.

Manifestly, the essence itself within a material existent also is strictly material, but only in the sense that it is *that by which* such an existent is material.[39]

* But such an essence is itself constituted of prime matter, substantial form and accidents. Can such components also be described as "material"? Since no essential component *in and of itself* has parts outside of parts or is actually extended or in place, each of them, when considered in itself, may be termed "immaterial" (thereby meaning simply "that which does not have extended parts outside of parts, and so on"). But since they actually go together to fashion a strictly material essence, each can also be called material through extrinsic denomination, meaning simply that it is a component of a material existent (to which the term is intrinsically applied) and, even more precisely, that it is a component of the essence within the existent. As a constitutive part of a material essence, it is within that by which a material existent is, precisely, material.[40]

---

[38] See Ch. III, Sec. 4, prgrs. corresponding to notes 31–33.

[39] Should "material" also be strictly predicated of quantity? Possibly, although differently than when predicated even of essence. The essence is material as "that by which that-which-is-of-such-a-nature as to have extended parts outside of parts does have such a nature." Quantity is material as "that by which that-which-is-of-such-a-nature as to have extended parts outside of parts does have such parts." It is the component within the essence which accounts for extension.

But one should remember that neither quantity nor essence is material as *that which* has parts outside of parts. Only the thing, the existent, is thus material.

[40] Although prime matter, substantial form and various accidents are all material through extrinsic denomination (see above, Ch. IV, n. 35), yet they are not all equally so because of the varying degrees of dependency they have upon matter, as will be clear in the following section, "Immateriality."

* But a material existent is not only made up of essence but also of an act of existing. Can this latter also be classified as "material"? Yes, and again through extrinsic denomination insofar as it too is a component of a material existent. But because it is other than the existent's essence (which is that by which the existent is material), the act of existence is not a component of the material existent as material, but only *as existent*. Consequently, one describes actual existence as material through extrinsic denomination in a different and weaker sense than when the term is applied through extrinsic denomination to the essential components.[41]

(b) Immateriality

But all the components can be described as immaterial when viewed in and of themselves, inasmuch as none of them has of itself such a nature as to be actually extended and directly in place or to have parts outside of parts. Yet that blanket description is not very helpful, for components are immaterial in varying degrees in view of the different connection they have with matter.

The human soul, together with its faculties of intellect and will and the operations and operative habits it produces through them, is only, so to speak, *extrinsically* dependent on matter.[42] True, it is the substantial form of the body; it can be created only within matter, and the source of its natural intellectual knowledge is data it receives from the senses. Nonetheless, it also is the intellectual principle; it does have intellection and free choice as its typically human operations; it continues to exist after the human composite itself is dissolved at death. Accordingly, it is intrinsically independent of matter. This kind of freedom from matter is traditionally described by the term *"spiritual,"* meaning *"a component which is within a material essence and yet which is immaterial* [it does not have parts outside of parts] *in such a way as to be intrinsically independent of matter."*

All other essential components except the human soul and the accidents immediately consequent upon it (the faculties of intellect

[41] One might designate this difference thus: essential components are material through extrinsic denomination as "within the essence," *esse* as "within the existent."

[42] We presuppose what is said here of the human soul and its faculties and operations to be discussed and established elsewhere (for example, in the philosophy of human nature or sacred theology). We make use of it so as to understand *esse* and its immateriality better.

and will, their operations and operative habits) are *intrinsically* dependent on matter insofar as they totally rely upon the material status of the essence of which they are constitutive parts. And this total reliance extends not only to prime matter, quantity and the physical qualities of, for example, this dog, but also to its soul, together with the sense faculties and other operative powers consequent upon it. This soul depends on matter from beginning to end in its very being and operations—it is educed from matter; it ceases to exist when the canine composite is dissolved through substantial change; all its operations occur necessarily within physical organs. Still none of those components, when considered in and by itself, has parts outside of parts or is actually extended and directly in place. Hence, each of them is in itself immaterial. But their immateriality cannot be described as "spiritual," because here the term "immaterial" expresses *"a component which is within a material essence and yet which is immaterial in such a way as to be intrinsically dependent on matter."* Let us say such a component is *"barely immaterial,"* the adverb differentiating its immaterial status both from that of the human soul and from that of the act of existing, to which we now turn.

This last component, too, is immaterial, because it obviously does not of itself have parts outside of parts and it is not actually extended or directly in place. Nevertheless, its immateriality is unique. True enough, in this man or this dog or this oak tree it is a constitutive part of a material existent, but it is there not because the existent is material but because he is an *existent.* In this it differs even from a human soul, which is a component of a material existent precisely *as material* (because it is part of his essence) and can begin to exist only through creation in matter as the substantial form of the body, and thus is at least extrinsically dependent upon matter. But the act of existing has no such dependency upon matter in any material existent whatsoever; hence it can hardly be described as "spiritual." Still less is it intrinsically dependent upon matter as is a canine soul or various other essential components. Hence it is not fittingly termed "barely material."

Such, then, is the extraordinary immateriality of the act of existing—*a component which is within a material existent and yet which is immaterial to such a degree as to be both extrinsically and intrinsically independent of matter* because it is other than his essence, whence arises his materiality. What is the best word for it? Manifestly, neither "spiritual" nor "barely immaterial" will do. Let us use *amaterial* and reserve it solely for the act of existing, thereby expressing that of itself it simply has no connection with matter whatsoever.[43]

Here, then, is a component whose unique status of immateriality arises from its unique nature and functions. All other components are within a material existent because he is material, whereas the act of existing is present in him because he is an *existent*.

Little wonder, then, in view of its uniqueness, that the act of existing has primacy over essence in an existent.

5. Summary and Conclusion

(a) In Chapter IV we aimed at showing that the act of existing is a component within an existent, really distinct from the essence it actualizes. In this chapter we have discussed the primacy which that act has within the existent.

(b) In what does that primacy consist? In the fact that the act of existing in any existent is such in nature and in function as to outrank the essence it actuates. It realifies and perfects; the essence is realified and perfected.[44] It is pure act, whereas an essence is solely potency in the order of being and even in its own order is always a combination of potency/act. Existence is absolutely necessary for any essence whatsoever, since no essence can be what it is unless it actually exists. But no one essence is absolutely necessary in order to have an act of existing; otherwise, existence would be confined to this one existent. It is a factor common to all existents; the quiddity is unique in each.

In short: existence precedes essence. In opposition to Sartre, we argue that material existents have genuine essences (concretized, intimate combinations of change and stability, of accidents and substance), but that they are subordinated to the acts of existing which actualize them and which relatively are more important.

---

[43] Traditionally, God and angels are also termed "spiritual" to express that the divine essence and an angelic essence are, each in its own way, entirely independent of matter. This is a legitimate and easily recognized extension of the term. They also can just as easily be described as "amaterial" through a similar extension of the latter term.

[44] Obviously, these remarks refer directly to cases in which essence is other than *esse*. But even in God *esse* is paramount as the heart of His reality and root of all His perfections (see Sec. 6 of this chapter).

(c) Can the reasons why *esse* is of greater importance and enjoys such precedence be stated more precisely and developed more thoroughly? First of all, the act of existing takes precedence because it is the perfection *par excellence* and because it is the source of all other perfections.

1. It is the perfection *par excellence* because it is what any and every existent must have if they are to exist. It is a transcendent perfection since of itself it contains no limitation and imperfection—it is limited only by the essence it actualizes, it is entirely independent of matter as such. Moreover, it is the only component which even *as a component* is a transcendent perfection and pure act.

2. It is the source of all other perfections because of the fact that it is the ultimate reason why an individual thing has those other perfections, as this consideration shows.

> A perfection is a possession due to (say) an individual man;
> But he has nothing unless he exists;
> But that by which he exists is his act of existing;
> Therefore, his act of existing is fundamentally that by which he has whatever he does have;
> Therefore, his act of existing is the ultimate source of all other possessions or perfections.

(d) The second reason for the primacy of the act of being is that it is autodetermining: it limits itself through the essence it actualizes. Why so? An essence limits the act of existing by specifying-individuating-individualizing it; but no essence can specify-individuate-individualize *unless it actually exists;* therefore the act of existing limits itself through the essence it actualizes by enabling it to be this or that essence and to carry out its causal function of specification-individuation-individualization (see note 18 above). Even in its uniqueness and particularity the essence of this man absolutely depends upon the act of existing, which, however, is relatively independent: in order to have an act of existing, there must be some essence or other, but it need not be this essence. Consequently, in any existent the essence is subordinate to the act of existing which is actualizing it, which thereby limits itself through the essence actualized and which is thus shown to have primacy in the existent.

(e) A final reason why the act of existing has primacy is its unique independence of matter even in a material existent: it has no direct connection with matter whatsoever, it is simply *amaterial.* Every component without exception is immaterial of and in itself in the sense that it itself has no extended parts outside of parts. But actual existence is extraordinary in that essential components are present in a material existent because the existent is *material,* whereas existence is present only because the existent is an *existent.* To express this diversity among components, let us say that

1. with the exception of the human soul (together with its intellect and will and their operations and operative habits), essential components are "barely immaterial" because *they are within a material essence and yet are immaterial in such a way as to be intrinsically dependent on matter;*

2. the human soul (as well as its intellect and will and their operations and operative habits) is "spiritual" because *it is a component within a material essence and yet which is immaterial to such a degree that it is intrinsically independent of matter;*

3. but *esse* is "amaterial" because *it is a component which is within a material existent but is other than the material essence, and hence is immaterial in such a way as to be both extrinsically and intrinsically independent of matter.* Accordingly, the act of existing has no direct connection with matter at all, and thus is a component with a unique status of immateriality and with a consequent primacy over all essential components.

6. Actual Existence and God

This primacy makes the act of existing an excellent basis for easily proving the existence of God, because it reveals material existents to be signposts pointing to an Existent Who is totally greater and significantly other than themselves. Why so? Because actual existence, which is perfection *par excellence* and which is autodetermining and amaterial, is other than the essence of a material existent; hence it does not belong to the nature of any such existent: none exists of its very nature. Nevertheless, they do exist, they do have that supreme and unique perfection. Therefore, there must be an Existent Whose very essence is to exist, Who of His very nature is actuality and thus needs no cause, and yet Who can and does cause all else to exist.[45]

---

[45] But why must the cause be an existent in whom actual existence and essence are identical? Why could no other material existents suffice? Because also in such existents existence is really other than essence and, hence, instead of a solution we merely have another question: Who causes *them* to exist? We

The situation here is like that which occurs when one sees a young, indigent, and (let us suppose) entirely honest child playing with a diamond necklace. We know that the youngster does not have those precious jewels of and from himself, and yet he now does actually possess them; therefore, someone must have given them to him. In a word, wherever there is a gift, there must be a giver. The gift with regard to the very existential status of material things is their actual existence, and the donor is an Existent Who *is* actuality.

Rather obviously, this line of reflection not only establishes that God actually exists but also enables us to know to some extent the sort of existent He is.[46] In order to be the cause of existents in whom actual existence is really other than what they are, He must Himself not be that sort of existent. He is necessarily a noncreature. As we have already stated, He is actual existence. His very nature is to exist, and in Him existence is identical with what He is. The conse-

---

have only managed to transfer the problem back one step. No solution is possible as long as the cause posited is merely a *creature:* an existent (whether material or immaterial) whose existence is really distinct from his essence. No creature can properly cause the existence of another because one properly causes only what he causes in acting according to his nature, and it is not the nature of any creature to exist.

But might not an infinite series of such existents be an adequate cause? No, because even if creatures are endlessly added to other creatures, they still remain creatures, just as the endless addition of zeros to other zeros never amounts to anything other than zero, and creatures are zeros when it comes to properly causing existence. In a word, an infinite series is no more powerful than any one of its members, each of which is a creature and, accordingly, incapable of properly causing another creature to exist, as we have just seen.

On the impossibility of an infinite series, see Henri J. Renard, S.J., *The Philosophy of God* (Milwaukee: Bruce Publishing Co., 1951), pp. 22–25; Maurice R. Holloway, *Introduction to Natural Theology*, pp. 83–84; Arnold Benedetto, S.J., *Fundamentals in the Philosophy of God* (New York: The Macmillan Company, 1963), pp. 44–49; G. Smith, *Philosophy of Being* (New York: The Macmillan Company, 1961), pp. 369–71.

For a nontechnical version of this line of reflection based upon the existentiality of things, see Jacques Maritain, *Approaches to God* (New York: Harper & Row, Publishers, 1954), pp. 1–15. It is what he calls, "The Primordial Way of Approach: Natural or Prephilosophic Knowledge of God." Also see Leo Sweeney, S.J., "God Does Exist," *Ensign*, 1 (1967), 5–10.

[46] This knowledge will be largely negative and indirect because derived through creatures. On the difficulties encountered in knowing God, see Leo Sweeney, S.J., "Metaphysics and God: Plotinus and Aquinas," *Die Metaphysik im Mittelalter*, Vol. 2 of *Miscellanea Mediaevalia* (Berlin: Walter de Gruyter, 1963), pp. 232–39.

quences of this identity are multiple and important. Actuality is being, its lack is nonbeing. Because God *is* actuality, He is Being, the subsistent and perfect fullness of reality. Moreover, since unity, truth, goodness, and beauty are all inevitable consequences of being (by the very fact and to the extent that something actually *is*, it is also one, true, good, and beautiful),[47] He is also subsistent unity, truth, goodness and beauty. Furthermore, He is endowed with intellection, volition, love and freedom, because these perfections[48] are ultimately rooted in and flow from actual existence. In order to know, choose, or love we must first actually *be*, but there are actual existents without knowledge, freedom or love. Again, intellection is intellection only because there actually *are* beings which know; love is love and freedom is freedom only inasmuch as there actually *are* existents who love and freely choose. In brief, then, actual existence is more common, more universally present than any other perfection, and it is the ultimate source for them all. Consequently, He Who is actuality is thereby also intelligent, loving and free.

Admittedly, this sketch of God needs much development in order to be satisfactory,[49] but enough has been said, we hope, to indicate that the act of existing in its primacy and real otherness from essence allows us to answer affirmatively to the question, "Is there a God?" Yes, God does exist, because how else could these material existents possess actual existence, that pearl of great price? It is other than what they are; it neither has been nor is now nor ever will be part of their natures. And yet they do exist. Hence, there must be an Existent Who by nature is actual existence and Who is giving them that gift.[50] This existent we call God, Who by

---

[47] On the transcendents, see Ch. VI, Sec. 3 sqq.

[48] On pure perfections, see Sec. 2 of this chapter.

[49] Such development can conveniently be found in the basic treatises on natural theology cited in n. 45; also see n. 46 above.

[50] Interestingly and significantly, James Collins has reviewed the positions taken by modern and contemporary philosophers on God and then concluded that one can legitimately attain a philosophical knowledge of God only by moving from the structure of material existents precisely as existents. See *God in Modern Philosophy* (Chicago: Henry Regnery Co., 1959), pp. 394 and 399: "[The proposition that God exists] rests upon an inference, the force of which comes from the given, actual existents of our experience. The proposition which gives meaning and validity to our philosophical conception of God ultimately gets its causal foundation and inferential warrant from our analysis of composite, sensible beings. There is no more radically determinate and relevant a basis for assent than this one, since the inference is made and

the very fact that He is *actuality* is also all-perfect (He possesses all pure and transcendent perfections) and by the fact that He is *subsistent* actuality is infinitely perfect (He possesses each perfection in an unlimited degree).

J. J. C. Smart, an Australian analytical philosopher, openly admitted the awe he experiences from reflecting upon actual existence.

> The only rational thing to say if someone asks "Why does this table exist?" is some such thing as that such-and-such a carpenter made it. We can go back and back in such a series, but we must not entertain the absurd idea of getting back to something logically necessary. However, now let us ask, "Why should anything exist at all?" Logic seems to tell us that the only answer which is not absurd is to say, "Why shouldn't it?" Nevertheless, though I know how any answer on the lines of the cosmological argument can be pulled to pieces by a correct logic, I feel I want to go on asking the question. Indeed, though logic has taught me to look at such a question with the gravest suspicion, my mind often seems to reel under the immense significance it seems to have for me. That anything should exist at all does seem to me a matter for the deepest awe. But whether other people feel this sort of awe, and whether they or I ought to is another question. I think we ought to. If so, the question arises: If "Why should anything exist at all" cannot be interpreted after the manner of the cosmological argument, that is, as an absurd request for the nonsensical postulation of a logically necessary being, what sort of question is it? What sort of question is this question "Why should anything exist at all?" All I can say is, that I do not yet know.[51]

---

the assent given to God as a consequence of inspecting some given sensible things in their composing principles of being. . . . A humanly developed philosophy of God must examine the structure of the existing sensible thing of our experience, discover its intrinsic composition and causal dependence in being for its concrete act of existing, and in this way infer the truth of the proposition that there exists a first, purely actual cause of this being." See *ibid.*, p. 387.

[51] J. J. C. Smart, "The Existence of God," in *New Essays in Philosophical Theology*, ed. A. Flew and A. MacIntyre (London: SCM Press, 1955), p. 46. Robert Nozick, more recently, has penned similar comments in his *Philosophical Explanations* (Cambridge, Mass.: Harvard University Press, 1981). See especially Chapter 2, "Why Is There Something Rather Than Nothing?"

The awe he feels before existence is, as he has rightly concluded, no request for a logically necessary being.[52] Yet it is the initial and valid step toward an Existent Who is necessarily known to exist and to exist of His very nature, because material things do exist and yet in such a way that existence is always other than what they are. And this Existent we call God.

Suggested Readings

Aquinas, Thomas, *Basic Writings,* ed. A. Pegis, Vol. I, pp. 18–24. New York: Random House, Inc., 1945. On the existence of God: the "Five Ways."

Augros, Robert M., and George N. Stanciu, *The New Story of Science,* ch. 4: "God." Lake Bluff, Ill.: Regnery Gateway, 1984.

Brady, S.J., Jules, *A Philosopher's Search for the Infinite.* New York: Philosophical Library, 1983.

Gilson, Etienne, *The Spirit of Mediaeval Philosophy,* trans. A. H. C. Downes, pp. 42–63. New York: Charles Scribner's Sons, 1940. On God: His existence and nature.

———, *God and Philosophy,* pp. 38–73. New Haven, Conn.: Yale University Press, 1941. On the primacy given by Aquinas to the act of existence.

———, *Being and Some Philosophers,* 2nd ed., pp. 152–215. Toronto: Pontifical Institute of Mediaeval Studies, 1952. On Aquinas' authentic existentialism: primacy given to the act of existence in existents and in metaphysics.

———, *Christian Philosophy of St. Thomas Aquinas,* pp. 29–45, 84–95. New York: Random House, Inc., 1956. On the act of existence: its primacy and autodetermination, its distinction from essence.

———, *Elements of Christian Philosophy,* pp. 43–87. Garden City, N.Y.: Doubleday & Company, Inc., 1960. On the "Five Ways" of Aquinas.

Hawkins, D. J. B., *The Essentials of Theism.* New York: Sheed & Ward, 1949.

Holloway, Maurice R., "Towards the Fullness of Being," *Proceedings of the Twenty-Fourth Annual Convention of the Jesuit Philosophical Association,* ed. Leo Sweeney, S.J., pp. 15–37 and 57–82. Woodstock, Md.: Woodstock College Press, 1962. An interpretation of autodetermination.

Jaki, Stanley L., *God and the Cosmologists.* Washington, D.C.: Regnery Gateway, 1988.

---

[52] See W. Norris Clarke, S.J., "Linguistic Analysis and Natural Theology," in *Proceedings of American Catholic Philosophical Association,* 34 (1960), 110–26.

Kovach, Francis J., "A Novel Argument from Contingency for the Existence of God," in *Scholastic Challenges to Some Mediaeval and Modern Ideas,* Essay One, pp. 3–22. Stillwater, Okla.: Western Publications, 1987.

Maritain, Jacques, *Approaches to God,* trans. Peter O'Reilly. New York: Harper & Row, Publishers, 1954.

Owens, Joseph, *An Elementary Christian Metaphysics,* pp. 311–34, 335–64. Milwaukee: Bruce Publishing Co., 1963. On the meaning of "spiritual"; on God: His existence and nature.

Phelan, Gerald B., "The Being of Creatures," *Proceedings of the American Catholic Philosophical Association,* 31 (1957), 124 ff. On essence as an intrinsic limiting mode in subordination to the act of existence.

Sweeney, S.J., Leo, "Metaphysics and God: Plotinus and Aquinas." In *Die Metaphysik im Mittelalter.* Vol. 2 of *Miscellanea Mediaevalia,* pp. 232–39. Berlin: Walter de Gruyter, 1963 (forthcoming as ch. 19 in *Christian Philosophy: Nature, Origin, Developments* [hereafter: *Christian Philosophy*] [New York/Bern: Peter Lang Publishing, Inc., 1994]).

———, "God Does Exist," *Ensign,* 1 (1967), 5–10.

———, "Existentialism: Authentic and Unauthentic," *The New Scholasticism,* 40 (1966), 36–61 (forthcoming as ch. 23 in *Christian Philosophy*).

———, "Gabriel Marcel's Position on God," *ibid.,* 44 (1970), 101–24 (forthcoming as ch. 24 in *Christian Philosophy*).

———, "The Christian Existentialism of Jacques Maritain," in Jean-Louis Allard (ed.), *Jacques Maritain: A Philosopher in the World* (Ottawa: University of Ottawa Press, 1986), 31–42 (forthcoming as ch. 25 in *Christian Philosophy*).

———, "Bonaventure and Aquinas on the Divine Being as Infinite," *Divine Infinity in Greek and Medieval Thought* (New York/Bern: Peter Lang Publishing, Inc., 1992), ch. 19, pp. 413–37, especially pp. 432–37.

———, "Surprises in the History of Infinity: Anaximander to Cantor," *ibid.,* ch. 23, pp. 539–64, especially pp. 539–53 and 560–64.

Wild, John, *Introduction to Realistic Philosophy,* pp. 356–91. New York: Harper & Row, Publishers, 1948. On God as First Cause.

———, *Challenge of Existentialism.* Bloomington: University of Indiana Press, 1959.

Wilhelmsen, Frederick D., *The Metaphysics of Love.* New York: Sheed and Ward, 1962.

———, *The Paradoxical Structure of Existence,* 2nd ed. Irving, Texas: University of Dallas Press, 1973.

VI

Primacy of Existence in Metaphysical Knowledge

In the previous chapter we have aimed at unveiling the primacy that the act of existing has within existents. After indicating what such primacy entails (Ch. V, Sec. 1: existence has pre-eminence because of its nature and function), we developed reasons why existence precedes essence: the former is the source of all other perfections (Sec. 2), it is autodetermining (Sec. 3), it is amaterial (Sec. 4). We concluded by mentioning that the act of existing in its otherness from essence and its primacy provides a valid basis for knowing that God exists and what sort of Existent He is (Sec. 6). In this chapter we shall emphasize its primacy in metaphysical knowledge. The foundation upon which this pre-eminence rests is completely solid, as this consideration shows. Existence has primacy within existents; but metaphysical knowledge is the intelligible representation of those existents; hence, existence has primacy also in our metaphysical knowledge, as well as in the definitions, descriptions, and other expressions of that knowledge. In other words, the act of existing should somehow (either explicitly or implicitly) enter into all discussions inaugurated by a metaphysician and into all definitions elaborated by him.

* This entrance can be easily illustrated by listing the descriptions of various components we previously formulated in terms of change/stability (see Ch. III, Secs. 3–5) and translating them into metaphysical language.

Previously: "Substance is that by which a material thing is and remains what it is specifically and generically and yet receives various individual perfections."

Now: "Substance is that by which an existent so exercises its act of existing[1] that it is and remains what it is specifically and generically while receiving various individual perfections."

Previously: "An accident is that by which the thing, while remaining what it is specifically and generically, is actually modified through an individual perfection, which is either contingent or necessary."[2]

Now: "An accident is that by which an existent so exercises its act of existing that, while remaining what it is specifically and generically, it is actually modified by some or other individual perfection (either contingently or necessarily)."[3]

Previously: "Prime matter is that by which a physical thing receives a substantial form and yet which is capable, through

---

[1] The English phrase "exercises its act of existing," here and in the subsequent definitions, is an attempt to put across the dynamic relationship between an existent and its existence. Other expressions might be: an existent "carries out," "fulfills," or passively, "is actuated by." Josef Pieper's word is "does": "The factor [of existence] is not co-ordinal with the others; it is something fundamentally different. It has something of the quality of doing. The tree, determined by all those contextual peculiarities, also 'does' something: it grows, turns green, bears fruit. And in addition it 'does' something else before all these other individual acts: it exists. This act of existing is not only something 'of the nature of doing'; it is 'doing' in a distinctive and wholly unique sense. The ancients called it 'doing' without restriction or further specifications; they simply termed it *actus*" (*Guide to Thomas Aquinas* [New York: Pantheon Books, Inc. 1962], pp. 135–36).

No expression so far discovered is completely successful, but at least this should be clear: to exist is not merely something static, not simply to be outside nothingness. Rather it is a dynamic, vibrant actualization and realification of the entire being; substance and the other components within essence function merely in reference to it.

[2] On the force of "contingent . . . necessary," see Ch. III, n. 25.

[3] One should recall that a single act of existing actualizes both substance and accidents within an existent. There is no so-called "accidental act of existing." See Ch. IV, n. 44.

Existents show themselves to be perfected by at least four sorts of accidents: quantity, various qualities, operations, and relations. See Ch. VII below, Sec. 4.

subsequent substantial change, of receiving other substantial forms."

Now: "Prime matter is that by which a physical existent so exercises its act of existing that it receives a substantial form and yet which is capable, through subsequent substantial change, of receiving other such forms."

Previously: "Substantial form is that by which a physical thing is of such-and-such a specific nature."

Now: "Substantial form is that by which a physical existent exercises its act of existing in such a way as to be specifically such-and-such."

Previously: "Essence is that by which a thing is what it is as a member of some or other species."

Now: "Essence is that by which an existent precisely as an existent is what it is,"[4] or "Essence is that within an existent by which the act of existing is received and limited."

These definitions are not the only ones a metaphysician could work out for substance and the other components, but they are simple enough and have the added advantage of showing how differently a philosopher of nature and a metaphysician view such components. The former conceives them solely in terms of the change and stability encircling a material thing. The latter sees them only in relationship to the act of existence. They function solely under its influence. They immediately account for the fact that each material existent exists uniquely—specifically similar to some existents but individually different from all.

1. Actual Existence and "Being"

Nowhere must the primacy of the act of existing be clearer or more important than with respect to our metaphysical awareness of "being." Existence must occupy the prominent place within "being" because it holds that spot in beings. That which makes any being be being is the fact that it actually is, and provided it does actually exist, it is being and is real, no matter how significant or insignificant it may be in what it is. God, this man, this insect, the soul within this dog, its prime matter, its accidental perfection of

---

[4] On essence, see Ch. IV, n. 54.

quantity—all differ greatly in what they are, which determines their way of existing. But all are alike in that they all actually are, and thus each is real and being.[5] The term "being," then, must express a meaning sufficiently supple and rich to fit any and all of them. Let us settle on "being" as meaning "an actually existing item." In that phrase the noun points to what is existing (for example, God, this man or any other such existent, prime matter or any other component, this machine or any other accidental unity); the other words point to actual existence, that whence such items derive their perfection, reality, and being. In understanding and interpreting that definition, one must remember that these words ("actually existing") are to be given emphasis and prominence. They point to the very heart of reality in each being.

* If "being" has that meaning, one must conclude that the term cannot be properly and directly predicated of the intentional universe. One may not apply it to the content of any concept except through extrinsic denomination.[6] This conclusion is diametrically opposed to the radical essentialists, for whom the possibles alone are fully real and are true beings. Because of this opposition let us spend some time on this point.

* First of all, how can there even be a question of predicating "being" of concepts if it means "an actually existing item"? One describes oxidized iron as "rusty" and various household furnishings as "plastic," but no one says meaningfully that this knowledge is rusty or plastic. On the other hand, we sometimes depict the conclusions to which we assent as "probable" but we do not say

---

[5] This status of diversity and similarity is the basis of analogy. See Sec. 2 below: "Analogy of Being."

[6] With regard to human knowledge, one must carefully distinguish between its concepts and operations (a) as actually existing and (b) as to their content. Because they actually exist within the knower, they are real, and "being" is predicated of them through intrinsic denomination, as it is of such operations as freely choosing, loving, becoming angry, and of any other accident. But knowledge has this peculiar and wonderful characteristic: through the operations and concepts which comprise it and which actually are within the knower, the thing known exists intentionally within the knower, who thereby becomes the known. Knowledge, then, has a *content*: what-is-known as it is intentionally within the knower. Of this content (for example, Mother Teresa-as-known, Pope John Paul II-as-known, prime matter-as-known, mathematical infinity) "being" is predicated only through extrinsic denomination. On the latter see Ch. IV above, n. 35, last prgr.

this wire fence or this barking dog is "probable." The intramental and the extramental universes are so disparate that adjectives apt for one cannot be applied to the other. Why, then, predicate "being" of the intentional world at all?

* Throughout the history of thought such predication has often been made because philosophers conceived "being" differently. For instance, being to Plato was coterminous with immutability, and thus he called separate essences "beings" and linked actuals as such with nonbeing and unreality.[7] He turned from the sensible to the intelligible universe, and those he influenced automatically applied "being" to the latter and questioned whether the term could fittingly be extended to sensible existents at all. Thereafter the inquiry of whether and how "being" is predicated of the intelligible realm became a commonplace.

* But even one who views "being" as signifying "an actually existing item" can reasonably and usefully apply the term to the intramental universe, provided proper safeguards are observed, in order to express the fact that it is similar and is related causally to the one outside. The similarity lies in the fact that each universe has, so to speak, its own inhabitants. One is full of actual existents, caught in skeins of relationships (cause-effect) to one another. The other is full of *cognita*, things known, and these too are interrelated: for example, the cause-effect relationships between the fictional characters in *Hamlet*, in William Faulkner's *As I Lay Dying*, in Graham Greene's *Heart of the Matter*;[8] the various functional relations between elements within modern mathematical systems; and so forth. The inhabitants of each world also involve an actuation: in the one it is that of actual existence, in the other it is that of being-known.[9]

* The relatedness between the two universes consists in the fact that knowledge is both the cause and the effect of actual existents. Knowledge within an artist causes artifacts (for example, the vision

---

[7] See Ch. II, Sec. 3: "Plato and Radical Essentialism," especially n. 39; also Ch. IV, n. 35.

[8] Perhaps in this interrelatedness of fictional characters whom we become through reading lies the reason why literature offers an escape from the humdrum, broadens one's perspectives, and enriches one's experiences and eventually one's personality.

[9] With respect to the latter, Berkeley is right: here *esse* is indeed *percipi, cognosci*.

of beauty a painter wishes to communicate helps produce the painting), whereas speculative knowledge is caused by existents (for instance, metaphysics arises from the reflection which beings as being initiate).

* In the light of the similarity and especially of the causal relatedness between the intelligible and actual universe, then, "being" can be transferred to the former, but this only through extrinsic denomination (see Ch. IV above, note 35, last paragraph): items within it can be called "beings" insofar as they are such as to be either the causes or the effects of actual existents, to which alone the term pertains properly and directly. Thus a possible can be described as "being" or "real" inasmuch as it is the blueprint of what can actually exist, or the memory of a past existent is "being" inasmuch as it is an awareness of what once was actual. And this predication through extrinsic denomination admits of various degrees, which depend upon how closely linked various contents of our intellection are to actual existents. The first degree is that of nonconstructural knowledge—that is, awareness based proximately on actual existents and exemplified by actual-existents-as-known (these can be past, present, or future existents, which are known either spontaneously or philosophically). The other and lower degrees are occupied by various kinds of constructural knowledge, since these are awarenesses only remotely based on actual existents.[10] This entire intramental universe is that of "intentional being."

* Let the following table clarify and summarize the previous paragraphs.

---

[10] What is constructural knowledge? From reflection upon various sorts of constructs found in logic, mathematics, physics, and other empiriological sciences, as well as in our spontaneous knowledge of physical and moral evils, constructural knowledge seems to consist in these two factors: (a) The mental activity involved helps constitute (and thus affects) the very content of the intelligibilities in question, within which it shows up as an integral part. (b) Consequently, the basis of those intelligibilities is not directly any actually existing item, but rather that mental activity.

By contrast, in nonconstructural knowledge (a) the mental activity involved is merely the means the knower uses to receive the intelligible message which actual existents themselves deliver; (b) accordingly, the basis of the content of such knowledge is directly those actual existents.

On content-determining-cause of knowledge, see below, Ch. X, Sec. 2.

"BEING" or "REAL" = "an actually existing item"

is predicated

A: *strictly and through intrinsic denomination*

of all actual existents (e.g., God, this man, that lion)
of all the components within each (e.g., prime matter, accidents)
of all accidental unities (e.g., a family, an artifact)

B: *with qualification and through extrinsic denomination* of the content of all concepts

1° actual-existents-as-known past present future (possibles)	nonconstructural knowledge	INTENTIONAL BEING
2° conceptions of logic, mathematics, empiriological sciences, etc. 3° Contradictory notions (e.g., square circle)	constructural knowledge	

* "Being," then, is predicated in two widely different ways, depending upon whether the subject of the predication is an actually existing item or is the content of knowledge. The primacy of actual existence with respect to our knowledge and predication of "being" dictates that the term be properly and intrinsically applied to nothing except whatever actually is.

* Two subsidiary points remain to be made. It already is obvious that we differ greatly from a radical essentialist with respect to the possibles. In his position they are supremely real and, in the last analysis, constitute the subject of metaphysics, because being-as-being is being in its immutability, its intelligibility, its possibility.[11] As we have often said, for us they are in themselves nonbeing,[12] they achieve reality only in relation to what is actual and at best are

[11] To a radical essentialist the treatise on the possibles is at the heart of his metaphysics. For example, Carolus Frick, S.J., devotes approximately one-fourth of his metaphysics book to them (*Ontologia* [Friburgi Brisgoviae: Herder and Co., 1934], pp. 67–101).

[12] See Ch. IV, Sec. 3, especially n. 35. Aquinas speaks similarly—see *S.T.*, I, 14, 9: "Whether God has knowledge of nonbeings" (*Utrum Deus habeat scientiam non entium*). As the body of the text makes clear, the nonbeings referred to are possibles. Also see Norris Clarke, "What Is the Really Real?" pp. 61–90.

on the fringe of metaphysics.[13] But there is another way in which we differ from an essentialist on the possibles, and this has to do with their very inner constitution. For him they are blocks of permanency and intelligibility, not yet actualized and hence still isolated from fluency and unreality. They are essences in an intelligible status, each of which exhausts the entire reality of the thing capable of existing, each of which *is* the thing. To our way of thinking, a possible is not just an essence. It is rather a composite of [essence/act of existing] which currently is not but which can be. Each is [an essence/act of being]-known-as-capable-of-existing. Each is an *existent*-which-is-possible, each is an *existent* which can be and perhaps will be.

* The reason why the act of existing as-known enters into the internal constitution of a possible seems indestructible. It is a constituent (in fact, the most important constituent) of an actual existent. But a possible existent is a future actual existent, or, stated from the other side, an actual existent is what was once a possible existent but now actualized. Therefore, the internal make-up of an existent as possible should match that of an actual, with the sole (but important) difference that the components of the former are there only as-known, whereas those of the latter are actual. Accordingly, a possible existent is [an essence/existence]-known-as-capable-of-existing.[14]

---

[13] They play an important role only in that section of metaphysics which is natural theology, where they enter into discussions of divine knowledge, freedom, and causality. See Henri J. Renard, S.J., *Philosophy of God, passim* and especially pp. 119–37, 152–61; Maurice R. Holloway, *Introduction to Natural Theology*, pp. 290–306, 319–32.

[14] The only reason why the act of existing (as-known) could be omitted from the make-up of a possible existent is if it were not a component of existents. As long as it is a constitutive part of them, no existent, whether actual or possible, can be accurately understood without it. See E. Gilson, *Being and Some Philosophers*, pp. 182–83: "Ideas represent possible beings, including both their actual existence and their becoming. In other words, if *esse* (to be) is the supreme act of creatures, their idea must needs include it as the active energy through which the corresponding essence shall progressively receive all its determinations. . . . The second error [in wrongly conceiving 'possibles'] is to forget that the essence of a possible being necessarily includes the possible existence through which alone it can achieve its essential determination. To repeat, essential possibility is no sufficient reason for existential possibility, and, since its essence is what a being is going to become, if it exists, existence itself necessarily enters the calculation of its essential possibility."

* The importance of this conclusion is apparent. Within authentic existentialism the very structure of a possible is radically modified.[15] No longer is it just an essence, it is now an essence/*esse* in the intelligible order. No longer is it real in and of itself, but only by relationship to the status of actuality it can and perhaps will attain. And the presence of *esse*-as-known within even its intentional make-up is a sign and a reminder of that radical modification. Within a possible existent *esse*-as-known assumes a primacy over the essence-as-known which is analogous to that assumed by *esse* over essence in an actual existent.

* The second subsidiary point involves the problem of how "being" is to be predicated of artifacts. Take literature or music. In what sense can *Hamlet* or the *Ode on a Grecian Urn* or any other poem be said to be actually existing and thus be describable as real and being? "In the beginning, everything is simple: a poem exists while somebody reads it or hears it being read. . . . But while it is not being actually read, or heard, in what sense can it still be said to exist?"[16] In what sense can a musical piece be said to actually exist? "A sonata, a symphony, or an opera endures as long as the time of its performance. As soon as an orchestral mass and the choirs it supports have sounded the last chord of Beethoven's *Ninth Symphony*, the whole structure vanishes into nothingness. Nothing of it is left except grateful memories and the hope to hear the same masterpiece again, or, rather, another rendering of it."[17] Moreover, "a musical piece has no simultaneous existence. . . . What do we actually hear of a sonata? Not the sonata as a whole. Not even one of its movements, its themes, or its bars; all that we actually hear of it at a time is one of its chords. While this one is actually sounding, the next one has not yet come and the preceding one has already ceased to be."[18]

* If "being" signifies "an actually existing item," it is applicable to literature, music, and other artifacts only because each of them is

---

[15] This modification parallels a similar one in the very structure of *essence* itself, already referred to (see Ch. II, Sec. 3: "Plato and Radical Essentialism," and Ch. V, Sec. 1, "Existence Precedes Essence"). An essence does not consist merely in stability, as a radical essentialist would have it, but is an intimate fusion of stability with change, of substance with accidents.

[16] Etienne Gilson, *Painting and Reality* (New York: Pantheon Books, Inc., 1957), pp. 5–6.

[17] *Ibid.*, p. 7.

[18] *Ibid.*, p. 8.

something which actually is, and this in its own way. The problem is to ascertain what each is and how each does actually exist.

* The artifacts listed are accidental unities; hence, let us begin by studying such commonplace unities as a family or an automobile. What is the unique reality of a family but the sum of the real relations binding together mother, father, and children and expressed by the collective noun "family?" Why, then, is "being" predicable of a family? Because that complex of relationships is an actually existing item, to which the term is applied properly and through intrinsic denomination.[19] What is the unique reality of an Oldsmobile? It is the ordering and arrangement of suitable parts in such a way as to form an attractive and sturdy vehicle capable of self-propulsion. Why is "being" applicable to it? Because that good order is an actually existing item, of which the term is said properly and intrinsically.

* Moving over to the area of fine arts, let us ask what the unique reality of a mosaic is. The answer: a decorative arrangement of small pieces of colored glass or stone inlaid into cement or plaster. Why can "being" be said of it? Because that arrangement is an actually existing item, aptly expressed by "being" through intrinsic and proper predication. What is a painting? It is the right ordering of various pigments upon a canvas or some other background material. Once again, "being" is predicable through intrinsic denomination because that good order is an actually existing factor.

* To summarize: "Being" is predicated of all such accidental unities (and this through intrinsic denomination) because all their parts are actual existents in their own right and yet coalesce to fashion a new actually existing item, designed for utility or for beauty. Now we should be ready to consider those same questions concerning literature and music.

* What is the unique reality of *Hamlet?* It is twofold: first the definite order of letters, syllables, and words upon a printed page; second and especially, the actual production of the play—those words uttered by actors and heard by an audience. Why can "being" be predicated intrinsically and properly of it? Because in those two states it is an item which exists actually and in its own fashion. What is the unique reality of music? Again, it is twofold: first, the definite order and sequence of notes as they are written on a score:

---

[19] Of course, "being" is also applied through intrinsic denomination to the members of the family (who are the subjects of the relationships expressed by "family") as individual existents and intrinsic unities.

second, and more important, an actual performance of the piece: those notes as played by an orchestra and heard by the audience. Why can a musical piece be properly described as "being"? Because however tenuous and fluent it may be ("Music [is] the very type of that which, because it never is but ceaselessly becomes, is much less a being than an existent striving to be without ever quite doing it"),[20] still it is an actually existing item, and thus deserves the name "being."

* "Being," then, is any actually existing item, and this fact has two important consequences. First, it is properly and directly predicable of any such item, whether it be this man, his components, his family, his automobile, his portrait, the literature he writes, the music he plays. Second, it is thus predicable only of such items. The possibles and the contents of all other intelligibilities are real, at best, through extrinsic denomination.

2. The Analogy of Being

We shall next discuss the primacy which actual existence enjoys in our metaphysical knowledge of truth, goodness and beauty, which together with being are the transcendent traits characterizing all actual existents and triggering corresponding awareness in the human knower (see Section 3 below). Before that step, though, let us briefly consider analogy. This is a consideration which is needed for a more adequate understanding of being, (and, for that matter, of the other transcendents too); it has in fact been prepared for by Section 1 of this chapter as well as by Chapters IV and V.

From what has gone before, it is clear that actually existing items are many in number and extremely different in kind. Some we directly perceive: ourselves, other men and women, animals, plants, inanimate things,[21] as well as the machines we use, the buildings we dwell and work in, the masterpieces of painting and music we enjoy.[22] Others we know only intellectually (although working within data furnished by perception) either through reflection (the components: the act of existing, substantial form, prime matter, various accidents—see Chs. III and IV) or through reasoning (for ex-

---

[20] Gilson, *ibid.*, p. 8.

[21] All these we have technically said to be or to involve "intrinsic" or *per se* unities. See Ch. III, Sec. 2.

[22] These we call "extrinsic" or accidental unities.

ample, God—see Ch. V, Sec. 6). The diversity between these existents is too manifest to need comment—for example, that between God and any other actual item, no matter what it is; that between an intrinsic and extrinsic unity (this man and this typewriter); that between two such intrinsic unities as this man and this mosquito, or even between this man and that man, who are numerically distinct and individually unique; that between such extrinsic unities as this typewriter, that garage, Leonardo da Vinci's *Mona Lisa*, Beethoven's *Violin Concerto;* that between this man and his substantial form or other components, or even that between one component and another, each of which has its own causal function to perform, each its own nature.[23] And yet, however diverse they are in what they are, they are similar in that they all do actually exist.

The extramental world is, then, everywhere shot through with similarity and diversity. But it is the content-determining-cause of our metaphysical knowledge of "being," which, as "an actually existing item," is deliberately designed to be predicable of all existents (be they God, an intrinsic unity, an extrinsic unity, or a component)[24] and, equally important, to signify everything within each ("item" refers to *whatever* each is, "actually existing" to the fact *that* each is).[25] Accordingly also, our awareness of "being" is marked by a parallel similarity and diversity.

---

[23] Besides Chs. III and IV, see also Ch. V, Sec. 3: "Actual Existence and Autodetermination."

[24] On the deliberate elaboration of the meaning given to "being," see Appendix B.

One should note that in subsequent pages the noun "existents" is restricted to men and women, animals, and other intrinsic unities, whereas "actuals" is applied also to components and to extrinsic unities—in brief, to any actually existing item, whatever it be.

[25] This dog is actually similar to and diverse from all other dogs and is the content-determining-cause of our awareness of him as "dog." Still that awareness is not analogous but univocal, because it grasps this dog only in his similarity to other dogs: in a word, it does not signify everything in each dog. But our awareness of this dog as "being" catches him not only in his similarity to all other beings (the fact that he actually exists) but also in his diversity from them (the fact of what he is: this dog [although not precisely as this dog but as actual]): rightly interpreted, it signifies everything in him. (Incidentally, our *perception* of him as "this dog" would seem to be describable in its own way as analogous, for we are aware of him in his similarity to other dogs ["dog"] and in his diversity from them ["this"].)

For a fuller explanation of this important point, see below, n. 29, second prgr.

But to predicate "being" is simply to reverse the initial movement from actuals to the knower: by affirming "God is real" or "This man is real," we simply apply back to actuals the knowledge gained from them. Hence, our predication of "being" involves similarity/diversity. When directed to God or to this man, his act of existing, and his portrait, "real" or "being" has a meaning which is neither completely identical nor totally different, but which weds diversity to similarity.

In brief, actual beings, our knowledge of them as beings, and our affirmation of "being" concerning them are all characterized by similarity/diversity. How can this characterization common to those three distinct areas be conveniently described? By the single term "analogy." Actual existents are analogous to one another; our metaphysical knowledge of them is analogous; our predication concerning them is analogous. In each case the adjective simply points to that situation of similarity/diversity. Analogy is nothing more than the condition of similarity/diversity in actuals, in knowledge, and in predication.[26]

One can even speak legitimately and usefully of various *kinds* of analogy in view of the various kinds of similarity/diversity which are to be found among actuals (as well as in the ensuing knowledge they cause and in the predications they receive). Why so? Similarity/diversity is a relational situation, and relational situations vary from one another insofar as their ingredients vary, one set of which is the *relata*—the existents which are referred to one another. That is to say, the sort of similarity/diversity obtaining between a creature and God is not identical with that between two creatures, with that between a creature and his components, or with that between the components themselves. Consequently, the analogy between God and creatures is somewhat unlike that between two creatures or between the other two sets of actuals. There are, then, various sorts of analogy, some of which we shall now try briefly to elaborate by reflecting upon the various kinds of similarity/diversity that actually existing items manifest.

---

[26] Traditionally, analogy seems restricted to knowledge and predication; thus it is contrasted with the univocal and equivocal: a *notion* is analogous if its *meaning* is similar/diverse, whereas a *notion* is univocal if its *meaning* is similar but equivocal if its *meaning* is diverse. In view of the facts, though, it is better to say that analogy is any sort of similarity and diversity, whether found within existents, knowledges, or predications.

First of all, God and a creature differ with respect to being inasmuch as actuality is of the former's very nature, whereas it is really other than the latter's. God *is* perfectly and subsistently, whereas the creature *is* only through an act of existing limited by what he is. Despite this grave difference, though, they are alike in that each *is*, each *does actually exist*. Here, then, is truly a situation of similarity/diversity, but one in which diversity is almost maximal, similarity minimal. It is a similarity/diversity which might be termed "eminence" if we describe it from the side of God, Who is being pre-eminently.[27] But analogy is nothing more than similarity/diversity. Accordingly, the analogy between God and a creature can be called one of *eminence:* namely, *the similarity/diversity in being* (as well as in consequent metaphysical knowledge and predication) *between the Existent Whose very essence is to exist and an existent whose existence is really distinct from his essence.*[28]

Another sort of similarity/diversity is that between two creatures. For example, take these two men.[29] They differ with respect to being inasmuch as each is numerically distinct and individually unique: although each is human, still each is so differently, singu-

---

[27] It might just as easily be called one of "participation" or of "dependence" if viewed from the side of the creature. The lesson to be learned is that descriptions of the kinds of analogy are somewhat arbitrary. Our criterion should be to choose the one which best fits the situation of similarity/diversity in question.

[28] If we interpret it more generally, the analogy of eminence might be depicted as the similarity/diversity between the more and less perfect, between the entitatively higher and lower. If so, it can for obvious reasons be applied to substance/accidents, matter/form or to existence/essence; in its strict interpretation, however, it is reserved for God/creature.

[29] What is true of individuals within the same species will *a fortiori* be true of other creatures. They will differ not only individually but also specifically (for example, this man and this dog), generically (this man and this tree) or even more drastically (this man and this angel).

Even though two individuals of the same species are specifically alike, still they are individually different, and this is more than sufficient to cause them to differ also in being. Being encompasses their very individuality; for them to be actual is precisely to exist each in his own way. Being is not formulated simply as "actually existing," but as "an actually existing item." It embraces both existence and essence, and this latter in its actual and hence individual and singular status. To refuse to ascribe an analogy of proportionality to individuals of the same species is a serious mistake. For further discussion see L. Sweeney, S.J, "Analogy and Being," *The Modern Schoolman*, 39 (March, 1962), 259.

larly, in a manner never to be exactly reduplicated. Still they are also alike in being—each actually exists, and this in the same fashion: in each the act of existing really differs from essence. Here, then, is another situation of similarity/diversity, but one in which neither diversity nor similarity is extreme. It is a similarity/diversity which has traditionally been described as "proportionality"—somewhat as with mathematical proportionality (for example, 2 : 4 : : 5 : 10), whence the name seemingly was derived—there exists within each creature a similar proportion between existence and essence: that of real distinction and composition (John : existence : : Paul : existence). Since similarity/diversity is equivalent to analogy, the analogy in being (as well as in the metaphysical knowledge and predication paralleling being) between one creature and another can be termed that of *proportionality: the similarity/diversity between existents in each of which actuality is really other than what they are.*[30]

* Still another sort of analogy is that between a creature's components. Consider within this man the act of existing by which he actually exists, prime matter by which ultimately he actually exists as substantially individuated, substantial form by which he exists as man, various accidents by which he exists in an individual fashion. They differ in being insofar as each is really distinct from the others, each has its own causal function to perform, each is what it is and nothing more. But they also are similar, for each actually exists and does so within one and the same human existent: they are intrinsic causes of the same effect (this man), upon

---

[30] Frequently, it is called "*proper proportionality,*" the point of the adjective being to distinguish it from the proportionality involved in metaphor. In the latter (for instance, "John is an ox") what is signified by the predicate is not found intrinsically in the subject. With regard to being, though, what is signified by the predicate is intrinsic to the subjects ("John is a being and Paul is a being"). (For a different interpretation of metaphor, see Robert Boyle, S.J., "The Nature of Metaphor," *Modern Schoolman*, 31 [May, 1954], 267–80; *idem, Metaphor in Hopkins* [Chapel Hill: University of North Carolina Press, 1960].)

Can the analogy of proportionality also be applied to God/creature? Yes, provided one realizes that this analogy is itself analogous and one broadens its definition a bit: "the similarity/diversity between existents in each of which actuality is somehow *other* (whether really or conceptually) than what they are." On this controverted point, see L. Sweeney, S.J., "Analogy and Being," pp. 257–58; John J. O'Brien, S.J., "Analogy and the Fourth Way," *Wisdom in Depth: Essays in Honor of Henri J. Renard,* S.J. (Milwaukee: Bruce Publishing Co., 1966), pp. 174–86.

which they in turn depend and within which they actually are. Because they all are and are what they are only *with reference to the single existent they constitute,* this similarity/diversity (and hence analogy) can aptly be described as one of "reference." Accordingly, the analogy of *reference* is *similarity/diversity between the components of one and the same existent.*[31]

* A final type of similarity/diversity with respect to being is that found between the extramental and the intramental universes.[32] These two are similar because each has so to speak, inhabitants. As we have already remarked (Ch. VI, Sec. 1), one is full of actual existents caught in webs of relationships (for example, cause-effect) to one another; the other is full of *cognita,* and these too are interrelated: for example, the cause-effect relationships between the fictional characters in (say) *Macbeth,* in J. D. Salinger's *Catcher in the Rye,* in Graham Greene's *End of the Affair* or between the various functional relations between elements within modern mathematical systems. The extramental and intramental universes are also alike because of their dependence on one another, which arises because knowledge is both the cause and effect of actual existents. Knowledge within an artist, whether human or divine, helps cause his artifacts (for example, the vision of beauty a painter wishes to communicate helps produce the painting), whereas speculative knowledge is caused by existents (for instance, metaphysics arises from the reflection which beings-as-being initiate).

* Yet these two universes also differ inasmuch as the "inhabitants" of the former (that is, actual existents) are genuinely real: they actually exist and their actuation is actual existence. But the "inhabitants" of the latter (that is, the content of our knowledges—

---

[31] We have lumped all components together in reference to the existent they constitute, but additional comparisons are possible (and hence additional kinds of analogy) because the components are variously interrelated to one another—for example, substance to accidents, existence to essence, existence to prime matter (as pure act to pure potency), and so on. But not enough profit would be gained from working out these other comparisons and analogies to warrant the labor and tedium.

[32] Actuals involve still other types of similarity/diversity—for example, that between this man and any one of his components, that between this man and any of the components of another man, that between two extrinsic unities, and so on. But as was the case with regard to the components (see previous note), so here too: too little profit would be gained for the amount of energy expended. Besides, it should be clear now how such types of similarity/diversity and of analogy can be worked out if there is need.

see note 6 above) are unreal: precisely as what-is-known they do not actually exist and their actuation is nothing more than being-known (*cognosci*).

* Thus there is another situation of similarity/diversity with respect to being, but one which joins minimal similarity to extreme diversity. Because of the similarity "being" is predicated through intrinsic denomination only of actuals and of *cognita* merely through extrinsic denomination: these latter are, strictly speaking, nonbeing and unreal.[33] How can we best describe this similarity/diversity? Since it issues into such disparate predications that actuals are named (denominated) "beings" intrinsically but *cognita* are so named only extrinsically, let us call it one of "denomination." Consequently, the analogy of *denomination* is *the similarity/diversity between the extramental and intentional universes,* and "being" is predicated of the former through intrinsic denomination but of the latter through extrinsic denomination (see Ch. IV above, note 35, last paragraph).

Such, then, are several kinds of analogy. Although elaborating them is a somewhat intricate task, still its fundamental methodology should be clear: one works out the kinds of analogy by investigating various kinds of similarity/diversity. And despite its grave importance,[34] analogy itself is easy to understand in its basic mean-

---

[33] From one point of view the diversity here is greater than that found between God and creatures, where despite their great dissimilarity "being" is predicated intrinsically of both. But not so of the *cognita,* which are so far removed from entity as themselves to be nonbeings and to be termed "beings" only through extrinsic denomination. See Ch. IV above, n. 35, last paragraph.

We might note that the predication of "being" here is counteracted by that of "true," which is predicated through intrinsic denomination of knowledge and of actuals only through extrinsic denomination. See Sec. 3 of this chapter.

[34] For example, Karl Barth declares analogy to be the crucial difference between Catholicism and Protestantism. See Niels C. Nielsen, "Protestant Faith and Catholic Unity," *America,* August 14, 1954, p. 479: "Barth made one central idea the essential point of difference between the Protestant and Roman Catholic positions. He announced that he regarded the rejection of the analogy of being, central in Thomistic analysis, as the only valid reason for refusing to accept the claims of Roman Catholic authority." Walter Lowrie, *Kierkegaard* (London: Oxford University Press, 1938), p. 9: ". . . The Catholic doctrine of the *analogia entis* . . . Barth accounts the dividing line between Protestantism and Catholicism." On Barth's views of analogy, see Sebastian A. Matczak, *Karl Barth on God: The Knowledge of the Divine Existence* (Staten Island, N.Y.: Alba House, 1962), Ch. V: "Abyss Between God and Man (Analogy)," pp. 173–221; B. Mondin, *The Principle of Analogy in Protestant and*

ing: it is simply the status of similarity/diversity found in actuals, as well as in the knowledge they cause and the predication they receive, with respect to being. In fact, it is a mere corollary, an automatic consequence of the rest of one's metaphysics. That is to say, one's acceptance or rejection of it is already determined by the stand he takes on the nature of existents and the meaning of "being." If one holds, as do monists, that existents are all identical with one another or with some basic stuff of which they are mere manifestations, then diversity is lacking and analogy is impossible. Or if one maintains, as do Ockham and other nominalists, that existents are totally diverse from one another (here, to be real is to be entirely other and different), then similarity is lacking and so too is analogy. But if one views existents as really distinct and yet also similar, he has the requisite combination of diversity and similarity and a doctrine of analogy is possible, although this possibility is still dependent upon the second point—the meaning one gives to "being."

If one restricts "being" to one level of existents (for example, Neo-Platonists define "being" as "one-many" and thus God is above being because of His utter unity and absolute simplicity,[35] whereas others reserve it for God with the result that creatures are unreal, no-good),[36] then it is not analogous. Or if its content consists of a

---

Catholic Theology (The Hague: Martinus Nijhoff, 1963); J. M. Robinson, "The German Discussion of the Later Heidegger," in *The Later Heidegger and Theology* (New York: Harper & Row, 1963), pp. 40–41.

[35] For a Catholic version of this Neo-Platonic position, see Meister Eckhart, "Sermon on Renewal in the Spirit," quoted in J. F. Anderson, *The Bond of Being* (St. Louis: B. Herder, 1949), p. 264: "If I say God is good, it is not true: I am good, God is not good. I say more: I am better than God is, for what is good can be better, and what is better can be best. But God is not good, therefore, He cannot be better, therefore He cannot be best. These three: good, better, best, are remote from God Who is above all. And if, again, I say that God is wise, it is not true: I am wiser than He. Or if I say, God is a being, it is not true: He is a transcendental essence, a superessential nothing."

[36] The position of those Lutherans who hold that original sin has cast humans into a condition of total ruin and intrinsic worthlessness would seem to fit here. Perhaps Barth's declaration (see n. 34) becomes intelligible in the light of this position.

The doctrine of Christian Scientists also appears to be a case in point. See Rosemary Lauer, "The Philosophy of Christian Science," *The Thomist*, 20 (1957), pp. 194 and 201: "From the original principles of Christian Science, if one interprets them in a univocal sense, certain metaphysical conclusions follow as surely as night follows day: *If God is, then whatever is not God is not*; if all

single factor—if it means simply "something" rather than "something actually existing"—then it still need not be analogous, even though it is not confined to any one area of existents. It could be equivocal if "something" is taken as including all the individual differences of each thing, or it could be univocal if understood as prescinding from individual and even specific and generic differences. Thus "being" in its content would be the most indeterminate, most indigent concept possible. Pushed to the ultimate of abstraction and of indefiniteness, it is predicable of everything (whether infinite or finite, whether spiritual or material, whether human or nonhuman) because it in no way expresses those differences. It points simply to the fact that each subject of which it is predicated is "something" rather than "nothing."

But if the content of "being" consists of two factors, if it means "an actually existing item," then it is analogous. "Item" has to do with the diversity of existents since it points to what each is (and in this each differs from all else). "Actually existing" deals with their similarity since it indicates that each is (and in this they are all alike, no matter how disparate they may otherwise be).

Still there is more. This last factor has to do with existents also in their diversity. Nothing actually exists except in a determinate, concrete, unique, individual fashion, thereby making it different from all else. Hence, its status of actual existence is one also of diversity. In expressing existents as "actually existing," then, "being" also expresses their diversity.[37] Accordingly, "being" is truly

---

reality is God, then all reality is intelligent, or Mind; if God is all reality and good, then evil is nothing; if God is immaterial, then matter is nonexistent. . . . In the realm of pedagogy [Christian Science] serves the teacher of metaphysics as a superb example of the consequences to be expected from taking univocally such terms as 'being,' 'real,' 'truth,' and 'good.' "

[37] Manifestly, the autodetermination of existence (see Ch. V, Sec. 3) is at the basis of analogy. Because existence is independent of any one particular essence, it essentializes itself through whatever essence it does actualize. But essence is the direct source of diversity in an existent. Therefore, the act of existence also causes its own diversity. But existents, together with the knowledge they cause and the predication they receive, are analogous as combining diversity with similarity. But actual existence is the mediate source of their diversity, as well as the immediate source of their similarity: all are diverse in that each exists in its own way, all are alike in that they do exist. Therefore, analogy of existents, knowledge and predication is based on actual existence in its autodetermination and its primacy within the existent.

Underlying the analogy of being in whatever sphere is the fact that to be actual is, in the last analysis, to be both similar and diverse.

analogous and its analogy rests mainly[38] on the second factor of its content.

Also because of that second factor, because it signifies all actuals precisely as actual, "being" has this prerogative: it is as rich in content as is possible for a concept having maximal extension, for it is designed not only to be predicable of all but also to signify everything in each. As we have seen, what an actual is is always determinate, concrete, unique, individual. Hence by signifying an actual in what it actually is, "being" catches it in its very determinateness, concreteness, uniqueness, individuality, for nothing exists except in a determinate, concrete, singular, individual way. But if it signifies everything in each, how can it still be predicated of all? Because it does not signify an actual in what it is precisely as determinate, as concrete, as unique, as this—if it did, it would only be predicable of this one existent. Rather, it signifies an actual in what it is (which actually is determinate, concrete, and so forth) precisely *as actual*, and thus is predicable of all actuals, because all agree in being actual (even though, we must add, their status of actuality is simultaneously one also of diversity).

Consequently, because "being" expresses actuals as actuals, it is predicable of all, since all actuals are being inasmuch as they are actual. And yet it also signifies everything in each because the actual status of each encompasses each in its very individuality, uniqueness and determinateness. Therefore, "being" is a concept which is maximal in extension and in comprehension.

In its signification of what is actual precisely as actual is also rooted its analogy, as we have already mentioned. In its status of actuality an actual is similar to and yet also diverse from all else: all actuals are alike in that they do exist, all are diverse in that each exists in its own way. Therefore, by expressing actuals precisely as actuals, "being" signifies actuals in their similarity and diversity, and hence is analogous.

Such is the analogy of being. Let us now move on to the other transcendents.

---

[38] Mainly, I say, but not entirely, because "item" too is necessary as indicating what is actualized. Essence functions as the immediate source of diversity, and this function actual existence could itself usurp only at the price of no longer being actual existence. (Similarly, actual existence is relatively independent of essence, but it can be autodetermining only if there is some or other essence. The act of existing can itself usurp the limiting function of essence only if it is no longer actual existence.)

3. Actual Existence and Other Transcendents

Manifestly, the analogy of being reaffirms the primacy of actual existence. Existents, together with ensuing metaphysical knowledge and predications, are analogous by reason of the similarity/diversity they entail. Actual existence is not only the immediate source of their similarity (all are alike in that they exist) but also is the mediate source of their diversity (each exists in its own way) because of its autodetermination: the act of existing essentializes itself through whatever essence it actualizes, and thus also diversifies itself and the existent. Therefore, actual existence is at the heart of analogy and is thereby again shown to have primacy.

Let us next consider the primacy of existence in the transcendents other than being.

*** (a) Transcendents as Known Spontaneously**

Whenever we are unexpectedly confronted with what is unknown (for example, suppose we return to our room to find an object concealed under a sheet on the floor), our spontaneous knowledge gradually moves from a condition of relative indetermination to one of determination, from the more to the less general, as the object in question gives off more and more evidence of itself. Let us say that the object under the sheet is an injured, bleeding man, which we observe without removing the sheet. Our first awareness would be, "something or other actually there," followed by "which is living . . . sentient . . . human," as it slowly moves about under the sheet, stains the sheet with blood, then groans and speaks.

There is, then, in our human knowledge a movement with respect to content from the less to the more definite; there is a cognitional growth. Subsequent awarenesses are added to prior ones, and these additions are immediately based upon the thing manifesting itself to the knower. They are useful, even necessary, in our coming to know things and in our communicating with one another about them. The terms we use to express them are not synonyms, since each subsequent one has a fuller and hence somewhat different meaning.[39] As our knowledge grows, subsequent

[39] What sort of distinction or difference is there between such awarenesses? As we have previously seen (Ch. V, n. 29), it is a mental one in view of the fact that what "rational" signifies is not really other in this man than what "sentient" and other such intelligibilities signify. A human's rationality permeates his entire sentient, living, chemical and material constitution. His nature as

awarenesses contain more than prior ones (for instance, "something actually present which is living" says more than merely "something actually present"). But they are predicable of fewer things (the former awareness can be applied only to what is living, the latter to the nonliving as well). As a logician would state it, their increase in comprehension is matched by a decrease in extension. In view of this situation, let us call such subsequent awarenesses and the words signifying them *"restrictive"*—they are *restricted* to definite classes of things.

But we also experience another sort of spontaneous knowledge, as reflection upon our reactions to that previous scene discloses. On coming upon that object hidden under the sheet, our first awareness is that of "something or other actually present," which then develops into the additional restrictive awareness already listed as we come to know the kind of thing it actually is. But that initial awareness also issues into that of "real," of "one," of "other than." These we find ourselves to spontaneously have if anyone questions us later about the scene and we reply that no, it was not just something we imagined, but was *real:* something actually *was* there; no, there were not several, but only *one;* no, it was not merely the sheet: there was something there *other than* the cloth.

Here, then, is a second type of cognitional growth, a movement from what is implicit to the explicit.[40] The subsequent awareness of "one" and "other than" are added to what is prior,[41] and these

---

rational is not really different from his nature as sentient, as living, and as material. The terms are descriptions of that single nature from a more or less determinate point of view.

For a contrast with transcendent awareness, see below, n. 42.

[40] This movement is also one from a condition of relative indetermination to one of determination, as is that in restrictive knowledge. But the awarenesses in which it terminates are to some extent different from those encountered in the latter (for instance, an increase in comprehension does not lessen extension). To emphasize the difference, we shall arbitrarily reserve the phrase "from the indeterminate to the determinate" for restrictive awareness and "from the implicit to the explicit" for transcendents. Besides, the latter words are especially apt, since subsequent transcendents merely explicate what "being" implicitly contains. In designating all actuals as *actual,* "being" also embraces them as "undivided," as "other than," and so on.

[41] "One" and "other than" (as well as the other subsequent transcendents still to be investigated) are added to "something actually present," but not so "real," which is not subsequent to but rather concomitant and on a par with it. "Something actually present" is what "real" or "being" means. Hence, "real" or "being" is prior to the other transcendents and is that to which they add.

additions are directly based upon the thing exhibiting itself to the mind. They are useful and necessary in our knowing things, as well as in our communicating with one another about them. The terms we use to signify them are not synonyms, because each subsequent awareness has a fuller, more explicit and, therefore, somewhat different meaning.[42] As our knowledge grows, the subsequent awarenesses contain more than the prior one—for instance, "something actually present and other than all else" explicitly says more than merely "something actually present." But even so—and this is their extraordinary characteristic—they remain predicable of an equal number of things—for example, "something actually present and other than all else" is applicable as extensively as is "something actually present," since every actual thing automatically is also distinct from everything else by the very fact that it is an actual thing. Here, increase of comprehension does not lessen extension. These awarenesses and terms, accordingly, are not confined to any

---

At least as far back as Avicenna (born A.D. 980) philosophers were saying that "being" is what a human knower first knows. In light of the fact that our initial spontaneous awareness is "something or other actually present," which the terms "real" or "being" designate, one can understand why they so spoke. Yet the content of that knowledge is not "being" so much as "something actually present." The former is the term, the latter the content of the awareness.

[42] What sort of distinction is between such awarenesses? As with restrictive intelligibilities (see n. 39), it is a mental one, since what "being" designates is not really other in this actual thing than what "one" and "other than" designate: its entity, unity and otherness all revolve around its actuality: each merely highlights now one, now another aspect of it.

They differ, though, from restrictive awarenesses (see n. 40), and hence the mental distinction between them is divergent from that between the latter. Some express this divergence by calling the first a "minor," the other a "major" mental distinction. Others express it by depicting the first as a "mental distinction only imperfectly grounded in reality," whereas the second is a "mental distinction perfectly grounded." This description is drawn from the fact that the second rests upon really distinct components within the existent (that is, substantial form and prime matter, from which issue the specific and the generic perfections respectively), whereas the first has no such basis. Rather, it results from the fact that an actual is so complex and rich in its very actuality that it cannot be grasped by a human knower in a single concept but only in a series of them.

Either description is satisfactory. What is important is to remember that the transcendent awarenesses only conceptually differ from one another, and differ in a way unlike that of restrictive ones.

certain classes of things, but rather transcend them. Let us call them, then, "transcendents."[43]

Besides "real," "one," and "other than," our automatic knowledge of things also entails several other awarenesses of an identical nature, although these are more easily illustrated and substantiated by stepping outside the previous example and by simply showing that they too transcend any one type of thing. Consider "good." We meaningfully ascribe it to such divergent things as food and drink, houses, apple trees and other plants, dogs and almost any other animal, men and women. When listening to Jascha Heifetz play a cadenza or watching an expert skater do a Triple Sal Chow, we instinctively exclaim, "A good job!" We speak also of a good choice, of good attitudes, of a good scholar. To be applicable to such various classes of things, then "good" also must be a transcendent.[44]

So too is "beauty," since a sunset, a landscape, trees and flowers, race horses and other graceful animals, men and women are all described as beautiful. Likewise with "truth." Although it is primarily a mark of knowledge ("The District Attorney knows the truth about the incident"), still we also say things are "true" or "false" (for example, a father after investigating his teen-age son's handiwork in the basement reports to his wife, "Yes, it's a true bomb, all right!"). And the things so described are many in kind, as evi-

---

[43] Other authors call them "transcendentals." For example, see Martin O. Vaske, S.J., *An Introduction to Metaphysics* (New York: McGraw-Hill Book Company, 1963), Ch. VII, pp. 178–208; Robert J. Kreyche, *First Philosophy*, Chs. 8 and 9, pp. 167–204; Henry J. Koren, *An Introduction to the Science of Metaphysics* (St. Louis: B. Herder Book Co., 1955), Ch. 2, pp. 48–103; Herman Reith, *Metaphysics of St. Thomas Aquinas* (Milwaukee: Bruce Publishing Co., 1958), Ch. 6, pp. 109–40. Because of Kant's use of it (as well as for other reasons), though, this term can be misleading. I prefer to call them "transcendents" (which, incidentally, is Aquinas' term—see, for example, *Disputed Questions on Truth*, 21, 3 resp.). They simply *transcend* any one class of things and for that reason are in contrast with restrictive ones.

[44] Upon additional reflection such divergent examples fall into three categories: (a) those in which "good" means "that which is perfect because it is the effect of love"—for instance, the cadenza, the figure skating; (b) those in which "good" means "that which causes love because it is perfect"—for instance, food, drink, buildings, and so forth; (c) those in which "good" is predicated only through extrinsic denomination—for instance, a free choice, which is called good because a human person freely chooses a good object (#b). See below, n. 54 and prgrs. corresponding to it.

On the meaning of "perfect," see Ch. V, Sec. 2.

denced by such phrases as "a true Rembrandt," "a true likeness," "true, not fool's gold," "a true rocket," "a true or a false friend," "a true Republican," "false teeth," "false storefront," "a true Socialist," and so on.[45]

"Good," "beautiful," and "true," then, are also transcendents and share in all the above-mentioned characteristics of "real," "one," and "other than."[46]

All six transcendents testify to two complementary factors as their causes: the complexity of things and the nature of human knowledge. Things actually are undivided within themselves, and thus each is somehow one; are distinct from one another; are perfect to some extent and thus worthy of appreciation and love; are intelligible and thus can cause true knowledge; are well proportioned and thus trigger admiration and joy. They are, in brief, so rich and complex in themselves and in their multiple interrelations that they cannot be adequately caught except in multiple intellections, and these are the various transcendents. Second, if the human mind were so powerful as to exhaust in a single intuitive grasp all the intelligible wealth of things, there obviously would be only one transcendent awareness. Although it is a tribute to man's cognitive ability that he can spontaneously achieve such transcendent awarenesses at all, still his knowledge is comparatively imperfect and weak: it is gradual, progressive, and piecemeal. The multiplicity of the transcendents testify to that aspect of human cognition.

---

[45] If truth is a property of knowledge, it can be applied to things only through extrinsic denomination. This application occurs in a twofold manner. Something can be called "true" insofar as it is the result of truth (for example, the bomb with respect to the teenager, who must know truly what a bomb is and how to make it in order for there to be a bomb) or insofar as it causes truth (the bomb with regard to those witnessing an explosion for the first time). In reference to this second application, some things are of such a nature as easily to deceive, to convey an erroneous impression, to cause a false judgment, as their very names imply—false teeth, fool's gold, false storefronts, a mirage, counterfeit money, a wig, a forged signature, and so on. See Sec. 3b of this chapter, especially notes 51 and 53 and prgrs. corresponding to them.

[46] This list of transcendents is not intended to be complete. Most likely "cause" is another, since it is predicable of everything—of agents, goals, components (see Ch. VIII). So too, perhaps, is "love" or "tendency"—on this, see William Rossner, S.J., "Love and Being," *Wisdom in Depth: Essays in Honor of Henri J. Renard, S.J.* (Milwaukee: Bruce Publishing Co., 1966), pp. 187–202.

b) Transcendents as Known Metaphysically

Such, then, are the transcendents on the spontaneous level—awarenesses which all persons automatically achieve and the meaning of which transcends any one of the various classes of things. By making the implicit be explicit they add to prior knowledge and thus are not synonyms. In them the content of our knowledge grows, but its extension remains constant: all of them are predicable wherever any of them is predicated. Because of the fact that these awarenesses are the direct reactions of the human knower to the actual universe itself, we can accurately say that in the last analysis the transcendents are nothing more than actual things re-presenting themselves within our minds in all the rich complexity of their interrelations. In the light of this, transcendents will necessarily be found wherever the actual universe confronts attentive minds.

They will be found, then, on the metaphysical level too, for metaphysics is the result of such a confrontation. It is the science of existents precisely as existent, immediately caused by actuals registering themselves in their very status of actuality upon our intellect. The effect is awarenesses which in a special manner transcend any definite kind of thing, which explicate what previously was only implicit, which add to prior knowledge, which mark a growth in comprehension with no decrease in extension. In a word, they are transcendents.

Let us briefly look at some of these. The initial awareness which actually existing items set up within the metaphysician has as its content "an actually existing item" and is expressed by "real" or "being." On the spontaneous level those terms mean "something or other actually present": "something" points to something material (be it an intrinsic unity such as a man or an extrinsic unity such as a wristwatch) because known only through direct perception; "actually present" points to its actual existence merely as a fact. No longer, though. Now they signify "an actually existing item": "item" indicates any sort of actual whatever, whether material or immaterial, whether a man, a clock, a component or God; "actually existing" now highlights actual existence as the heart of the item's reality, whether this be identified with that actuality (as in God) or really other than it (as in other actuals).[47] Manifestly, such an awareness is predicable of absolutely every sort of actual because it has

[47] See Appendix B: "How the Meaning of 'Being' Is Worked Out."

been consciously derived from them and signifies each in its very actuality, whence all are similar.[48] It is, in short, a transcendent.

Every actual *is* also in an undivided and cohesive way, whether this indivision, cohesiveness, togetherness be that of an extrinsic unity (this telescope, this mosaic), an intrinsic unity (this man), or of simplicity (as in God or in a substantial form or any other component).[49] Addressing themselves in that condition to a metaphysician, actuals add to the previous notion, and the result is the awareness of "an actually existing item as undivided," expressed by the word "one." "Item" still points to any sort of actual whatsoever and "actually existing" to actual existence as the center of its reality, but "as undivided" indicates what is both a condition and a consequence of actuality, for whatever is actual could be divided only at the risk of not being what it is and, above all, of not be-ing at all. This awareness continues to be predicable of all actuals because it too has been deliberately derived from them so as to be reapplied to them in their varying states of unity. It is, then, a second metaphysical transcendent.

Inasmuch as it actually exists and does so in a unique fashion, every actual also is other than all others. This fact is clear from even a mere inventory of them. Various intrinsic unities such as this man and that woman, as well as various extrinsic unities such as this pipe organ and that electric fan, are all known to be distinct through direct perception: we see them as physically separate. The act of

---

[48] Since "being" also designates them in their diversity, such predication is analogous, of course, and this according to the kinds of analogy previously outlined. See Sec. 2 of this chapter.

[49] Manifestly, such actuals are not all equally one, but are analogous in their unity. They are similar in that all are to some degree undivided and cohesive. They differ in that each is so in its own way—for example, the members of a family are themselves individual persons, held together by relations arising from common origin, love, and other factors; the integral parts of an individual man depend entitatively upon a single human nature, which is itself specifically one because informed by a single substantial form, itself actualized by a single act of existence simultaneously existentializing all the other components and all integral parts; God is totally free of diverse parts and thus is subsistent unity.

For portrayal of a philosophy in which unity holds primacy, see L. Sweeney, S.J., "Basic Principles in Plotinus' Philosophy," *Divine Infinity*, ch. 11, pp. 243–56; *idem*, "Are Plotinus and Albert Magnus Neoplatonists?" in L. P. Gerson (ed.), *Graceful Reason*, pp. 181–91 (forthcoming as ch. 17 in my *Christian Philosophy*).

existing and other components within this man we know to be distinct through intellection: we reflect upon the diverse evidences he gives of change/stability, of actual existence.[50] By reasoning, we know God to be totally other than all else because He alone exists of His very nature. In their otherness, then, actuals cause within an alert metaphysician the awareness of "an actually existing item as other than all else." "Item" and "actually existing" retain their previous meanings, but the addition, "as other than all else," points to a second condition and consequence of actuality: every actual is distinct from all else by the very fact it actually *is* and is *what it is*. Because it can be predicated of all actuals (and this for the same reasons which held good for "being" and "one"), this awareness is also a metaphysical transcendent.

With respect to their status of actuality, actuals entail relationships also to knowledge. As we previously saw when analyzing situations on the spontaneous level, truth when strictly interpreted is a characteristic only of knowledge—the conformity of the mind to what actually is ("The prosecutor knows the truth about the racial incident"). But what actually is (a bomb made by a disgruntled teenager) is the result of true knowledge in the mind of its maker (unless the youth had true knowledge of what a bomb is and how to make it, there would be no bomb, and this fact is recognized in the father's statement, "Yes, it's a true bomb, all right"). What actually is also is the cause of true knowledge in other minds (as indicated by the mother's remark after the bomb exploded: "Now, I truly know what a bomb is"). Because of its relationship to truth, then, what actually is can be termed "true" through extrinsic denomination (see Ch. IV above, note 35).[51]

---

[50] Components differ really from one another by what can be described as a "real but minor distinction"; intrinsic, as well as extrinsic unities, differ really among themselves by a "real major distinction." See Ch. IV, Sec. 2a.

[51] No one should imagine that this mode of predication is arbitrary or meaningless or without objective foundation. When we apply health to medicine through extrinsic denomination (for example, "Declomycin capsules are health-giving for anyone having the flu"), that application is grounded in and points to the very chemical constitution of the medicine. Change the chemical formula and the application is no longer possible. Likewise, the application of truth to an actual is grounded in and points to its very entity, which *is* and is exactly *what* it is because it conforms to its maker's true knowledge, and which in turn causes our minds to be conformed to itself because of the fact that it *is* and is *what* it is. To say an existent is true is to limelight the connection which *being* has to knowledge and truth.

Once we ascend to the philosophical level and discover that all actual existents whose essence is really other than existence have been made by an Existent Whose very nature is Actuality and thereby is also knowledge (see Ch. V, Sec. 6), then we realize that all such existents can be called "true." They actually *are* and are what they are because in knowing Himself perfectly God knows them truly as finite representations of His infinite actuality, and He produces them in accordance with that knowledge.[52] They are, then, the effect of truth in the mind of Him Who makes them. As the content-determining-source of human cognition, they also are the cause of truth in the minds of us who observe them. They are situated midway between divine and human truth.

When this situation in which all creatures are located gets through to a metaphysician, the result is the awareness of "an actually

---

Some define truth as any type of conformity. In such an approach, it can be predicated through intrinsic denomination not only of knowledge (conformity of the mind to things), but also of things (conformity of things to the mind). But this approach does violence to the primary connection truth seems to have to knowledge. We depict the conclusions to which we intellectually assent as "probable," "certain," and "doubtful" but we describe a barbed-wire fence or a barking dog as rusty or loud but not as probable or certain or dubious through intrinsic denomination because these are clearly properties of knowledge. So too is truth, which should accordingly be reserved, in its intrinsic predication, for knowledge.

[52] For a substantiation and development of God's knowledge and its link with His causality, see the treatises in natural theology referred to in Ch. V, n. 45.

Why bring God into a consideration of truth (as well as goodness and beauty, soon to be considered)? Because His existence has already been proved, and the sort of Existent He is has also been sketched, at least in a general fashion (see Ch. V, Sec. 6). His knowledge, love and joy in contemplation add a necessary dimension to the transcendents.

They can, nonetheless, be validly (although incompletely) viewed without God—that is, in relation to the truth, love, and joy through contemplation which they cause in us. Existents themselves actually are intelligible, and as the content-determining-causes of our knowledge they bring it into conformity with themselves. Existents themselves actually are perfect and thereby capable of exciting in us love and desire. Existents themselves actually are splendent (for the force of that word, see n. 56) and call forth joy and admiration when we behold them. Consequently, transcendent descriptions of things in their relations to human knowledge, love and delight as true, good and beautiful are not only possible but also accurate, valid, worthwhile, philosophically necessary. Seeing them against the background of divine truth, love and delight simply completes and balances the picture.

existing item in its relationship to truth." "Item" continues to indicate any kind of actual and "actually existing" indicates actuality as the heart of its reality, whereas "in its relationship to truth" stresses that in their existential status actuals are linked with true knowledge—either as its effect or as its cause. Nothing *is* or is what it is unless its maker knows truly; no one else knows truly unless things actually *are* and are what they are. Since this awareness has arisen from the universal condition of all actuals, it is predicable of all, and thus is another transcendent on the metaphysical plane.[53]

Actuals also are immersed in a context of love. Let us momentarily return to the spontaneous plane. Whatever actually *is* (for example, the cadenza bowed by Heifetz, the Triple Sal Chow executed by a champion figure skater, the pirouette of an expert ballerina) is the result of love in its maker (one does not endure the long hours of practice unless he loves music, skating or dancing, and the perfect cadenza, Triple Sal Chow or pirouette does not occur except from painstaking practice). Whatever actually *is* also is the cause of love in us witnessing it (because perfectly executed, a cadenza, Triple Sal Chow, or pirouette can trigger in us a desire to do likewise: "How wonderful! I would love to do that too").

Upon moving to the metaphysical plane, we realize that the context of love encompasses absolutely every creature. As existents whose existence differs really from what they are, they point to God, Who by His very essence is Actuality and thus is Love and Freedom also. They actually exist and are what they are because in

---

[53] The subject of this predication through extrinsic denomination (notes 45 and 51) is not only this man but also his components, each of which is known truly by God and can cause us to know them truly.

Can we also say God is true? Creatures are said to be true because they are the effect of God's true knowledge and the cause of ours. They are conformed to divine truth and bring our knowledge into conformity with themselves. Can we apply this twofold situation in any way to God? Clearly, God is true with reference to us inasmuch as through creatures He causes us to know Him truly. What of the first sort? Yes, if properly understood. Within God there can be no question of cause/effect between knower/known. Moreover, conformity is replaced with absolute identity: what is known and the knower are identical because each *is* God, subsistent Actuality. God knows Himself by actually being Himself (whereas we know only by intentionally being the known). Hence, God could no more not know Himself than He could not be Himself. Here, truth is predicated of God's very being no longer through extrinsic denomination, because knowledge here is identified with actuality. God *is* truth.

loving Himself God also loves them as limited reproductions of His limitless perfections, and He effects them according to that love. In brief, they are the result of His love. Because their perfections initiate love in us, they also are the cause of our love. They occupy a halfway house between divine and human love.

When existents bring home to the metaphysician the place they thus occupy, there ensues an awareness of "an actually existing item as perfect and thus in relationship to love," designated by the term "good." "Item" and "actually existing" preserve their former significations, but the addition, "as perfect and thus in relationship to love," emphasizes the connection all actuals in their very actuality have to love: they are perfect because they are the effects of love or they cause love because they are perfect. Nothing is perfect unless its maker loves, no one else loves except because existents are perfect. Issuing from that common situation in which all existents find themselves, this awareness can be predicated of all and is, clearly, still another metaphysical transcendent.[54]

Finally, existents prove also to be inserted into a third milieu—that of joy and contemplation. As is clear with regard to a human artist, what he actually makes (a painting, a poem, a sonata) results from his compelling inspiration, from his vision of beauty and the thrill and delight it instills. In turn, what he actually makes communicates delight and joy to us beholding it. Simply stated, what actually *is* is at once the effect of the artist's joy through contemplation and the cause of the spectator's joy from contemplation. For both reasons it can be named "beautiful."[55]

---

[54] Manifestly, good is predicated of all actuals without exception (men and all other material existents, their components, God) through intrinsic denomination, and this analogously, since all are perfect, each in its own way. This analogous predication would be according to the same kinds of analogy as that of "being"—namely, eminence, proportionality, and reference.

Is good predicated of anything through extrinsic denomination? Apparently it is so predicated of our free choices, which can be depicted as good or bad with reference to whether the objects chosen are good or evil. If so, a moral good is something objectively, entitatively good in relation to freedom.

[55] The beautiful has traditionally been described as "that which pleases upon being seen" (*id quod visum placet*). On the spontaneous level that description concerns aesthetic beauty and consists of three elements; (a) *"That which"* points to the beautiful thing itself, whether in nature (a sunset, a landscape, a person) or an artifact (a painting, a sonata). Beauty in those objects resides in their having at least these three properties: integrity or abundance of perfections; proportion, order or harmony; clarity and refulgence. (b) *"Upon being*

To a metaphysician, that environment of joy and contemplation is the habitat of every created existent. By their very existential status as creatures, such existents establish the existence of an Existent Who by nature is Actuality, and thereby is subsistent Perfection, Order, Harmony, Clarity—in a word, Beauty—issuing into joy through self-contemplation. They actually *are* and are what they are because God, in beholding and rejoicing in Himself, also rejoices in them as partial mirrorings of His beauty, and He produces them in accordance with His joy and delight. They are the results of His joy in beholding the splendor of His beauty. Because their order, right proportions, clarity and integrity stimulate joy in us beholding them, they are the source of our joy. They reside between divine and human joy.

When actuals address themselves in this condition to a metaphysician, they set up the awareness of "an actually existing item as splendent and, hence, in relation to joy and contemplation," signified by "beautiful."[56] "Item" and "actually existing" again express

---

seen" indicates any sort of artistic perception (seeing, hearing, and the like). (c) *"Pleases"* points to the effects of #a and #b: joy, delight.

When transferred to the metaphysical level, the same three elements should be present, but in a different manner: (a) *"That which"* indicates any actual whatsoever in the very force of its actuality (which for God *is* His very nature and for creatures is the act existentializing all other components, through which it in turn essentializes itself). Thence reside the actual's perfections, unity, right order and harmony, luster. (b) *"Upon being seen"* points no more to mere artistic perception but to the austere, heightened intellection by which a metaphysician understands all actuals in their very actuality (see #a). (c) *"Pleases"* signifies the resultant delight and joy.

On beauty, see Jacques Maritain, *Art and Scholasticism* (New York: Charles Scribner's Sons, 1937); *idem, Creative Intuition in Art and Poetry* (New York: Pantheon Books, Inc., 1953); E. Gilson, *Painting and Reality;* G. Smith and Lottie Kendzierski, *The Philosophy of Being* (New York: The Macmillan Company, 1961), pp. 359–63; M. Vaske, *An Introduction to Metaphysics*, pp. 197–205.

[56] This definition is only an attempt to explicate the traditional one just discussed (see previous note). "Splendent" (as well as the noun, "splendor") is used in the original force of the Latin word: "*splendere*: to shine, to be bright." The integrity, perfections, right proportion and good order inherent in their actuality enable all actuals to be bright, to shine forth upon human knowers sufficiently prepared to behold them, with resultant joy and admiration. See G. Smith and L. Kendzierski, *op. cit.*, p. 360: "Only some knowledge acts are delightful. The question is, why is this so? The explanation seems to lie here. Some knowns are integral wholes, with properly proportioned parts

what we would expect; the other words highlight the liaison which actuality has with joy and contemplation: all actuals as actual are splendent because they result from joy through contemplation or because they effect joy from contemplation due to their splendor. Whatever actually is flashes forth in splendor only because of its maker's delight in contemplation; we take delight in contemplating whatever actually is only because it does so flash forth. Since this awareness has issued from a characteristic common to all actuals, it is predicable of all, and thus is another (and final) transcendent.[57]

(c) In Retrospect

Here, then, are the metaphysical transcendents:

being	an actually existing item as actual
one	an actually existing item as undivided
individual[58]	an actually existing item as other than all else
true	an actually existing item in relation to truth
good	an actually existing item as perfect, and thus in relation to love
beautiful	an actually existing item as splendent, and thus in relation to joy and contemplation

Together with their counterparts in one's spontaneous knowledge, they have the following characteristics. They are awarenesses whose meanings are not restricted to any of the various classes of things. They explicate what previously was only implicit. They add to prior knowledge and hence are not synonymous. In them knowledge grows in comprehension, extension stays constant: all of them are predicable wherever any of them is predicated.[59] They are the

and bathed, so to say, in their own light. The knowledge of such knowns causes an intense knowledge and delight."

[57] See n. 46 as to the number of transcendents. The present list is not exhaustive.

[58] A single word is needed to express "other than," and "individual" is the adjective we have chosen as sufficiently appropriate to be applied to God in His otherness from all else, to material things, even to components. Each actual is *individual;* in saying this we mean simply that each is *other than* all others. On "individuated," see n. 87.

[59] Because "one" and the other transcendents subsequent to "being" merely explicate what "being" already implies, they also share in the properties of "being." But "being" is as rich as is possible for a concept with maximal extension: it signifies everything in each actual of which it is predicated, and

immediate reactions of the human knower to the actual universe itself—things actually are divided, are distinct from one another, are perfect and intelligible and well proportioned. In fact, they are actual things reproducing themselves intentionally within us in all their complex richness. This reproduction, though, is no longer through mere direct perception, as that which occurs when the transcendents are spontaneously known and which results in matter showing up in their content. Rather it is through intellection (initiated, however, and nourished by data gained perceptually, and thus inductively). Through analysis, reflection and reasoning the human knower becomes (to paraphrase Maritain) sufficiently purified, sufficiently empty, sufficiently attentive to listen to actual existents speaking directly in terms of their very actuality, and the science of metaphysics is begotten within him.[60]

That status of actuality is the core of reality in all actuals, and therefore all their other transcendent marks are its sequels. This man is one not only because a single substantial form specifies his nature, but also and especially because the single act of existence actualizing that substantial form also actualizes all of his other components. Why is he really distinct from other members of the human species? Proximately because his quantified matter physically sets him apart from them, although quantified matter exercises its intrinsic causal function of substantial individuation only if it actually is.[61] The fact that he is a *man* enables others to know truly what human means, but humanity and its ability to communicate itself intentionally are anchored in the fact that humans do exist. Why is he virtuous, witty, wise, and perfect in various other ways? Because granted that he actually is, then virtue, keen wit, wisdom *are* and are virtue, wit, and wisdom. Whence his ontological splendor? From the right proportion, good order, ontic integrity to be found (among other places) in the harmonious subordination of all other components to actual existence (they are, are what they

---

it is predicable of all. Therefore, the other transcendents too are as rich in content as is "being": although predicable of all, they too signify everything in each, even though they do so each from its own point of view.

[60] Jacques Maritain, *Preface to Metaphysics*, p. 48.

[61] As we have already seen, substantial form individuates itself through prime matter (see Ch. V, especially n. 30). But since this cannot specify unless it actually exists, its self-individuation rests upon the act of existing, which is thereby shown to embrace individuation within its own autodetermination.

The role of actual existence in regard to otherness is even more clearly seen when one considers a human's otherness as a person. See Sec. 5 of this chapter.

are and are causally functioning because existentialized), which in turn autodetermines itself through them. In brief, the act of existing is the fundamental source not only of reality but of unity, of otherness, of intelligibility, of perfection, and of beauty as well. Its primacy in existents is reaffirmed.

But metaphysical transcendents are nothing more than actually existing items immediately re-presenting themselves within the human knower in their very actuality. Hence, actuality should have primacy in those awarenesses too. If it would not be too complicated, the phrase "as actual" should show up not only in the definition of being but in that of one, individual, true, and all the rest: "an actually existing item *as actual* and thus undivided . . . *as actual* and thus other than everything else . . . *as actual* and thus with relations to truth," and so on. At least henceforward their definitions should be so read and interpreted that prominence be given that phrase, whether expressed or not.

4. Actual Existence and Evil

If actual existence indeed is the source of reality and thereby of perfection and of splendor, the inevitable result should be that the universe is full of goodness and beauty by the very fact that it is actual.[62] But to realize that such is not the case we need only scan our daily newspapers, even in times of what we now call "peace." A relentless hurricane lashes the southern coast with incalculable damage to buildings, property and crops. On the west coast savage fires race through tinder-dry forests, leaving only blackened hillsides in their wake. In a Far East city a *coup d'état* replaces one

[62] This optimistic mood is well expressed by Augustine, *On the Trinity*, VIII, Ch. 3 (from *Basic Writings of St. Augustine*, ed. W. J. Oates [New York: Random House, Inc., 1948], II, 775–76): "Since good is the earth, with the loftiness of its mountains, and the due measure of its hills, and the level surface of its plains; and good is an estate that is pleasant and fertile; and good is a house that is arranged in due proportions, and is spacious and bright; and good are animal and animate bodies; and good is air that is temperate and salubrious: and good is food that is agreeable and fit for health; and good is health, without pains or lassitude; . . . and good is the mind of a friend, with the sweetness of agreement, and with the confidence of love; and good is a righteous man: and good are riches . . . ; and good is the heaven, with its sun and moon and stars; and good are the angels, by their holy obedience. . . ."

corrupt regime with another possibly just as corrupt, while its streets run red with blood and its stores are invaded by looters. And in an American city, a gang of juvenile delinquents knife two helpless youths in an alley. A nationwide network of hoodlums is uncovered. Within the walls of a major hospital a mother of three children is dying from cancer; a newly married couple are injured when the drunken driver of an oncoming car careens into theirs; a middle-aged man attempts suicide because of unemployment, loneliness or anxiety.

Despite the many perfections it does contain, then, our universe is not totally perfect. Its inhabitants are, for one reason or another, deprived of many goods they should have. In a word, it is marred by evils, and the question now arises of *what* evil is.[63] We ask the same question concerning a substantial form, a cabbage or a man, or running or thinking or courage. Now the inquiry has to do with the blindness, sickness, death, destruction, injustice, dishonesty and the like which scar our world. What is meant by tagging each of them as "evil"? How can it find a place within a universe which, theoretically at least, should be a plentitude of goodness and perfection? In view of its apparent omnipresence and its far-reaching effects, some have granted evil a positive status and made it a co-principle with good.[64] Others, perhaps no less aware of its extent and force, have thought the only way to cope with evil is simply to ignore it, to deny its existence, to reckon it as an illusion which can be overcome by positive thinking.[65] What is the answer? Can one find a middle position between those two extremes?

---

[63] Evil initiates other questions too. For example, from what causes does evil flow? Does it have an efficient or final cause? (See Ch. IX, Sec. 4, n. 78.) How can we reconcile the presence of evils in the world with God's power and love? For answers to this last, see the natural theology treatises listed on Ch. V, n. 45.

No solution to the problem of evil can be satisfactory without bringing in truths from divine revelation (especially the doctrines of original sin and Christ's redemption of mankind through suffering and death), as well as points from the philosophy of man and ethics on the nature and condition of human freedom and moral activity.

[64] This is the position of the Manicheans. Perhaps Sartre also fits here, although he pushes the position to its extreme: nothing is good, all reality is evil, and the result is the boredom, forlornness, nausea overwhelming us. See Ch. IV, n. 34.

[65] This stand is that apparently taken by Christian Scientists and by other religious groups who spurn medicine and doctors (see n. 36 above).

Some items are known and described in themselves—for instance, a cabbage, a vertebrate, a man, his visual power, his actual seeing, his operative habit of mathematics, and the like. Others are known only through reference to something else with which they are contrasted. For example, darkness is the absence of *light*, a hole is the absence of *earth* or *cloth* or *dough*, nonbeing is the absence of *being*. In order to understand this sort of item, one must be acquainted with whatever positive factor is missing (light, earth, cloth), realize that such are absent, and then affirm that these items *are* that very absence. Evil fits here, for it is the absence of a *good* which an existent ought to have.[66] Consequently, as the first step to understanding evil, let us consider again what good consists in.

As previously defined "good" is "an actually existing item as perfect, hence in relation to love," and is predicable through intrinsic denomination of all actuals—a human person, his components, God (see Sec. 3 of this chapter). For greater maneuverability, let us rephrase this definition as follows: *a good is a perfection which an existent ought to have*. Suppose we now concentrate momentarily upon this man. He is composed of various components (actual existence, substantial form, prime matter, multiple and various accidents), each of which is a perfection, and hence a good. When compared to one another, some are recipients (that is, essence, prime matter, substance) of other perfections, others are the perfections received (that is, act of existing, substantial form, accidents).[67] Through his own efficient causality and that of agents external to him, he can gradually increase in accidental perfections—for example, he can grow in virtue and become more open to God, he can gain intellectual operative habits in speculative or practical matters, he can contemplate what is beautiful (whether in nature or in artifacts) and thus avoid sinking to a merely impersonal, superficial, inhuman way of living.

What is important for our present purpose is to garner two facts from the preceding. Such an increase is also an increase in goodness, since a good is nothing more than a perfection which one should have. Second and more significantly, to grow in goodness is also to grow in reality and being. Goodness involves the *presence* of

---

[66] For instance, blindness is the absence of seeing, deafness, that of hearing; a fever is the absence of the degree of temperature suitable to the human organism; blasphemy is a blatant absence of reverence and adoration toward God.

[67] See Ch. V, Sec. 2.

due perfections which *actually exist* within whatever is perfected; but presence and actual existence are coterminous with being and reality; therefore, goodness too is coterminous with being or reality, and an increase in the former is simultaneously also an increase in the latter. Because a newly acquired accident is received by the human existent, and because both what is received and the recipient are good, an increase in goodness is equivalent to a perfection-in-perfection, a good-in-good, a being-in-being.

In contrast, an evil is the *absence* of a good which an existent should have: some or other perfection does not actually exist within a subject. But absence and nonexistence are coterminous with nonbeing and unreality; therefore, evil is also coterminous with nonbeing or unreality. Accordingly, to become somehow evil is simultaneously a decrease in being and reality, as well as in perfection. Although evil itself is the absence, nonexistence, nonbeing, still it involves the subject or recipient which is deprived of the perfection and yet which itself is composed of other perfections and thus is good.[68] Consequently, evil is equivalent to imperfection-in-perfection, nongood-in-good, absence-in-presence, nonbeing-in-being.[69]

Perhaps it is now somewhat clear what evil is. It entails three factors.

---

[68] For example, the subject of blindness is the human and, more immediately, his visual sense, which for some reason or other cannot see. The more immediate subject of poor vision, though, is his actual activity of seeing as without the degree of vision that could and should be there. The immediate subject is always that which directly lacks the perfection in question, that which would itself receive the perfection were it there. On the human level this frequently is a faculty or its operations.

[69] This method of describing evil reveals how heinous evil is when freely chosen. By preferring what is entitatively not good for us (see n. 54), we deliberately insert imperfection into perfection, absence into goods already present, nonbeing into being. Knowingly and freely we begin to destroy and (literally) to annihilate ourselves, to downgrade our degree of reality. These privations are unlike those which come from alien or inescapable sources: because they could have been prevented, they are our own doing.

To stress this difference, as well as their seriousness, freely chosen privations are given the special name of *moral evils* and thereby distinguished from physical evils. A moral evil is the absence of due perfection in a free choice, as well as in any operation which comes under its direct influence. All other absences of due perfections (whether in human or in subhuman existents) are physical evils.

(a) *In itself* it is the very absence, nonexistence, privation, lack of a due perfection.[70]

(b) It has a *subject*—the existent which is deprived of its due perfection and thus is affected by and suffers from the privation. But the subject in itself is good, and hence is something positive and real.[71]

(c) It is known through a *concept or idea*, the content of which is "the absence of a due perfection" but which is itself an actually existing awareness within our minds, and, accordingly, is also something positive and real.[72]

---

[70] In the phrases above (*imperfection*-in-perfection and so on), the first word designates evil *in itself*.

One should take care not to invest evil itself with anything positive. This investiture is not liable to occur with reference to, say, total blindness, which is the absence of all vision, but it can occur when we think of poor vision. Evil there is not the actual vision itself: this the man does have and is a good to the extent it is there—in fact, it is the subject of the privation. Rather it is the amount of vision which is lacking, which he should have but does not. Similarly, the evil connected with such a disease as fever is not the high temperature itself but rather the absence of well-being brought on by that temperature in this type of animal, the lack of suitability and proportion between that temperature and this human being.

[71] In the phrases referred to in the preceding note, the last word indicates the subject of the evil (imperfection-in-*perfection*). On the subject, see n. 68.

[72] Obviously, we can easily (although unwittingly) project this concept out upon the actual subject affected and begin to imagine evil itself as something positive and real.

This concept is itself a construct (see n. 10). In order to understand this, let us contrast our awareness of "seeing" with that of "blindness." The direct basis of the first is an actually existing item—the operation of seeing which this man is now performing. That of the second is no such actually existing item (in fact, blindness is its very absence) but is the mental activity by which we produce the concept—namely, our knowledge of what seeing is; our affirmation that seeing is absent here, that this man does not see; our concomitant awareness that blindness is "not seeing," "the absence of seeing." Obviously, the mental activity involved helps constitute the very content of the intelligibility in question, within which it shows up as an integral part ("seeing-*denied*," "*not*-seeing," the *absence* of seeing").

On this point see Aquinas, *S.T.*, I, 48, 2 ad 2: "In another sense, *being* is said to be that which signifies the truth of a proposition which consists in composition, revealed by the verb *is*. In this sense, being is what answers to the question, *Does it exist*? It is in this sense that we speak of blindness as being in the eye, or of any other privation. In this way even evil can be called a being." The only "is" that blindness itself has is the "is" in the intellect's affirmation that, for example, "Helen Keller *is* blind," whereas seeing has a double "is":

Here, then, is the intermediate position sought. With the Christian Scientists one can agree that *in itself* evil is nothing—an absence, a lack. To the Manicheans, though, we concede that evil has a positive side—the subject it afflicts and (frequently, at least) the awareness it produces in those observing that subject. Without a real subject, there could be no evils. Without the positive, there could be no negative. And even though evil itself is a mere absence and a nothing, still it does affect its subject, it does generate a tension, a seeking or reaching out for what is not there but should be. And there lies part of the mystery of evil. If the actual universe were not permeated with reality, perfection and goodness, evils would be impossible. But it is so permeated, and evils not only can be, but, alas, actually are found in it—privations of perfections in existents which make those very privations possible.[73]

---

that of the intellect affirming "Anne Sullivan is seeing" and that of the visual operation within her.

[73] The picture is not entirely bleak, however. Evils offer us the challenge needed to become better human beings. "[The fundamental purpose of education is] to introduce a human being to the secrets of his own power to create and thereby to win, through freedom and through suffering, if necessary, the will which is inseparable from all greatness: the will to suffer in creation. Unless we have that will to suffer in creation, we are unworthy to take our part in the travail of humanity" (William E. Hocking in an interview to R. L. Hartzell, Jr., quoted in the *St. Louis Post-Dispatch*, March 20, 1960).

Frequently evils are a great obstacle to assenting to the existence of God. For example, see Raissa Maritain, *We Have Been Friends Together* (New York: David McKay Co., Inc., 1942), p. 26: "Toward the age of fourteen I started asking myself questions about God. Now that I knew how unhappy or wicked men could be, I wondered if God really existed. I recall very clearly that I reasoned thus: If God exists, He is also infinitely good and all-powerful. But if He is good, how can He permit suffering? And if He is all-powerful how can He tolerate the wicked? Therefore He is not all-powerful nor infinitely good; therefore He does not exist."

Nonetheless, others prove there must be a God from those very evils. See Nicholas Berdyaev, *Dostoievsky*, trans. Donald Attwater (New York: Sheed & Ward, 1934), p. 87: "The argument everlastingly used against God is the existence of evil in the world, and the whole of Dostoievsky's work is an answer to that argument. I would sum it up, in a paradoxical form, thus: *The existence of evil is a proof of the existence of God. If the world consisted wholly and uniquely of goodness and righteousness there would be no need for God, for the world itself would be god. God is, because evil is. And that means that God is because freedom is.*

"Thus does Dostoievsky arrive at the existence of God through a consideration of the freedom of the human spirit: those of his characters who deny this freedom deny God, and inversely."

5. Actual Existence and the Individual

Of the six transcendents, the one which deserves special attention and needs more detailed discussion is "other than" or "individual." It indubitably is a transcendent, for it is a trait common to all extramental items, and, we may add, even to intramental ones. For example, in their content our awareness of "animal" is conceptually somewhat *other than* that of "rational"; similarly, our awareness of "being" is *other than* that of "good" or of the other transcendents; our awarenesses of "rational animal" and "man" or of "being" and "real," although identical in content, still are at least expressed by terms which are *other than* one another.[74] But otherness is especially operative in the extramental world. The heart of this man is somehow really *other than* his liver, feet, and other integral parts. His substantial form is really *other than* his prime matter, actual existence, and other components. He himself is really *other than* his twin brother, mother, father, and all other humans.[75]

* (a) Data from Revelation

This last otherness it is which demands special discussion, since it actually is twofold. As we learn from divine revelation, this man is really other than that one as an individual member of the human species and, second, as an individual human supposit or person. Those two othernesses are really different: nature and supposit are not identical, as revelation in its elaboration and statement by the Catholic Church makes clear. Although we shall discuss this nonidentity only with regard to Christ for reasons of convenience and for obviously direct relevance to our inductive approach in philosophy, still it is to be found also in the Trinity, and this in a

---

[74] The otherness in the first set of awarenesses ("animal"/"rational") is that of a "major mental distinction" (see n. 29 and n. 42); that in the second set ("being"/"good") is a "minor mental distinction" (see n. 42); that in the third ("rational animal"/"man") might be called a "purely arbitrary" or a "merely semantic mental distinction"—that between synonymous terms (see Ch. IV, n. 27).

[75] The otherness between integral parts can be described as an "inadequate real distinction" or a "potentially real distinction." Such parts are actually united in and to the whole they constitute; still they are extended and thus are spatially other than one another. Hence, they *can* become really other than the whole when severed from it. The otherness between components is that of a "minor real distinction"; that between two things, a "major real distinction" (see Ch. IV, Sec. 2a).

magnificent way. Let us quote a few of the Church's statements on the Trinity before turning to Christ. "This is what the Catholic faith teaches," we read in the Athanasian Creed. "We worship one God in the Trinity and the Trinity in unity; we distinguish among the *persons*, but we do not divide the *substance*. For the Father is a distinct *person;* the Son is a distinct *person;* and the Holy Spirit is a distinct *person*. Still, the Father and the Son and the Holy Spirit have *one divinity*, equal glory, and coeternal majesty."[76] Some centuries later the Fourth Lateran Council stated: "We firmly believe and profess without qualification that there is only one true God . . . the Father, the Son, and the Holy Spirit: *three persons but one essence and a substance or nature* that is wholly simple."[77]

But, as we said, we are confining our discussion to Christ. Briefly, how does the Church speak of Him? After its declarations on the Trinity, the Lateran Council turns to the Incarnate Word. "The only begotten Son of God, Jesus Christ, made incarnate by a common action of the Holy Trinity, and conceived by Mary ever Virgin with the cooperation of the Holy Spirit, became a *true man* composed of a rational soul and human flesh, *one person in two natures*."[78] The Church takes pains to emphasize that His human nature is complete in every way: it consists of soul and body and all the properties any human has.

> [In Christ] the proper character of each *nature* [both divine and human] was kept inviolate, and together they were united in *one person*. Thus was lowliness assumed by majesty, weakness by power, mortality by eternity; and a *nature* that could not be defiled was united to one that could suffer in order to repay the debt attaching to our state. . . . In the full and perfect *nature of true man*, therefore, the *true God* was born—perfect in every characteristic proper to us as well as in every one proper to himself.[79]

---

[76] John F. Clarkson, S.J., *et al.* (trans.), *The Church Teaches: Documents of the Church in English Translation* (St. Louis: B. Herder Book Co., 1955), #6. [Emphasis added here and in the next three quotations.] The Athanasian Creed was probably written in the fifth or sixth century. In this and subsequent documents "supposit" and "person" are equivalent. "Nature," "substance," and "essence" are also equivalent.

[77] *Ibid.*, #306. The Fourth Lateran Council was held in 1215.

[78] *Ibid.*, #455.

[79] *Ibid.*, #412. The quotation is from St. Leo's Letter to Flavius in 449, accepted by the Council of Chalcedon as an accurate expression of the Church's teaching on Christ. Also see the Athanasian Creed: "Our Lord Jesus Christ . . .

However little inclined philosophers may be to attend to divine revelation, nevertheless here is a fact revealed by God that casts an important light on existents and hence cannot be ignored: a Man once actually existed Who had a complete human nature and essence but Who was not a human supposit. Because of that human nature He was really other than every other member of the human race. By reason of His quantified matter He was physically separate from them. By reason of His soul, together with His intellect, will and other faculties, He had his own operations—His own knowledge, His own free choices, His own prayers, His own feelings, His own sufferings. But He was not really other than them as a human supposit for the simple reason that, as revelation informs us, He was not a human supposit. The question is, then: what makes a nature be a supposit? What is added? How, precisely, do supposit and nature differ?

Revelation itself does not explicitly answer that question, and theologians have given various answers. According to Scotus and others, supposit adds to nature solely the negative characteristic of incommunicability, of noncommunication—my human nature is supposit because I do not share it with someone else; it has not been assumed by another, whereas Christ's human nature was taken up by God and thus is no supposit.[80] For both Suarez and Cajetan, as well as their modern followers, supposit adds a really distinct mode to nature—according to the former it is a sequel to existence; according to the latter it is preparatory for existence: it

---

is a perfect man, with a rational soul and human flesh" (*The Church Teaches*, #7). Council of Chalcedon in 451: "We declare that He is perfect both in His divinity and in His humanity, truly God and truly Man composed of body and rational soul; that He is consubstantial with the Father in His divinity, consubstantial with us in His humanity. . . . We declare that the one selfsame Christ, only-begotten Son and Lord, must be acknowledged in *two natures* without any commingling or change or division or separation; that the *distinction between the natures* is in no way removed by their union, but rather the specific character of each *nature* is preserved and they are united in *one person* and *one hypostasis*. We declare that He is not split or divided into two persons, but that there is one selfsame only-begotten Son, God the Word, the Lord Jesus Christ" (*ibid.*, #414).

Such declarations are against those who would make Christ be one existent by eliminating part either of His divine nature or of His human nature.

[80] For a clear account of Scotus' position, see M. de la Taille, S.J., *The Hypostatic Union* (West Baden Springs, Ind.: West Baden College, 1952), pp. 15–16. On Scotus (as well as other positions), see L. de Raeymaeker, *Philosophy of Being*, pp. 240–47; H.J. Renard, S.J., *Philosophy of Being*, pp. 222–34.

enables essence to exist independently.[81] For theologians whose philosophical approach is an inductive one and to whom material existents have shown themselves to be composed of an act of existing really distinct from what each is, the answer is simple and ready-made. Supposit adds to nature or essence the act of existing: a supposit is a nature actualized by its own act of existing.

> The difference between a human nature that is a person (as in the case of Peter) and a human nature that is not a person (as in Christ's case) is reducible to this: in the one case the nature exists through an existence of its own, in the other through the existence of an uncreated Being. . . . In the first case (the case of Peter) the humanity is possessed of an existence of its own: it exists, not only as a substantial power of action, but as an agent, with its own initiative and its own ends; it exists, in a word, for its own sake, because it exists independently of any one existing, except the Creator as such. Clearly it does not exist of itself, or without cause: that is God's exclusive privilege. But it exists *by* itself, apart from any companionship or partnership in existence, it is *self-enclosed:* which is the definition of a person.[82]

Again:

> What do we call a person, or a subsisting individual, in opposition to a mere nature? We mean one that exists as a complete whole: not as a part of a whole, like my hand, nor as an associate only, like my body; nor as a mere belonging or dependency, like Christ's humanity. We mean one existing separately as well as independently: self-governed no less than self-contained. All that is verified at once when you have, in the created sphere, a complete nature fitted with what is required to make it exist by itself and for itself. What then is required for this? Nothing more than the ordinary connatural existence of a human nature. Have that, I would say to the nature, and at once you are a man, you are some-

---

[81] See M. de la Taille, *Hypostatic Union*, pp. 16–19. One of Cajetan's most prominent followers is J. Maritain. See his *Existence and the Existent*, pp. 62–68; *Degrees of Knowledge*, Appendix A.

[82] M. de la Taille, *Hypostatic Union*, p. 19.

body: because to exist in such manner is to subsist as a whole, as an independent unit.[83]

Several philosophically important conclusions can be drawn from the preceding theological excursion. By following the inductive methodology already outlined (see Chs. III and IV), one can have achieved the realization that a material existent involves more than a mere essence or nature: it also comprises an act of existence, which existentializes that essence and is the heart of reality in that existent. When he comes upon the revealed dogma that nature is not supposit, that they are different, that the latter adds still further independence to the former, he can easily agree. Of course, they are not identical: nature or essence is only part of the existent, which also involves actual existence. A supposit is the entire existent—the essence as actualized by existence. Unlike a philosopher who follows the lead of Scotus or of Cajetan, he need add nothing to his philosophical interpretation of existence when he encounters divine revelation.[84]

---

[83] *Ibid.*, p. 20.

[84] The matter actually is not that simple, since historically the revealed dogma came first and the philosophical contrast between nature and person was worked out under its influence. This influence produced what Gilson calls *Christian* philosophy. See E. Gilson, *Spirit of Mediaeval Philosophy*, p. 37: "If [Christian philosophy] is to deserve that name the supernatural must descend as a constitutive element not, of course, into its texture, which would be a contradiction, but into the work of its construction. Thus I call Christian, *every philosophy which, although keeping the two orders formally distinct, nevertheless considers the Christian revelation as an indispensable auxiliary to reason.* . . . It includes in its extension all those philosophical systems, which were in fact what they were only because a Christian religion existed and because they were ready to submit to its influence." See *ibid.*, Chs. I, II, and XX; *idem, Reason and Revelation in the Middle Ages, passim; Christianity and Philosophy* (New York: Sheed & Ward, 1939) in its entirety.

Despite this historical priority, though, a student who works out the authentic existentialist philosophy presented in this book *before* he learns of, or at least meditates upon revelation could experience the reactions indicated—a ready assent to revelation with no change in his philosophical analysis of existents.

One should remember that prior to revelation philosophers showed no awareness of the otherness issuing from person or supposit. The terms were known, but they had quite a different meaning. *Persona* in Latin and *prosopon* in Greek mean a mask—literally, "that through which sound comes" and "that which is placed before the face." *Suppositum* is "that which is placed

Does he learn nothing new from that encounter, then? Yes, he discovers that not only does nature differ from supposit as part from whole, but also that a nature can, absolutely speaking, actually *be* and yet not be in a supposit, since once at least there actually was a human nature which was not in a human person. Accordingly, emphasis is placed upon the fact that every human (for that matter, every material existent) entails two sorts of otherness, of independence, of autonomy, of individuality: that of his human nature, by which he is really other than the members of any other species, human or otherwise, and that of his human personality, by which he is really other than all other supposits, human or otherwise. However much contemporary thinkers may lump both sorts together[85] and however difficult or even impossible it is for anyone

---

under." Aristotle was aware of the otherness issuing from nature (see, for example, *Metaphysics*, VII, Ch. 8, 1034a5–8; V, Ch. 6, 1016b32; VII, Ch. 9, 1035b30; X, Ch. 3, 1054a33; X, Ch. 9, 1058b5; XII, Ch. 8, 1074a33). But even for him an individual member of the human species was important not so much in himself but as a link in the endless chain of the species. This attitude to individual humans is still to be found in Averroës—see Roland J. Teske, S.J., "The End of Man in the Philosophy of Averroës," *New Scholasticism*, 37 (October, 1963), 431–61.

[85] Perhaps one might more correctly say they simply are ignorant that there are two sorts. They are, though, keenly alive to the importance, validity, and value of the individual. Upon that keen awareness is built democracy as a form of government. Karl Marx: "Political democracy is Christian in the sense that man, not merely one man but every man, is there considered a sovereign being, a supreme being. . . . Creations of fantasy, dreams [are] the postulates of Christianity [as to] the sovereignty of man—. . . all these become, in democracy, the tangible and present reality, secular maxims," *Marx-Engels Reader*, R. C. Tucker (ed.), 2nd ed. (New York: W. W. Norton, 1978), p. 39. Adolph Hitler said: "To the Christian doctrine of the infinite significance of the individual human soul . . . I oppose with icy clarity the saving doctrine of the nothingness and insignificance of the human being" (quoted by Hermann Rauschning, *The Voice of Destruction* [New York: G. P. Putnam's Sons, 1940], p. 25). See also Moorhouse F. X. Millar, S.J., "The History and Development of the Democratic Theory of Government in Christian Tradition," in *The State and the Church* (New York: The Macmillan Company, 1924), pp. 99–144.

From that awareness flow modern approaches to education. See Ralph Harper, "Significance of Existence and Recognition for Education," *Modern Philosophers and Education* (Chicago: National Society for the Study of Education, 1955), Part 1, p. 250: "Both students and teacher are individuals. . . . The teacher should recognize the student . . . as an individual. . . . To see another man as an individual is to treat him as if he personally mattered, as if he was irreplaceable, as if he was different from all others. This requires a sensitivity perceptually and experientially to discern their difference, nonetheless different they are. Divine revelation is there to assure us that this is so, and an authentically existentialist philosophy helps explain how this is so.

Finally, actual existence is again disclosed to have primacy because it proves to be the source of the otherness which existents have as supposits. The nature of this human existent is that by which he exists in such a way as to be independent and autonomous as a member of the human species. But his act of existing is that by which he subsists—that is, that by which he exists not in someone else, but in, for and through himself: that by which he exists in such a way as to be independent and autonomous also as a human person. Rightly understood, it is the cause of his human personality.[86]

---

to differences, a humor, and even a certain tenderness that one does not extend to a person in so far as one is thinking of him as one of a type."

[86] Throughout Section 5a we have rather constantly linked supposit with person, and especially with human person. No one should think, though, that supposit and person are synonymous. A person is a certain kind of supposit, one with an intellectual nature; but its having an intellectual nature, its transcendence through knowledge, love and freedom are not what make it a supposit—this comes from its independence in existence. Analysis solely in terms of such transcendence is inadequate or even irrelevant to its status as supposit. Accordingly, supposit is broader than the human level. It extends to all existents who subsist, whatever their natures—whether divine, angelic, human, or subhuman.

Accordingly, the fact that the presence or absence of knowledge, love and freedom in an existent flows directly from his nature explains how it was possible for there to have been a human Existent (Christ) Who had such human operations and yet was not a human supposit. But that same fact also emphasizes a point to us who are human supposits: our transcendence through knowledge, freedom, and love, our ability to enter into an "I-Thou" dialogue with other selves, our subjectivity and openness to other subjects issue immediately from the *sort of existents* we are and not from our existential status itself, not from the fact that we subsist, that we exist in, for and through ourselves because each has its own act of existence. The result is that the consideration of supposits precisely as human, precisely as persons, as subjects *vs.* objects, as selves *vs.* nonselves does not pertain to metaphysics, which studies existents qua existent and not qua this or that kind of existent. Such a consideration can (and should) be made after one has studied metaphysics, philosophy of man, ethics and philosophy of God. It then serves as an informative and inspiring synthesis of those other philosophical disciplines. But it is itself not metaphysics, and those who locate it at the heart of metaphysics thereby reveal that theirs is not authentically existential. "To be real" then is

(b) The Principle of Individuation

Material existents have, then, two kinds of otherness or individuality, the first of which issues from their status as supposits, the other from their natures or essences.[87] This latter sort we experience constantly. Because of his concrete nature a human being is this material, living, sentient and rational existent. By reason of his quantified matter he is physically separate from everything else. His vegetative powers nourish and develop him and not others. Through his sensitive powers, together with intellect and will, he

---

no longer "to be actually existing" but "to be a subject," with the unfortunate result that "real" or "being" can have become univocal (see Sec. 2) and is predicable only of subjects (and, consistently, perhaps only of *human* subjects). Whatever is not a subject, whatever is subhuman or even transhuman, is unreal and nonbeing. Such a price is too high to pay even for the most attractive feature which a metaphysics of subjectivity or personalism has to offer: the primacy of being human, "the manwardness, the natural or intrinsic predestination of all physical things to be humanized" (Jerome Diemert, S.J., "Comments," *Proceedings of the Twenty-fifth Annual Convention of the Jesuit Philosophical Association*, ed. John E. Gurr, S.J. [Woodstock, Md.: Woodstock College Press, 1963], p. 78).

For further comparison of nature/supposit with subject/object, see Leo Sweeney, "Existentialism: Authentic and Unauthentic," *New Scholasticism*, 40 (1966), 44–52; *idem*, "Gabriel Marcel's Position on God," *ibid.*, 44 (1970), 110–17. From those two articles (which are forthcoming as chs. 23 and 24 in my *Christian Philosophy* volume—for publishing data see "Suggested Readings" below) one may infer that "person" can refer either to the entitative structure itself of a human existent (in this sense Christ is not a human person or supposit) or to his psychological individuality constituted by unique free choices (thus Christ can be called a human person). In human existents other than Christ entitative and psychological personalities complement one another.

[87] In our interpretation "individuality" is an analogous awareness. All individual items, whether intramental or extramental, are similar in that they are other than one another, and yet are diverse in that they are so each in its own way. This holds true even with respect to nature and supposit. The otherness which marks existents because of their individuated natures is both like and unlike that which marks them as supposits. The first is like the second because both are othernesses; they differ, though, in that the one issues from the sort of being the existent is, the other from his existing independently.

Incidentally, "individuation" and the adjective, "individuated," are restricted solely to the otherness of nature or essence. Although one can talk about both nature and supposit as "individual," one should not speak directly of a supposit as "individuated." Every individuated item is individual, but not every individual is individuated.

has his own knowledge, his own feelings, his own free choices, his own appreciation of beauty, his own sufferings. As this corporeal, living, sentient, rational existent, then, he is other than all other existents, human or otherwise.

Accordingly, the fact of difference seems beyond doubt, and the question is rather: what is its intrinsic cause? If the act of existing is the source of independence and autonomy in an existent as a supposit, what is their source in him as a distinct member of a species? Within a concrete nature what is there to ground otherness and individuality?

First of all, one should note that by one's nature one is specifically different from members of other species. Our inquiry does not concern this difference since, obviously, its source is the substantial form—that by which an existent is human and thus is not canine, feline, and so on. By his nature, though, one also is specifically like members of the same species and yet is unlike them individually. Both John and Paul are similar in that both are men and yet differ because one is this and the other is that man. This difference is the problem.

In its general outline the solution seems foolproof. The natures of John and of Paul are not simple but are composed of substantial form and prime matter. If his substantial form is that by which John is specifically similar to Paul (and, we may add, specifically unlike a dog or a tree), then prime matter should at least basically be that by which he substantially is individually dissimilar to him. Materiality plays such a function in artifacts.

> Each and every [painting] is a distinct entity, which cannot be duplicated, even by its own author. However carefully he may copy himself, a painter can turn out only another painting. Now, the fundamental cause assigned by philosophers to this character of physical substances lies in the very matter that enters their composition. The classical formula—matter is the principle of individuation—means something quite simple. *It merely expresses the fact that each definite portion of matter, delimited by certain dimensions, exists only once.* A man, or even a machine, can turn out any number of similar chairs made out of the same kind of wood, but the same kind of wood is not the same piece of wood. The number of similar chairs it is possible to make depends only on the available quantity of wood, *but the particular piece of wood that goes into the making of one particular chair cannot enter the structure of another one.* This

> is what the philosophers give us to understand in saying that, on account of its fundamental incommunicability, matter is the principle of individuation.[88]

What is true of artifacts is *a priori* or even *a fortiori* true of intrinsic unities. By the very fact that it is educed from *this* sperm/ovum, a canine substantial form is unique—no other will ever be educed from identically the same sperm/ovum, and hence no other will ever be totally like it. The very fact that a human soul is created within a particular sperm/ovum (with *its* store of genes) eliminates the possibility of another soul being created within the same matter; thus it is unique and differs from all others. Once a substantial form is educed or created within this or that matter, individuation has so thoroughly marked every fiber of its being, as well as that of its faculties and other properties, that the nature it specifies will develop thenceforward in a singular, never-to-be-reduplicated fashion.

* But there are difficulties in this theory, as this series of questions reveals.

* *First:* "Is prime matter the sole principle of individuation? If so, how can that which is itself pure potency accomplish such a feat?" *Answer:* Prime matter is only the ultimate principle of individuation. The proximate principle is quantified matter[89]—matter at its lowest degree of essential perfection, matter in such a state that besides whatever other perfections it may have it has extended parts outside of parts. The result is that *this* parcel of matter is other than *that* parcel[90] and, hence, what happens in and develops from this parcel is necessarily other than what happens in and develops from that parcel.

---

[88] E. Gilson, *Painting and Reality*, p. 47. (Emphasis added.)

[89] Traditionally, this principle has been called "matter signed by quantity" (*materia quantitate signata*)—matter made definite by quantity, matter "delimited by certain dimensions" (Gilson, *ibid.*), matter in such a condition that it can be designated and pointed out. This is what we intend by "quantified matter." For a survey of Aquinas' texts, as well as of those of many other authors, see M. D. Roland-Gosselin, O.P., *La 'De Ente et Essentia' de S. Thomas d'Aquin* (Paris: J. Vrin, 1948), pp. 51–134.

[90] Gilson, *Painting and Reality*, p. 47: "[The principle of individuation] merely expresses the fact that each definite portion of matter, delimited by certain dimensions, exists only once. . . . The particular piece of wood that goes into the making of one particular chair cannot enter the structure of another one."

* *Second:* "But is not matter quantified only when substantial form is present in the composite? If so, is not form the principle of individuation? Or how can substantial form somehow be genuinely necessary and yet matter remain the individuating principle?" *Answer:* Substantial form is necessarily present as conferring the specific perfection which inevitably carries along with it the generic perfection of corporeity—that by which the existent is of such a specific nature as to have extended parts outside of parts, as to have quantity as a property. In and through its proper function of specifying, then, form is also that by which a composite is of such a nature as to have extended parts outside of parts. The composite as so constituted individuates the additional perfections of life, sensitivity and rationality by receiving them in a unique way. This it can do because, by reason of the quantity, it is physically separate from and is thus other than any other composite receiving its own set of essential perfections. The intrinsic cause which is directly responsible for individuation, then, is the composite itself in that initial stage of composition—the composite as being of such a nature (whatever specifically it may be) as to have extended parts outside of parts, as to have quantity as its property. And this is what we call "quantified matter."

* *Third:* "But such an answer only suggests a new difficulty. Either those essential perfections are really distinct from one another (and then one has as many really different substantial forms as there are such perfections; thus man is no longer an intrinsic unity). Or they are solely mentally distinct (and, in that case, they are merely arbitrary disjunctions and theoretical constructs—just different synonyms for one and the same reality); if so, they cannot be real factors in causing individuation within actual existents." *Answer:* There is a third possibility: their mental distinction is not arbitrary but is such as to be objectively grounded in actual existents, as this evidence shows. Although rationality, sensitivity and the rest are only mentally distinct in this human existent, they are sources of faculties and other properties which are really distinct—for example, his intellect and will (which flow from rationality) differ really from his sense faculties (which flow from sensitivity), from his vegetative operative powers (which come from life), and so forth.[91] Again, even though such perfections are not really distinct in this man, they show themselves to be genuinely different

[91] See Ch. V, n. 29.

when those in a human being are contrasted with those in a dog, a plant, or a chemical compound. The lower perfections *are actually found to exist without the higher ones* and thus they cannot be totally identical—for instance, a dog has sensitivity but not rationality, a geranium lives but is not sentient, water has various chemical properties but is without life. Moreover, when found within one and the same nature, the higher perfections are never found without the lower (no rationality without sensitivity, no sensitivity without life, no life without an apt chemical constitution in the body), and the higher depends on the lower, which receives, affects, and influences the higher. Accordingly, although various essential perfections are only mentally distinct when considered in any one nature, that distinction is not merely constructural but has a real basis in actual existents.[92] Among these perfections the higher depends upon the lower, and in this sense the lower is to the higher as the prior to the posterior. Because of this atemporal dependence and priority, quantified matter can individuate the further essential perfections which it receives and from which it is genuinely and objectively (although mentally) distinct.

* *Fourth:* "But a problem remains. If substantial form is the source of the essential perfection of corporeity (as we indicated in the answer to the second question) and hence is the reason why matter is quantified, then form still seems to be the principle of individuation." *Answer:* This might be true were it not for the fact that prime matter is more directly the cause of corporeity and quantity than is the substantial form. True enough, quantity is a property of the composite and thus comes from both. Nonetheless, it flows more proximately from matter than from form. The latter is the proximate principle of specific perfection and properties; but "quantified body" is not a species—nothing actually exists simply as "quantified body" but always as such-and-such a body—as a hydrogenous body, a geraniaceous body, a canine body, a human body; consequently, the substantial form is not the proximate principle of body or quantity. This role must be filled by its partner-component in the nature or essence—prime matter.[93] Accordingly, quantity is a property of the composite itself and yet is more directly the result of prime matter than of form because it is a non-specific and generic perfection. Prime matter is pure potency, yes,

---

[92] It is the mental distinction we previously called "major" or "perfectly grounded"—see n. 42 and n. 74.

[93] See Ch. V, Sec. 3a.

but it is not merely a negation. It is an actually existing and hence real component, now revealing itself to be capable of more immediately causing quantity than does substantial form, provided the latter is informing it and specifying the existent. True enough, substantial form, because it is autodetermining, individuates itself through prime matter, since this latter can individuate only if it is in an existent which is specifically such-and-such, which has been formally and essentially perfected. Still, as the more direct cause of quantity prime matter performs a function which the form could itself take over only at the price of no longer being substantial form.

Such, then, is the intricate answer to the question of what causes the otherness and individuality which issues from the natures or essences of material existents. The intricacy of the solution is proportioned to the intricacy of the problem. No principle of individuation is needed at all if with Plato one says there are no individuals but only Natures, or if with Ockham and Sartre one says there are no natures but only individuals. In the first case there is only unity, in the second sheer multiplicity.[94] A principle of individuation is demanded only when unity mingles with multiplicity, when individuals share a common specific nature. Each is truly and equally human, although one is this human, the other that human. All are specifically alike, although individually different. How can these disparate characteristics arise from the single, concrete natures they have? Because that nature is itself composed of two components. Substantial form is that by which this man is human and thus specifically similar to all other humans; prime matter, because the more immediate source of quantity is that by which ultimately and substantially he is *this* man and thus is unique and singular. Embedded within the concrete and composite nature itself is the intrinsic cause not only of specific perfection, similarity and unity, but also of individuation, dissimilarity and multiplicity.

---

[94] Plato equivalently says there are no individuals by viewing them as unreal. To Ockham nature is nothing but a name, a term. Sartre explicitly eliminates natures (*Existentialism*, p. 18: "There is no human nature, since there is no God to conceive it"). Although in his interpretation individuals are alone real, theirs is a reality heading toward unreality, for they are mere series of fluid appearances, streams of chance events. See pp. 22 sqq. On Plato and Ockham, see L. Sweeney, S.J., "Existence/Essence in Aquinas' Early Writings," *Proceedings of the American Catholic Philosophical Association*, 37 (1963), pp. 110–11 (forthcoming as ch. 20 in my *Christian Philosophy*).

6. Summary and Conclusions

(a) Our intention in Chapter VI has been to reveal the primacy which the act of existing has in metaphysical knowledge. This primacy rests upon unshakable foundations: actual existence has primacy in actual existents (see Ch. V); but metaphysical knowledge is nothing more than the reaction set up in the human knower by existents precisely as existent; therefore, actual existence has primacy also in metaphysical knowledge—it should somehow (either explicitly or implicitly) enter into all discussions inaugurated by a metaphysician and into all definitions elaborated by him, where it should occupy a prominent place. He studies (and subsequently describes) all other components only in relation to the act of existing.

(b) The metaphysical definition of "being" is a clear illustration of this pre-eminence, for in its signification of "an actually existing item" it is designed to express all actuals in their *very actuality*—whether this be really other than (as in creatures) or identified with (as in God) what they are.

(c) Because it signifies all actuals in their very actuality, "being" also expresses them in their similarity and diversity, and thus is analogous. How can this be shown?

1. Actuals themselves are similar and diverse to one another; they are similar in that they do exist, but diverse in that each exists in its own way. They are, in a word, entitatively analogous.

But actuals as actuals are the content-determining-cause of our metaphysical knowledge of "being."

Therefore, the metaphysical notion of "being" as "an actually existing item" combines similarity with diversity and thus is analogous: "item" has to do with the diversity of existents since it points to what each is (and in this each differs from all else), whereas "actually existing" deals directly with their similarity because it indicates that each is (and in this they are all alike).

2. But "actually existing" also has to do with existents in their diversity, as this line of argumentation shows.

Nothing actually exists except in a determinate, concrete, unique, individual fashion, and thereby is different from all else.

Therefore, its status of actual existence is one also of diversity.

Hence, in expressing existents as "actually existing," "being" also expresses their diversity—it catches them in their very determinateness, concreteness, uniqueness, individuality.

Therefore, by designating all actuals in their actuality, "being" expresses not only their similarity but also their diversity and, thus, is analogous.[95]

(d) There are as many different kinds of analogy as there are different kinds of similarity/diversity in actuals, as well as in the ensuing knowledge they cause and in the predications they receive. Some of these are:

1. *Analogy of Eminence:* the similarity/diversity in being (as well as in consequent metaphysical knowledge and predication) between the Existent Whose very essence is to exist and an existent whose existence is really distinct from his essence.

2. *Analogy of Proportionality*: the similarity/diversity in being, knowledge and predication between existents whose actuality is really other than what they are.

3. *Analogy of reference:* the similarity/diversity in being, knowledge and predication between the components of one and the same existent.

4. *Analogy of denomination:* the similarity/diversity in being, knowledge and predication between the extramental and intentional universes.

(e) Actual existence is the basis of all analogy, and thus again reveals its primacy, as is clear from the following.

Actuals themselves are analogous because they are both similar (all do actually exist) and yet diverse (each exists in its own unique fashion).

---

[95] Another way of stating the same thing is this:

The characteristics of determinateness, concreteness, singularity, and individuality (which account for the diversity of existents) directly flow from what each is, and by expressing what each is precisely as actual, "being" expresses each in its diversity.

But the fact that something actually exists accounts also for its similarity with all other actuals.

Accordingly, by expressing actuals in their very actuality, "being" also expresses them in their similarity.

Because it deals with an actual precisely qua actual, then, "being" expresses both the diversity and the similarity within existents, and hence is analogous.

But actual existence is the source of both similarity and diversity—
immediately of similarity inasmuch as it is that by which they actually exist;
mediately of diversity inasmuch as it essentializes (and, thus, diversifies) itself through whatever essence it actualizes.

Therefore, actual existence is the chief source of analogy in actuals, as well as in the metaphysical knowledge they cause and the predication they receive, and its pre-eminence therein is manifested.

(f) That pre-eminence is also clear in metaphysical transcendents other than "being," which these merely amplify. They explicate additional aspects and consequences of actuality. "Being" stresses actual existence as the source of all reality; these emphasize its role as the source of undividedness, of otherness and independence, of intelligibility, of goodness, and of beauty.

being	an actually existing item as actual
one	an actually existing item as undivided
individual	an actually existing item as other than all else
true	an actually existing item in relation to truth
good	an actually existing item as perfect, and thus in relation to love
beautiful	an actually existing item as splendent, and thus in relation to joy and contemplation

(g) Whereas "good" is "an actually existing item as perfect, and thus in relationship to love," an evil is "an actually existing item as lacking perfection, and hence as out of step with love." If the item without due perfection is one's free choice (together with operations it directly influences), the evil is called *moral;* absences of due perfection in any other item are *physical evils*.

1. Every evil entails three factors. (a) *In itself* it is nothing but the very absence of a due perfection. (b) But it has a *subject*—the existent which is deprived of the perfection but which is composed of other perfections, and hence is good and is something positive and real. (c) It is known through *a concept or idea,* the content of which is "the absence of a due perfection," which is accordingly a construct, but which is itself an actually existing awareness within our minds and consequently is also something positive and real.

2. Since evil itself is nothing (#1a), it would seem to lie outside the primacy of actual existence. Nonetheless, that escape is only apparent, because evils require actual existents as the subjects of

which they are predicated and without which they would be impossible.[96] Consequently, the primacy of actual existence is maintained, however mysteriously and indirectly, even with regard to evil, the very privation of perfection, goodness and reality.

(h) That primacy is not merely indirect in the otherness or individuality arising from one's status as a person, or, more generally, as a supposit. Actual existence is the intrinsic cause of that very status. A supposit is the existent in its entirety, the existent as consisting of a complete nature or essence actualized by its own act of existing. The act of existing is that by which this man exists in such a way as to be independent and autonomous as a person. It is that by which he *subsists*—exists not in another, but in and thereby through and for himself.

(i) Because it is autodetermining, actual existence has primacy even in the second sort of otherness and individuality—namely, that springing from nature or essence. Prime matter is the basic principle of that individuation because it more directly causes quantity than does substantial form, which is the cause of specific perfection and properties. However, because matter can perform its own causal function only if it is within a specific nature, prime matter relies upon substantial form, which thus individuates itself through matter. But the intrinsic causality of both form and matter is dependent on that of actual existence: unless they actually exist, matter cannot quantify, form cannot specify. Consequently, by actualizing a complete essence or nature and thereby essentializing itself, the act of existing also individuates itself and also helps ground the otherness and individuality indigenous to essence and nature.

(j) This primacy which the act of existing has in supposits and natures should register in their definitions. However variously these are formulated, actual existence should have a prominent place. For example, *supposit* is "that which subsists," "that which exists in, by, through and for itself," "an existent which is independent and autonomous in the order not only of essence but also of existence itself." *Nature,* though, is "that by which an existent exists in such a way as to be independent and autonomous solely as a member of some species or other," "that by which an existent exists in an individuated fashion." The *act of existing* is "that by which an existent (immediately) subsists and is a supposit, and (mediately—through prime matter and substantial form) exists also in a substantially individuated way, as a particular member within a species."

---

[96] They also have actual existents as their extrinsic causes. On the causes of an evil, see Ch. IX below, Sec. 4.

Suggested Readings

Anderson, James F., *The Bond of Being: An Essay on Analogy and Existence.* St. Louis: B. Herder Book Co., 1949; reprinted Westport, Conn.: Greenwood Press, 1984. On the analogy of being.

———, *Metaphysics of St. Thomas Aquinas,* pp. 44–98. Chicago: Henry Regnery Co., 1953; reprinted 1969. Aquinas on the transcendents.

Augros, Robert M., and George N. Stanciu, *The New Story of Science,* ch. 3: "Beauty." Lake Bluff, Ill.: Regnery Gateway, 1984.

Bobik, Joseph, "Dimensions in the Individuation of Bodily Substances," *Philosophical Studies* (Maynooth), 4 (1954), 60–79.

———, "Matter and Individuation," in *The Concept of Matter,* ed. Ernan McMullin, pp. 277–94. University of Notre Dame Press, 1963.

———, "St. Thomas on the Individuation of Bodily Substances," in *Readings in the Philosophy of Nature,* ed. Henry J. Koren, pp. 327–40. Westminister, Md.: Newman Press, 1958.

Bourke, Vernon J., *The Pocket Aquinas,* pp. 261–82. New York: Washington Square Press, Pocket Books, Inc., 1960. Aquinas on beauty and art.

Cajetan, *Analogy of Names,* trans. E. Bushinski and H. Koren. Pittsburgh: Duquesne University Press, 1953. A sixteenth-century interpretation of Aquinas' doctrine on analogy.

De la Taille, S.J., Maurice, *The Hypostatic Union,* trans. Cyril Vollert, S.J. West Baden Springs, Ind.: West Baden College Press, 1952. On individual, nature, and supposit.

De Raeymaeker, Louis, *Philosophy of Being,* trans. E. H. Ziegelmeyer, pp. 61–69 and 212–25. St. Louis: B. Herder Book Co., 1954. On unity and distinction; on good and evil.

Eco, Umberto, *The Aesthetics of Thomas Aquinas,* trans. Hugh Bredin. Cambridge, Mass.: Harvard University Press, 1988.

Gilson, Etienne, *Elements of Christian Philosophy,* pp. 145–63. Garden City, N.Y.: Doubleday & Company, Inc., 1960. On God and the transcendents.

———, *Painting and Reality.* New York: Pantheon Books, Inc., 1957.

———, *The Spirit of Mediaeval Philosophy,* trans. A. H. C. Downes, pp. 108–27, 189–208. New York: Charles Scribner's Sons, 1940. On good and evil; on individuality, supposit, and individuation.

Gracia, Jorge J. E., *Introduction to the Problem of Individuation in the Early Middle Ages.* Washington, D.C.: The Catholic University of America Press, 1984.

Johann, S.J., Robert O., "The Problem of Love," *Review of Metaphysics,* 8 (1954), 225–45. With reference to a philosophy of subjectivity, where "to be real" is equivalent to "to be a subject."

———, "Subjectivity," *Review of Metaphysics,* 12 (1958), 200–234.

Journet, Charles, *The Meaning of Evil,* trans. Michael Barry. New York: P. J. Kenedy & Sons, 1963.

Klubertanz, S.J., George P., *St. Thomas Aquinas on Analogy,* pp. 157–293. Chicago: Loyola University Press, 1960. Useful collection of texts on analogy from Aquinas.

Kovach, Francis J., *Scholastic Challenges to Some Mediaeval and Modern Ideas.* Stillwater, Okla.: Western Publications, 1987. Essay 5: "The Transcendentality of Beauty in Thomas Aquinas," pp. 67–80; Essay 6: "Divine and Human Beauty in Duns Scotus' Philosophy and Theology," pp. 81–110; Essay 11: "The Empirical Foundations of Thomas Aquinas' Philosophy of Beauty," pp. 199–210.

Lyttkens, H., *The Analogy Between God and the World.* Stockholm: Almquist and Wiksells, 1952. One of the first authors to challenge Cajetan's interpretation of analogy in Aquinas' writings.

Maritain, Jacques, *Art and Scholasticism,* trans. F. J. Scanlon. New York: Charles Scribner's Sons, 1937. On beauty and our perception of it; on art and related questions.

———, *Creative Intuition in Art and Poetry.* New York: Pantheon Books, Inc., 1953.

———, *Existence and the Existent,* trans. Lewis Galantiere and Gerald B. Phelan, pp. 70–91. Garden City, N.Y.: Doubleday & Company, Inc., 1956 (Image Books Edition). On subject and supposit (on this latter Maritain follows Cajetan).

———, *The Person and the Common Good,* trans. J. Fitzgerald. New York: Charles Scribner's Sons, 1947; Reprinted; University of Notre Dame Press, 1966.

———, *St. Thomas and the Problem of Evil,* Aquinas Lecture, 1942. Milwaukee: Marquette University Press, 1943.

McInerny, Ralph M., *The Logic of Analogy.* The Hague: M. Nijhoff, 1961. A study made of analogy from a logician's point of view.

O'Neill, Martin S., "Some Remarks on the Analogy of God and Creatures in St. Thomas Aquinas," *Mediaeval Studies,* 23 (1961), 206–15.

Owens, Joseph, *An Elementary Christian Metaphysics,* pp. 43–67. Milwaukee: Bruce Publishing Co., 1963. On the apprehension and conceptualization of "being" (multiple references are given there to other authors).

———, "Thomistic Common Nature and Platonic Idea," *Mediaeval Studies,* 21 (1959), 211–23. Valuable study with reference to the possibles.

Pegis, A., "The Dilemma of Being and Unity," in *Essays in Thomism,* ed. R. E. Brennan, pp. 151–83. New York: Sheed & Ward, 1942.

Phelan, Gerald B., *St. Thomas and Analogy.* Milwaukee: Marquette University Press, 1941.

———, "Verum Sequitur Esse Rerum," *Mediaeval Studies,* 1 (1939), 11–22.

Reichmann, James B., "St. Thomas, Capreolus, Cajetan, and the Created Person," *The New Scholasticism,* 33 (1959), 1–31, 202–30.

Ricoeur, Paul, *The Symbolism of Evil.* New York: Harper and Row, 1967.

Salmon, Elizabeth G., *The Good in Existential Metaphysics,* Aquinas Lecture, 1952. Milwaukee: Marquette University Press, 1952.

———, "Metaphysics and Unity," in *Progress in Philosophy,* ed. James A. McWilliams, pp. 47–60. Milwaukee: Bruce Publishing Co., 1955.

Sciacca, M. F., "Individuality and Personality," in *The Human Person and the World of Values,* ed. B. V. Schwarz. New York: Fordham University Press, 1960.

Siwek, Paul, *The Philosophy of Evil.* New York: The Ronald Press Company, 1951.

Smith, Gerard, "Avicenna and the Possibles," *The New Scholasticism,* 17 (1943), 340–57.

Sweeney, S.J., Leo, "Analogy and Being," *The Modern Schoolman,* 39 (March, 1962), 261–69.

———, "Basic Principles in Plotinus' Philosophy," in *idem, Divine Infinity in Greek and Medieval Thought* [hereafter: *Divine Infinity*] (New York/ Bern: Peter Lang Publishing, Inc., 1992), ch. 11, pp. 243–56. A study of a philosophical position giving primacy to unity.

———, "Plato, Plotinus and Aristotle on the Individual," in W. J. Carroll, J. Furlong and S. Mann (eds.), *Quest for the Individual: Roots of Western Civilization* (New York/Bern: Peter Lang Publishing, Inc., 1992, pp. 35–87 (forthcoming as ch. 5 in my *Christian Philosophy: Nature, Origin, Developments* [New York/Bern: Peter Lang Publishing, Inc., 1994]).

———, "*Summa de Bono* (Codex Vaticanus Latinus 4305): An Anonymous Amalgam of Alexander of Hales, Aquinas and Bonaventure," in *Divine Infinity,* ch. 20, pp. 439–72.

Symposium: *The Principle of Individuation,* Aristotelian Society Proceedings, Suppl. Vol. 27 (1953).

Tournier, Paul, *The Meaning of Persons,* trans. Edwin Hudson. New York: Harper & Row, Publishers, 1957; reprinted 1973. On the difference between persons and things.

Wilhelmsen, Frederick D., *The Metaphysics of Love,* pp. 13–52, especially 23–24, 46–49. New York: Sheed & Ward, 1962. On supposit, nature, and individuation; against an exaggerated primacy to subject.

VII

Existence and Relations

In the light of Section 5 of the preceding chapter, existents show themselves to be independent and autonomous because of the two-fold otherness and individuality they enjoy. Each of us is "an unsurrenderable core which in the end determines everything."[1] Each is himself—unique, self-centered (literally), self-enclosed, self-reliant, resistant to what is alien, inviolable in his innermost depths, mysterious.

Nevertheless, each also is open to the outside. Each is necessarily exposed to what is without. This openness, this vulnerability is not a characteristic just of human beings but of subhumans as well. All inanimate things, plants, and animals are affected by their space-time environment.[2] All are used by others—absorbed, cooked, eaten,

---

[1] Edwin O'Connor, *Edge of Sadness* (Boston: Little, Brown & Co., 1961), p. 249. See also Virginia Woolf, *To the Lighthouse* (New York: Harcourt, Brace & World, Inc., 1927), p. 95: "*She could be herself*. And that was what now she often felt the need of—to think; well, not even to think. To be silent, to be *alone*. All the being and the doing, expansive, glittering, vocal, evaporated; and one shrunk, with a sense of solemnity to *being oneself*, a wedge-shaped core of darkness, something invisible to others." (Emphasis mine.)

[2] A science has, in fact, grown up to study just that—*ecology*, described as "the study of these interrelations of plants and animals with their environment." And what is the environment? "In referring to the natural environment one tends to think first of the broad aspects of the landscape, such as water, soil, desert, or mountain. These types of environment can be more exactly described in terms of physical influences—difference in moisture, temperature, texture of material, and the like—and of biological influences.

intussuscepted, grafted, trained, harnessed, driven, and so on. But with man it is especially clear, frequent and profound because of his knowledge and love.[3] Although remaining ourselves, we *become others* through these tremendous powers. Thereby we are affected for better or for worse. We are helped or we are hindered but, no matter what, we are influenced by them, and deeply so. And other human existents too, while continuing to be themselves, *become us* through their cognition and love, and thereby we affect them. Complex webs of interrelationships are spun, and we are caught in their powerful strands.

> Nobody has the power to leave another . . . So much to answer for! . . . All these personal relationships between men and women, between man and man, for which each one of us will, separately, have to answer. The question—"What has thou done

---

[But] other organisms form part of the environment just as much as the soil or the rocks. . . . Modern ecology goes beyond the mere description of the habitat, or the listing of its inhabitants, to an analysis of causal relationship and a coordinated understanding of constructive and destructive processes in the community" (George L. Clarke, *Elements of Ecology* [New York: John Wiley & Sons, Inc., 1954], pp. 2 and 3). Again: "Ecology is a broad field—the study of the relations of organisms with their environment. . . . It has been divided into smaller fields, including plant and animal ecology and marine and fresh-water ecology" (Allen H. Benton and William E. Werner, *Principals of Field Biology and Ecology* [New York: McGraw-Hill Book Company, 1958], p. 56). Both books give abundant examples.

Also see W. K. Brooks, "Heredity and Variation: Logical and Biological" (quoted by Benton and Werner, *ibid.*, p. 56): "Every reflective biologist must know that no living being is self-sufficient, or would be what it is, or would be at all, if it were not part of the natural world. . . . Living things are real things . . . but their reality is in their interrelations with the rest of nature, and not in themselves."

On humans, too, as subject to cosmic influences, see Pierre Teilhard de Chardin, *The Divine Milieu* (New York: Harper & Row, Publishers, 1960), pp. 27–29.

[3] E. Gilson, *The Spirit of Mediaeval Philosophy* (New York: Charles Scribner's Sons, 1940), Chs. 12–14; Robert O. Johann, *Meaning of Love* (Westminster, Md.: Newman Press, 1955); Frederick D. Wilhelmsen, *Metaphysics of Love* (New York: Sheed and Ward, 1962); Joseph de Finance, S.J., *Être et agir*, 2nd Ed. (Rome: Libraire Ed. de l'Univ. Greg., 1960), pp. 266–72, 295–312, 326–41.

with thy brother" will be asked of us as often as in the course of our existence we have influenced anybody, have exercised power over another's heart or body, have used, and abused, a body.[4]

I underwent, during the summer that I became fourteen, a prolonged religious crisis. . . . What I saw around me that summer in Harlem was what I had always seen; nothing had changed. But now without any warning, the whores and pimps and racketeers on the Avenue had become a personal menace. It had not before occurred to me that I could become one of them, but now I realized that we had been produced by the same circumstances. . . . My friends were now "downtown," busy, as they put it, "fighting the man." They began to care less about the way they looked, the way they dressed, the things they did; presently one found them in twos and threes and fours, in a hallway, sharing a jug of wine or a bottle of whiskey, talking, cursing, fighting, sometimes weeping: lost, and unable to say what it was that oppressed them, except that they knew it was "the man"—the white man. And there seemed to be no way whatever to remove this cloud that stood between them and the sun, between them and love and life and power, between them and whatever it was that they wanted.[5]

They were four and a family—the man, the woman, the small boy, the small girl, and [as with all families] there was something wrong with the whole thing, only now it was too late. In each of them there seemed to be a secret anguish about the struggle it was, everyday, to understand the others. By turns they were enchanted and perplexed, delighted and outraged, entertained and bored; and yet most of the time in the most unaccountable manner *all* of it was fun of one kind or another, or at any rate could become pleasantly memorable, as when after the stupidest fight imaginable the man and woman be-

---

[4] François Mauriac, *The Lamb* (New York: Farrar, Straus & Co., Inc., 1955), pp. 134–35.

[5] James Baldwin, "Letter From a Region in my Mind," *New Yorker*, November 17, 1962, p. 59; later published as "Down at the Cross" in *The Fire Next Time* (New York: The Dial Press, 1963), pp. 29–33.

> gan to move about in the house in silence, as if in memory of chances lost from long before they had met, and suddenly they looked at one another and each saw a total stranger but loved the stranger because now they were tangled in time and held captive by the two kids, and therefore laughed softly about it all, or hummed or sang or said strange words.[6]

The stark otherness and distinction we experience in ourselves, then, are matched by an almost total vulnerability and openness to others, which terminate in intricate skeins of countless relationships.[7]

These relations are our next topic of study. Somewhat surprisingly, perhaps, some philosophers deny their existence. They see in friendship or marriage or a family or Harlem nothing more than the mental activity of a human knower when confronted with two or more existents in a definite sort of situation. The question which ultimately awaits us, then, is whether or not a relation is itself genuinely real. Is it a perfection actually existing over and beyond the existent at which it terminates, the subject of which it is predicated, the source within the subject from which it flows? Or is it merely a name given those factors when an observer grasps them together in a single awareness?[8]

---

[6] William Saroyan, "Boys and Girls Together," *Saturday Evening Post*, January 19, 1963, p. 38.

[7] See Cassius Jackson Keyser, *Mathematics as a Culture Clue and Other Essays* (New York: Scripta Mathematica, Yeshiva University, 1947), p. 219: "Most words, perhaps all of them, denote relations either directly or indirectly. Familiar specimens are: father, mother, child, brother, sister, uncle, king, subject, citizen, inhabitant, author, above, below, in, out, greater, less, better, worse, mayor, taller, shorter, area, diameter, derivative, integral, volume, lower, sweeter, savior, president, premier, and so on and on.

"The number of relation-denoting terms is huge; yet, compared with the multitude of relations, it is exceedingly small, for most relations are nameless. . . . C. W. Wood [has said]: 'The web of reality is woven of relations, and the so-called things or individuals which the relations connect are themselves composed of relations, being, so to say, only branch-points or nodes or knots or ganglia formed by the web by the meeting and intersection.' "

[8] See the second paragraph of n. 28 for the serious consequences of this position.

1. The Relational Situation

In order to understand the problem better, let us consider various descriptions given an individual human existent.

1. "Stephen is blind."
2. "Stephen is an oak."
3. "Stephen actually is human."
4. "Stephen actually is quantified,
healthy,
a mathematician."
5. "He actually is smaller than the hoodlum lurking in the alley
and larger than his wife."
6. "He actually is more intelligent than his brother."
"He actually is similar to him as a man and as a being."
7. "He actually is a friend of Bernard,
the husband of Grace,
the father of Mary,
the teacher of eighty-nine students in geometry."
"He actually is an inhabitant of St. Louis' Harlem."
"He actually is a creature of God."

Statement #1, obviously, is negative; #2 is affirmative but figurative; #3 is affirmative, literal, and describes what he is substantially; #4 is affirmative, literal, and describes what he is accidentally. Statements #5 to #7 likewise are affirmative. They are as literally true as #3 and #4—if I affirm the opposite of them, I either am in error or I misrepresent the man in question. Like #4, they are in the accidental order, but unlike #4, they are relational—they have to do with him in reference to various other existents. The relational situations they express arise actually from various reasons—from quantity (#5), from the presence of perfection other than quantity (#6), from efficient causality (#7).[9] These reasons let us call the

[9] Actually, causality other than efficient causality is also operative in many situations. For example, there is the influence exercised upon us by the place where we live—an Iron Curtain country affected its inhabitants' attitudes, values, psychological moods, and culture differently than does Italy or France or the United States. And the same holds proportionally true of where one lives within the country—whether in a rural or urban area, in what city, in what district in the city, and so on. There is also the effect

foundation of the relation—that which grounds and causes them, that from which they flow. Their *subject* is that in which they inhere, or at least that of which they are predicated (in this case, Stephen). Their *term* is that to which the subject is referred—the hoodlum, wife, brother, student and so forth. The *relation* itself is that which is expressed by "smaller than," "similar to," "friend of," and so on—the order, the being-open-toward, the liaison between subject and term.

Let us keep such information at hand as we approach the problem.[10] Manifestly, the question of whether relations are real does not arise in situations in which the *S*, *F* and *T* (one or all of them) are only mental—for example, friendship between Snoopy and Lucy in the comic strip is no more real than are Snoopy and Lucy themselves.[11] But it does arise when those three factors do actually exist—when my acts of knowledge and love (*F*) make me (*S*) a friend (*R*) of another (*T*), when your entrance into a marriage contract (*F*) causes you (*S*) to be the husband (*R*) of Lenore (*T*), when your quantity (*F*) makes you (*S*) smaller than (*R*) the bully next door (*T*), when a young man's environment (*F*) turns him (*S*) into rebellion (*R*) against his fellow men (*T*). Does "friend of," "husband of," "smaller than," or "rebellion against" express an actually existing perfection which is over and above the *S*, *F* and *T*? If not, then the *R* is itself not genuinely real. If so, it is. For example, friendship would be the actual entitative condition of my entire person through knowledge and love toward another. It would be an accident really

---

brought about in us by the times in which we live. We who live in the High Tech Age are thereby different from those living in the Depression or in the nineteenth century, and so forth. Such causes are not efficient ones, or if they are, are greatly different from those generally encountered (the sculptor, carpenter, and so on).

[10] In subsequent pages we shall use these obvious abbreviations: *S* = subject, *F* = foundation, *T* = term, *R* = relation.

[11] Mental relations are especially important in logic (both Aristotelian and modern) and in mathematics. In the latter, a relation is defined as "the class of couples (x, y) for which some function $\Phi\ (x, y)$ is true." See Louis Kattsoff, *A Philosophy of Mathematics* (Ames: Iowa State College Press, 1948), p. 35. A class or set is in turn described as any collection into a whole, *M*, of definite distinguishable objects *m* (which will be called "elements" of *M*) of our intuition or thought.

Robert W. Schmidt, S.J., has suggested that "mental relations" be called "*rationate relations*"—see "The Translation of Terms like *Ens Rationis*," *Modern Schoolman*, 41 (November, 1963), 73–75.

distinct[12] from its *S* (me), from its *F* (operations of intellect and will), and from its *T* (the other person): it is that by which I so exist as to be orientated to another through cognition and love.

Let us consider those two answers more in detail, beginning with the affirmative one.

2. The Affirmative Reply

Although this position is commonly associated with Thomists, some modern non-Thomists also espouse it.[13] Unless I misread him, one such is John Wild. After listing those who denied the reality of relations in favor of an atomism and essentialism,[14] he explains why noetic relations must be real:

> If we drop our *a priori* prejudices as to what cognition must be, and turn to the examination of any given instance of those recurrent facts which are commonly referred to as cognitive, we shall find that they are all relational in character. Something in the knowing organism, a sensation or a concept, is related in some very intimate way to something distinct from itself. This cognitive relation is normally expressed in our language by the word *of*. All knowledge is *of* something. Take the case of tactual feeling. When I press this table there is something in my finger, the sensation or sense impression. But this is definitely not all there is. The sensation is not an isolated atom. *It is a relation to something quite distinct from itself, and quite distinct from my finger.* The sensation is of something external pressing.
>
> Now the relation and its term are not merely added on to the impression as external atomic accretions or inferences.

[12] This distinction would, of course, be a real minor one because the relationship is a component, an accident. See Ch. IV, prgr. corresponding to n. 28.

[13] For an excellent survey of nonscholastics on relation, see C. Kossel, S.J., "The Problem of Relation in Some Nonscholastic Philosophies," *Modern Schoolman*, 23 (1946), 61–81.

[14] John Wild, "A Realistic Defense of Causal Efficacy," *Review of Metaphysics*, 2 (June, 1949), 1–9, especially 4–5. In his list he names Antisthenes, Nicolaus of Autrecourt, Ockham, Descartes and Hume. Wild is concerned with relations in the following three areas: human knowledge, efficient causation and logical inference.

> They are essential parts of the complex, initial datum which cannot occur without them. I cannot touch without touching *something*. Nor does the relation succeed the impression in time. *They occur all together and simultaneously, as the foundation, the relation, and the term of any relation occur all at once and simultaneously, as distinct but inseparable aspects of one composite structure.*[15]

He ends by urging philosophers to put off their *a priori* atomism and to acknowledge the real relations which actual existents reveal so strikingly.

> This false assumption [that every part of a whole must ultimately be an atomistic globule, merely juxtaposed with the rest] has been laming and distorting our analysis, and blinding it to the rich relational structure of reality, especially its causal dependence. Why not free our analytic methodology from the shackles that chain it to the prejudices of an *a priori* atomism trying to disguise itself as an empiricism? Experience fairly flaunts her complex relational structure before our eyes with little or no concealment. We cannot express ourselves intelligibly or scientifically without recognizing this in the very form of our expressions. Why not then sharpen up our tools of analysis, and refine them? Why not a truly empirical and relational mode of analysis?[16]

However infrequent this acknowledgement may be elsewhere, it is rather common among contemporary Thomists. Aquinas himself leads the way and even indicates the methodology to be followed. "Are names implying relations to creatures [for example, 'Creator,' 'Lord'] predicated of God temporally?" he asked early in the *Summa Theologiae*.[17] After answering affirmatively, he states: "In order to see this we must realize that some have held relation is not something real but only mental. This position is plainly seen to be false

---

[15] *Ibid.*, pp. 5–6. (Emphasis mine.)

[16] *Ibid.*, p. 14. Also see *idem*, *Introduction to Realistic Philosophy* (New York: Harper & Row, Publishers, 1948), pp. 347–51. (After ca. 1958 Wild moved from realism to phenomenology. Perhaps this move affected his position on relations, too.)

[17] *Summa Theologiae*, I, 13, 7.

from the very fact that things themselves have a natural ordering and reference to one another." By opposing that false opinion Thomas shows his own hand, and this in strong Latin. A relation is not a mere thing of the mind (*res rationis tantum*), but is itself a thing of nature (*res naturae*)—an accidental perfection actually existing in things. And the methodology by which to proceed? Simply observe the actual ordering, reference, openness, liaison to be found among existents themselves.[18]

However little some of those who call themselves Thomist may have followed an inductive procedure in other areas, still down through the centuries and up to the present day many conclude with him that friendship, marriage, family, larger than, and the like are accidents really other than the *S, F* and *T*.[19] Let us quote one of the most prominent:

> Two sugar cubes, in their real being, are equal to each other regardless of any consideration by the human mind. If they are both white, moreover, they are like each other in color without the human intellect's help. They are therefore related to each other in reality as equal and as similar. Their equality and similarity are accordingly real relations. Real relations, of course, add no absolute reality to their subject, but they do add relative reality. They make the subject really related to something else, as the cubes are really equal to each other and really like each other in color. . . . Because it is a referring, a relation requires a subject, ground, and term. As a real accident, it is really distinct from its own being as well as from its

---

[18] "Ad cuius evidentiam sciendum est quod quidam posuerunt relationem non esse rem naturae sed rationis tantum. Quod quidem apparet esse falsum ex hoc quod ipsae res naturalem ordinem et habitudinem habent ad invicem." Also see *De Potentia*, 7, 9 resp. For a list and exegesis of Thomas' texts, see A. Krempel, *La doctrine de la relation chez saint Thomas: Exposé historique et systématique* (Paris: J. Vrin, 1952); William J. Kane, *Philosophy of Relation in the Metaphysics of St. Thomas* (Washington, D.C.: Catholic University Press, 1958); C. Kossel, S.J., "Principles of St. Thomas' Distinction Between the *Esse* and *Ratio* of Relation," *Modern Schoolman*, 24 (November, 1946 and January, 1947), 19–36 and 93–107; *idem*, "St. Thomas' Theory of the Causes of Relation," *ibid.*, 25 (March, 1948), 151–72.

[19] For a historical survey of positions within scholasticism on relations, see A. Krempel, *op. cit.*, especially pp. 179–79 and 245–71. On Scotus, see *ibid.*, pp. 249 sqq. and 270.

subject, and its being is really distinct from the being of the substance in which it inheres.[20]

How can we establish this affirmative answer? What reasons can be offered to show that it is true?

First of all, how do we know other accidents? How are we sure that an operative habit such as mathematics, acts of free choice, a musical talent, good health, color, and so on actually exist within us? By direct experience of ourselves and others in the concrete circumstances of our day-by-day lives. We are directly aware that now we are working quantitative problems with facility and accuracy, that now we are freely choosing to turn from such problems to study metaphysics, that now we are strumming a tune on a guitar, and so on. In those direct awarenesses we realize that such accidental perfections exist within us and hence are real, we realize what they are (within sufficiently exact limits) and we are aware that they are really other than one another.[21]

The same hold true for relations. In the give-and-take of daily life we experience the actual order, reference, being-orientated-to, dependence-upon, openness-to between ourselves and others.[22] I am directly aware of the bond (as well as of consequent duties and rights) I have to my parents and you have to yours;[23] of the orienta-

---

[20] Joseph Owens, C.Ss.R., *An Elementary Christian Metaphysics* (Milwaukee: Bruce Publishing Co., 1963), pp. 180 and 189. Other authors in this group include Henry J. Koren, *An Introduction to the Science of Metaphysics* (St. Louis: B. Herder Book Co., 1955), pp. 216–26; Charles A. Hart, *Thomistic Metaphysics* (Englewood Cliffs, N.J.: Prentice-Hall, Inc., 1959), pp. 232–39; P. B. Grenet, *Ontologie* (Paris: Beauchesne, 1959), pp. 114–23; Maurice Holloway, *Introduction to Natural Theology*, pp. 350–52 and 360–61; John A. Peters, *Metaphysics* (Pittsburgh: Duquesne University Press, 1963), pp. 382–86.

[21] These realizations are, of course, intellection upon data supplied by the immediate awarenesses. No accident, technically understood, is itself directly perceived. See Ch. III, prgrs. corresponding to n. 14. What is said there also applies to relations.

[22] This is, after all, Thomas' advice. See n. 18.

[23] Filiation is quite complex. It can be viewed as springing solely from the act of reproduction or, secondly, from that act plus the knowledge and love between parents and child. When does it cease? In the first interpretation, when the offspring has physically developed to a certain stage, as is especially evident on the subhuman level: at a definite point of time the female of various species rebuffs her offspring and physically separates from them. In the second interpretation, filiation ceases when knowledge and (especially) love have broken down. Of course the *R* may also disappear when the mother

tion of my very being to Christ by my status as a religious;[24] of a liaison with my fellow humans because of my priesthood and with these students because I am their teacher; of my openness toward and communion with a certain person because of the love of friendship. That bond, orientation, openness are relations; and thus in directly perceiving them we understand that relations do exist within us as accidental perfections (and hence are real) and that they are really other than the subject which they perfect, the activity from which they result, and the terms at which they point.

Some may say, "Granted that we are directly aware of such situations. Still their real constituents are *S*, *F* and *T* and nothing more. For example, the son-parent complex is equivalent really to the fact that you (*S*) have been begotten (*F*) by this man and woman (*T*). It is adequately explained by those three factors alone." I must disagree. Something more is entailed and experienced in such situations. My sonship is not the mere fact that I have been produced by such parents, but the actual ordering to and dependence upon them which are consequent upon that production. My status as a religious is not merely the fact that I have pronounced vows at such-and-such a date, but the ensuing actual condition of belonging to God, of being oriented-toward and dedicated to Him. Your state of husbandhood is not solely the fact that at a definite point of time you freely exchanged marriage vows with your bride, but the resultant ontic conditioning of yourself, body and soul, by which you belong to her and are orientated toward her. Your being bigger than she is not merely the fact that you both have quantity, but also the actual physical, comparative status we express by "bigger than." Such ordering, dependence, belonging to, dedication, reference, orientation or openness are entitative: they are there whether we think of them or not. The mind does not construct them but only recognizes them for what they actually are.

* A second way of substantiating this position is the following inference.[25]

---

or father dies. See G. Marcel, *Mystery of Being*, Vol. One: *Reflection and Mystery* (Chicago: Henry Regnery, 1960), pp. 242–49.

[24] Each one must dwell upon and utilize the unique orderings and references which personally affect him or her.

[25] This process seems especially helpful with respect to quantitative and other relational situations where the actual ordering and reference are not so vividly experienced. When I meet an enormous stranger in a dark alley and realize that I am smaller than he, my experience of "smaller than" is sufficiently vivid. But in less perilous circumstances my awareness of such orderings based on quantity is more subdued.

Actually existing items are the content-determining-causes of our immediate knowledge and predication.
But one may validly move from effect to cause.
Therefore, we may validly go from our immediate knowledge and statements to actually existing items.
But we have direct, perceptual knowledge issuing
not only into these affirmative, literal statements:
[4] "Stephen actually is quantified, healthy, thinking, freely choosing, a mathematician,"
but also into these equally affirmative and literal statements:
[5] "Stephen actually is smaller than the hoodlum and larger than his wife"
[6] "He actually is similar to his brother in intelligence and in being"
[7] "He actually is a friend of Bernard, the husband of Grace, the father of Mary, the teacher of certain students, a member of St. Matthew's Parish, and so forth."
Therefore, among actually existing items are to be counted
not only quantity, entitative and operative habits, other qualities, various activities;
but also smaller than, greater than, similar to, friend of, husband of, and the other accidental perfections we call "relations."

* Through the direct perception and statements they cause, then, existents show themselves to possess not only such accidents as quantity, various qualities, and operations (all of which are really distinct from one another), but also *relational accidents*, which also are distinct from one another, from other accidents and from the subject which they perfect and in which they inhere. Such immediate awarenesses and statements are nothing more than those actually existing accidents (relational and otherwise) as intentionally representing themselves within the human knower.

3. The Negative Reply

There is another view on relations, though. Some have denied to them any reality other than that of their *S*, *F* and *T*. They can be

In the inference the number in brackets refer to the statements as previously listed in Section 1, "The Relational Situation."

called real only because those three factors do actually exist. The relation itself is, at best, the mental activity stimulated by the *S*, *F* and *T* situation. When a human knower observes that Stephen (*S*) loves (*F*) someone (*T*), he affirms that Stephen is a friend of the other. But "friend of" expresses no unique ontic condition or status within him. When contrasted with the *S*, *F* and *T*, friendship is "an abstraction, the work of the intelligence,"[26] "a product of our mental comparison of subject with term,"[27] a construct imposed by the mind upon the *S-F-T* complex.[28] The same holds true for all other so-called real relations.[29]

Historically, those upholding this negative position have mainly been essentialists, especially those in the Suarezian tradition.[30] Recently, though, some Thomists have made the same denial. One such is the prominent British author, Denis J. B. Hawkins, who ends his chapter on relations with this paragraph:

> It seems that there are three questions which we can ask about the reality of relations and to which the answers are as follows. Are there real relations? Yes, relatedness is as much a feature of the real world as terms in relation; the world is presented to us as an interconnected whole from which terms and their relations have to be analytically distinguished. Are relations ever the source of new reality? Yes, that is precisely

---

[26] Fernand Van Steenberghen in the passage cited in n. 32.

[27] P. Coffey in the passage cited in n. 36.

[28] George P. Klubertanz, S.J., *Introduction to Philosophy of Being*, p. 315: "In metaphysics itself, we deal with pure intelligibilities; this is especially true in the case of the predicaments. For example, *relation* as a form is a construct."

This author is perfectly correct in describing relations as constructs if they are not in themselves anything real beyond their *S*, *F* and *T*. But one must also face the result of this description: whatever is relational (for example, the family, the state, the Mystical Body of Christ, morality, analogy) would be, *of and in itself*, also constructural. On constructs, see Ch. VI, n. 10.

[29] Therefore, "spouse of," "son or daughter of," "parents of," "smaller than," "similar to," and so on are likewise abstractions, mental products, constructs.

We should recall that "real" here means those relations which are contrasted with the *purely* conceptual or rational kind, as well as those in logic and mathematics. In all of these *S*, *F* and *T* are intramental. See n. 11.

[30] On Suarez and his followers, see Krempel, *op. cit.*, pp. 253–54. Albert the Great, together with early Dominicans he influenced, is also a fellow traveler of Suarez (*ibid.*, p. 248 sq.), as well as Ockham and other nominalists (*ibid.*, p. 172 sq. and p. 245), together with John of St. Thomas (*ibid.*, p. 253).

> the nature of the orginative type of relation, and, wherever we find a relation which gives rise to novelty, we should look for the originative relation or relations involved in it. Are the relations which we discover in the world of experience ever really distinct from the terms which they relate? No, for to say so would be to convert relations into pseudo-absolutes; they are logically distinct aspects of the things in their togetherness.[31]

Across the Channel his Belgian counterpart, Fernand Van Steenberghen, is of the same opinion.

> The scholastics asked whether there were *real* predicamental relations, that is, relations which would constitute *real accidents,* distinct from the two related subjects. Such entities, however, are superfluous. The relation as such is an abstraction, the work of the intelligence. It is real when it rests upon real foundations. Thus the relation of filiation between a son and his father is real, because this son was actually begotten by this father. It is based upon a real biological activity, of which the father is the principle and the son is the result.[32]

But many of those taking this negative view have been Suarezian essentialists. Let us take as representative of them P. Coffey, who is the author of a once widely used textbook, *Ontology or the Theory of Being: An Introduction to General Metaphysics,* and who acknowledges that his greatest intellectual debt is to two nineteenth-century Suarezians, Urraburu and Kleutgen.[33] His long chapter on relations (pp. 332–56) consists of six sections, two of which are especially pertinent to us. In the first (pp. 341–43) he defines a real relation.

> A real relation is *one which is not a mere product of thought, but which obtains between real things independently of our thought.* For a real relation there must be (a) a *real, individual subject;* (b) a

---

[31] D. J. B. Hawkins, *Being and Becoming* (New York: Sheed & Ward, 1954), pp. 71–72.

[32] Fernand Van Steenberghen, *Ontology* (New York: Joseph F. Wagner, Inc., Publishers, 1952), pp. 252–53. Also see L. de Raeymaeker, *Philosophy of Being,* p. 202; G. P. Klubertanz, S.J., *op. cit.*, 269–76.

[33] (London: Longmans, Green & Company, Ltd., 1918); his acknowledgement to Urraburu and Kleutgen, p. viii.

> *real foundation;* and (c) a *real, individual term,* really distinct from the subject.[34]

He then proceeds to vindicate its existence against "the specious sophistries of . . . Subjective Idealism" by emphasizing that at least some relations "are not merely logical, are not a mere product of our thought." In the second section (pp. 349–56), he faces this question. Precisely in what sense are those relations real? Do such predicamental relations embody "any mode of real being adequately distinct from those modes which constitute the other categories"?

> Considered adequately, the predicamental relation adds to the reality it has in its foundation the *actual reference* of subject to term. In fact, it is in this reference of subject to term, this *"esse ad,"* that the relation *formally* consists. The question therefore may be stated thus: Is this formal relation of subject to term, this *"esse ad,"* a real entity *sui generis,* really distinct from the absolute entities of subject, term, and foundation, and in contradistinction to these and all absolute entities a "relative entity," actually existing in the real universe independently of our thought? Or is it, on the contrary, itself formally a mere product of our thought, a product of the mental act of comparison, an *ens rationis,* an aspect superadded by our minds to the extremes compared, and to the foundation in virtue of which we compare them?[35]

The question could hardly be formulated more clearly, and Coffey's reply is just as lucid. Although "a good many scholastics . . . have espoused the former alternative," still he personally agrees with

> the great majority of scholastics [who] espouse the second alternative: that the relation, considered *formally, "secundum esse ad,"* is a product of our mental comparison of subject with

---

[34] *Ibid.*, p. 341. Relation is not a *mere* product of thought, as it will turn out, because of the real *S, F* and *T*. The *R itself,* though, is a product of thought.

[35] *Ibid.*, p. 349. In the phrase "actual reference," the adjective is to be understood as equivalent to "mental," as is clear from the text cited in the next note: the actual reference is "a product of our mental comparison of subject with term. It is not itself a real entity or a real mode, superadded to the reality of extremes and foundation."

> term. It is not itself a real entity or a real mode, superadded to the reality of extremes and foundation.[36]

And his reasons?

> In the first place there is no need to suppose the reality of such a relative entity. *Entia non sunt multiplicanda praeter necessitatem.* It is an abuse of realism to suppose that the formal element of a relation, its "*esse ad*," is a distinct and separate reality. The reality of the predicamental relation is safeguarded without any such postulate. Since the predicamental relation, considered *adequately*, i.e., not merely formally but fundamentally, not merely *secundum esse ad* but *secundum esse in*, involves as its foundation an absolute accident which is real independently of our thought, the predicamental relation is not a mere *ens rationis*. It has a foundation in reality. It is an *ens rationis cum fundamento in re*. This is a sufficient counter-assertion to Idealism, and a sufficient reason for treating relation as a distinct category of real being. . . . In the second place, if a subject can acquire a relation, or lose a relation *without undergoing any real change*, then the relation considered formally as such, or *secundum "esse ad,"* cannot be a reality.[37]

We have quoted from Coffey rather extensively because he states the negative, essentialist position so lucidly. Moreover, the reasons he lists for maintaining it provide a transition to our next consideration. Why do philosophers hold this view? What arguments do they offer?

In his second reason Coffey gives an important clue: ". . . the relation considered formally as such . . . *cannot be* a reality."[38] One of the basic convictions that influences them is that it is *impossible and unintelligible* for a relation to be itself a real perfection distinct from *S*, *F* and *T*.

> There are thousands of eggs in existence, all of which are like each other. When a new egg is laid, all the other eggs are now

---

[36] *Ibid.*, p. 352.

[37] *Ibid.*, pp. 352–53.

[38] We shall consider Coffey's first reason in the next section, "The Predicaments." Emphasis has been added to the quotation taken from the second reason.

> similar to it. How many relations of similarity does each egg have? It seems *foolish* to say that there are thousands of perfectly similar accidents in each egg, differing only in their term, and it is *impossible* to say that there is a general relation of similarity, because a general relation is abstract and cannot be found in the real order, but only in a mind. *These absurdities and impossibilities* should be enough to show us that the question has been wrongly understood.[39]

In what does this impossibility, absurdity, contradiction consist? In at least two points: first, a relation so conceived would have to be a form, and, second, would be almost totally influenced by its term. Let us consider each separately.[40]

If a relation were an actually existing accident really other than its *S*, *F* and *T*, then, it would necessarily be a *form*.

> Relation is understood as a kind of form which is between two beings, and joins or unites them like a bridge or a rope.[41]

> If the "*esse ad*" were a separate real entity, a relative entity, really distinct from extremes and foundation, what sort of entity could it be? Being an accident, it should inhere in, or be a mode of its subject.[42]

But its being a form or, what amounts to the same, an intrinsic mode of a subject, puts a relation in an embarrassing predicament.

---

[39] G. Klubertanz, S.J., *op. cit.*, p. 271. Interestingly enough, Owens finds no trouble with a similar situation in sugar cubes: see text cited in n. 20.

[40] Each consideration will proceed as follows: first, the explanation given by those holding this negative view, followed by my own comments and evaluation.

[41] Klubertanz, *op. cit.*, p. 273. Also see G. Smith and L. Kendzierski, *op. cit.*, p. 278: "As referred to George's, John's size 'stretches' towards George's, and this 'stretch' is precisely an *esse ad*, a new category of accident, a relation. A relation is thus a sort of 'in-between' being, in between an accidented subject and its correlative, a sort of metaphysical antenna by which John's size 'feels' George's (this 'feeling' is the *esse ad*), and by which even *before* John's size 'feels' George's it is all set *(esse in)* to do the 'feeling' without the slightest change in John's size, even when it 'feels' differently, that is, even when John's size is differently related to George's."

[42] Coffey, *op. cit.*, pp. 352–53. An inherent, absolute mode is the same as form, as is clear from the context.

A form is an inward-looking, self-enclosing modification of a subject, but by a relation a subject goes out and opens up to what is without. As a form, then, either a relation would no longer be relational or it would simultaneously be inward-outward and shut-open.

> [But if a relation were a form,] it would lose its formally relative character by becoming an inherent mode of an absolute character. While to conceive it as an entity astride on both extremes, and bridging or connecting these together, would be to substitute the crude imagery of the imagination for intellectual thought.[43]

In view of such patent contradictions and impossibilities, one must conclude (they say) that a relation is nothing real in itself, but is only the mental reaction set up in a human knower by a *S, F* and *T* complex.

What can be said by way of *comment*? All must readily sympathize with Coffey's aversion to substituting "the crude imagery of the imagination for intellectual thought." To conceive of relation as a bridge, rope, antenna, and so on is not to think but to imagine, and no philosophical problem can be decided by the imagination. If it proves to be a real accident, a relation is a *component*, a *that by which*, and accordingly can no more be accurately known through imagination or even through mere direct perception than can any of the other accidents.[44]

But to judge that a relation, if real, must be a form is, we admit, entirely consistent with essentialism. They say that to be real is to be intelligible and thereby also to be form, because intelligibility accrues to a thing from its form. This equivalence between form

---

[43] *Ibid.*

[44] See n. 21. See H. Koren, *An Introduction to the Science of Metaphysics*, p. 223: "How can we represent such things [entities having nothing absolute and merely pointing to something else] in our mind? As a kind of gossamer web linking every creature to all other creatures by innumerous threads, possessing a higher degree of elasticity than the best grade of bubble gum, so that they can stretch and shrink with every move of every correlated being without becoming hopelessly entangled in one another? The answer is that we should beware of using our imagination in metaphysical problems. Just as any effort to imagine what potency and act, essence and 'to be,' substance and accident, look like if taken by themselves can end only in disaster, so also any effort to draw a mental picture of real relations."

and reality determines the rest of their metaphysics. If real, prime matter must itself have a form or act, however imperfect, and thus is not pure potency.[45] Actual existence (*esse*) cannot be a real component, because if real it would have to be a form, and what function would it perform when added as another form to a human soul or to any other substantial form? A relation too, if it is to be real for an essentialist, must also be a form, but then the patent absurdities and contradictions already alluded to would arise.

But having granted that consistency, what can we say? The equivalence between reality and form vanishes in an authentic existentialism, where to be real is to be actually existing. Thus relations can be real (they actually exist), can be accidents (they perfect the *S* in which they inhere), and still need not be accidental *forms*. There are, then, various components which are real (because actually existing) but which are not forms—for example, the act of existing itself, prime matter, our operations,[46] as well as various relationships. Of course, some components are forms (for example, human soul and other substantial forms; such accidents as color, operative habits, intelligible and sensible species), although they are real not because they are forms but because they actually exist. In our existentialism, what is a *form*? By contrasting the various components just listed as forms with those which are nonforms, we arrive at this description: strictly speaking, a form is that [a] by which a subject or recipient is perfected [b] within the essence [c] in a quiescent [d] and totally intrinsic way.[47]

---

[45] See C. Frick, S.J., *Ontologia*, p. 45; T. Pesch, S.J., *Institutiones Philosophiae Naturalis* (Friburgi Brisgoviae: Herder & Co., 1880), pp. 241–43 (Pesch there gives prime matter both an *essential* and an *existential* act of its own).

[46] Operations are dynamic actuations of our operative powers, and thus seem to be so different from accidents which are obviously forms (for example, color, intelligible and sensible species, operative habits, and so forth) as to be nonforms. In the parenthesis, "intelligible and sensible species" is Thomas Aquinas' language for what is better described as "the entitative actuations which knowledge entails"—see Ch. X below, prgrs. corresponding to notes 22–23, and *idem*, "Preller and Aquinas: Second Thoughts" in *Christian Philosophy: Nature, Origin, Developments* (New York/Bern: Peter Lang Publishing, Inc., 1994), ch. 22.

[47] Because of the words in #a, prime matter is not a form: it is itself a subject or recipient. The words in #b eliminate the act of existing, which is other than and hence outside the essence; #c eliminates operations, which are dynamic actuations (see n. 46); #d excludes relations.

In view of that definition friendship, fatherhood, similarity, smaller than, and other relations are not accidental forms: even though each is that by which a subject is perfected within the essence in a quiescent way, still they do not perfect it in a *totally* intrinsic fashion. True, they do inhere in, and thus perfect, the subject (hence, they have an intrinsic side), but their unique nature is to orientate, refer and open up the subject to what is without. In Aquinas' excellent language: *Forma ponit aliquid sed relatio ponit ad aliquid* ("A form places a 'something' but a relation places a 'to something'").[48] Hence, they are real because they do actually exist. They are accidents because they are individual perfections of the substance in which they inhere. Yet they are not accidental forms and, accordingly, we rather easily escape the absurdity and impossibility their reality might entail in an essentialistic conception.

Let us move on the second point which the proponents of this negative position see as a cause of unintelligibility and impossibility: a relation, if a real perfection distinct from *S*, *F* and *T*, would be almost entirely dominated by its term. For example, [1] an *S* acquires an *R* solely because of changes in the *T*.[49]

> A child already born is neither larger nor smaller than its brother who will be born two years hence. But after the birth of the latter child the former can acquire those relations successively *without any real change in itself,* and merely by the growth of the younger child. Again, one white ball *A* is similar in color to another white ball, *B*. Paint the latter black, and *eo ipso* the former loses its relation of resemblance *without any real change in itself*.[50]

> One white page of paper is *like* another, but if the other turns brown with age, the white page is *unlike* the brown one. The white page has changed from like to unlike without any cause influencing the white page. How can this be?[51]

---

[48] See *In I Sent.*, d. 20, q. 1, a. 1 sol. (Mandonnet Ed., p. 504); *ibid.*, d. 26, q. 2, a. 1 sol., p. 630; *ibid.*, d. 30, q. 1, a. 1 sol., p. 702; *Quodl.*, IX, 2, 3, resp. (Marietti Ed., p. 182); *S.T.*, I, 28, 1 resp.

[49] Numbers in brackets are affixed to sentences in the paragraph for easy reference in my subsequent comment.

[50] Coffey, *Ontology or the Theory of Being: An Introduction to a General Metaphysics*, p. 353.

[51] Klubertanz, *op. cit.*, p. 271.

[2] Again, an *S* loses an *R* when its *T* disappears: the paternity which a man acquires by an act of reproduction is lost when the offspring dies. [3] Moreover, multiple relations arise from a single *F* because of the multiplicity of terms: in this man one and the same quantity grounds the triple relations of smaller than, equal to, larger than when he is referred to his father, twin, and wife. [4] This last example discloses even further complications, because by reason of that same quantity he is smaller than, equal to, and greater than *many other men* (to say nothing of trees, various animals, buildings, machines, and so forth). How many relations of smaller than, equality, greater than does he have? If there were as many relations as there are terms, they would be infinitely numerous.[52]

In view of such difficulties, how much simpler and more intelligible to withdraw from relations any reality which would be distinct from their *S*, *F* and *T* and to affirm that the relations *are* those factors as grasped together by the mind in a single awareness? Such is, in fact, precisely what the upholders of the negative view do.

Comment: Although offering matter for serious consideration, such examples also provide an opportunity for further clarifying the affirmative side. Let us briefly take them up one by one.

[1] First, when a new *R* is produced by a change in the *T*, the *S* also changes: it acquires a new accidental perfection—that of the *R*, which comes to inhere in it and which perfects it by ordering it to another. Of course, it does not change absolutely or formally, as the *T* does by increasing in quantity or by acquiring a different color. Second, such examples reveal that the *T* genuinely helps cause the *R*. What sort of cause is it? It appears to fit into none of the Aristotelian classification of causes (efficient, final, exemplary, formal, material), which should, then, be enlarged to cover this new evidence. We might aptly call it a *"presential* cause"—*by its very presence* the *T* brings the *R* into existence. The *F* is an "emanative cause" of the same *R*, which emanates or flows forth from the quantity or quality in the *S*.[53]

---

[52] A man having several children would offer a similar problem (although not because of the multiple terms so much as because of the multiple foundations: the individual acts of generation which produced the children): does he have several relations of paternity? Similarly, how many relations does a teacher instructing sixty-five students have?

[53] On emanative cause, see Ch. V, prgr. corresponding to n. 32. Also see n. 9 above for a list of causes which overlap or even escape Aristotle's list. Moreover, the physical universe offers several cases of causality which are

[2] If a *T* is truly a cause of an *R*, there is nothing strange about the latter vanishing when the former disappears. The *T*, which causes the *R* by its presence, is no longer present, and hence is no longer causing the *R*, which the *S* thus loses.

[3] The fact that many terms produce many relations from one *F* is not surprising in view of the fact that the *T* is a *presential* cause of the *R* and in view of what quantity is. Although a quantitative continuum such as a man is a unity, the very nature of quantity is such as to have extended parts outside of parts and to be potentially multiple.[54] Because of this it can do what it shows itself actually to be doing: when helped by several terms, it grounds several relations.

[4] Finally, no matter how many terms there may be, an individual existent has only three quantitative relations (smaller than, equal to, greater than), each of which however has multiple "respects" insofar as each "looks toward" (the literal force of *respicere*, from which *respectus* is derived) its multiple terms. The multiple "lookings-toward" of each *R* are its "respects."[55] Take the actually existing relation of "smaller than" in this man. In him it is his entitative condition of actually having such "respects" to *A*, *B*, *C*,

---

accepted as facts but which still have no adequate explanation—gravity, extrasensory perception (ESP), magnetic forces, dowsing, and so forth. One attitude toward such instances is to deny that they can be causes because they do not fit traditional categories of causes. Another is to grant the fact that they *are* causes and then enlarge the categories and explanation to include these newly discovered instances of causality.

[54] Not only is quantity potentially multiple, but it is also virtually and (in a literal sense) radically (*in radice*) related before the terms exercise their causality. See Aquinas, *In V Phys.*, lect. 3 (Leonine Ed., no. 8): "If someone through change in himself [*T*] becomes my size, while I undergo no change [in quantity], this equality was somehow in me beforehand, that is, in its root, from which it has real being" (*ista aequalitas primo erat in me quodammodo sicut in sua radice*). For an exegesis, see Kossel, "St. Thomas' Theory of the Causes of Relation," *Modern Schoolman*, 25 (March, 1948), 158.

[55] "Respects" translates Thomas' *respectus*—for example, see *Quodl.*, I, 2, 1, p. 3: "Propter unam enim quantitatem est in uno corpore una aequalitas tantum, *quamvis sint respectus plures,* secundum quod diversis corporibus dicitur esse aequale. Si autem secundum omnes illos respectus multiplicarentur realiter relationes in uno corpore, sequeretur quod in uno essent accidentia infinita vel indeterminata." Other English equivalents would be "exposures" or "facets."

One should note that at times Thomas identifies *respectus* with the relation itself—see *In I Sent.*, d. 33, q. 1, a. 1 sol., p. 765; *In III Phys.*, lect. 5, no. 618; *S.T.*, I, 28, 1 resp.; *ibid.*, a. 2 resp.; *ibid.*, a. 3 resp.

and so on. It is no general, abstract relation,[56] but one which is definite and concrete because it inheres in and perfects a particular *S*. Someone observing it in reference to those terms recognizes those "lookings-toward" and applies them now to this, now to that term by saying, "He actually is smaller than *A*, than *B*, than *C*, than *D*. . . ." Those objective "lookings-toward," now recognized and applied by an observer, are its "respects," which are as many as there are terms. The same can be said of equality and greater than.[57]

Such, then, is at least one basic reason why some philosophers withhold from relation any reality which would be other than that of its *S*, *F* and *T*: conferment of such reality is impossible, absurd, unintelligible, contradictory. Why so? Because an *R*, if real in itself, would have to be a form, an inherent and absolute mode of a subject and, second, would be under the complete domination of its term. Such an approach appears to square best with a radical essentialism, where intelligibility is the criterion of reality and where philosophy keeps itself protected from the actual universe. But whether or not relations are real is not only a question concerning such innocuous things as eggs and balls and pieces of paper. It has also to do with marriage and family and friendship and slums and religion. If a philosopher should say to a lover or a husband or a mother or an African-American, "The relationships which give you your name and make you what you are are themselves only abstractions, mental comparison, constructs," he might well have Hamlet's words addressed to him: "There are more things in heaven and earth/Than are dreamt of in your philosophy."

In his approach the authentic existentialist tries to listen to those things of heaven and earth and then simply records what he hears.[58]

---

[56] See Klubertanz, *op. cit.*, p. 271: "It is impossible to say that there is a general relation . . . because a general relation is abstract and cannot be found in the real order but only in a mind."

[57] The same explanation answers the problem of a father and his several children or of a teacher and his numerous students (see n. 52)—a single *R* with several or even numerous "respects." See Owens, *An Elementary Christian Metaphysics*, p. 184, n. 19.

One should remember that the sole function of the mind observing a relational situation with many terms is to recognize and apply (not to construct) the multiple "respects" of the single *R* which are actually there.

[58] Proponents of the negative view also offer another reason why it should be accepted: it does (for them) adequate justice to actual relation situations. We have already seen this reason as an objection to the affirmative view—see prgr. immediately after the prgrs. corresponding to notes 22–24 above.

4. The Predicaments

Before formulating the conclusions which the previous sections warrant, we must briefly turn to the predicaments. This necessity arises from the powerful role some authors offer them when deciding the fate of relations. According to Coffey, relation "is a product of our mental comparison of subject with term" and "is not itself a real entity" because "there is no need to suppose the reality of such a relative entity." Why not? Precisely because "the reality of the predicamental relation is safeguarded without any such postulate."[59] And what is predicamental relation? It is a concept, an intelligibility: although "it is not a mere *ens rationis*," nonetheless "it is an *ens rationis cum fundamento in re*."[60] As long, then, as the predicament, the concept, the genus of relation is saved, nothing else really matters. In such a perspective, relation has little chance of gaining a hearing for itself as an actual perfection.

Or consider Klubertanz, who apparently proposes moving from the predicaments to existents as the proper methodology for evaluating the nature of relations. First comes a general remark:

> [1] When we consider substance and accident as principles *by* which something has *esse* in itself and *by* which something is modified, we are trying to understand them according to the manner in which things exist. Such an understanding is difficult and roundabout—a fact which is manifested by the awkward circumlocutions necessary to express it. On the other hand, it is very easy to understand and deal with these principles when they are *conceived as things;* in other words, it is easy to deal with the principles of things *by means of intelligibilities*. When we classify these intelligibilities according to what they represent, we have the predicaments. The predicaments, therefore, are *conceived in the manner proper to the human understanding*.[61]

---

[59] *Op. cit.*, p. 212. What he says immediately thereafter shows that he is primarily interested in the *category* of *R* (p. 212): "[*R* as an *ens rationis cum fundamento in re*] is a sufficient reason for treating relation as a *distinct category* of real being." And "real being" for him? It is " 'being' considered *substantially as essential* (whether possible or actual)."

[60] *Ibid.* Also see pp. 207, 212 and 349.

[61] *Op. cit.*, pp. 246–47 (emphasis added). Dealing with accidents "when they are conceived as things" is equivalent to treating them as substances: "By

After several pages he begins to study relations.

> [2] Our particular problem then is: What is "relation" considered in itself? It is, of course, a predicate, and so something understood, an *intelligibility* (a *ratio*). But our question means more than this: it means, Is a real relation *as such* and *according to its mode of intelligibility* to be found in the order of being?[62]

After depicting the havoc which newly laid eggs create upon the metaphysical scene, he continues:

> [3] These absurdities and impossibilities should be enough to show us that the question has been wrongly understood. Let us go back briefly to accidents. The *intelligibility,* "accident," which is *mentally understood after the manner of a form,* is variously and differently realized in existent material beings. In saying that accident is *conceived after the manner of a form,* we mean that it is *thought of* as a form or quasi-form determining and modifying a substance, in a way somewhat like that in which substantial form determines and specifies matter. . . . The way in which these three principles of relation [*S, F* and *T*] are *understood* is unlike the way in which they are in the real order. *Relation is understood* as a kind of form which is between two beings, and joins or unites them like a bridge or a rope. What is there in the real order which corresponds to the *intelligibility conceived after the manner of a form*?[63]

In the light of those quotations, there seems little doubt but that such is the procedure this author proposes: go from intelligibilities to actual accidents, and, more relevantly, from relation as an intelli-

---

means of formal abstraction, we can consider these modifications (accidents) in themselves apart from any substance. Indeed, we can consider them as if they were substances (*per modum substantiae*); and it is precisely as considered in this way that they are placed in the predicaments" (*ibid.*).

Numbers in brackets are affixed to this and the two later quotations for easy reference in my subsequent comments.

[62] *Ibid.*, p. 270.

[63] *Ibid.*, p. 271 and p. 273. See also *ibid.*, p. 315: "In metaphysics itself, we deal with pure intelligibilities: this is especially true in the case of the predicaments. For example, *relation* as a form is a construct."

gibility and predicament to actual relational situations.[64] But this procedure already predetermines one's position, and it is negative. If a relation in itself is "a predicate, and so something understood, an intelligibility (a *ratio*)" (see #2), of course it is not an accidental perfection other than its *S*, *F* and *T*—it is what it is defined to be from the very start: a predicate, an intelligibility, a *ratio*. Nor can a relation be that sort of accidental perfection if a relation in itself is "understood as a kind of form" (#3), for, as we have already noted, such a situation would be contradictory: either the relation would not be relational or it would be inward-outward at one and the same time.

However easy this methodology may be and however difficult and roundabout understanding relations and other accidents may be according to the manner in which they exist (see #1), still the very aim of the metaphysician is knowing them precisely as they do exist, understanding them precisely qua actual. The difficulties and hardships of attaining that knowledge he must bear if he is to achieve his goal. There is no shortcut.

But what is a predicament? Where do they fit into an authentically existentialist metaphysics? Have they any function to perform? Those are the questions we shall now answer briefly.

What are the predicaments? In my interpretation, they are intelligibilities, *rationes*, the content of awarenesses which emerge when one reflects upon various grammatical predications made about material existents. For example, take these statements.[65]

(a) "Terence actually is the father of Helen."
(b) "He actually is also the sculptor of this statue."
(c) "He actually is an inhabitant of St. Louis County."
(d) "He actually is politically conservative."
(e) "Yet he actually is a yuppie, too."

---

[64] This is also equivalent to going from relations conceived as a substance (see n. 61) to them as actual accidents.

[65] We shall concentrate upon the last six predicaments in traditional Aristotelian lists—relation, action/passion, time, place, posture, and state. "Posture" (*situs*) is not explicitly treated, but what is said of place is true of it, *mutatis mutandis*.

A good treatment is to be found in Owens, *op. cit.*, pp. 191–209. Also see his article, "Aristotle on Categories," *Review of Metaphysics*, 14 (1960), 73–90.

All those statements are grammatically intended to express the actual relationships he has to various terms.[66] But those same relational situations can also be stated in such a way as only to imply the relations and explicitly to express their foundation or terms. For instance:

(a) "Terence did actually beget Helen."
(b) "He actually is carving this wood (which also is simultaneously being carved)."
(c) "He actually lives here in St. Louis."
(d) "He actually is late twentieth-century in his attitudes and outlook."
(e) "He actually wears such-and-such clothes."

The difference between these two series of predications, then, is merely one of grammatical expression. They both involve relations, but the first explicates the relation (and implies the *F* and sometimes the *T*), whereas the second explicates the *F* and/or *T* (and implies the *R*). By reflection upon the first series there emerges the awareness or predicament of "relation," whereas by reflection upon the second there emerges the awareness or predicament of "action" (#a and first clause of #b), of "passion" (second clause of #b), of "place" (#c), of "time" (#d), and of "state" (#e).[67] In view of their origin from statements which differ only grammatically, these all have to do with relational situations and merely designate them from different points of view.[68] Despite this mental distinction,

---

[66] Even #c, #d and #e involve relations, since each expresses a cause-effect complex. On #c and #d, see n. 9. With respect to #e, the clothing one wears may cause him to be warm, to be protected, confident, vain, and so on. The adage "Clothes make the man" is relevant here.

[67] "State" is Owens' word (*op. cit.*, p. 208) for *habitus*.

[68] The mental distinction operative here is somewhat like the "minor" one between the transcendents (see Ch. VI, prgr. corresponding to n. 42): they all have to do with relational situations, but "relation" is primarily concerned with the actual relations themselves, whereas "action" and the others are concerned with the *F* and/or *T*. But the distinction is also like the "major" one between restrictive awarenesses (see *ibid.*, prgr. corresponding to n. 39): the distinction, although only mental or rationate, ultimately entails really distinct items—the *R* itself, the *F*, and the *T*, all of which are really other than one another.

One should carefully note that the distinction in question here is not between an actual *R*, *S*, *F* and *T* (which of course is real), but between

though, they are not constructural intelligibilities because there is an actually existing item which directly corresponds to them—namely, the real relation explicated or implied in each situation.[69]

Can they meaningfully be called "accidents"? Yes, if one remembers he is viewing "accident" against a grammatical, predicational background. A predicate which is essentially constitutive of its subject is "substantial" (for example, "Terence is a man"),[70] and consideration of this sort of statement produces the predicament of "substance." Predicates which are not essentially constitutive of their subjects "happen to" them, and thus are "accidental" (for instance, "Terence actually is quantified, actually is a mathematician," as well as the two series of statements [#a–#e] in the penultimate paragraph above). Consideration of this sort of

---

"relation," "action," and the rest precisely as predicaments. In their content all of them deal with a relational situation, but some explicate the *R* and others the *F* or *T*. Thus they somehow differ. They are not identically the same predicament.

[69] Of course, that direct correspondent also is the *S, F* and *T,* which too are actually existing items.

"But [someone may ask] are not the predicaments which are accidents all constructural by the fact that they are abstract rather than concrete? For example, everyone agrees that 'humanity' is constructural because in contrast to 'man' it is abstract. So too, 'quantity,' and not 'quantified,' is the predicament, or 'fatherhood,' and not 'father.' " Although the accidental predicaments are abstract rather than concrete, they are still not constructs. The difference between them and such an intelligibility as "humanity" is that what immediately corresponds to the latter is one's mental activity, whereas what immediately corresponds to the former is actual accidents. An actual man is subsistent, is a composite and a whole, and the concrete awareness of "man" intentionally represents him directly in those characteristics. But "humanity" results from one's concentrating solely on what makes this man be *man* and by *prescinding* from his individuality and all else. "Humanity" then, stands for what is merely a *part* (the *forma totius*) and not for the whole of man. But any actual accident is itself inherent, simple and a part. To match those properties directly, knowledge must be abstract rather than concrete. Hence, the very abstraction of an accidental predicament proves rather than disproves it to be nonconstructural.

On "humanity," see Aquinas, *De Ente et Essentia,* c. 2 (Roland-Gosselin Ed., pp. 21–23); on the accidental predicaments, see *ibid.,* c. 6 (Roland-Gosselin Ed., pp. 46–47).

[70] If spelled out, one would say: "A predicate which signifies that which is essentially constitutive of what is signified by the subject of a proposition. . . ." But the shorter version used here (and in the subsequent sentence) is sufficiently clear.

proposition gives rise to the predicaments of various "accidents"—"quantity," "quality," "relation," and so on. They are not directly, however, accidents in a metaphysical or (perhaps) even a philosophical sense.[71] They are not components but are mere awarenesses, intelligibilities, predicaments.

Can they be termed "forms"? Again, yes, if one recalls he is using "form" and "matter" solely in a predicational, grammatical signification. Outside a proposition a subject is of itself indeterminate—for example, "Ali" says nothing about whether it designates a parrot or a man, white or black, metaphysician or pugilist. But it is determinable, and this occurs through predicates, the very function of which is to determine the subject of a proposition—"Ali is a *man*, is *black*, is a *prizefighter*, and so on." But the determinant is to the determinable as form is to matter. Therefore, the predicament is to subject as form is to matter. Accordingly, predicaments which emerge from meditation upon the function of predicates within propositions can be called "forms." Remember, however, that here we meet "form" and "matter" solely in a grammatical context. They are not the components encountered in the philosophy of nature and in metaphysics.

What function do these predicaments perform in metaphysics? Absolutely none, as far as I can see. They certainly play a role in logic and, possibly, in a philosophy of nature. But they are totally missing from the cast of metaphysics.[72]

---

[71] A logician, though, would accept them as his nine categories of accidents.

[72] But what about the use made above (prgrs. corresponding to n. 25) of statements in arriving at a knowledge of relations? Does it not insert the predicaments into metaphysics? Direct statements can be utilized in two different ways. (a) When considered in a strictly grammatical fashion, they can lead to the elaboration of intelligibilities, formalizations, predicational classes called "predicaments." These in turn can be used as guidelines for returning to the actual existent and for deciding whether or not he has various accidental perfections and what they consist in. This use is, I suggest, a metaphysical mistake. (b) But they can also be considered as the effects of actually existing items, which are their content-determining-causes, and thus are revelatory of those very causes. Hence they can serve as a starting point for a direct inference, which terminates in one's assenting: "Yes, accidental perfections of both relational and nonrelational caliber do actually exist, and they have such-and-such natures." This utilization seems legitimate and is quite different from the former.

But what about the contrast between "predicamental" and "transcendental" relations? If predicaments are dropped from metaphysics, what of this

Does that mean, then, that metaphysics has no predicaments? Yes, although at the end of his study a metaphysician may separate accidents into various classes. But notice that this occurs at the end, not at the beginning of metaphysics and, second, that these classes are mere summaries of knowledge already gained about actually existing accidents and not initial steps toward acquiring that cognition. The metaphysician observes change/stability on the accidental level—the loss and acquirement of various individual perfections (operations, operative habits, color, and so on) in an existent remaining generically and specifically what it is. Thereupon he realizes both *that* the existent is composed of two components conveniently named "substance" and "accident" and *what* they are (each is a component, a "that by which," and so forth). His knowledge of various accidents grows through reflection upon individual perfections lost and acquired (for example, all are components, all are known through intellection based upon data gained through perception, and so on); what the special characteristics of some are (for example, quantity as entering into substantial individuation, relations as accidents but not accidental forms); finally, that accidental perfections show themselves to be either (1) quantity, (2) various qualities, (3) operations or (4) relations. These last are the four classes which accidents themselves thrust upon the metaphysician toward the conclusion of his science. They are not predicaments.

---

contrast? The notion of "transcendental" relation became popular among Renaissance authors, where at least one of its functions appears to have been to unite components within a thing. When a philosopher conceives of components as themselves "things" (for example, of prime matter as having an act of its own), something is required to coalesce them into a single existent. One way of meeting that requirement is to call upon transcendental relations: "Of course, the components are united—they are *transcendentally related to one another.*" But if one accurately conceives of a component as "that *by which*" and not as a "thing," then unity is no problem, and the need for the doctrine of "transcendental" relation drops. (On transcendental relations, see Krempel, *op. cit.*, "Table Analytique" [p. 799] for multiple references; especially see "Appendice: L'intrusion de la relation transcendentale dans l'école thomiste," pp. 645–70; also see Adriaan Pattin, O.M.I., "Contribution à l'histoire de la relation transcendantale," *Revue de l'Univ. d'Ottawa*, 28 [Juillet-Septembre, 1958], pp. 137*–55*.)

Accordingly, all the relations touched on in the present chapter would be called "predicamental," in contrast to "transcendental." I prefer to speak of them simply as "relations."

5. Summary and Conclusions

Despite their independence and autonomy, material existents are immersed in multiple and deep-seated relationships because of an almost total vulnerability and openness with respect to their fellow existents in space and time. What is the nature of those relations?

(a) A relation involving an *S*, *F* and *T* which are within the mind is itself merely mental. In contrast, a relation which has an actually existing *S*, *F* and *T* is real.[73]

(b) It genuinely depends upon those three factors. The *S* is that in which it inheres and exists. The *F* (which can be quantity, nonquantitative perfection, and causality of various kinds and complexity) is that which helps cause it. The *T* is that to which the *S* is referred and also that which at times helps cause the *R* by its very presence.

(c) Nonetheless, the *R* is really distinct from those three factors. Why so? The distinction is in certain cases experienced by us, as well as inferred from our direct statements about relations.

(d) In itself, then, the relation

1. is a component—for example, fatherhood is *that by which* a man is so ordered to another as to have such-and-such rights and duties;
2. is, accordingly, known by intellection working upon actual relational situations directly perceived;
3. is real because it actually exists;
4. is an accident because it is an individual perfection of the *S* in which it inheres;
5. yet is not an accidental form because although it is that by which a subject is perfected within its essence in a relatively quiescent way, it does not perfect it in a *totally* intrinsic fashion: its unique nature is to orientate, refer, and open up the subject to what is without.

---

[73] Real relations are either bilateral or unilateral (mutual or nonmutual, double or single), depending upon whether or not the relation in the *S* to *T* is matched by a relation in the *T* to *S* (which *T*, of course, is the *S* of the second relation). An example of bilateral relations: filiation and fatherhood; of a unilateral relation: that of creature to God, of knowledge to what is known.

(e) Whenever a single real relation has many terms (as happens when a man is the father of several children, is bigger than all the people in Missouri), it has many "respects": the multiple "lookings-toward" which the single *R* actually has to its multiple terms and which the mind progressively recognizes.

Suggested Readings

Aristotle, *Basic Works*, ed. Richard McKeon, pp. 7–37. New York: Random House, Inc., 1941. On the categories.

Berry, K. K., "The Relation of the Aristotelian Categories to the Logic and the Metaphysics," *New Scholasticism*, 14 (1940), 406–11.

Blackwell, Richard J., "The Methodological Function of the Categories in Aristotle," *ibid.*, 31 (1957), 526–37.

Kane, William J., *Philosophy of Relation in the Metaphysics of St. Thomas.* Washington, D.C.: The Catholic University of America Press, 1958.

Kosman, L. A., "Aristotle's First Predicament" in *Substance and Things: Aristotle's Doctrine of Physical Substance in Recent Essays,* M. L. O'Hara (ed.), pp. 17–44. Washington, D.C.: University Press of America, 1982.

Kossel, S.J., Clifford, "Principles of St. Thomas' Distinction between the *Esse* and *Ratio* of Relation," *Modern Schoolman*, 24 (1947), 19–36 and 93–107.

———, "The Problem of Relation in Some Nonscholastic Philosophies," *ibid.*, 23 (1946), 61–81.

———, "St. Thomas' Theory of the Causes of Relation," *ibid.*, 25 (1948), 151–72.

Owens, Joseph, *An Elementary Christian Metaphysics*, pp. 178–90. Milwaukee: Bruce Publishing Co., 1963. On real relations. Also pp. 191–209 on the relative categories other than relation itself.

———, "Aristotle on Categories," *Review of Metaphysics*, 14 (1960), 73–90.

Scheu, Sr. M. Marina, *The Categories of Being According to Aristotle and St. Thomas*. Washington, D.C.: The Catholic University of America Press, 1944.

Wild, John, *Introduction to Realistic Philosophy*, pp. 330–55. New York: Harper & Row, Publishers, 1948. On relation and other categories.

———, "A Realistic Defense of Causal Efficacy," *Review of Metaphysics*, 2 (1949), 1–14. On real relations.

Part III

Causality

VIII

Efficient Causality

Whenever something unknown confronts us,[1] several questions spontaneously come to mind. The first is, "What?" What is it? What is inside? Of what is it made? This question we already have technically answered concerning material existents. They are composites of various components—substance/accidents, prime matter/substantial form, essence/act of existing. This last is the direct source of each existent's reality and being, as well as of its unity, individuality, truth, goodness and beauty.[2] All these components are its intrinsic causes. They *cause* it because they help produce it; they make it *be* and be *what* it is. They are its *intrinsic* causes[3] because they are its constitutive parts—they are not really other than the whole they constitute, which is the sum of its parts.[4] More precisely, in what does their causality consist? It consists in the fact that they actually are present within the existent, that they are what they are so that each can perform its own function (for example, the substantial form specifies, prime matter individuates, the act of

---

[1] For example, we return to our room and find an object concealed under a sheet on the floor (see Ch. VI, Sec. 3a), or we unexpectedly receive a package in the mail.

[2] On actual existence, see Chs. IV and V; also Ch. VI, Secs. 2 and 5; on the other components, see Ch. III.

[3] "Intrinsic" with reference to the effect: they *are* the effect, they are the parts which go to make it up. They are contrasted with efficient and final causes, which are really other than the effect and hence are "extrinsic" to it.

[4] At best there is between them and the whole a real distinction which is "inadequate" or "potential." See Ch. VI, n. 75.

existing actualizes and realifies), that thereby they join forces actually to constitute the existent. In the light of their functions, intrinsic causes are of two sorts: they either are *actuating* causes (actual existence, substantial form, accidents—these are acts and obviously cause the existent by their actuations) or *limiting* causes (essence, prime matter, substance—these are potencies and manifestly cause the existent by receiving and limiting the acts).[5]

Although all these points are clear at this stage of our metaphysics, nevertheless the fact that actual existence and the other components are intrinsic causes is important. It emphasizes that they are not negations or mere intramental constructions but that they are real constitutive parts of the existent, each with a unique contribution to make.

But an unknown object triggers another question in our minds—namely, "Who?" After we know what it is, we instinctively wonder who is responsible. Who did it? Who made it? What agent constructed it? This is the consideration of *efficient cause,* to which we now turn. However well we may understand material existents in their internal, componential makeup, we still have not accounted for them completely until we study the efficient causality which brings them into being and by which they in turn produce other existents.

Many find this sort of causality baffling.

> The obscurity of the idea of causality is notorious. No idea has so persistently challenged analysis and criticism. To dispel its nebulousness by tracing its origin and defining its features has been the ambition of many subtle thinkers. Yet its genealogy and its nature are still matters of great uncertainty. The

---

[5] With the advent of the act of existence into metaphysics, Aristotle's description of intrinsic causes as "formal" and "material" is no longer adequate. "Prime matter" and "substance" can be suitably designated as "material" causes, "substantial form" and "accident" as "formal causes" (although even here it breaks down, for not all accidents [for example, relations] are forms); however, the act of existing is not a form, and hence can hardly be called a "formal" cause. One way of handling the problem is to deny that the act of existing is an intrinsic cause (as has been done by Joseph Bobik, "Some Disputable Points Apropos of St. Thomas and Metaphysics," *New Scholasticism,* 37 [October, 1963], 428–30). But this is unfortunate, for what other component is so influential in producing an existent? Another way is to enlarge the description of intrinsic causes to include actual existence. Then they are either *actuating* or *limiting* causes.

> ancestry of causality has been imputed to various sources. What is its actual genesis? Shall we look for it in the logical relation between ground and consequent, or in the psychological connection between our wills and our acts, or in the given conjunction between individual facts and events? The question presupposes different conceptions of the nature of causality. Concerning its importance, too, how diverse the assertions! Causality has been eulogized as the highest principle of explanation; it has been accepted only as a descriptive law of limited applicability; it has been disparaged altogether as being either otiose or self-contradictory. While all agree that there is something opaque about the idea of causality, its darkness has been accounted for in different ways, some ascribing it to profundity, some to confusion, and others to mystery. No wonder, then, that in some quarters causality has assumed the character of a *bête noire*.[6]

Such a philosopher as Harold Chapman Brown even finds it dangerous: "The concept of causation is the most treacherous concept that man has fabricated to interpret his experiences in the physical world."[7] Hume overcomes both obscurity and danger by reducing it entirely to something merely intramental.

> Necessity [and, *a pari,* power and efficacy] is . . . nothing but an internal impression of the mind, or a determination to carry our thoughts from one object to another. . . . The efficacy or energy of causes is neither placed in the causes themselves nor in the deity nor in the concurrence of these two principles; but belongs entirely to the soul, which considers the union of two or more objects of all past instances. 'Tis here that the real power of causes is placed, along with their connection and necessity.[8]

---

[6] J. Loewenberg, "The Elasticity of the Idea of Causality," in *Causality,* ed. George P. Adams *et al.* (Berkeley, Calif.: University of California Press, 1932), p. 3.

[7] "Causality and the Cosmos," *ibid.,* p. 41.

[8] *A Treatise of Human Nature,* I, Part 3, Section 14 (Open Court Ed., pp. 214 and 215). Hume performs a similar reduction on beauty ("Beauty is no quality in things themselves; it exists merely in the mind which contemplates them") and on substance ("The idea of a *substance* . . . is nothing but a collection of simple ideas that are united by the imagination and have a particular name

Is there any alternative to Hume's reduction? How, in fact, does one achieve a valid knowledge of efficient cause? The answer is simple: by following the same inductive methodology used with the components—namely, turn to the actual universe, where the efficient-cause situation repeats itself constantly before our very eyes. Phosphorus bursts into flame on combining with oxygen; radioactive particles affect photographic plates, as well as living tissue; cosmic and light waves bombard us from outer space.[9] Plants grow, flower, and produce the seeds which will reproduce

---

assigned them by which we are able to recall, either to ourselves or others, that collection"—*ibid.*, I, Part 1, Section 6, p. 16).

For an explanation and critique of Hume's position, see D. J. B. Hawkins, *Causality and Implication* (New York: Sheed and Ward, 1937), pp. 65–88; also *idem*, *Being and Becoming* (New York: Sheed & Ward, 1954), Ch. X: "Causality in Aristotle and Hume," pp. 137–49 (also see pp. 150–62); James Collins, *A History of Modern European Philosophy* (Milwaukee: Bruce Publishing Co., 1954), pp. 423–33; J. de Finance, *Connaissance de l'être* (Paris: Desclée de Brouwer, 1966), pp. 370–72; T. J. Richards, "Hume's Two Definitions of 'Cause,'" *Philosophical Quarterly*, 15 (1965), 247–53.

Hume's position on efficient causality (as on substance and other topics) is largely predetermined by his twofold attitude on human knowledge; human reason operates (as Collins observes, *ibid.*, p. 429) "in a purely abstract and *a priori* way, entirely apart from the guidance of sense observation" and, secondly, human cognition terminates immediately at the human knower himself, since "the immediate object of experience is the mental percept" (*ibid.*, p. 431). The first causes him to conclude that reason cannot formulate a theory of efficient causality which would be valid for the actual universe, because it does not and cannot discover it within that universe. The second forces him to picture efficiency on the horizon of his own mind. He restricts it to an intramental association: the conjunction of the *ideas* of cause-effect, of prior-posterior, and so forth.

Because Hume's metaphysics or causality rests upon his epistemology and psychology, it collapses when one realizes from his own actual cognitive operations that the human intellect is constantly nourished by the senses and spontaneously moves in an inductive direction and that nonconstructural human knowledge terminates directly at actual existents themselves. On induction see Ch. X below, prgrs. corresponding to notes 25–28.

[9] To many scientists causality tends to be identified with predictability. For example, Max Born, *The Restless Universe* (New York: Dover Publications, Inc., 1951), pp. 163–64: "We now have a *new form* of the law of causality, which has the advantage of explaining the objective validity of statistical laws. It is as follows: if in a certain process the initial conditions are determined as accurately as the uncertainty principle permits, then the probabilities of all possible subsequent states are governed by exact laws. If the experiment is repeated a great many times with the same initial condi-

the species. Birds build nests, lay eggs, hatch their young. Human beings erect houses, beget children, write poetry, carve statues, build rockets, pilot spaceships.

> Causal efficacy is a *relational* concept. What it means is the diffusion of something from one being (the cause) to another which is able to receive it (the effect). To the atomic analyst [Hume and his modern counterparts] such relational potencies and powers are sheer nonsense. Reality is made up of perfectly actual atomic capsules which are entirely insular and self-enclosed. Nature however is constantly confronting us with evidence of causal efficacy. The colorless gases O and H act on one another in certain ways to bring into existence a new fused substance quite distinct from any mere juxtaposition of O and H. Stones break windows, and murderers slit their victims' throats. No one who really disbelieved in causal efficacy would ever read a detective story.[10]

---

tions, the frequency of occurrence of the expected effects (and its fluctuations) can be predicted."

Such a conception of causality is in keeping with modern empiriological sciences and is valuable within that context. It is not, however, in conflict with a philosophical conception of causality, which has to do with the here-and-now situation of an agent's actually producing something new and with the ensuing real relationship between the new product and him.

On the extremely complicated question of the meaning of "cause" in empiriological sciences, see Ernest Nagel, *Structure of Science: Problems in the Logic of Scientific Explanation* (New York: Harcourt, Brace & World, Inc., 1961), pp. 73–78 and 277–335, especially pp. 316–24; Philipp Frank, *Philosophy of Science: The Link Between Science and Philosophy* (Englewood Cliffs, N.J.: Prentice-Hall, Inc., 1957), Ch. 11: "Causal Laws" (pp. 260–77) and Ch. 12: "The Principle of Causality" (pp. 278–96); John G. Kemeny, *A Philosopher Looks at Science* (Princeton, N.J.: D. Van Nostrand Company, Inc., 1959), pp. 48–53; Andrew G. Van Melsen, *Philosophy of Nature* (Pittsburg, Pa.: Duquesne University Press, 1953), pp. 206–42; Victor F. Lenzen, *Causality in Natural Science* (Springfield, Ill.: Charles C. Thomas, 1954); L. de Raeymaeker, *Philosophy of Being* (St. Louis: B. Herder Book Co., 1954), pp. 262–70. Also see publications of Jaki and Lerner listed in "Suggested Readings" below.

[10] John Wild, "Realistic Defense of Causal Efficacy," *Review of Metaphysics*, 2 (June, 1949), 6–7. Also see Paul Weiss, *Modes of Being* (Carbondale, Ill.: Southern Illinois University Press, 1958), p. 40: "To deny causation is thus to deny current evidence, to ignore an omnipresent category, to be faced with an inexplicable world, and to have an inexplicable belief that it is a mistake to say there is causation in fact."

It is, then, from nature itself that we derive knowledge of causes. The doctrine we formulate is, in fact, nothing more than the intelligible representation of actual existents as they are produced by the activity of others and as they in turn produce still others by their activity.[11] Let us, then, concentrate upon actual cases of productivity.

1. Six Causal Factors

Let us begin with the simple case of a sculptor carving a statue from a piece of walnut. First of all, it is an instance of *causality*, because the sculptor does bring it about that there is a statue. With him present and working, the slab of wood turns into the figure of Nolan Ryan. Without him it remains a slab of wood. It is, moreover, *efficient* causality, for he produces the artifact through his activity.[12] An *efficient cause*, then, is *"that which produces another through activity."*

But the statue has at least two efficient causes, for the knife used by the sculptor also helps produce it. No matter how talented the sculptor may be, no matter how thrilling and compelling a vision of beauty he may be experiencing, no matter how plentiful the supply of wood, there would still be no statue without a knife, or at least some sharp instrument. And the very condition the instrument is in (sharp or dull, nicked or smooth) affects the final product. No less true is the fact that the artist's use of it affects its efficacy: he communicates to it his own exemplarity and finality (for instance, today the knife is carving Nolan Ryan's features, yesterday it carved William Bennett's), as well as actual motion.[13]

---

[11] Our knowledge of other causes, too, is derived from the actual universe, where aluminum causes a canoe to be durable yet lightweight (intrinsic causes), money causes us to work (final cause), the fact that Boris Pasternak lived in Communist Russia makes *Doctor Zhivago* the novel it is (exemplary cause).

[12] Carving is such an activity as to perfect something which is other than the agent itself, and hence is called "transient" activity. But other activities (for example, assimilation of food, thinking) perfect the agent himself and are called "immanent." Efficient causality involves both sorts, since even the latter produce something new (for example, increase of size, concepts and propositions), although this is within the agent. In subsequent paragraphs we shall more frequently use transient activities as examples because their causal nature is more apparent and easier to work with.

[13] Actual motion is not communicated to such instruments as are active of their own nature (living things, acids, and so forth), but exemplarity and finality are communicated to all.

In view of those facts, let us designate the knife as *"instrumental* cause," the artist as *"principal* cause." With reference to the single activity issuing from them, the former "acts when and as acted upon" (*movens motum*), the latter simply "acts" (*movens*). The efficacy of the former is colored both by its own nature (for example, it is a knife and is this particular knife) and by the exemplary and telic direction it receives by being moved.[14]

But there being a statue also demands the artist has at hand wood or some other sort of material from which to make it. Of course this is not an efficient cause,[15] but still the material chosen makes a unique contribution to the final product (for example, a statue made from wood has different characteristics than one of bronze, marble, or aluminum). Also, it determines to a large measure what an efficient cause can do—for example, a cook can make clam chowder only if the pantry is stocked with clams, a male and female collie can beget collies from their sperm and ova but not French toy poodles, someone shooting an elephant in his parlor is responsible for different kinds and a greater quantity of chemicals than if he steps on a mouse. What this boils down to is that the material upon which efficient causes work is also a factor in the efficient cause complex.

Still another factor is the activity itself, in which efficient causality consists. It is the actual carving, begetting, writing, cooking, and similar operations by which agents (both principal and instrumen-

---

[14] See James S. Albertson, "Instrumental Causality in St. Thomas," *New Scholasticism*, 28 (1954), 409–35.

With respect to the human soul, which is not educed from matter but is directly created by God, human parents are manifestly not principal causes, nor are they even instrumental causes. Why not? An agent is an instrument by educing a new perfection from the potency of matter, but the sperm and ovum do not potentially contain the human soul and, accordingly, the parents are not its instrumental cause. What sort of cause are they, then? The answer lies in what they do with regard to the soul: they furnish the matter within which the human soul is created and substantially individuated. Let us call them, then, efficient "furnishing" causes.

Accordingly, efficient causes are at least threefold: principal, instrumental, and "furnishing."

On the causality of human parents, see William Reany, *Creation of the Human Soul* (New York: Benziger Brothers, 1932); Henry J. Koren, C.S.Sp., *Introduction to the Philosophy of Animate Nature* (St. Louis: Herder, 1960). On other sorts of efficient causes, see above, Ch. VII, note 9.

[15] Because it is a constitutive part of the effect, the material is an intrinsic limiting and receiving cause. See n. 5 above.

tal) bring forth the product. Looked at from one point of view, such an operation is in the agent itself in act insofar as it originates in the agent and is aligned with a state of actuation and perfection in him. But viewed from the other side, it is in the very thing which is being produced and precisely as being produced, precisely as changing from a state of potentially to one of actuation. In this sense, obviously, the change, perfection, actuation resides in the product—in fact, the product is the operation, change, actuation as realized, externalized, concretized.[16]

A further factor is the real relation between the product and its agents, and it is one of origin, of belonging to, of dependence, of similarity. It is an unilateral relation (see Ch. VII, n. 73), since, as we have just seen, the change, actuation and production is in the thing being changed, actuated and produced. Thus, the agent *as agent* is not changed or produced and hence has no real relation to the product.[17] But efficient causality consists essentially in that change, actuation and production. Accordingly, such causality also consists in that relation of effect to agent. It is present in every efficient situation, whereas a real relation exists between agent and his product only when and because the agent is himself changed and perfected in the very act of producing the effect. Such a real relation exists in an agent as finite or as material, but never in him *precisely as agent*. The real relation of an effect to its agent is, then, at the very heart of efficient causality.[18]

---

[16] This property of an operation by which it is in both agent and patient is the background for the Aristotelian position that one and the same motion can be described as both action and passion. See J. Owens, *An Elementary Christian Metaphysics*, pp. 192–204. This description works most easily, of course, with transient operations—see n. 12.

[17] The agent *as agent* is without a real relation to the effect because he is without the foundation required—namely, being changed, modified, perfected. Between the agent as agent and his product there is a mental relation—that put there by the mind as balancing the real relation between the product and agent. The real relation entailed in the effect-cause situation is, then, unilateral (see Ch. VII, n. 73).

Of course, the real relation between effect and agent is interpreted differently by the negative and affirmative views on relations. According to the former it consists in the *S*, *F* and *T*, plus the mental activity of the one considering those three factors (see Ch. VII, Sec. 3); according to the latter it is an accidental perfection besides the *S*, *F* and *T* (Ch. VII, Sec. 2).

[18] Efficient cause would, then, be more completely defined if a reference to the relation is included—for example, an efficient cause is "that through whose activity something new is produced, which thereby is really related to it."

The influence of those factors terminates in the product, which at times is an artifact, an extrinsic unit (the statue), where a new accidental perfection (the shape) has been drawn from the potency of second matter, now inheres in it, and is existentialized by the acts of existence actualizing the individual intrinsic units which make up that matter. But on occasion it is an intrinsic unit (this collie pup), where a new substantial form has been educed from matter (the sperm/ovum), is received and substantially individuated by it, and is actualized by the act of existence existentializing the entire composite. Or it is the various chemical compounds resulting from the death of a living thing, where new substantial forms have been brought from a state of virtual presence to one of formal presence, are now individuated by the quantified matter of those compounds, and are existentialized by the acts of existence which actualize them.[19] Whatever the effect produced, it is the culmination of various causes, some of which are intrinsic (that is, the components which make it up, whether their function is to *actuate* [accidents, substantial form, actual existence] or to *receive and limit* [substance, prime matter, essence]). Others are extrinsic in the sense they are really *other than* the product, and these are the efficient causes (both principal and instrumental), together with the exemplarity and finality which efficiency involves.[20]

Here, then, are at least six factors which always are operative when material existents efficiently cause something:

Principal agent: "that which acts without qualification."
Instrumental agent: "that which acts while simultaneously being acted upon."
Preexisting matter: that from which a new perfection is educed and in which it inheres and exists.
Activity, whether transient or immanent.

---

[19] With regard to human parents, the product is a new human existent, but many distinctions must be made. Because they furnish the matter within which the human soul is created and individuated, they are efficient "furnishing" causes of the soul (see n. 14). Because man consists of soul/body and because the parents furnish the matter, these parents are the principal causes of the body, while their generative powers, together with sperm/ovum, are its instrumental causes. These last—sperm/ovum—also become one of the new human existent's intrinsic causes (limiting, individuating) at the instant of conception and of the creation of the human soul.

[20] On final and exemplary causes, see Ch. IX.

Real relation of origin, dependence and similarity between the product and its agents.

The product itself—the new accidental perfection or substantial form, existing in and individuated by its recipient.[21]

2. Some Corollaries

There are several points of information which additional reflection upon actual cases of efficient causality uncovers. These can be stated as corollaries to the basic causal factors already listed. In fact, the first has already been mentioned in connection with that list.

(a) *An agent precisely as agent is not changed by his activity.*[22] He may undergo changes inasmuch as he is material—for example, he expends energy while working. He may change insofar as he is finite: his operative powers pass from a state of potentiality to one of actuation in order that he be actually acting, and his activity can perfect his art and other operative habits so that the artifact he produces next time will be even better. But granting all that, an agent precisely as agent does not himself change. Why so? Because the very nature of his activity (carving, writing, and so forth) is to be outgoing, perfecting another. Second, the activity is *in the thing which is being produced*. It is, actually, the thing's very change from the potential to the actual, its being actuated and perfected under the influence of the agent.[23] Because of what such activity is, then, an agent as agent undergoes no change by acting, an efficient cause precisely as efficient cause is not itself perfected in causing.

(b) *Whatever an agent produces is similar to himself.* At first sight this point is extremely simple and what one would expect, as this argument shows.

> In order to be an agent, something must actually *be* (obviously, since how could that which does not exist possibly act?) and must be *in a definite way* (since no one can simply produce but must produce something—crab apples or collies or statues).

---

[21] This list has to be carefully interpreted when applied to human parents. See notes 14 and 19.

[22] This corollary is concerned primarily with principal and not instrumental agents, and with transient and not immanent operations. See n. 12.

[23] As Aristotle remarked accurately, motion or change is the very actuation of a potency as it continues to be in potency. See *Physics*, III, I, 201A10–11.

But one is in a definite way either by nature (by its very nature, a crab-apple tree is a definite sort of tree and has its own type of natural operative powers) or through cognition (because of the singular vision of beauty and creative inspiration he is currently experiencing, this painter is the unique artist he is and is capable of producing a unique canvas).

Accordingly, an existent's status as an agent originates in, flows from, is colored and influenced by what he is by nature or by cognition.

Hence, an existent's very activity is in line with its nature or with its current state of knowledge. The activity is, in fact, nothing more than the agent projecting itself, externalizing what it itself is here and now.

But the product is the result of that activity—it is, actually, the activity itself in a concretized and realized state.

Therefore, the product also is basically nothing more than the agent-as-projected-and-externalized.

Therefore, the product is similar to the agent, or, to say the same, whatever an agent produces is similar to himself.

But the point is not as simple as it looks when one inspects the product of various agents. A collie pup is similar to its collie parents, a child resembles his parents in myriad ways—but how is the statue of Mother Teresa like its sculptor, and, also, like the knife he used? How is the patient's good health like the medicine which helped him recover it? How is my chill similar to the wind, or the growth this geranium has undergone similar to the sun?[24]

Such instances indicate that there are varying degrees of likeness between effect and cause. [1] At times the perfection found in the effect is intrinsically also in the agent, and this in the same manner and to the same degree (for example, the collie dogs). This class of causes let us call "univocal" (for obvious reasons). [2] At other times, the perfection of the effect is intrinsically found also in the cause, but in a different manner (for example, the statue and its sculptor). This class of causes let us call "analo-

---

[24] Other instances could be listed: an animal nourishing itself, someone seeing a red object or thinking on a philosophical problem, someone producing in his intellect the operative habit of geometry through working quantitative problems, and so on. What sort of similarity do these effects have to their cause? These instances indicate that perhaps the second corollary has reference only to transient operations. Since an agent perfects *himself* by immanent operations, what he produces by them is clearly like the agent.

gous."[25] [3] On occasion the perfection of the effect is not as such in the cause, although something equivalent is there (for example, the patient's health and medicine, the statue and the knife, plant growth and the sun). This class of causes let us call "equivocal."[26]

What is responsible for those varying degrees of similarity? It is the fact that the agents themselves are so different. Some work through knowledge and art (#2), others through natural powers (#1 and #3). Even among these last, though, there is a difference. Some are principal and proximate causes (#1), while others are principal but remote (the sun with regard to the plant growth) or proximate but instrumental (medicine in relation to health, the knife in relation to the statue).

Despite these diversified levels of similarity, though, it remains true that every effect resembles its efficient cause to some extent or, in other words, that whatever an agent produces is somehow similar to itself.[27] And why so? Because the activity involved is the

---

[25] In general all artists are analogous causes. The perfection in question is found both in the artist and in the artifact—in the former, though, as contemplated and experienced; in the latter as concretized and incarnated. For example, *Oedipus Rex* is nothing but the dramatist's experience of grief as externalized in written and spoken symbols. *Death of a Salesman* is Arthur Miller's feeling of frustration and anger similarly expressed. *Heart of the Matter* is Graham Greene's vision of the complexity of the human situation projected into external expression. (We might add that each creature is likewise nothing but the divine Artist's vision of His own infinite perfection externalized in finite existents.)

At least one reason why the similarity between artifacts and artists is not as great as that between offspring and parents is that the latter produce the very matter of the offspring: the sperm and ovum not only are instrumental causes of the offspring but also become constitutive parts and thus intrinsic causes of him, and hence enter into his very makeup. See n. 19.

[26] Causes of this type would more consistently be entitled "extrinsically *analogous* causes," because their effects are not totally dissimilar to them. Actually, the perfection of the effect is predicated of the cause through extrinsic denomination because the cause has some equivalent perfection. For example, the chemical make-up of the medicine corresponds to health.

[27] This point may also be stated thus: "A cause contains in some way all the perfections of its effects." Plotinus disagrees with respect to The One, Who is God and First Cause. If He is to cause the perfections of His effects, He must contain none of them. This position is necessary where to be real is to be one: that which is supremely real must also be supremely one, and thereby is unable to contain in any way the multiple perfections of the effect. It also suggests that the causality exercised by the One is not efficiency. See L. Sweeney, S.J., "Some Basic Principles of Plotinus' Philosophy," in my *Divine*

agent projecting and externalizing itself, and the product is the same activity in a concretized and realized condition.

(c) *Whenever a single effect is produced by two or more different agents* (for example, by principal and instrumental causes), *each agent makes a unique contribution to that effect* because each acts according to what it is if it is to act at all, and what each is makes it unique and diverse from everything else. *The unique contribution which an agent makes by acting according to what it is is called its "proper effect."* No matter what other effect it may have, then, *every agent has a proper effect, since an agent always acts according to what it is.*

By way of example, consider a teacher using a piece of red chalk to write "dog" upon the blackboard. The effect produced is composite and yet one. It is composite inasmuch as it is a symbol which is both meaningful and colored. It is one insofar as it is a single symbol where the color expresses the meaning, which in turn determines the precise position of chalk particles on the board. That effect is wholly caused by the principal and instrumental agents, since each causes both meaning and color, but differently. The teacher causes the color through the chalk but the meaning directly and of himself; the chalk causes the meaning only as moved by the teacher, and the color directly in virtue of its own nature. By directly causing the meaning, then, the teacher also causes the color; by directly causing the color, the instrument also causes the meaning. What is the *proper effect* of each cause? For the teacher it is the meaning, because by nature he is an intelligent being and agent. For the chalk it is the color because by nature it is a piece of red chalk.[28]

Whatever an agent causes in virtue of what it itself is, then, is its proper effect. But the act of existing is really other than what any material existent is. Therefore, the act of existing is not the proper effect of any material existent. No such existent (or, for that matter, no creature) can properly cause anything to exist. But more of this in the next section.

Infinity in Greek and Medieval Thought (New York/Bern: Peter Lang Publishing, Inc., 1992), ch. 11, pp. 243–56; *idem*, "Metaphysics and God: Plotinus and Aquinas," *Die Metaphysik im Mittelalter*, Vol. II of *Miscellanea Mediaevalia* (Berlin: Walter De Gruyter, 1962), pp. 232–39; forthcoming as ch. 19 in my *Christian Philosophy: Nature, Origin, Developments* (New York/Bern: Peter Lang Publishing, Inc., 1994).

[28] This reflection on proper effect furnishes another definition of principal and instrumental causes: a principal cause is one which properly causes the higher perfection in an effect; an instrumental cause is one which properly causes the lower perfection.

3. Co-operation with God

When we realize that creatures cannot properly cause existence, an entirely new dimension is added to our understanding of efficiency. That realization is the basis for proving that God exists and for knowing to an extent the sort of existent He is. No material existent can properly cause existence, because the act of existing is really distinct from what each is and thus belongs to the nature of none of them. Nevertheless, they do exist, they do have that supreme perfection. Therefore, there must be an Existent Whose very nature is to exist, Who Himself needs no cause but Who can and does properly cause all other existents to exist.[29]

The sequel to this proof is that any material existent is caused both by God and by other material things. God properly causes them to *exist*, creatures properly cause them to exist *as thus and so*. Accordingly, God and creatures *co-operate* (work together), and the question is how this co-operation takes place. There are difficulties. In some instances agents are said to work together because they work side by side—for example, two students writing two exams, three horses pulling three carts. Such is not the case here, which is more like two students writing one and the same exam paper or three horses pulling the same cart. But the current case differs even from these instances, obviously, in that these agents are all creatures and thus are on the same level of reality, whereas here one agent is infinite and the other finite, one the Creator and the other a creature. The danger in such co-operation is that either the higher cancels out the lower or the lower impedes the higher. What is to be said?

Manifestly, the parallel most relevant to God working with a creature is that of a principal agent working through an instrument to produce one and the same effect. This relevance is, actually, confirmed by these facts. As has already been indicated, God properly causes this dog *to exist* whereas its parents properly cause it to exist *as this dog*. But the act of existing is itself a greater perfection than what determines and limits it. Therefore, God properly causes what is more perfect in the effect, whereas material things properly cause what is less perfect.[30] But that which causes what is more

---

[29] On God, see Ch. V, Sec. 6, especially, n. 45; L. Sweeney, "God Does Exist," *Ensign*, 1 (1967), 5–10; *idem*, "Metaphysics and God: Plotinus and Aquinas," II, 232–39.

[30] One's decision of what God properly causes is determined by his position on what it means to be real. If to be real is to be actual, then God's proper

perfect is the principal agent, whereas the instrumental agent causes what is less perfect.[31] Consequently, God is to the creature with which He works as principal to instrumental cause.

The result of this parallel is that the characteristics of the principal/instrumental cause relationship are attributable, when rightly understood, to God and creatures. Consider a sculptor carving wood with a knife. A mutual dependence exists between them. If a sculptor is to carve, he needs a knife, which in turn can carve only if moved and directed by the artist. Far from hampering him, the tool complements him. On the other hand, the artist does not annihilate the influence of the instrument because he uses it according to its own nature as a sharp instrument (otherwise, why choose it?). Simultaneously he is enabling it to bring about an effect (a statue) which is well above its own mere sensible and immobile nature. The tie-up, then, between a principal agent and his instrument is mutually beneficial, as well as one of mutual dependence.

How are those properties verified with regard to God and creatures? Of course, God could directly create all existents (as He did the initial stuff from which the present universe has evolved, and as He still does with reference to human souls). Absolutely speaking, then, He does not need creatures as co-workers. But in the present economy of things He has chosen to work through and with creatures and has given them requisite operative powers. Within the context of that free decision, then, He relies upon sculptors that there might be statues, upon plants that there might be seeds and eventually new plants, upon subhuman parents that

---

effect is that the thing actually exists. But if one holds that to be real is equivalent to being immutable and intelligible, then God properly causes creatures to be immutable and intelligible, whereas created agents properly cause them to actually exist.

One may note that this latter equivalence apparently generates difficulties in explaining creation, the process by which possibles become actuals. If possibles, by reason of their intelligibility and immutability, are already real, then creation is a passage from the real to the unreal, from the perfect to the imperfect (see Ch. IV, n. 35). But how can one then credit God with creation, Who would thereby be downgrading rather than ameliorating things? Or how can God's proper effect be, as the essentialists say, to confer immutability and intelligibility upon things? Or what would creation be? In the essentialist's interpretation, is it not going from being to nonbeing rather than from nonbeing to being?

[31] See n. 28. One should remember that God works *with* creatures because He works *in* and *through* them.

there might be animal offspring, and even upon human parents that there might be matter within which He can create human souls (and thus that there might be new human existents).

From the side of creatures the dependence is, of course, absolute, since they cannot *be*, let alone act, without Him. The benefits likewise are extreme, for as instruments in the hands of God, they help bring about what is well above their nature—that countless things *actually exist*. This is a perfection which only God can properly cause but which He achieves through them, who simultaneously are properly causing things to exist in a determinate, limited fashion.

Let us illustrate this co-operation briefly. Consider a newly existing statue. By properly causing the wood to be *this statue*, the sculptor also (instrumentally) causes this statue to exist. By properly causing the statue to *exist* (as well as the wood, the sculptor, and the carving to exist), God also (through the sculptor) makes the wood *be a statue*. Or take this existing collie pup. Its parents properly cause it to be this collie pup and thereby instrumentally cause it to exist. God, though, properly causes it to exist, and thereby causes it to be this pup through its parents. Other illustrations could be given, but enough has been said to indicate that such co-operation benefits both God and creature.

This, then, is the new dimension given to a doctrine of efficient causality when one realizes that no creature properly causes existence. Because they do cause other actually existing creatures, they must literally *co-operate* with God in their causality. This co-operation is like that between an instrument and the principal agent—the former properly producing the lower perfection and the latter the higher, and yet each producing the entire effect. Applied to God and creatures: God properly causes the thing to be, and, through the created agent, to be this thing; the creature properly causes it to be *this thing*, and, through God, actually to *be*.[32]

---

[32] A further problem arises when one tries to determine the co-operation more closely. There are at least two kinds of instruments—those which need to be physically moved, as well as directed exemplarily and telically (for example, a knife); and those which need only the latter because they are physically active of themselves (acids, radioactive materials, living things). Which kind do creatures resemble in reference to God? Are they like knives or like those things which already are physically active of themselves? Discussing those questions must be reserved to natural theology.

Incidentally, when speaking throughout this section of creatures as instrumental causes of existence, we do not intend that such instrumentality applies also to creation. Creatures cannot co-operate with God in creation, even

"Harmony," then, is the word best suited to describe the co-operation between material agents and God. As with any principal and instrumental causes, each is, rightly understood, dependent upon the other: God upon the creature as that *through which* He works, the creature upon God as Him *by Whom* it is used. Each has its own proper function because each acts in accordance with what it itself is. Yet each helps the other. God assists creatures so that by their activity other creatures begin *to be;* creatures assist God so that *these* creatures it is which come into being.[33]

In all this efficacy, though, God has primacy—He sustains, initiates, moves, directs all else. The basic reason for this primacy is the same as for that He enjoys in being: He is subsistent Actuality. Priority in being, then, spells priority in activity. Creatures' posteriority in efficient causality flows from their posteriority in being. They *are,* and because they are, they are active and thus efficiently cause others. But the act of existing by which they are and thereby are active[34] is really other than what they are, and thus is constantly caused by Another. Their efficiency, no less than their being, is itself *caused.*

4. The Efficient Cause Proposition

So far in this chapter we have been considering material existents as *efficient causes*—what the six factors are in a causal situation

---

instrumentally, for an agent is an instrument only by educing a new perfection from the potency of pre-existing matter. But creation, strictly understood, is a production which precisely excludes anything pre-existent. Hence, a creature cannot be an instrumental cause in strict creation. (See *S.T.*, I, 45, 5 resp.; also above, second paragraph of n. 14.) Creatures instrumentally cause actual existence only within noncreative causal situations.

[33] There are thus two sets of principal and instrumental causes: the one between God and creatures, the other between two creatures (for instance, between a sculptor and his knife—see Sec. 1 of this chapter). For the sake of clarity, let us call the causes in the first set "primary" and "secondary"; those in the other set simply "principal" and "instrumental." God is, then, the primary efficient cause, creatures are secondary causes, among which some are principal but others are instrumental agents.

See Robert O. Johann, "A Comment on Secondary Causality," *Modern Schoolman*, 25 (1947), 10–25.

[34] The act of existing is, then, the root also of all efficient causality. See Sec. 5g of this chapter; also J. de Finance, *Être et agir*, 2nd Ed. (Rome: Libraire Éditrice de l'Université Grégorienne, 1960), pp. 70–77, 241–53, 356 ff.

(Sec. 1); that precisely as agents such existents do not change, that whatever they produce is somehow similar to themselves, that they always properly cause something in the effect—namely, what it is (Sec. 2); finally, that they are co-workers with God (Sec. 3). The question we now face concerns existents *as effects*. How widespread is efficiency? How many existents are, actually, products of efficient causes? From one point of view, the answer is ready at hand: all of them, with one exception. Why so? Because all except God exist through an act of existence which is really other than what they themselves are. Actuality is not and never will be a part of their very nature. But they do exist, and therefore they must be efficiently caused by an Existent Who is actuality and Who properly causes them all to be actual. This convincing and obvious reply comes as a mere sequel to the real distinction between existence and essence.

*** (a) Another Approach**

But another way of answering is frequently used, which substitutes deduction for induction and which elaborates a "*Principle* of Causality" rather than a corollary and a conclusion. This approach thrives best in a Cartesian atmosphere, where the human knower is not the body/soul composite but solely the soul; where data for human knowledge comes not from the senses but from ideas innate within the mind; where additional knowledge is achieved by deducing from those ideas the self-evident truths which they contain, which are formulated as analytic and *a priori* principles and to which one assents immediately.[35] This approach is that taken, for

---

[35] For a history of the "Principle of Causality," see E. Gilson, "Les principes et les causes," *Revue Thomiste*, 52 (1952), 39–63; Joseph Owens, C.Ss.R., "The Causal Proposition—Principle or Conclusion?" *Modern Schoolman*, 32 (January, 1955), 159–71. Also see John Gurr, S.J., "Genesis and Function of Principles in Philosophy," *Proceedings of American Catholic Philosophical Association*, 29 (1955), 121–33; *idem*, "Some Historical Origins of Rationalism in Catholic Philosophy Manuals," *ibid.*, 30 (1956), 170–80; *idem, The Principle of Sufficient Reason in Some Scholastic Systems, 1750–1900* (Milwaukee: Marquette University Press, 1959). These scholars show that Leibniz and Wolff, besides Descartes, play important roles in this history. According to Gurr ("Some Historical Origins," pp. 171–75), textbooks in the years 1750–1900 can be classified as follows in terms of the predominant influence at work upon their authors: 1750–1800—influence of Wolff; 1800–1850—influence of Descartes; 1850–1900—influence of Wolff again.

What I call a "*Cartesian* atmosphere" for reasons of convenience and simplification, Gurr in the studies cited above calls rationalism, primacy-of-essence position, geometry of being, and so forth. Despite that difference we

example, by John McCormick in his once widely used textbook, *Scholastic Metaphysics*.[36] First he turns to the Principles of Identity and Contradiction in a section entitled, "First Principles Derived from Notion of Being."

> Certain first principles of being are derived from the consideration of the notion of being. Comparing "being" with itself we find that it is identical with itself, and hence we derive the Principle of Identity: "Whatever is is," or, "If a being is, it is." Comparing "being" and "nothing" we find that they are directly opposed. What one affirms the other denies; one removes from a subject what the other predicates of it. They are therefore mutually exclusive and contradictory, and hence cannot be predicated of the same subject at the same time. From this comparison we derive the Principle of Contradiction as a self-evident principle. It may be formulated thus: "A thing cannot be and not be at the same time."[37]

In a later chapter he deals with the Principle of Sufficient Reason and the Principle of Causality.

> The Sufficient Reason
>
> If reality is intelligible, there must be reason for things. It must be possible for intelligence to account for things, to find some intelligent answer to the question: Why is it? asked in regard to any being. The answer to this question will be the Sufficient Reason for the thing. On our assumption, then, that reality is intelligible, it will be possible to formulate a

---

are both describing the same thing. See Gurr, "Some Historical Origins," p. 178: "The ultimate source of first principles is within the realm of the rational, that is, the realm of the mind—more specifically, within the concept, which upon analysis yields a content whose necessity and universality is guaranteed because of the mind itself and the way it knows, that is, conceptually, that is, with a universality and a necessity which escapes the contingence and singularity of the sensible object by belonging to a realm distinct from it. Sometimes this process is explained in terms of an analysis made of the concept of being which yields the principle of contradiction, which, in turn, guarantees the principle of sufficient reason and thereby the mind can put itself in possession of the principle of causality, which by definition expresses the necessity and a universality the world of sense experience itself is incapable of yielding."

[36] Chicago: Loyola University Press, 1940.

[37] *Ibid.*, p. 21.

self-evident principle in regard to the reason for things, to the effect that: Everything that is has a sufficient reason for its being. Now reality . . . comprises the possible and the actual. Therefore, if a thing is possible, there must be reason for its possibility; if it is actual, there must be reason for its existence. . . .

The Principle of Causality

This sufficient reason [for the actual existence of things] may be looked for either in the being's own essence, or in something outside the being. . . . If we find the reason for existence completely within the being's own essence, we have a self-existent being, one which exists by reason of its own essence, by the necessity of its own essence. The answer to the question, Why does it exist? is, Because of the essence which it has. Its own essence is the completely sufficient reason for its existence. We know, however, that beyond the actually existing things, there are things which could exist and do not, beings, therefore, which have not the complete reason for existence in their own essence. If then such beings come to have existence, this cannot be entirely due to themselves, but, in part at least, to something else. They must also be extrinsically possible, that is, there must exist some other being that can give them existence, and the influence of this other being must have been exerted in their favor. Now the reason for existence of a being, which is found entirely or in part outside that being, is called a cause. A being, then, which begins to be must have a reason for its existence outside itself. But though this principle is thus shown to be a special application of the Principle of Sufficient Reason to a special class of beings, that is, beings that begin to be, it is really self-evident in its own right, for the two concepts, "to begin to be," and "to be without a cause," are evidently contradictory.[38]

---

[38] *Ibid.*, pp. 140–41. McCormick is not a Cartesian in other respects (for example, he holds that the human soul is the substantial form of the body—*ibid.*, pp. 235–37). Still his essentialism seems clear even from the paragraphs quoted. He there comes close to identifying reality with intelligibility ("If reality is intelligible, . . . On our assumption, then, that reality is intelligible. . . ."). Essence is for him the heart and center of a thing's existence (". . . a self-existing being, one which exists by reason of its own essence, by the necessity

We have quoted McCormick at length because he illustrates sufficiently well the approach we have called "Cartesian." Its starting point is the notion of being, its procedure is comparison of various notions,[39] its cognitive movement is a descent from simple to complex awarenesses, its culmination is a series of self-evident and necessary principles, the last of which is called the "Principle of Causality: Whatever begins to be must have a reason for its existence outside itself."[40]

---

of its own essence. The answer to the question, Why does it exist? is, Because of the essence which it has").

On the importance of isolating a "pure position," but on the difficulty of finding it in any one philosopher, see Gurr, "Some Historical Origins," p. 175 and n. 13; *idem, The Principle of Sufficient Reason,* p. 160.

[39] He not only compares the notion of being with itself and with nonbeing ("Comparing 'being' with itself we find that it is identical with itself. . . . Comparing 'being' and 'nothing' we find that they are directly opposed"). In working out the Principle of Causality he also compares "beginning to be" with "causeless" and discovers that they violate the Principle of Contradiction ("[The Principle of Causality] is really self-evident in its own right, for the two concepts, 'to begin to be,' and 'to be without a cause,' are evidently contradictory").

[40] *Ibid.*, p. 141. Also see C. Frick, S.J., *Ontologia* (Friburgi Brisgoviae: Herder & Co., 1934), pp. 204–12. Not only does he derive the Principle of Causality by deduction from the Principle of Sufficient Reason, the Principle of Contradiction, and the intelligibility of "being" (in that order—pp. 204–5), but on p. 208 he makes the strong statement that one knows the Principle of Causality to be certain only from the ideas involved: *Ea certitudo autem nequit hauriri nisi ex ipsis ideis.*

Also see P. Coffey, S.J., *Ontology* (London: Longmans, Green & Company, Ltd., 1918), pp. 359–60 and 369–70. In the earlier reference two statements make clear the relationship between the Principle of Sufficient Reason and that of Causality: "To understand all the intrinsic principles which constitute the *essence* of anything is to know the *sufficient reason* of its *reality.* To understand all the extrinsic principles which account for its actual *existence* is to know the sufficient reason of its existence; and to understand this latter adequately is to realize that the thing depends ultimately for its actual existence on a Reality or Being which necessarily exists by virtue of its own essence." These statements also illumine his radical essentialism: reality is something apart from existence and is located in a thing's essence and ultimately in the Essence or Reality of Being. In the second reference he establishes the Principle of Causality to be "a self-evident, axiomatic, necessary principle" by stating that its opposite is "positively unthinkable and absolutely repugnant to our intelligence; all this our reason peremptorily declares to be intrinsically impossible." The result? "The Principle of Causality is therefore a necessary, *a priori,* self-evident principle." Also see H. Renard, *Philosophy of Being,* 2nd ed. (Milwaukee: Bruce Publishing Co., 1946), p. 123.

Suppose, though, that the human knower is not solely the soul but also involves the body, that he has no innate ideas, and that his way of knowing shows itself to be at best empirical—then this *a priori* approach to causality collapses, and skepticism (or even disdain) sets in. Such has been the attitude of many philosophers from Hume on down to Bertrand Russell, who finds that "the law of causality, I believe, like much that passes muster among philosophers, is a relic of a bygone age, surviving, like the monarchy, only because it is erroneously supposed to do no harm."[41]

The history of the doctrine of efficient causality consisted pretty much of those two stages (the Cartesian approach and its rejection) until recently, when some Thomists advised going back to what Aquinas had affirmed long ago: the human knower is a composite of body/soul; data for natural human knowledge (both spontaneous and philosophical) come to him from the senses; knowledge largely entails induction. Accordingly, knowledge of efficient causality is not *a priori* but *a posteriori*, is not analytic but (rightly understood) synthetic, is not a principle but a conclusion.

> For St. Thomas, then, the basic metaphysical formulation of the causal proposition is that everything for which to be is other than its nature has its being (*esse*) from another. This is the conclusion of a strict demonstration. The first step in that demonstration is to show that a thing abstracts from its being without prescinding from it. This itself is a difficult demonstration in which the nature of the thing is compared with its different ways of being. The being which is attained in the judgment and which is other than that nature is used as the middle term. The second step is to show that the being of a thing is accidental to it, not in the sense of a property or a predicamental accident, which would be subsequent to the nature, but in the sense of an accident which is in its own way absolutely prior to the nature. The notion of accident in this sense is used as a middle term. The conclusion is that to be for such a nature is *ab alio* [from another]. This is the causal proposition. . . . Where, in contrast [to the Cartesian and Leibnizian background], sensible things are the origin of all human knowledge, and where those things are of a nature which is different from, but always open to, the act of being, they provide the

[41] Bertrand Russell, "On the Notion of Cause," in *Mysticism and Logic* (New York: W. W. Norton & Company, Inc., 1929), p. 180.

basis for a rigorous demonstration in which the causal proposition follows as a conclusion from the accidental character of their being.[42]

As far as it goes, this Thomistic advice is all to the good by reemphasizing that man is a mind/matter complex, by reaffirming the inductive character of human knowledge[43] and, most relevantly, stressing that the causal proposition ("Everything for which to be is other than its nature has its being from another") is a *conclusion*.[44] It is that, as we have already indicated.[45] It is a sequel to the real otherness between existence and essence, as this inference shows.

> The act of existing in a material existent is really other than the essence of that existent, because the fact that this man *exists* is genuinely different than the fact that he is *this man*.
> But that which is really other than the essence of something must somehow be efficiently caused.
> Therefore, the act of existing in a material existent must somehow be efficiently caused.
> But it cannot be efficiently caused by that existent itself, because nothing can efficiently cause unless it actually exists.[46]

---

[42] J. Owens, "The Causal Proposition—Principle or Conclusion?" *Modern Schoolman*, 32 (May, 1955), pp. 335 and 339. E. Gilson initially advised returning to Aquinas in the article cited in n. 35 above.

[43] Our approach in other areas of metaphysics has been inductive and thus confirms this reaffirmation. On the components as inductively known, see Ch. III, Sec. 5, and Ch. IV, Sec 5; on the transcendents, see Ch. VI, Sec. 3; on relations, see Ch. VII, Secs. 1 and 2.

[44] Owens' substitution of the phrase "causal proposition" for "principle of causality" is helpful. A proposition is any statement in which a predicate is affirmed or denied of a subject, whether that statement be a conclusion of a syllogism, one of its premises or independent of any process. That substitution works well for Owens, to whom the Causal Proposition is a conclusion. It also works well for me, to whom the Efficient Cause Proposition (I prefer the more explicit expression) in one of its formulations is also a principle (see Sec. 4b of this chapter).

Owens interprets *De Ente et Essentia* accurately with respect to the Causal Proposition, but questionably with respect to the real distinction (see *art. cit.* [March, 1955], pp. 265–70). On the latter see L. Sweeney, S.J., "Existence/Essence in Aquinas' Early Writings," referred to in Ch. IV above, n. 3.

[45] See the beginning of this section.

[46] Actual existence is necessary not only for efficient causality, but also for intrinsic causality (for example, substantial form cannot specify and prime

Therefore, material existents are efficiently caused to exist by existents other than themselves (who eventually turn out to be God, since no existent whose existence is really distinct from its nature would suffice to properly cause existence).

Such, then, is the Efficient Cause Proposition—"Every material existent is efficiently caused by another," or, more technically, "Every existent whose existence is really other than what it is is efficiently caused by another." In the light of the process it terminates, it is a conclusion and not a principle; it is mediately known through reasoning and is not self-evident. It is inductive and *a posteriori*, initiated as it is by our direct perception of two facts which material things disclose: *that* they exist and *what* they are.

*** (b) Is the Causal Proposition Immediately Known?**

That approach to the Causal Proposition, then, is valid and important, as well as highly metaphysical, for it deals with existents precisely as existent, that is, precisely as existentially structured of existence and essence. Yet it is incomplete, since there is evidence that the Causal Proposition when differently formulated is also known immediately, and is, in fact, a self-evident principle of further cognition.

What is that evidence? The fact which we saw early in this chapter: when confronted with something new (for example, a raincoat pocket filled with syrup, a freshly baked cake in the cupboard, a smashed vase in the front hallway), everyone spontaneously and immediately asks, "Who?" Who is responsible? Who did it? Who made it? This question appears to follow from a syllogism, the major premise of which is the Causal Proposition:

> Every new item comes about because of some agent;
> But here is a new item;
> Therefore, some agent is responsible, and my question is: *Who*?

True enough, that proposition is operative on the purely practical level: it directs us with respect to the events we encounter in our day-by-day life. Also, it ordinarily is only implicit (we do not go

---

matter cannot individuate unless each actually exists), for emanative causality (quantity cannot flow from the composite of form/matter unless there actually is such a composite; intellect and will cannot come from the human soul unless the latter actually is), and so on.

about our daily tasks, repeating, "Every new item comes about because of some agent")—it becomes explicit solely under the force of such reflection as we are now making. Nonetheless, it is operative in our practical lives, and it must *be* there implicitly so as to be able to become explicated. Moreover, it must *be known* immediately, spontaneously and by all, because everyone immediately and spontaneously does ask "Who?"

What would be the origin of that knowledge? In line with the nature of the human knower as a body/soul composite and in keeping with the fact that human knowledge grows out of data obtained through perception, it would be a concrete case we observe of some agent constructing (or demolishing) something.[47] There we notice first the ingredients upon which he will work—the shortening, sugar, milk, flour, and so on which now and of themselves are nothing but shortening, sugar, and so forth, but which (unlike putty, lead, steel) can become a cake. We then see that the agent's activity of measuring, sifting, stirring, and so on transforms them from mere separate, sometimes distasteful ingredients into a delicious, edible combination. While observing such a concrete case, we become aware not only that *this* new item has resulted from *this* agent, but that in general every new item comes about through *some agent*, and this because of the very nature of ingredients and of an agent's function.[48] This awareness is the Causal Proposition, which becomes operative from then on in our everyday lives, so that whenever any new event touches us personally, we automatically know that some agent or other is responsible, and we instinctively inquire who it is.

---

[47] An instance of either construction or destruction would serve. In the first the many become one; in the second what is one becomes many.

[48] In this interpretation of the evidence, a child has accomplished a good deal in coming to know the Causal Proposition, in grasping the reasons why it must be true (the nature of ingredients as such and the function of an agent). Of course, all this he has done inarticulately and darkly, but he *has* done it, and this when a case (or cases) of an agent actually making something confronts him when he is psychologically and neurally ready for it.

For a child's knowledge of causality as interpreted by cognitive psychologists, see J. Piaget, *The Child's Conception of Causality* (London: Routledge & Kegan Paul, Ltd., 1930); Piaget and R. Garcia, *Understanding Causality* (New York: Norton, 1974); A. Karmiloff-Smith and B. Inhelder, "If you want to get ahead, get a theory," in P. N. Johnson-Laird and P. C. Wason (eds.), *Thinking: Readings in Cognitive Science* (New York: Cambridge University Press, 1977), pp. 293–306; D. N. Stern, "Diary of a Baby," *Reader's Digest* (July 1991), 135–40.

As so formulated and known, that Proposition is inductive, for we know it from and within a concrete case (or cases). It is immediately known because it is known without reasoning. It is self-evident, not through mere analysis either of the terms used in its formulation or of the concepts they express, but because it is cognized immediately through the light of intelligibilities present within a concrete case of an agent making something. It is a principle because it serves as the major premise of the practical syllogism already discussed.[49]

It retains those properties even when philosophical reflection makes it explicit, speculative and formally certain. While in the presence of a cook making a cake, a philosopher can concentrate technically upon the efficient causality taking place, upon the change being effected in the ingredients by the agent. That technical reflection would uncover at least these four facts: (1) that change is a process by which what is potential becomes actual; (2) that what is potential is not simultaneously and of itself also actual; (3) still that it has become actual when the change is terminated; (4) that, accordingly, the potential becomes actual not of itself but from something else—an agent.[50] Manifestly, the last fact is the Efficient Cause Proposition and can be formulated in various but synonymous ways—"Whatever goes from potency to act does so because of some agent,"[51] or "Whatever changes, changes because of the influence of an agent," or "Whatever is moved is moved by another," and so on. However formulated, it is explicit, technical, speculatively operative,[52] and

---

[49] Thus it is the initial step of a deductive process. Note that deduction has a place in human knowledge, but it is a subordinate one and generally begins from and deals with truths furnished by induction. On induction and deduction, see Ch. X, Sec 3. From this chapter it will be clear that I do not intend "induction" to have the meaning it has in the writings of scholastic rationalists: "They make it a kind of appendage to the syllogistic process. Induction involves the deduction of universality and necessity from a principle possessed prior to and independently of the experience supposed to yield this intelligibility" (Gurr, *The Principle of Sufficient Reason*, p. 173).

[50] See G. Klubertanz, *Philosophy of Being*, p. 158. Also see n. 54 of this chapter.

[51] In the light of this formulation, cannot one also express it as, "Whatever is *composed of potency/act* demands an agent"? If so, the Efficient Cause Proposition known through reflection here meets that known through reasoning ("Every existent whose existence is really other than what it is is efficiently caused by another").

[52] That is, it is used in speculative philosophical processes. See n. 54 for an example.

formally certain (one not only assents to it without fear of erring, but one can also give a technical account for that absence of fear). Nevertheless, it remains inductive because it is initiated by concrete instances of efficiency. It still is immediate and self-evident, for it arises not from reasoning but from mere reflection upon evidence directly presented within those concrete cases.[53] It is a principle because it can and does serve as a premise within reasoning processes.[54]

(c) Résumé

The topic discussed in this fourth section has been existents as effects of efficient causality. How widespread is efficient causality? How many existents result from the activity of others? From one point of view, the answer is direct and easy: they all do, with the exception of God, because in all save Him actuality is really other than essence, and because all except Him change, going from potency to act on one or many levels.

---

[53] On the difference between reflection and reasoning, see Ch. X, Sec. 3.

[54] For example, Aquinas uses it as a premise in his First Way for proving the existence of God (*S.T.*, I, 2, 3, resp.): "It is certain and evident to our senses, that in the world some things are in motion. *Now whatever is moved is moved by another.*" Immediately thereafter he spells out the reflection by which one arrives at that proposition: "For nothing can be moved except it is in potentiality to that towards which it is moved, whereas a thing moves inasmuch as it is in act. For motion is nothing else than the reduction of something from potentiality to actuality. But nothing can be reduced from potentiality to actuality, except by something in a state of actuality. . . . Now it is not possible that the same thing should be at once in actuality and potentiality in the same respect but only in different respects. . . . It is therefore impossible that in the same respect and in the same way a thing should be both moved and mover."

It also furnishes the basis for psychoanalysis. See Charles Brenner, *Elementary Textbook of Psychoanalysis* (New York: International Universities Press, 1957), p. 2: "Let us start with the principle of psychic determinism. The sense of this principle . . . is that each psychic event is determined by the ones which preceded it. . . . Mental phenomena are no more capable of such a lack of causal connection with what preceded them than are physical ones. . . . If we do understand and apply [this principle] correctly, we shall never dismiss any psychic phenomenon as meaningless or accidental. We shall always ask ourselves, in relation to any such phenomenon in which we are interested: 'What caused it? Why did it happen?' We ask ourselves these questions because we are confident that an answer to them exists. Whether we can discover the answer quickly and easily is another matter, of course, but we know that the answer is there."

On the other hand, the reply is more complicated if one takes into account the Cartesian tradition and discusses the knowledge involved. Then one must reject a cognition which would be immediate and self-evident in a deductive, analytic, *a priori* sense. Rather, one finds it to be inductive and *a posteriori* because it entirely issues from our observing agents which actually are producing things by their activities. This inductive cognition is at least twofold. Either it is a conclusion to the reasoning process by which one realizes the impact which the real distinction between existence and essence in existents has upon their origin, in which case it is formulated as "Every existent whose existence is really other than what it is is efficiently caused by another." Or it is a self-evident principle known inductively through immediate insight into or technical reflection upon what change itself entails, as manifested in concrete cases of various changes effected by agents, and it is then formulated in some such fashion as "Every new item comes about because of an agent," or "Whatever goes from potency to act does so under the influence of an agent."

5. Summary and Conclusions

(a) However thoroughly a philosopher may have studied existents in the light of their intrinsic causes (the act of existing and the other components), he must still investigate their efficient causes if he is to understand them completely. The question "Who?" comes as automatically to mind as does "What?"

(b) The investigation of efficient causality made in this chapter centers around two problems—existents as efficient causes (Secs. 1–3) and also as effects of efficiency (Sec. 4). Let us review the discussion of the second problem first.

1. How many existents result from efficient causality? With the exception of God, all of them, and this for two reasons. First, all except Him entail change—the transition from potency to act. Second, all besides Him actually *are* in such a way that the act by which each *is* differs really from the essence by which each is *what* it is.

2. Through what sort of knowledge is the answer achieved? Through induction, which is either immediate insight or reflection—then the knowledge is an immediate, self-evident principle, and can be formulated as "Every new item comes about because of an agent," or "Whatever passes from potency to act does so under the influence of an agent"; or through inductive reasoning—then

the knowledge is a conclusion, and can be formulated as "Every existent whose existence is really distinct from what it is is efficiently caused by another."

(c) Granted, then, that all material existents are effects of efficient causes, but in what exactly does that causality consist? How does it come about? In what way do material agents produce their fellow existents? There are several preliminary points of information to be considered. First of all, when physical existents efficiently cause other existents, at least six factors are involved:

Principal agent: "that which acts without qualification" or "that which causes the higher perfection in an effect."

Instrumental agent: "that which acts while simultaneously being acted upon" or "that which causes the lower perfection in an effect."

Pre-existing matter: that from which a new perfection is educed and in which it inheres and exists.

Activity, whether transient or immanent.

Real relation of origin, dependence and similarity between the product and its agents.

The product itself: that which is produced through activity and which is really dependent upon and similar to the agents (with respect to physical agents, it is a new accidental perfection or substantial form, existing in and individuated by its recipient).

(d) Still additional preliminary information can be stated in these corollaries:

1. *An agent precisely as agent is not changed by his activity,* because the activity is in the thing being produced—it is, actually, the thing's very change from the potential to the actual.

2. *Whatever an agent produces is similar to itself.* Why so? Because the activity involved in the production is the agent projecting and externalizing itself, and the product is that same activity in a concretized and realized condition. According to the degrees of similarity, agents are called univocal, analogous, and equivocal.

3. *Every agent, whether principal or instrumental, has a proper effect in the product*—that which it produces by acting precisely according to what it is.

(e) The last corollary has important and relevant consequences. Because the act of existing is really other than what any material existent (or, for the matter, any creature) is, it is not the proper effect of any material existent. No such existent can properly cause anything to exist. It is the proper effect only of that Existent Whose very nature is to exist—namely, God, Who is subsistent actuality. But we know from direct perception that material existents help produce other material existents; hence they must literally *work together* with God as His instruments.

(f) In that co-operation between God and other existents lies the reply to how material existents are efficient causes. Instrumentally they account for the fact *that* other existents do exist, and properly they account for *what* they are. God properly accounts for the fact *that* they exist, and through His created and material co-workers He accounts for *what* they are.

(g) Obviously, actual existence is at the heart of all efficiency, created and divine. Creatures are active, ultimately, because they *are*. But since they *are* through an act which is really other than *what* they are and which must continuously be efficiently caused by God, their very efficiency is efficiently caused, and they only instrumentally cause others to exist. God's activity too is rooted in His actuality, which, being perfect (because subsistent), issues into efficiency which is perfect and totally uncaused. He properly causes existence in others. Accordingly, although creatures are secondary efficient causes, He alone is the primary Cause.

Suggested Readings

Albertson, James S., "Instrumental Causality in St. Thomas," *The New Scholasticism*, 28 (1954), 409–35.

Anderson, James F., *The Cause of Being*, pp. 1–31. St. Louis: B. Herder Book Co., 1952. On God as primary efficient cause; on the co-operation of creatures with God.

Bunge, Mario, *Causality: The Place of the Causal Principle in Modern Science.* Cambridge, Mass.: Harvard University Press, 1959.

De Finance, Joseph, *Connaissance de l'être: Traité d'ontologie.* Paris: Desclée de Brouwer, 1966. Pp. 351–95 *re* efficient causes.

De Raeymaeker, Louis, "The Metaphysical Problem of Causality," trans. A. J. Heiman, *Philosophy Today*, 1 (1957), 219–29.

Gilson, Etienne, *The Spirit of Mediaeval Philosophy*, trans. A. H. C. Downes, pp. 128–47. New York: Charles Scribner's Sons, 1940. On creatures as efficient causes in relationship to God.

Gurr, S.J., John Edwin, "Genesis and Function of Principles in Philosophy," *Proceedings of the American Catholic Philosophical Association*, 29 (1955), 121–33.

———, *The Principle of Sufficient Reason in Some Scholastic Systems,* 1750–1900. Milwaukee: Marquette University Press, 1959. On "sufficient reason" in reference to the Efficient Cause Proposition as a Cartesian "principle."

Hawkins, D. J. B., "Causality in Aristotle and Hume" (Ch. X), "Simultaneous and Successive Causation" (Ch. XI), "Principles of Causality and Intelligibility" (Ch. XII), in *Being and Becoming,* pp. 137–49, 150–62, 163–76. New York: Sheed & Ward, 1954.

Jaki, Stanley L., *God and the Cosmologists.* Washington, D.C.: Regnery Gateway, 1988. Ch. 5, pp. 111–41, and *passim*—see "causality" in "Index of Topics."

Johann, Robert O., "A Comment on Secondary Causality," *Modern Schoolman,* 25 (1947), 19–25.

Lerner, Daniel (ed.), *Cause and Effect: The Hayden Colloquium on Scientific Method and Concept* (New York: The Free Press, 1965)—see especially Ernest Nagel, "Types of Causal Explanation in Science," pp. 11–32; Abraham Kaplan, "Noncausal Explanation," pp. 145–54; Herbert A. Simon, "Causal Ordering and Identifiability," pp. 157–89.

Meehan, F. X., *Efficient Causality in Aristotle and St. Thomas.* Washington, D.C.: The Catholic University of America Press, 1940.

Owens, Joseph, "The Causal Proposition—Principle or Conclusion?" *Modern Schoolman,* 32 (1955), 159–71, 257–70, 323–39.

Smith, S.J., Gerard, *Natural Theology,* pp. 77–100 and 116–56. New York: The Macmillian Company, 1951. Concerning efficient causes.

Wild, John, *Introduction to Realistic Philosophy,* pp. 297–318. New York: Harper & Row, Publishers, 1948. On efficient causality.

———, "A Realistic Defense of Causal Efficacy," *Review of Metaphysics,* 2 (1949), 1–14.

IX

Final Causality

"What?" and "Who?" are not the only questions which arise when we are confronted with an unknown object.[1] We also ask "Why?" Why did the agent do it? For what reason? What is his goal and motive in acting as he does? This third question concerns final causality, which we shall now consider.

* 1. Several Opinions

Finality is totally rejected by many contemporary philosophers and scientists. No one has stated and explained this rejection better than the once prominent American philosopher, W. T. Stace at Princeton University. "Why is religion disappearing?" he asks.[2] Why, consequently, must the universe be purposeless, man's ideals be his own creation, man himself be alone and friendless in the world? Because of modern science, he answered, and this not because of any "particular discoveries or theories, such as the Darwinian theory of evolution, or the views of geologists about the age of the earth," but rather because of the "general spirit of science and certain basic assumptions upon which modern science, from the seventeenth century onwards, has proceeded." Who, in particular, was responsible for that general spirit of science and thus destroyed "the old comfortable picture of a friendly universe governed by spiritual values?" Galileo and Newton, by the "general

[1] See Ch. VIII, prgrs. corresponding to notes 1–5.

[2] W. T. Stace, "Man Against Darkness," *Atlantic* 182 (September, 1948), 53.

picture of the world which these men and others of their time made the basis of the science, not only of their own day, but of all succeeding generations down to the present."

> Neither the Copernican hypothesis nor any of Newton's or Galileo's particular discoveries were the real causes. Religious faith might well have accommodated itself to the new astronomy. The real turning point between the medieval age of faith and the modern age of unfaith came when the scientists of the seventeenth century turned their backs upon what used to be called "final causes." The final cause of a thing or event meant the purpose which it was supposed to serve in the universe, its cosmic purposes. What lay back of this was the presupposition that there is a cosmic order or plan and that everything which exists could in the last analysis be explained in terms of its place in this cosmic plan, that is, in terms of its purpose.
>
> Plato and Aristotle believed this, and so did the whole medieval Christian world. For instance, if it were true that the sun and the moon were created and exist for the purpose of giving light to man, then this fact would explain why the sun and the moon exist. We might not be able to discover the purpose of everything, but everything must have a purpose. Belief in final causes thus amounted to a belief that the world is governed by purposes, presumably the purposes of some overruling mind. This belief was not the invention of Christianity. It was basic to the whole of Western civilization, whether in the ancient pagan world or in Christendom, from the time of Socrates to the rise of science in the seventeenth century.[3]

How did Galileo, Newton, and the other founders of modern science accomplish this revolution? Although they were mostly pious men who did not doubt God's purposes, nevertheless

> they took the revolutionary step of consciously and deliberately expelling the idea of purpose as controlling nature from their new science of nature. They did this on the ground that inquiry into purposes is useless for what science aims at: namely, the prediction and control of events. To predict an eclipse, what you have to know is not its purpose but its

[3] *Ibid.*, pp. 53–54.

> causes. Hence, science from the seventeenth century onwards became exclusively an inquiry into causes. The conception of purpose in the world was ignored and frowned upon. This, though silent and almost unnoticed, was the greatest revolution in human history, far outweighing in importance any of the political revolutions whose thunder has reverberated through the world.[4]

And the result?

> For the past three hundred years there has been growing up in men's minds, dominated as they are by science, a new imaginative picture of the world. The world, according to this new picture, is purposeless, senseless, meaningless. Nature is nothing but matter in motion. The motions of matter are governed, not by any purpose, but by blind forces and laws. Nature on this view, says Whitehead, . . . is "merely the hurrying of material, endlessly, meaninglessly. . . ."
>
> If the scheme of things is purposeless and meaningless, then the life of man is purposeless and meaningless too. Everything is futile, all effort is in the end worthless. A man may, of course, still pursue disconnected ends, money, fame, art, science, and may gain pleasure from them. But his life is hollow at the center. Hence, the dissatisfied, disillusioned, restless, spirit of modern man. . . . Along with the ruin of the religious vision there went the ruin of moral principles and indeed of all values. . . . If our moral rules do not proceed from something outside us in the nature of the universe—whether we say it is God or simply the universe itself—then they must be our own inventions. Thus it came to be believed that moral

---

[4] *Ibid.* See also Robert B. MacLeod, "Teleology and Theory of Human Behavior," *Science* 125 (March 15, 1957), 478, col. 1: "The revolution of the New Science banished Aristotle's final cause, at least so far as physical nature was concerned, and even Aristotle's formal causes were laid open to question. The physical world that Newton envisaged was a world that could be described in terms of material and efficient causes, in terms of particles of matter that exist in space and time and are moved by force. Since Newton's day matter has lost much of its materiality; space and time have ceased to be absolutes, and force has been transmuted into a mathematical formula; but for all practical purposes the Newtonian scheme still works, and deep down we still have the conviction that Newton had his fingers on the fundamentals."

> rules must be merely an expression of our own likes and dislikes. But likes and dislikes are notoriously variable. What pleases one man, people or culture, displeases another. Therefore, morals are wholly relative.[5]

Stace goes on to suggest two remedies to help us in enduring those evils of our times (first, face the truth that such *is* the universe in which we live and, second, learn to live with that truth as best and as decently as we can),[6] but limits of space forbid following him. Even so, the points relevant for our purposes have been made amply clear: the root of our contemporary *malaise* is the rejection by modern science of final causes, of cosmic purposes; this was done because of the very aim of science—to predict and control events; the result is that modern sciences became an inquiry into causes other than final ones.

Since Stace's article, some have tried to insert finality into at least one of the modern sciences. Robert B. MacLeod, an experimental psychologist of Cornell University, tentatively suggested at the 1956 New York meeting of the American Association for the Advancement of Science that the concept of finality be introduced into the social sciences.

> In reviving the old question of teleology, I realize that I am venturing down a pathway that for some centuries has appeared forbidding even to the angels, and that in taking a hesitant step in this direction I am identifying myself with a nonangelic group. Teleology means the explanation of natural events in terms of purposive constructs. This is a currently unpopular approach. I submit, however, that we should from time to time look again at the phenomena that invite a teleological explanation and make sure that we have done full justice to them.[7]

The social sciences lack the significant upheavals and advances that mark the histories of astronomy, physics and biology, and MacLeod locates that lack precisely in the fact that the social scientists, slavishly imitating the natural scientists, have apriorily excluded Aristotle and his theory of causality.

---

[5] Stace, *art. cit.*, pp. 54–55.

[6] *Ibid.*, pp. 57–58. Also see *idem, Religion and the Modern Mind* (Philadelphia: J. B. Lippincott Co., 1952), where Stace covers much the same ground.

[7] *Art. cit.*, in n. 4, p. 477, col. 1.

> We look for [the great revolution of the social sciences] in vain because it has not yet taken place. Why? I suggest that it is because the students of man have cravenly tried to pattern their fundamental concepts and methods after those of the natural sciences. I do not propose to canonize Aristotle, as the medieval theologians nearly did; but I do think that, just as the Renaissance was sparked by the rediscovery of the real Aristotle, so the social sciences of today can profit from a fresh look at Aristotle's argument for the unity of man and nature [which rests upon] a fourfold theory of causality.[8]

He then proposes that social scientists should at least consider whether teleology would not help their very science.

> I am not arguing that science should suddenly have a change of heart and reinstate Aristotle's final causes. The physical sciences have done fairly well without them. The biological sciences seem to be admitting formal causes without yielding to final causes, although some biologists are striving manfully to reduce formal to material and efficient causes. What I do suggest is that the social sciences, dealing as they do with the very phenomena that invite a teleological explanation, should not scurry away from these phenomena but should look at them fearlessly and be prepared to think in more global terms. A quarter of a century ago a much maligned psychologist, William McDougall, analyzed what he called "the marks of behavior," the most important of which was purposive striving. I think he was right. Among the many things that are characteristic of organisms is that they strive toward goals. We may deduce goals from the observed behavior of simpler

[8] *Ibid.*, p. 477, col. 3. See *ibid.*, p. 479, col. 3: "The most influential of contemporary psychologists, the American behaviorists, are still trying to stuff the science of man into a Newtonian bottle. They would like to see all of human behavior plotted bidimensionally within a simple scheme of space-time coordinates. I do not really deplore this. The scheme works well with rats, and with human beings who have the fortitude to memorize endless chains of nonsense syllables. It is a healthy and humbling experience to know that human, as well as animal, organisms can be made to behave like well-oiled machines. In a world that cries for a deeper understanding of man, however. . . , I think it is high time that the students of man stop pretending to be scientists in the traditional sense and settle down to the business of looking at man as he really behaves."

> organisms or we may observe them directly in our own experience. The fact remains that goal directedness is something we can observe. If science is to include the behavior of man, it must include the fact of purposive striving. Sticks and stones do not strive, but people do.[9]

Even this proposal he tempers with the suggestion that if the time is not yet ripe for the direct introduction of final causes, let social scientists begin with formal causes and eventually move over to final causes.

> My present feeling is that, if we were to reintroduce final causes now, we would be moving too fast. Some day we may have a natural science that is broad enough, both in its concepts and in its methods, to include the facts of human purpose. For the time being, I think it is expedient to concentrate on Aristotle's formal causes, and I suspect that the solution of formal causality may automatically resolve the problem of final causality.
>
> One's thinking is always culture-bound. My own bias is against any sort of teleology. I do not want to admit transcendent, or even immanent, purposes into the universe. This may be a relic of my Newtonian upbringing. Nevertheless, the facts of human behavior and experience reveal purposiveness. Shall we consider these facts of nature, or shall we deny them? If we accept them, shall we reduce them to "purposeless" terms, or shall we try to discover a unified science that is broad enough to encompass the full richness of experience?[10]

MacLeod's suggestion has not been universally welcomed by his fellow scientists. In an address at the 1959 convention of the same American Association for the Advancement of Science and later published also in its organ, *Science,* George Gaylord Simpson, Professor of Vertebrate Paleontology at Harvard, showed himself to be uninfluenced by MacLeod—in fact, he made statements directly opposing the latter's thesis that "What is most challenging about Darwin . . . is his reintroduction of purpose into the natural world.

---

[9] *Ibid.,* p. 479, col. 3.
[10] *Ibid.,* p. 480, col. 2.

He may not have intended to do this . . . but this was clearly one of the consequences."[11] Simpson rejoins:

> The sort of testable evidence that would suggest vitalism or finalism would be the steady progression of life, and of each of its evolving lineages, toward a final and transcendentally worthy goal. That is not, in fact, what the known record of life's history shows. There is no clear over-all progression. . . . [The sort of evidence Simpson offers in rebuttal] convinces me, at least, that the hypotheses of vitalism and finalism are not necessary. Everything proceeds as if they were nonexistent. . . . [Vitalism and finalism] are sometimes advanced with the avowed hope of retaining something from the world of superstition. Vitalism then pretends to find a place in nature for the supernatural. Finalism tries to bring in by the back door *the teleology that Darwin swept out the front door*.[12]

In the following year and in the same journal Ernst Mayr, professor of zoology at Harvard, shows a direct acquaintance with MacLeod and reduces "teleology" to "teleonomy" in an important and interesting paper on "Cause and Effect in Biology." First he indicates the evidence generally adduced for final causes.

> No discussion of causality is complete which does not come to grips with the problem of teleology. This problem had its beginning with Aristotle's classification of causes, one of the categories being the "final" causes. This category is based on the observation of the orderly and purposive development of the individual from the egg to the "final" stage of the adult, and of the development of the whole world from its beginning (chaos?) to its present order. Final cause has been defined as "the cause responsible for the orderly reaching of a precon-

---

[11] *Ibid.*, p. 478, col. 3.

[12] George Gaylord Simpson, "The World Into Which Darwin Led Us," *Science*, 131 (April 1, 1960), 973, col. 2. On the link between vitalism and finalism, see *ibid.*, p. 973, col. 1: "There is no absolute logical necessity that vitalism and finalism should go together, but the ideas are related if only because both are to some degree nonnaturalistic, and in that sense nonmaterialistic. More often than not, vitalists are finalists and finalists are vitalists." On this point, see the entire section, p. 972, col. 3, to p. 973, col. 2.

> ceived ultimate goal."... Thinkers from Aristotle to the present have been challenged by the apparent contradiction between a mechanistic interpretation of natural processes and the seemingly purposive sequence of events in organic growth, in reproduction, and in animal behavior.[13]

But "what is the *x*, this seemingly purposive agent, this 'vital force,' in organic phenomena?" It is not *élan vital* or *entelechia*, whereby "the finalistic and vitalistic philosophies of the past merely replaced the unknown *x* by a different unknown, *y* or *z*. . . . The supernaturalistic conclusions drawn from these observations are altogether misleading."[14] What, then, is it?

> Where, then, is it legitimate to speak of purpose and purposiveness in nature, and where is it not? To this question we can now give a firm and unambiguous answer. An individual who—to use the language of the computer—has been "programmed" can act purposefully. Historical processes, however, can *not* act purposefully. A bird that starts its migration, an insect that selects its host plant, an animal that avoids a predator, a male that displays to a female—they all act purposefully because they have been programmed to do so.[15]

In what does this "programming" consist?

> The completely individualistic and yet also species-specific DNA code of every zygote (fertilized egg cell), which controls the development of the central and peripheral nervous systems, of the sense organs, of the hormones, of physiology and morphology, is the *program* for the behavior computer of this individual.[16]

It is completely mechanistic.

> The purposive action of an individual, insofar as it is based on the properties of its genetic code, therefore is no more nor less

---

[13] Ernst Mayr, "Cause and Effect in Biology," *Science* 134 (November 10, 1961), 1503, cols. 2 and 3.

[14] *Ibid.*, col. 3.

[15] *Ibid.*, col. 3–p. 1504, col. 1.

[16] *Ibid.*

> purposive than the actions of a computer that has been programmed to respond appropriately to various inputs. It is, if I may say so, a purely mechanistic purposiveness.[17]

It is in fact better not to call such a mechanistic purposiveness "teleological" but "teleonomic."

> It would seem useful to [substitute *teleonomy* for *teleology* and then to] restrict the term *teleonomic* rigidly to systems operating on the basis of a program, a code of information. Teleonomy in biology designates "the apparent purposefulness of organisms and their characteristics," as Julian Huxley expressed it.
>
> Such a clear-cut separation of teleonomy, which has an analyzable physico-chemical basis, from teleology, which deals more broadly with the over-all harmony of the organic world, is most useful because these two entirely different phenomena have so often been confused with each other.[18]

He then turns to MacLeod's position on Darwin.

> The development or behavior of an individual is purposive, natural selection is definitely not. When MacLeod stated, "What is most challenging about Darwin, however, is his reintroduction of purpose into the natural world," he chose the wrong word. The word *purpose* is singularly inapplicable to evolutionary change, which is, after all, what Darwin was considering. If an organism is well adapted, if it shows superior fitness, this is not due to any purpose of its ancestors or of an outside agency, such as "Nature" or "God," Who created a superior design or plan. Darwin "has swept out such finalistic teleology by the front door," as Simpson has rightly said.
>
> We can summarize this discussion by stating that there is no conflict between causality and teleonomy, but that scientific biology has not found any evidence that would support teleology in the sense of various vitalistic or finalistic theories.[19]

In the light of those articles by MacLeod, Simpson and Mayr, there are within the realm of modern science two opposing camps.

---

[17] *Ibid.*

[18] *Ibid.*, p. 1504, col. 2.

[19] *Ibid.*

One of these, numerically smaller and almost apologetic, timidly suggests reinstating finality. The other vigorously opposes that move, or at least wants it reduced to merely a mechanistic, psychochemical, immanent condition of material things.[20]

Another attitude toward finality is that of those Scholastics whose way of proceeding fits best into a Cartesian atmosphere[21] and for whom finality is a genuine and obvious factor in all reality. That every agent acts necessarily for the sake of an end is a self-evident and *a priori* principle. Consider what R. Garrigou-Lagrange, O.P., says in his well-known book *God: His Existence and His Nature.*[22]

> As soon as we understand what is meant by the word *end*, this principle ["Every agent acts for an end"] is self-evident. End is not only the terminus or result of an action, but the reason why the action has taken place. . . . It is a *definite perfection*, which directly *refers* to the agent as its own good, and for the sake of which the agent acts. . . . Now every agent . . . produces a *definite* effect according to its own natural law. . . . It cannot produce this definite and appropriate effect rather than any other, except on condition that it has a *tendency* to produce this particular effect rather than any other. It is not necessary for the agent to know the cause of this tendency, but at least that it is by its nature *ordained towards* this object. Thus the sense of sight produces an act which is not indifferent, but determined. . . . The reason why the sense of sight perceives colors instead of hearing sounds is because it is naturally *ordained to* seeing and not to hearing, because seeing is its very *raison d'être.* This is a self-evident truth, which certainly transcends the range of sense perception, but is perceived at once by the intellect, a faculty of being, when it considers such an organ as the eye or ear. . . . The mind has intuitive knowledge of this fact.[23]

---

[20] For other representatives of those two camps, see Edmund W. Sinnott, *The Biology of the Spirit* (New York: The Viking Press, Inc., 1955) and Lecomte DuNoüy, *The Road to Reason* (New York: David McKay Co., Inc., 1949), who energetically champion telism. On the other side is Leo Francis Koch, "Vitalistic-Mechanistic Controversy," *Scientific Monthly*, 85 (November, 1957), 245–55.

[21] On this attitude with reference to the Efficient Cause Proposition, see Chap. VIII, Sec. 4a.

[22] St. Louis: B. Herder, 1934. All the references are to volume I of this work.

[23] *Ibid.*, pp. 200–201.

The Principle of Finality is for him immediately evident also because of its direct connection with the Principles of Sufficient Reason and of Contradiction.

> This principle of finality . . . is not only self-evident as soon as the terms of the proposition are understood, but it can also be proved indirectly by showing that to deny it leads to the absurdity of denying the principle of sufficient reason, which latter cannot be rejected without necessarily rejecting the principle of contradiction.
>
> If every agent produces, not an indifferent effect whatsoever, but a determined effect which belongs to it by right, *though it does not tend towards this effect*, and is not *ordained* for it, . . . it follows that there is no way of explaining by *the principle of sufficient reason* how it is that the effect is definitely established and essentially refers to definite cause. . . . If the agent did not *tend* towards its effect, if it did not have at least a natural *intention* for it, if it were not naturally ordained to produce it, it would no more produce this particular effect than any other, except by accident or chance. . . . In other words, action is essentially *intentional*, that is, ordained towards some end. Without this tendency not only the effect, but the activity itself, would be without a sufficient cause, that is, without determination or congruity, or, to put it differently, it could no more be said to be an attraction than a repulsion, vision than audition, digestion than respiration. . . .[24]

Our author draws his final conclusion.

> Therefore, every agent acts *for* an end. The word *for* has a meaning, not only when applied to human activity, in which the end is known and intended, but also when applied to any other kind of activity. Whereas the efficient cause is the sufficient reason as a realizing principle (or that by which a thing is accomplished), the final cause is the sufficient reason for the thing which is accomplished. The eyes are made for seeing and not for hearing. Therefore, the principle of finality, like that of causality, is an analytical one in the Aristotelian sense.[25]

---

[24] *Ibid.*, pp. 201–2.
[25] *Ibid.*, p. 203.

This third group could be illustrated by other authors,[26] but the paragraphs from the Dominican writer disclose with sufficient clarity its diversity from the previous groups. They are hesitant or even hostile with regard to finality; their approach tends to be *a posteriori*; they fear any tie teleology might have with God, with the supernatural, the transcendent. But the last group welcomes finality wholeheartedly; they approach it in an *a priori*, analytic way so that it is formulated as a self-evident principle; they use it as a way of knowing God, the intelligent designer of the finalized universe.

Such, then, are various opinions on finality, which can serve as an introduction to our study of it. The excerpts from Stace indicate how important that study is if religion and morality hinge upon it, as well as how its rejection by modern scientists came about. The selections from the other authors set up some of the questions we must discuss. What is finality or teleology? Is it synonymous with teleonomy, or does it involve more? Is finality found only on the cognitive level, or is it found also among living existents and even among inanimates? What is its relation to God? Does it lead to God, or does knowing Him lead us to it? Are the charges of superstition and supernaturalism valid?

Contact with these authors also confirms that the methodology to be followed is not an *a priori* descent from innate ideas to a so-called self-evident, analytic but largely gratuitous Principle of Finality. Rather, it should be that of a hardheaded but open-minded student of nature: an *a posteriori* and inductive observation of actual cases. As MacLeod advised,

---

[26] For example, see Kevin J. O'Brien, C.Ss.R., *The Proximate End of Education* (Milwaukee: Bruce Publishing Co., 1958), p. 48: "The Principle of Finality is traditionally and best formulated: *Omne agens agit propter finem*. . . . Its validity, though impugned in diverse ways by some writers—materialists, pantheists, positivists, evolutionists—is in practice an accepted part of daily life. It is of itself evident according to the second mode of perseity; its denial leads to absurdity and to a violation of the principle of sufficient reason." Also see *ibid.*, pp. 32–33. See J. Maritain, *Preface to Metaphysics*, "Fifth Lecture: The Principles of Identity, Sufficient Reason, and Finality," pp. 90–109, and "Sixth Lecture: The Principle of Finality (Second Aspect)," pp. 110–31; R. Arnou, S.J., *Metaphyisca Generalis* (Romae: Typis Pontificiae Universitatis Gregorianae, 1941), pp. 231–34. Interestingly enough, P. Coffey, *Ontology*, p. 370, holds that the Principle of Efficient Causality is self-evident but not so with finality: "We shall see that as a matter of fact nothing happens without a *final* cause; that intelligent purpose pervades reality through. This, however, is a conclusion, not a principle."

> [We] should not scurry away from these phenomena [which invite a teleological explanation] but should look at them fearlessly and be prepared to think in more global terms. . . . Among the many things that are characteristic of organisms is that they strive toward goals. We may deduce goals from the observed behavior of simpler organisms, or we may observe them directly in our own experience. *The fact remains that goal directedness is something we can observe.* If science is to include the behavior of man, it must include the fact of purposive striving.[27]

2. Finality on the Cognitive Level

Let us begin by considering what happens when an industrious student in serious financial straits learns that a wealthy alumnus of the school is now on campus ready to give deserving students a gift of three thousand dollars with no strings attached. The student of course begins to *want* that money, but the coming about of that desire involves several stages which need explication. First of all, there is the student before he learns of the possible gift. Suppose that he is asleep in his room. In that condition he is not consciously desiring anything, and yet, unlike the bed upon which he is lying,

---

[27] *Art. cit.*, p. 479, col. 3. In the third sentence of the quotation, he does not mean "deduce" in the sense of an *a priori* deduction from innate ideas, such as a Cartesian would advise, but in the sense of an inductive inference.

As to methodology, also see John L. Russell, S.J., "The Principle of Finality in the Philosophy of Aristotle and Teilhard de Chardin," *Heythrop Journal*, 3 (October, 1962), p. 351: "The difference in approach to philosophy between Descartes and Aristotle can be summarized without too much oversimplification by saying that for Descartes the philosopher is a [mere] spectator of the physical world; for Aristotle he is a participant. The Cartesian philosopher seeks to detach himself from the world; he withdraws to his study and contemplates the mundane scene with a quasi-angelic intellectual regard which has been purged, as far as possible, from the distractions of sensible experience. The Aristotelian, on the other hand, goes out into the world; he picks things up and handles them; he pushes and pulls them about. He recognizes that he has, in varying degrees, a common nature with animals, plants, and even lifeless things. . . . The philosopher must go to school with the physicist, the biologist, and the artist if he is to acquire the 'feel' of the world which it is his business to elucidate. It is no accident that Aristotle the philosopher was also a first-class biologist and one of the world's great writers on aesthetics and political theory. His philosophy is essentially that of a man who knows the world from the inside, not simply as a spectator."

he is of such a nature as to be capable (when awake) of desiring, and of desiring many different objects (for example, he might desire to study, to swim, to dance, to earn money, and so on). The telephone rings, and someone informs him of the alumnus' generosity and tells him the alumnus is now present on campus. The result is that the student's appetitive powers become active, he now *actually wants the money*, and he hurries for an interview.

That is the sort of situation which "finality" is used to describe on the cognitive level—an agent who can know and love, his awareness of a good, his actual love of the good known.[28] The "final" or telic *cause* is the good-as-known.[29] The causality it exercises is the

---

[28] "Love," "desire," and similar terms can refer to different operations (see H. Renard, S.J., and Martin Vaske, S.J., *Philosophy of Man,* 2nd ed., pp. 212–13; G. Klubertanz, *Philosophy of Human Nature,* pp. 211–24). But it is more convenient for us to use them in the meaning which they have in common: they are all actuations of a cognitive agent's appetitive powers. For our purposes, then, they can be taken as synonymous. The distinction between will and sense appetites also is not crucial for our purposes, and we shall generally use these terms also without reference to that distinction. We shall also speak of love (or desire and so on) as an "operation" or "activity" or "act" without intending any difference in meaning.

Both humans and animals are cognitive agents because both have appetitive powers, the former having both will and sense appetites (concupiscible and irascible), the latter only sense appetites. (See H. Renard, *op. cit.*, Chs. VII and VIII; G. Klubertanz, *op. cit.*, Chs. X and XI.) Although we shall speak only of humans throughout these pages, what is said of them is also applicable, *mutatis mutandis,* to animals. But not all the operations of a human (or animal) are relevant to cognitive finality—only his appetition and those operations which it directly instigates. For example, in his vegetative functions (assimilation of food, growth, respiration, and the like), in his unconscious relieving of tension by yawning or scratching his head, even in his cognitive activity when actuated by stimuli from without and not by a will-act, he is not acting as a cognitive agent.

A cognitive agent, then, is *an agent with reference to its appetitive operations, as well as to other operations directly caused by them.* A noncognitive agent is an agent with reference to all other operations except these.

[29] The adjective "final" is ambiguous. It can mean what is chronologically last ("The final task of the day") or what is definitive ("His book is the final word on the subject"), and so on. It can also be derived from *finis* as "goal." This last is the meaning in which we shall be using it: a good-as-known is the *final* cause because it is the goal which initiates a human's love and ensuing activity. Since *telos* in Greek means "goal," we shall use the adjective "telic" also as a synonym. This latter term has been brought into prominence by Donald C. Williams in his phrase, "telic tugs" (see "Form and Matter," *Philosophical Review*, 67 [1958], 312).

attraction it exerts upon the agent. The final or telic *effect* is the agent's love for the good. The efficient cause of that act of love is the agent's appetitive powers—his will and/or sense appetites. Let us briefly touch upon each of these factors.

(a) Four Causal Factors

1. The final cause is, then, the *good-as-known*, in which phrase each word is important. As seen previously, a good is "an actually existing item *as perfect*, and hence in relation to love."[30] The goodness of an existent (money, a building, a person, and so forth) resides precisely in its perfections—those possessions which are due to it in view of what it is.[31]

But the final cause with respect to cognitive agents is not simply a good, but, more exactly, a good *qua known*. The addition of the last two words has several important consequences. First of all, they explain how we can love what is in itself evil—we *look upon* it as good, and thus it seems a good because of our erroneous knowledge. Second, some of the goods which are final causes by triggering love in us do actually exist—the money desired by the student in the previous example, the person living next door, the sports car in the show window, and so on. But in order actually to be final causes, they must be known: only then can they attract us and set up desire within us. Some goods which are final causes, though, do not yet exist—the house to be built, the statue to be carved, the fame to be achieved, and so on. In fact, bringing them into existence is exactly what we want, and thus enters into their final causality. This they can exert, even though they are not yet actual, because a final cause is not simply a good, but a good precisely *as known*.[32]

To sum up: a final cause is a good-as-known, because this is what causes love in a cognitive agent. This can be something which is objectively evil, provided it is viewed as good. It can also be something which is objectively good, and this in two ways:

---

[30] See Ch. VI, Sec. 3c.

[31] On perfections, see Ch. V, Sec. 2.

[32] The house to be built, the statue to be carved, and other final causes which do not yet exist are, strictly speaking, good only through extrinsic denomination: they are the awarenesses of what *will be* actual and thus good. See Ch. VI, prgrs. corresponding to notes 44 and 54. Also see R. Kreyche, "How the End Functions as a Cause," *First Philosophy* (New York: Holt, Rinehart & Winston, Inc., 1959), pp. 248–50.

either it is something which does not yet actually exist and we want to make it, or it is something which already is in existence and we want to obtain it.

The very last point opens up a further complexity which cognitive finality entails, because one can have many reasons for obtaining something already actually existing. For example, I may want the hundred dollar bill you have in order to spend it or deposit it or cut it up. I may want to own that house on the corner lot so as to burn it, remodel it, rent it, or live in it. But the complexity does not stop there, for the person for whom I want it can vary. I may desire that I myself own the house, but I also may wish that you or your mother-in-law or the Young Democrats Club may own it.

The precise use to be made of a thing, as well as the person for whom it is intended, then, enters into why a cognitive agent desires something. Accordingly, a final cause in its concrete circumstances (for example, I want you to deposit the money) involves not only the thing itself (the money) but also the person for whom (you) and the precise use to be made of it (its deposit).[33] In saying that a final cause is a *good-as-known*, one must intend the last phrase to embrace those three elements: the thing itself (*finis cuius* or *qui*), its use (*finis quo*) and the person for whom it is done (*finis cui*). They are not, though, three final causes: they constitute a single, concrete goal, for they constitute a single object of the agent's appetitive power.

An actual final cause involves a further intricacy, because one good is frequently desired because of another. For example, you can desire that you own this mansion so that your son may be socially accepted at an Ivy League school so that he may eventually find a place in the United States Foreign Service. Or an artist may want to carve a statue so that he may obtain money so that he can feed his family. Obviously, then, a single goal may be made up of a series of subordinated goods (each of which involves the three elements mentioned in the previous paragraph). However multiple that series may be, though, it constitutes a single object for the appetitive power, and thus is a single final cause.[34]

---

[33] Traditionally, the first is called the *finis qui*, or at times *finis cuius*; the second, *finis cui*; the third, *finis quo*. These three conceptions and terms can also be applied analogously to a good which is to be made. For example, if I wish to carve a statue out of oak, the *finis qui* is the statue, the *finis cui* is the slab of oak, the *finis quo* is the carving.

[34] For semantic reasons the main goal has traditionally been called *finis operantis* (literally, the "end of the agent," the end in which the agent himself

Despite the complexities that can mark a final-cause situation, though, this must be clearly understood: the final *cause* therein is the good-as-known which is attracting the cognitive agent and thus causing him to love and tend toward it.

2. In what does the final causality of that good-as-known consist? What does it do? It does not strictly *do* anything, for it is not an efficient cause. It is a cause, though, because it brings about an effect—immediately, the agent's love; mediately (that is, through him), his obtaining or making something or other. The question is, then, *how* does it produce that act of love? By the attraction it exerts upon the agent. Because of its perfections it attracts or draws him, although not in any physical way, because it is not an efficient cause.[35] The thing known and loved is not itself changed by being known and loved—for example, the bottle of beer that attracts the thirsty laborer undergoes no change in that attraction: the change occurs in him—upon seeing the beer, he begins now to want it.

On two points the situation here is somewhat parallel to what one finds with respect to the transient activity of an efficient cause. Although an agent is truly an efficient cause, still precisely as agent he undergoes no change; the change is entirely in the patient, in the thing worked upon. So too here: the good-as-known is truly a final cause, and yet it itself does not change—only the one loving changes. Also, on the level of efficient causality a single physical activity is both action and passion: it is the former insofar as it comes from the agent, it is the latter inasmuch as it is in and perfects the patient.[36] Likewise, the act of love which arises within a final-cause situation is both the attraction which the good exerts upon the lover and simultaneously the response of the lover to the good. It is the former insofar as the act is telically caused by the good-as-known; it is the latter insofar as that same act is efficiently caused by the

---

is primarily interested, whereas the others he considers as means); the subordinate goal (or goals, since they can be multiple) has been called *finis operis* (the "end of the work," the end which *is* the work). The original force of the latter phrase is clear in such an instance as this: a man wishes to fashion a mobile sculpture from metal rods and delicate wire in order to earn money. The *finis operis* refers to fashioning the sculpture—that is, a goal (hence, *finis*) which *is* the very object to be produced (hence, *opus*). The *finis operantis* is, of course, the sculptor's earning of the money.

[35] A final cause does not, then, attract or draw the agent as a magnet draws iron filings or horses a buggy.

[36] On action/passion, see Ch. VIII, n. 16.

agent through his operative powers. It is a single operation which is open to and the result of both causes.

The good-as-known is, then, a genuine cause because it helps produce the activity of love within a cognitive agent. Its causality is the nonphysical attraction which the agent experiences within himself and which is, actually, also his very act of love as produced not efficiently but telically by that good. The attraction is his act of love in reference not to himself but to the good.

3. That operation of love is, then, the final *effect*: that which the good-as-known produces precisely as a final cause. It has two important characteristics—it is a determination and it is a tendency. It is a determination because, along the lines of what precisely is to be loved, a cognitive agent is indeterminate: *as far as he himself is concerned*, he is not now loving *A* or *B*. Yet he is determinable: he is by nature such as to be able to love *A* or *B*, or, for that matter, almost anything else (the student in our previous instance is capable of wanting to study, to swim, to go to the cafeteria, to dance, and so on). What determines him? The good which he comes to know, which attracts him and causes him to love it rather than something else. Hence, that act of love is an actual determination within him, a state of definiteness which directs him to *this* rather than *that* object and which issues into a determinate way of acting in order to implement that love and to achieve that object. In a telic situation, then, the cognitive agent of himself is determinable, the good as known is the determinant, and the act of love it telically causes is the resultant determination.

But that operation of love is also a tendency, an inclination. Because of it an agent tends toward, is directed and orientated and pointed toward, some definite goal. It energizes his whole being, so that he undertakes labor and undergoes hardships in order to acquire or construct (as the case may be) the thing in question.[37]

The act of love is, accordingly, both a determination and a tendency. But that act is the telic effect in a final-cause situation; hence, determination and tendency are effects of finality. So truly are they

[37] As an example of the energy that love for a goal can release, consider Konrad Adenauer. This elderly man had already been Chancellor of West Germany for several years when a reporter asked him how he managed to keep going under hard work and pressure. He replied: "First, one must be of good stock. Second, one must have great patience. There is also a third necessity: one must do everything within one's power for an *ideal* that one believes in. In my case, it is the *ideal* of *saving Christian civilization*" (*Time*, August 31, 1953). "Ideal" I take to be synonymous with "goal."

thus linked with finality that they become a criterion of deciding whether or not finality is present in a situation.[38] If an agent acts in a determinate way and if he spontaneously tends to that activity, then he is finalized toward that activity. What we are then observing are the *effects* of finality. Finality is present in its results.

4. The efficient cause of that act of love is, as has already been mentioned, the agent through his appetitive powers (will and sense appetites). He is a *cause* because he helps produce it. He is an *efficient* cause because he produces it by his activity: in fact, love is the very activity and actuation of his appetitive powers.[39]

Such are, then, the causal factors in a teleological situation involving cognitive agents.

The telic cause:	a good-as-known.
Its causality:	the attraction it exerts on the agent (which is rooted in its perfections but which is the ensuing act of love as telically caused).
The telic effect:	the act of love (which is determinate and tendential).
The efficient cause:	the agent through his appetitive powers.

Manifestly, the act of love is midway between final and efficient causes:

[good as known]	⟶	[love]	⟵	[appetitive powers]
final cause		*effect*		*efficient cause*

[38] This criterion is useful not only for cognitive agents but for noncognitive ones as well. No matter where found, determination essentially entails that what is multiple is reduced to unity and what is potential becomes actual, with the result that the agent thus affected is pointed and directed to a definite goal. In a cognitive agent that multiplicity or potentiality resides in his appetitive powers with their ability to love all sorts of goods, whereas the unity or state of actuation is his loving one of them. In a noncognitive agent the multiplicity and potentiality are the materials, the basic stuff which constitute it, but which as far as they themselves are concerned could have formed various other sorts of things, which virtually they are even now and which they will formally become through eventual substantial change. The unity or actuation is the very entity of the agent itself, organized, structured, programmed to produce definite activities. See Sec. 3a of this chapter.

[39] As we shall see later, his appetitive powers (as well as all his other operative powers) are also final effects. They tend to operations and to determinate operations. See Sec. 2b2 of this chapter.

(b) The Final Cause Proposition on the Cognitive Level

Another question now emerges. How widespread is such finality? Is a known good absolutely necessary for bringing about love in a cognitive agent? Is this true: if no known good, then no love, then no ensuing activity?

One can easily answer that inquiry in the light of those four causal factors. A known good is absolutely necessary in order for a cognitive agent to love: such is the very nature of his appetitive powers and of a good as known. The former make him determinable with respect to what precisely is to be loved: they give him a capacity to love and yet they do not determine what exactly he is to love. This determination comes from something other than himself—from the good-as-known, which because of its perfections can attract him and settle what is to be the precise object of his love. The act of love is, then, a joint product of both his appetitive powers and the good. Without the former there is no ability to love; without the latter there is nothing to love. If either were absent, there would be no love. Hence, the good-as-known is absolutely necessary that there be love (and the consequent activities it initiates) in a cognitive agent. To say the same: every cognitive agent acts because of a goal which is a good-as-known.

* ***1. Is the Final Cause Proposition Immediately Known?*** Such an answer is simple and clear, based as it is upon what appetitive powers and a good-as-known show themselves to be in our experience. They are to one another as the determinable to the determinant, the perfectible to the perfective, the actuable to the actuating. Another way of replying is to set the question within the framework of the Cartesian tradition and to investigate the sort of knowledge involved. Although this approach is more intricate, it is profitable because of the additional information it affords.

In our discussion of the Efficient Cause Proposition (see Ch. VIII, Sec. 4a), we have seen the fundamentals of this Cartesian approach. In a Cartesianism which is a "pure position," the human knower is not the body/soul composite but solely the soul. Data for human knowledge come not from the senses but from ideas innate within the mind. Additional knowledge is achieved by deducing from those ideas the self-evident truths they contain, which are formulated as analytic and *a priori* principles and to which one assents directly. In this chapter on finality (see paragraphs corresponding to notes 22–26 above) it became clear that Garrigou-Lagrange and other scholastic authors take this approach to finality. According to them, every agent necessarily acts for the sake of an end, and this is a self-evident and *a priori* principle. It is immediately known to be true by analysis of its terms[40] and by consideration of its intimate connection with the prior Principles of Sufficient Reason and of Contradiction.[41]

Against that Cartesian background, the question we now face is how the Final Cause Proposition is in fact known. What sort of knowledge is our awareness of it? Is it immediately known in any of its formulations?[42] Within the inductive movement which characterizes all basic human knowledge (spontaneous and philosophic), is it a self-evident principle?

My answer is yes, because of this evidence. When confronted with something new (for example, a raincoat pocket filled with syrup, a freshly baked cake in the pantry), everyone spontaneously asks not only "Who?" but also "Why?" Why did the agent do it? For what reason? What is his goal and motive in acting as he does? This inquiry seemingly is a sequel to a syllogism, the major premise of which is the Final Cause Proposition:

> Every new item comes about through an agent acting because of a goal;
> But here is a new item;
> Therefore, the agent responsible for it had some goal in mind and my question is: "*Why* did he do it? What is his goal?"

What we said previously concerning the Efficient Cause Proposition can also be applied here.[43] The Final Cause Proposition which is the major in that inference ("Every new item comes about through an agent acting because of some goal" or, more simply, "Every cognitive agent acts because of a goal") is operative on the purely practical level: it guides us in the events we encounter in our daily lives. Also it normally is implicit, becoming explicit only under the force of such considerations as we are now making. Nevertheless,

---

[40] See R. Garrigou-Lagrange, *op. cit.*, p. 200: "This principle . . . is self-evident to all who correctly understand the terms. . . . As soon as we understand what is meant by the word *end*, this principle is self-evident."

[41] See Garrigou-Lagrange, *ibid.*, pp. 201–2. Also see the references to other authors in n. 26 above.

[42] We have already seen one formulation in the introductory prgr. immediately prior to this section #2b1.

[43] See Ch. VIII, Sec. 4b.

it is operative in our practical lives, and it *is* in our minds implicitly if we are able to make it explicit. What is more, it necessarily is *known* immediately, spontaneously, and by all, because everyone immediately and spontaneously asks "Why?"

What would be the genesis of that knowledge? In harmony with the basic inductive character of human knowledge, it would be a concrete case a child observes in which an agent makes (or breaks) something under the influence of the end he has in mind. Consider a child witnessing Mother reacting favorably to Father's telephoned message that his employer would dine with them that evening. Everything else being equal, Mother begins to *desire* to prepare a special dinner to please the boss, thereby gaining a raise for her husband, a winter vacation in Florida for herself, and so forth. The child would notice several stages in the coming about of that desire. To begin with, there is Mother before she learns of the employer's visit. She is sleeping on the sofa. In that state she is not consciously desiring anything, and yet, unlike the sofa upon which she is lying, she is capable (when awake) of desiring and of desiring many different things (for instance, she might want to view TV or to sew or to clean house or to rake leaves, and so on). The telephone rings and her husband delivers the news of the visit. The knowledge of this good actuates her appetitive powers. She *now actually desires* to fix a special meal, and she heads for the kitchen.[44]

While observing such a concrete case, the child becomes aware not only that *his mother's* desire (plus the efficiency into which it issues) is the result of *this* known good but, more generally, that desire in any cognitive agent results from a good-as-known, and this because of the very nature of a cognitive agent (indeterminate with reference to what precisely to desire and yet determinable) and of the very nature of a good-as-known.[45] This awareness is the Final Cause Proposition, which becomes operative from then on in his everyday life; thus whenever cognitive agents act in virtue of their cognitive natures, he automatically knows that they are acting

[44] The coming about of the meal itself would, of course, provide data for someone's coming to know the Efficient Cause Proposition in case he has not already achieved that knowledge.

[45] What we remarked previously with reference to the Efficient Cause Proposition also holds here: the child has achieved a lot in knowing the Final Cause Proposition. In an inarticulate but genuine way he grasped from a concrete case what a cognitive agent is and what a good-as-known is, as well as their mutual *rapport*.

under the influence of goals which are good-as-known. And he instinctively inquires what they are, *why* they are acting.

As so known and as so formulated ("Desire in any cognitive agent results from a good-as-known" or, less complexly, "Every cognitive agent acts because of a goal"), the Final Cause Proposition is inductive, since we know it from and within a concrete case. It is immediately known because it is known without reasoning. It is self-evident not through analysis of the terms and concepts involved, not through deduction from the Principles of Sufficient Reason and Contradiction, but because cognized immediately under the light of intelligibilities present within a concrete case in which a cognitive agent begins to love when influenced by a good-as-known. It is a principle inasmuch as it serves as the major premise of the practical syllogism already indicated.[46]

It keeps those properties even when philosophical reflection makes it explicit, speculative, and formally certain. While in the presence of that mother as she begins to *desire* to prepare the special meal for her husband's boss, a philosopher can concentrate technically upon the final causality taking place, upon the change occurring in her because of a known good.[47] Such technical reflection would disclose at least these four facts:

1. Change within such an agent is a process by which what is potential becomes actual (she who can desire *A* or *B* or *C* now actually desires C).
2. What is potential is not simultaneously and of itself also actual.
3. Still, it has become actual when the change is accomplished.
4. Accordingly, the potential becomes actual not of itself but from something else, which is, in this case, the goal, the good-as-known.[48]

Obviously, the last fact is the Final Cause Proposition; it can be formulated in various ways, all of which come down to the same

---

[46] See the prgrs. corresponding to notes 41–43 of this chapter. As we noted with reference to the Efficient Cause Proposition (Ch. VIII, n. 49), the Final Cause Proposition is also an initial step in a deductive process.

[47] This is no longer reflection on the "fieri *operis*" (the coming about of the thing), as is the case with the Efficient Cause Proposition, but on the "fieri *operantis*" (a coming about within the agent himself) or, more exactly, "fieri *amoris in operante*" (the coming about of the operation of love within the agent).

[48] See prgrs. corresponding to notes 41–45 of this chapter.

thing: "A cognitive agent goes from potency to act under the influence of a good-as-known" or "Every cognitive agent acts because of a goal." However formulated, it is now explicit, technical, speculatively operative, and formally certain (one not only assents to it with no fear of erring, but one can also give a technical account for that absence of fear). Nevertheless, it remains inductive because it issues from concrete instances of finality. It still is immediate and self-evident because it arises not from reasoning but from mere reflection upon evidence directly presented within those concrete cases. It is a principle because it can serve as a premise within reasoning processes.[49]

2. ***Is the Final Cause Proposition Known through Reasoning?*** Can this Proposition also be known through reasoning? Is it ever a conclusion to a reasoning process?[50] I would say yes, and substantiating that affirmative answer can add a deeper dimension to our understanding of finality.

Its substantiation rests on the inductively known fact that whenever a cognitive agent produces an object, that product is the goal he had in mind as concretized and realized and, consequently, it acts according to finality simply by acting according to what it itself is, merely by "doing what comes naturally." Suppose someone is shipwrecked on an island. What he desires is safe, dry, and convenient transportation across the water separating him from the mainland. With that in mind, he builds a wooden boat and a gasoline motor. His goal dictates his every move—his choice of materials and the construction of the boat and motor, all the parts of which are made to have and tend toward a determinate function. Because of its determinate, tendential and (to use Mayr's

---

[49] For example, Aquinas could have used it in a version of his "Fifth Way" for proving the existence of God, although what he actually used was finality in noncognitive agents (see *S.T.*, I, 2, 3 resp., last prgr.).

[50] Such as is the Efficient Cause Proposition—see Ch. VIII, Sec. 4a.

Two points should be remembered as we move into this section on knowledge of the Final Proposition through reasoning: (1) Such knowledge and our immediate knowledge of that Proposition (see Sec. 2b1 of this chapter) are each self-contained: each has its own basis for assent; each is, at bottom, independent of the other (although each complements the other); each is valid by and of itself. (2) We may legitimately introduce God into the consideration of finality in view of the fact that without relying on finality we previously have proved Him to exist and have some awareness of the sort of Existent He is (see Ch. V, Sec. 6).

word)[51] teleonomic nature, that product is the telic *effect* in the final-cause situation just outlined. It is nothing but the man's goal as externalized and realized in various materials. Hence, by acting precisely as a motorboat, it acts for a goal (that of its maker) and according to finality.[52]

But why is this relevant to the problem at hand? Because cognitive agents (as well, of course, as all agents) are products of God, Who makes them with definite goals in mind. Thus by acting precisely according to their natures as cognitive agents, they automatically act for a goal (God's) and according to teleology. Let us try to understand these points a bit.

What is the end God intends in making a particular human existent? It is not to receive anything, but to give. As subsistent Actuality and thus infinite perfection, God is completely self-sufficient. He does not need any creature, for creatures add nothing to Him. Consequently, the divine will to create is entirely free: it bases itself solely upon love—the love God has for Himself and for His creatures as finite re-presentations of the divine perfections. Hence, God's attitude toward creatures is a loving generosity: He wishes to give, to share with them His perfections until they become as like Himself as their created natures and capacities allow.

Coming back now to cognitive agents and more specifically to this human existent, what is the goal God has in mind in making him? It is to uniquely communicate Himself in a manner apropos to an existent who is cognitive and humanly so. That is to say, He is to be possessed through a contemplation and love achieved by the human existent in question going through sensible existents, which are to nourish him, to furnish data for his knowledge, and so on. In view of those various operations, God has constructed this man accordingly. So that he nourish himself, God gave him operative powers by which he could assimilate food; so that he

---

51 Ernst Mayr, *art: cit.*, p. 1504, col. 2. On determination and tendency, see prgrs. corresponding to notes 37–38.

52 Another example in which a thing's tendency to act is even more noticeable would be as follows. A man wishing to hurl an object across a narrow but deep crevice bends back a supple tree on the edge of the crevice and ties the object to it. When released, the tree will swing back into place and thus catapult the object across the space. Before its release, though, it strains to snap back into its former position (so much so that the man must use force to hold it back): it is a tendency to that motion. The point of the example is that all products are such tendencies to activity.

could propagate the human race, God gave him remarkable generative powers; so that he could see colors, hear sounds, and so on, God gave him various powers of sense cognition; so that he could know truth (and, eventually, Truth), God gave him an intellect; so that he could love goods (and, eventually, the Good), God gave him appetitive powers (sense appetites and will). Those operations are the goals God directly had in mind. The operative powers themselves, as well as the human existent himself from which they stem, are the telic effects. They are nothing more than those goals as concretized and realized. They are determinate tendencies to those operations. In simply acting according to what they are, in letting them do what comes naturally, in allowing them each to seek its own formal object, a human existent is acting for the goals God intended, that is, according to finality.[53]

But the appetitive powers are those by which a human being acts precisely as a cognitive agent (and this is the point under discussion), and they differ from all his other operative powers in this—that their very object is the *good-as-known.* Accordingly, simply by letting them act according to their natures as *appetitive pow-*

---

[53] We might add that this picture of God making man with definite operations in mind and fitting him out with operative powers orientated to those operations is paralleled in the supernatural order. Divine revelation tells us that man's possession of God is not merely to be through natural contemplation and love (that is, the kind achieved by going through material existents), but through a participation in the divine life itself and ultimately through direct union with God. He intends us to know and love Him somewhat as He knows and loves Himself. How is this plan to be carried out? He would personally come and dwell in each human soul, and His very coming and indwelling would necessarily and simultaneously result in the elevation and quasi-deification of the human person through sanctifying grace. (See M. de la Taille, *Hypostatic Union* [cited in Ch. VI, n. 80].) Such a man would, in a sense, truly live as God lives, and thereby would personally know and love God in Himself; through that love and knowledge he would thus be intimately united to God, Who would dwell within him.

Such are the supernatural operations God intends for man. What are the operative powers given him to achieve these operations? The theological virtues (faith, hope, charity), the infused moral virtues (prudence, fortitude, and so forth), and the gifts of the Holy Spirit. All of these flow from and complement sanctifying grace, the entitative change effected in man by God. All of these are determinate tendencies to these operations.

"Supernatural" aptly fits all such factors, since they genuinely transcend that to which human nature itself entitles man. For an erroneous use of the term, see Sec. 5b of this chapter, second prgr.

ers, a human person is not only acting for the goal God intended,[54] but he simultaneously is also acting because of a good-as-known.

What this comes down to is that the operation of love is unlike the operations of all other operative powers in that it is involved in two telic situations. [1] It is the telic *cause* of the appetitive powers insofar as it is the goal God intended in making those powers; they are that goal as achieved, they are its telic effects, they are tendencies to it. [2] It is also the telic *effect* here and now of a good-as-known: when some good or other is presented to a cognitive agent, he begins to desire and love it, and that act of desire and love is a determinate tendency to it. [3] It also is, we may add, the efficient effect of the appetitive powers, which however can efficiently cause it only because in God's plan they are its telic effect.[55]

[good as known] .... [love] .... [appetitive powers]

[1] *final cause* ⟶ *final effect*

[2] *final cause* ⟶ *final effect*

[3] *efficient effect* ⟵ *efficient cause*

Manifestly, then, when someone is involved in a final-cause situation, there are two tendencies operative—that of his appetitive powers themselves to love and that of the act of love itself to the good-as-known. In this, appetitive powers are unlike other operative powers, which are a tendency to their operations, but these operations themselves are not strictly further tendencies.

Let us now marshal the points made into an orderly sequence.

A product, in what it is, is the end its maker had in mind as concretized and externalized;

But activity flows from, is determined and influenced by, what something is;

Therefore, a product acts for an end (that of its maker) and according to finality by acting according to what it is;

But every cognitive existent is a product of God and thus is the end He had in view as realized and concretized;

---

[54] This property they have in common with all other operative powers, each of which is by nature a divine goal as concretized and realized.

[55] See Sec. 2a of this chapter.

Therefore, every cognitive existent, in acting according to its cognitive nature, acts for an end (God's) and in accordance with finality;

But in virtue of his cognitive nature every cognitive existent has among its operative powers appetitive ones, which are tendencies to known goods and whose function is to love those goods;

Therefore, every cognitive existent, when acting according to its cognitive nature, tends to and loves goods-as-known;

Therefore, a cognitive agent, when acting in accordance with what he is as a cognitive existent, acts for a goal which is a good-as-known and which simultaneously is also the goal intended by God;

That is to say, if a cognitive existent is to act at all, he must act in accordance with what he is; but for a cognitive existent to act in accordance with what he is is equivalent to his acting for the goal set up for him by his Maker, which in turn is equivalent to his acting for goods-as-known.

Obviously, then, every cognitive agent acts because of a goal.

Obviously, too, the last statement is the Final Cause Proposition, which terminates a long and complex reasoning process and, thus, is a conclusion and not a principle.[56] It is mediately known, and thereby is not self-evident. It is inductive and *a posteriori* inasmuch as that process is directly initiated by information on the tie-in between products and goals (see the first two propositions of the process) which is gathered within concrete cases and which governs our subsequent viewing of cognitive existents in relationship to God.

(c) Résumé

Let us bring the preceding sections into better focus by a survey.

1. There actually are situations in which cognitive agents begin to love because they become aware of some good or other. The result is a determinate tendency to that good through the act of

---

[56] This process allows us to know not only *that* cognitive agents act because of a goal but also *why*. That is to say, it affords not only *quia* but also *propter quid* knowledge.

On reasoning in contrast to mere reflection, see Ch. X, Sec. 3. We may note that the fifth proposition in the process is also a formulation of the Final Cause Proposition.

love they efficiently cause. How can we describe that sort of situation? Let us say it is one of "finality" or "teleology." The good-as-known is the telic cause. The operation of love is the telic effect and is also the efficient effect of the agent working through his appetitive powers.

No one can validly challenge the existence of such situations because everyone frequently experiences them in himself and observes them in others. No one should, then, challenge finality in this its initial meaning, because it is nothing but a direct description of those situations.

2. Those same situations entail another finality when they are viewed in relationship to God. Cognitive existents are the handiwork of God, and thus in what they are (especially in their operative and, above all, appetitive powers) they are His goals as concretized and incarnated. Hence, in acting in accordance with what they are as cognitive existents, they necessarily act for a goal (God's).

Let us emphasize that those existents, together with their operative powers, are telic effects. They are *determinate tendencies* to the operations He intended. Hence, when someone begins to love upon becoming aware of a good and through love begins to tend to it (#1), that tendency rests upon the deeper, prior tendency which is his appetitive powers themselves.

This second sort of finality is based upon the fact that God exists and makes us with goals in mind. Anyone who doubts that fact will also be skeptical of this finality. But this skepticism has to contend with the fact that we all experience our operative powers and their tendential character. Who has not felt the internal unrest caused by an unsolved problem (practical or speculative)? Until the mind finds an answer, it is uneasy, it probes and seeks, all of which reveals that it is a tendency to knowledge, to solutions. Or who has not experienced the disquiet brought on when there is no one or no thing to love? The will is a tendency to the good and is restless unless some good terminates that search.

But if one realizes through experience that his operative powers are determinate tendencies and if determination and tendency are marks of telic effects,[57] he should realize also that his operative powers are telic effects. In such an event his skepticism should be somewhat shaken.

---

[57] On determination and tendency, see Sec. 2a3 of this chapter and n. 38. On Plato's conception of operative powers as telic effects, see *Republic*, V, 477B–D; *Timaeus*, 46C–47E (the entire dialogue is devoted to teleology).

3. But however that may be, we can clearly affirm finality with regard to cognitive agents. They act because of goals, which are goods-as-known. This acting because of goals is absolutely necessary, since the very nature of the appetitive powers demands them: those powers are to a good-as-known as the determinable to the determinant, the perfectible to the perfective, the actuable to the actuant. This we know inductively and immediately (either through immediate insight or through reflection), and we formulate it in a self-evident principle: "A cognitive agent goes from potency to act under the influence of a good-as-known" or "In a cognitive agent love comes about because of a known good" or, simply, "Every cognitive agent acts because of a goal."

4. Second, cognitive agents act because of goals that are goods-as-known since they are products of God, and thus are His goals as concretized and realized. Hence, in acting as cognitive existents, by acting in accordance with their appetitive powers, they automatically act for goals (God's), which are, in fact, goods-as-known, for such is the formal object of those powers. This we know inductively but mediately as the conclusion of a reasoning process, and it is expressed simply as "Every cognitive agent acts because of a goal."

3. Finality on the Noncognitive Level

Cognitive agents' acting for a goal centers around the fact that they have appetitive powers, whose very formal object is the good-as-known. But what about existents which do not have such powers? Do they act because of a goal? In a word, is finality found on the noncognitive level? Such is the next question we face.[58]

An affirmative answer is obvious if we view noncognitive agents in reference to God. They are His products no less than cognitive existents (see Sec. 2b2), and thus He has made them with definite goals in mind—the various operations and activities He intends for them.[59] Consequently, by acting according to their natures as non-

[58] On what a noncognitive agent is, see n. 28. Chemicals and plants are not the only noncognitive agents. Humans and animals are too with reference to all operations save their appetitions and those under the direct influence of these last.

[59] We cannot tell what these operations are in an *a priori* way, but instead we know them from observation, from experience, and from the progress of science as it discloses more and more what material things are, the uses to which they can be put, and thus, gradually, what God intends through them.

cognitive agents, by acting in accordance with the operative powers or active qualities[60] which God has given them to perform those operations, they automatically act for a goal (those activities) and according to finality. They are tendencies to determinate operations. They are effects in a telic situation. The universe is shot through with finality.

(a) Causal Factors

But if we remove God from the picture and look at noncognitive agents merely in themselves, do they show any evidence of finality? If determination and tendency are signs of finality,[61] that question is the same as asking whether their activity entails those two factors.

Nothing is more evident than that noncognitive existents act, within limits, in a determinate and constant way.[62] Cherry trees

---

Also see R. Kreyche, *First Philosophy*, p. 256: "Neither must it be supposed that man must in every instance be able to 'read' final causes in nature, as though there were some peculiar significance for *man* in the formation of clouds or as though mosquitoes were made in order to try men's patience. True enough, there is abundant evidence of extrinsic finality in nature, by which things of a lower nature are ordered to the good of things of a higher nature, especially man. However, one must not be arbitrary in assigning specific ends to specific events." Because of the limits of human cognition we shall never be able to know the specific ends of all or even many subhuman agents and existents.

[60] For purposes of clarity, that by which living things effect an activity is called an "operative power"; that by which an inanimate thing effects an activity is an "active quality."

[61] On tendency and determination, see Sec. 2a3 and n. 38.

[62] The phrase, "within limits," is added mainly in view of outside interference. When this occurs (for example, by application of X-rays or radioactive materials or through grafting or genetic engineering) the activity of those existents will change (although the change in activity arises only from a prior change in the agents themselves).

On the "Principle of Indeterminacy" spoken of by empiriological scientists today, see M. Vaske, *Introduction to Metaphysics*, p. 136, n. 4: "The Heisenberg principle of 'uncertainty,' or 'indeterminacy,' does not seem to be a denial of determinacy of action, but a denial of certainty of observation, prediction, and manipulation of microcosmic events. Moreover, the principle (primarily at least) seems to be concerned with the measurable *phenomena* of action, not with the proper *causes* of the phenomena." Also see Stanley L. Jaki, *God and the Cosmologists* (Washington, D.C.: Regnery Gateway, 1989), ch. 5, especially pp. 115–35; *idem*, "Cosmology and Religion," *Athéisme et Foi*, 25 (1990), 252–65.

On indeterminacy in biology, see E. Mayr, *art. cit.*, p. 1505. He lists four reasons why a biologist meets indeterminacy in the objects of his study:

grow in a definite way and produce cherries. A Concord grapevine grows in its own fashion and produces grapes. A mixture of hydrogen and oxygen, when an electric spark is passed through it, turns into water, not into petroleum. And so on through countless other examples which could be given: plants and chemicals act in a determinate, constant manner so as to produce definite results.

In such things tendency is less easily observed, perhaps, but does manifest itself adequately enough. For example, sodium and phosphorus are so active (*tend* so strongly to activity) that they must be kept under kerosene to remain in a pure state. If exposed to air, phosphorus is so active that it bursts into flames. Sodium oxidizes slowly if exposed to air but bursts into flames when placed near water. Bromine must be kept in a dark bottle at ordinary room temperature or else it will oxidize. Fluorine is so active that chemists do not attempt to produce it in a pure state. Acids can burn spontaneously without any outside prodding. Plants also grow spontaneously, sending their roots down to water, pushing their stalks up through the soil to the sun. We may say, then, that noncognitive agents not only act determinately but also tend to their activities.[63]

---

randomness of an event with respect to the significance of the event; uniqueness of all entities at the higher levels of biological integration; extreme complexity; emergence of new qualities at higher levels of integration. But he adds: "Let us remember that indeterminacy does not mean lack of cause, but merely unpredictability." Also see M. Bunge, *Metascientific Queries* (Springfield, Ill.: Charles C. Thomas, 1959), pp. 232–40. Also see G. Klubertanz, *Philosophy of Being*, p. 173: "The results of nonvital activities are consistent results. Of course, there is not an absolute invariability of action and result. But there is a definite *constancy*, within limits, so much so that physicists and chemists can construct mathematical formulas for these activities, and so much so that in the past two generations entire industries have been built on the exact, universal knowledge acquired by scientists."

[63] What would tendency be on the noncognitive level? Do we have a parallel which might help us understand it better? Yes, since all our operative powers are the same sort of determinate tendencies to operations (see Sec. 2c2 of this chapter, third prgr.) and we directly experience them as such. In our awareness of our own determinate tendencies, then, we gain an insight into what such tendencies are in plants and chemicals. On this level we are like plants and chemicals, save that we experience our tendencies, whereas they do not experience theirs.

J. Russell, "Principle of Finality," p. 350, gives these examples of tendency on the nonliving level: "Gravitational attraction between two bodies is not the only instance of inorganic seeking or striving. This is a far more universal

This tendency or spontaneity, as well as the fact of determination, discloses that noncognitive agents are finalized. Their operations (together with the products to which these at times give rise) are the final causes.[64] Those very agents in themselves, in their structure, in their operative powers and active qualities, are the final effects: they are determinate tendencies to the operations they also efficiently cause.

[operations]		[noncognitive agent itself]
final cause	⟶	*final effect*
efficient effect	⟵	*efficient cause*

Those, then, are three causal factors in the teleological situation on the noncognitive level: final cause, final effect, efficient cause. If the final cause in a situation involving cognitive agents is "a good-as-known to which the agent tends through love," here a final cause is "a good to which an agent tends under the impulse of its very being." The good of a noncognitive agent is its operations, as well as the products which ensue from those operations.

---

property than Aristotle or the medievals could have suspected. It is present wherever there are forces of attraction or repulsion. Among the ultimate particles of matter, protons and neutrons seek each other, and this accounts for the great stability of most types of atomic nuclei. Electrons and protons are drawn to each other; hence arise all the chemical properties of matter. Magnetized bodies seek to orientate themselves in each other's field. The mutual repulsion of two electrons, or of two protons, is again a type of striving: in this case a striving to separate rather than to approach. Attraction and repulsion are both necessary for the manifold chemical and physical activities of matter. Seeking and striving are therefore to be found throughout all nature." In offering gravity as an example, Russell stresses (as well he should) that gravity as currently conceived has nothing to do with Aristotle's outmoded theory of natural place.

[64] Here lies the reason why so many refuse to see finality on the noncognitive level: it would inevitably lead them to God. If noncognitive existents are the telic effects of operations which do not yet exist, and if they are already structured today to produce tomorrow's operations, someone must have made them with those operations in mind. Consequently, finality on the noncognitive level demands God ultimately as its complement.

(b) The Final Cause Proposition on the Noncognitive Level

We are now confronted with the problem of how widespread such finality is. Do all noncognitive agents act according to finality? Is this necessarily so?

If we take into account the causal factors just discussed, the answer is yes. Because noncognitive agents act in a determinate and tendential way by acting according to what they are, they all act in accordance with teleology. They all act for a goal (the operations which they efficiently cause and to which they direct themselves).

* ***1. Is the Final Cause Proposition Immediately Known?*** Perhaps if we again place the question in a Cartesian perspective and consider the kind of knowledge at issue, we shall gain further information.[65] How, then, is the proposition, "Every noncognitive agent acts for an end," known? Do we have immediate cognition of it, so that it is a self-evident (although inductive) principle?

One can reply affirmatively as a result of the following evidence, which is complex and rather difficult to handle. When confronted with a change in the activity of a noncognitive agent, everyone spontaneously asks, "Why?" and looks to the structure of the noncognitive agent as the immediate explanation and to the cognitive agent responsible for the changed structure as the ultimate explanation.[66] For example, if I throw a cork into a basin of water, I notice that it floats. But suppose someone secretly fills the cork with lead and then throws it into the water. Seeing it sink, I inevitably ask, "Why did it happen?" and seek the reason by investigating the cork and eventually seeking the motive my friend had in mind when he made the change. This question and subsequent investigation appear as the sequel of a syllogism, the first premise of which is a version of the Final Cause Proposition:

> On the noncognitive level a change in activity comes about through a change in the thing acting, which in turn comes about because of the goal the cognitive agent making the change had in mind;

---

[65] See Sec. 2b of this chapter.

[66] Not all changes in activity are caused directly by cognitive agents; some are caused by deterioration of the thing itself (see n. 67), some by other noncognitive agents (which seemingly would be ultimately dependent upon cognitive agents, however). Then, too, the proposition can be known not only through a *change* in activity but also through *activity* (see n. 68).

But here is a change in activity;
Therefore, there is a change in the thing acting, coming about because of a cognitive agent's goal, and my inquiry is, "Why did it happen? What in the noncognitive agent accounts for it? Why did the cognitive agent change the thing?"

Several comments can be made concerning that major premise. Why is the first portion of it true? Why does a change in activity result from the thing's being changed? First, because an agent acts according to what it is, and this for the reason that it could hardly act according to what it is not; second, because its structure is a determination to that activity. Hence, the first part of the major is equivalent to stating that "Noncognitive agents act for an end (their activities) because they are determinate tendencies to it."[67] But why does a change occur in the thing? In some cases at least, because a cognitive agent engineers that change with an aim in mind. Because a product (here, the thing as changed) is the goal of its maker (here, the cognitive agent changing the thing) as concretized and realized, it acts for a goal by acting according to what it is, since what it is has been determined to that goal by the one changing it. Consequently, the major in its entirety is equivalent to affirming that "Noncognitive agents act for an end because they are determinate tendencies to it by reason of the fact that they are the end their maker intended as realized and concretized."

That major premise is, then, the Final Cause Proposition as formulated with regard to activity issuing from noncognitive agents. It is operative on the purely practical level: it guides our reactions to events we meet in our daily lives. Normally we do not go around repeating, "On the noncognitive level a change in activity comes about because of a change in the thing acting." Hence, it ordinarily is implicit, becoming explicit only when subjected to the sort of consideration we are currently making. However, it *is* influential in our daily lives, and it is implicit in our minds, for it can be explicated. Moreover, it must be known immediately, spontaneously, and by all if everyone immediately and spontaneously asks, "Why?"

What would be the origin of that knowledge? In line with the fundamental inductive orientation of human knowledge, it would

---

[67] This consideration would take care of cases in which change occurs through the thing itself (see n. 66). One should remember that the thing itself is not the final cause, but rather the *effect*.

be some concrete case in which a child observes that a cognitive agent changes the structure of a noncognitive agent so as also to change its activity. It could, in fact, be an actual incident as simple as the one involving the cork made to sink by the insertion of lead. There the child not only would become aware that the activity of *this* object is now different because the object itself is different due to the influence of this cognitive agent changing it. But he would also realize more generally that the activity of any noncognitive agent becomes different if that agent is itself modified by a cognitive agent acting for some good-as-known. And this realization stems from the necessary tie-in between a noncognitive agent and its activity and between that agent and the cognitive agent changing it. This realization is the Final Cause Proposition expressed in terms relevant to activity on the noncognitive level; from then on it becomes applicable in events which touch his personal life, enabling him spontaneously to ask, "Why did it happen? What in the noncognitive agent accounts for it?" and, eventually, even, "Why did the cognitive agent change the structure of the noncognitive agent?"

As so known and expressed, the Final Cause Proposition is inductive, since we know it from and within a concrete case (or cases). It is immediately known because known without reasoning. It is self-evident—not through analysis of terms and concepts, not through deduction, but because known directly under the light of intelligibilities present within a concrete case in which a cognitive agent modifies what a noncognitive agent is so as also to change its activity. It is a principle because it serves as the major premise of the practical syllogism already discussed.

It retains those marks even when philosophical reflection renders it explicit, speculative and formally certain. While in the presence of someone inserting lead into a cork so that it may sink when placed in water, a philosopher can concentrate technically upon these points:

1. The influence of the known good upon the cognitive agent involved (it determines, perfects, actuates him).
2. The fact that the product which results from his activity is nothing but his goal as realized and incarnated—it is a determinate tendency to definite operations.
3. The fact that, consequently, the product acts according to finality in acting in accordance with what it is—what it is is not only the efficient cause of its activities but is their final effect as well: it tends to them as to what is to be produced.

4. That, consequently, any change in what it is results in a change in what it does.

Such reflection brings it about that the Final Cause Proposition is now explicit, technical, speculatively operative and formally certain. It is, though, still inductive, because all those realizations are made within concrete instances of finality on the noncognitive level. It remains immediate and self-evident because it issues not from reasoning but from reflection upon evidence directly offered by those concrete instances. It is a principle because it can serve as a premise within reasoning processes.[68]

* 2. ***Is the Final Cause Proposition Known through Reasoning?*** Can the Final Cause Proposition itself be known through reasoning? Is it ever a conclusion to a reasoning process? The affirmative answer is so clear from previous discussions that here we need only organize the points made earlier[69] into an orderly sequence.

A product in what it is is the end its maker had in mind as concretized and externalized;

---

[68] Aquinas uses it within his "Fifth Way" for establishing that God exists. See *S.T.*, I, 2, 3 resp., final prgr.

The Final Cause Proposition can also be known immediately not merely through a *change* in activity but through activity itself, although probably this knowledge would first occur when we encounter something new. For example, when confronted with the activity of a new machine, we spontaneously ask, "Why the activity? Why does this agent act this way?" Then we investigate the structure of the thing for the immediate explanation. This question and subsequent investigation appear as the sequel to a syllogism, the first premise of which is a version of the Final Cause Proposition.

Every noncognitive agent acts according to what it is;
But here is an activity;
Therefore, the explanation of its activity lies in what it is, and this I shall investigate so as to understand its activity.

Behind the major premise stands the fact that an agent is not only the efficient cause of its activities but is also structured and programmed for them, is a determinate tendency to them. The major, then, is equivalent to: "Every noncognitive agent acts for an end by acting according to what it is, because what it is is a determinate tendency to its activity."

This process is implied in that elaborated above concerning a change in activity.

[69] Concerning cognitives, see Sec. 2b2 of this chapter; concerning noncognitives, see the initial paragraphs of Sec. 3.

But activity flows from, is determined and influenced by, what something is;
Therefore, a product acts for an end (that of its maker) and according to finality by acting according to what it is;
But every noncognitive agent is a product of God and thus is the end He had in view as realized and concretized;
Therefore, every noncognitive existent, by acting according to its nature as a noncognitive existent, that is, by acting in accordance with the operative powers and active qualities which God has given him as properties of that nature, acts for an end (God's) and according to finality.

The last statement, obviously, is the Final Cause Proposition, a conclusion which terminates a reasoning process. It is mediately known and thus is not self-evident. It is inductive and *a posteriori* insofar as that process is directly instigated by information on the link between products and goals which is gathered within concrete cases and which affects our understanding of noncognitive agents in relationship to God.

(c) Résumé

In cognitive agents finality is detected by the fact that they begin to love upon becoming aware of a good: this actuates their appetitive powers, and the resultant actuation is the very operation of love, telically caused by the good and efficiently caused by the appetitive powers (see Sec. 2a). Such detection is impossible in noncognitive agents, which do not have appetitive or cognitive powers and which therefore elicit no operations of love.[70]

What does finality consist in, then, with respect to these agents? It consists in the determinate tendencies to activities which they have and, in fact, are. Nothing is more obvious than that various noncognitive existents do act; that they act in a definite, programmed and spontaneous way; that, everything else being equal, they pro-

[70] "Love," as well as such terms as "appetite," "striving," and "seeking," seems so intimately linked with cognition that preferably it is not predicated of noncognitive agents. Other authors do not share this preference—for example, M. Vaske, *Introduction to Metaphysics*, p. 141; R. Kreyche, *First Philosophy*, pp. 195 and 252; J. Russell, "The Principle of Finality," *passim*. "Tendency" and "inclination," though, do not appear to have that intimate connection, and hence I apply them with reference to cognitives and noncognitives alike.

duce definite results.[71] Finality in them is that spontaneous, tendential, intrinsic, teleonomic determination to activities which is their very nature, structure, entity. They act according to finality by acting according to what they are, and this because what they are is a determined tendency to activity.[72] Hence, a noncognitive agent through its operative powers or active qualities is not only the efficient cause of its activities: together with those powers and qualities, it is also the telic effect of those very operations (how else can we explain the fact that it tends to produce them by reason of its structured nature?). They are its final causes, which it is programmed to produce efficiently and to which it tends.

Obviously, this picture of finality is incomplete. If these noncognitive existents are the telic effects of operations which do not yet exist, if they are already structured today to produce tomorrow's operations, Someone must have made them with those operations in mind, and this Someone must have a mind so as to make them. Thus, finality on the noncognitive level also requires an intelligent Agent (who ultimately proves to be God) as its complement. These noncognitive agents act for an end (God's) by acting according to what they are, because what they are is God's goal as concretized and realized.[73]

But even without this complement, finality in its initial phase is genuinely found on the noncognitive level. Just as all cognitive agents are determinate tendencies to a goal (the good-as-known) by reason of love, so too all noncognitive agents are determinate tendencies to a goal (their operations) by reason of their very entities, which are programmed for those very operations. Even one who withholds God from the picture can and should admit this teleonomic teleology.[74]

---

[71] The phrase "everything else being equal" is added to take care of external interference. When this occurs everything is not equal, and their activity is changed if their entity has been changed. See n. 62.

[72] This is the Final Cause Proposition, known immediately (either through immediate insight or through reflection).

[73] This is the Final Cause Proposition as known through reasoning.

[74] The adjective in the expression "teleonomic teleology" utilizes Mayr's term (see n. 51). The tendential determination of a noncognitive agent to operations, which is its structure and entity, is teleonomic precisely because it is that very entitative structure. It is woven into the very fibers of its being. But that determination is teleological too inasmuch as it is the result of finality: it is the telic effect of those operations. On the noncognitive level there is no conflict between teleonomy and teleology.

4. Chance in the Universe

If all cognitive and noncognitive agents act for an end, then one would expect that no event escapes finality. But such is not the case, as any daily newspaper testifies. Because its steering wheel locked, a southbound car swerved over into the path of a northbound car, which in turn pulled over onto the sidewalk and hit two pedestrians. Their deaths were not intended by the driver of either car, yet the second driver did hit them and their fatal injuries did actually occur. A delivery man steps from the back door of an apartment building after making a delivery and finds himself catching a three-year-old boy who had fallen from a fourth-floor window ledge. When he came to the building, his purpose was not to save the boy, yet he did actually catch him—another actual occurrence which is over and beyond the finality of the agents involved. Such events which escape finality we shall call "chance." Now let us investigate them more thoroughly in order to know how widespread chance is.

Suppose that someone invites two of his former classmates to his home for dinner. These two men have not seen each other for years, and neither of them knows the other will be there. The meeting will be chance as far as the two guests are concerned because neither had intended to see the other, but it will not be chance on the part of the host because he planned the meeting. But suppose the moment they meet in the driveway, the host's wife hurriedly backs her car out of the garage and accidentally runs over them. Their injury is still another chance event, but this time involving not only the two guests and the wife, but even the host. He did not intend it, but he could not have prevented it because of a lack of either knowledge (he did not know it was going to happen) or power (he saw what was about to occur but was too far away to stop the car or to warn his guests).

This instance enables us to make several points.

1. A *chance event* is *the crossing-over of two or more lines of efficient causality, so that the crossing-over itself (as well as that which results from it) is not intended by any of the agents directly involved.*
2. Chance events are of at least two sorts:
   (a) only two lines of efficient causality are directly involved (one guest meets another unexpectedly)—let us call these "*relative* chance";

(b) more than two lines are directly involved (the wife runs over the two guests against her own and her husband's intention)—let us call these "*absolute* chance."

3. Evidently, an event which is chance on one level may not be so on another (the meeting of the two guests is accidental with respect to them but not to the host; the injury of the two guests is a chance event to them and to their host, but not to his wife if she intended it).
4. A chance event occurs because the agents involved lack knowledge or power—otherwise they would stop it, since it is over and beyond or even against their wishes.

Now to the question of how widespread chance is. Relative chance events are, of course, frequent enough in our own lives as to need no additional comment. What about absolute chance events? If taken in a sufficiently restricted sense (involving three or four chains of efficiency), they too occur occasionally, as each one can testify from his own experience. Whenever finite cognitive agents with ability to make frequent and disparate decisions by reason of free will are close to one another in space and time, the various lines of efficiency they initiate are bound to intersect one another with unintended results.

But is absolute chance on what might be called a "global" scale possible? For example, might a nuclear war be triggered accidentally? It would be against the wishes of every nation, yet none of them could prevent it—either because they are unaware of the chain of events leading up to the accidental launching of the first missile or because they are powerless to stop it. Obviously, it could happen, for each government has only limited knowledge and power. Despite the precautions currently taken (for example, no one person at a launching site or at military headquarters has full access to the crucial machines or information, a direct telephone line has been installed between Washington and Moscow, and so forth), still it is conceivable that a chain of events could get out of control of any and all persons, and thus a nuclear war could be started accidentally. Just as obviously, though, no series of events can escape the control of God, Whose knowledge and power are both infinite. Therefore, what might be called "total" chance is impossible.[75] All the happenings in this universe (even those which

[75] "Total chance" aims at expressing an event which would escape the finality even of God. "Relative," "absolute," and "total," arbitrary terms though

are chance as far as we created agents are concerned) are framed, stabilized, guided by the infinite wisdom, love and power of divine providence.

Is chance found on the noncognitive level? In order to answer, we must first establish what chance there would be. It would be an event which escapes finality. But noncognitive agents act according to finality by acting according to what they are, and since they act according to what they are whenever they act, they act in accordance with finality every time they act. The only way in which a noncognitive agent could escape finality, then, would be not to act at all. But in that case there would be no event, either. Hence, every event brought about by noncognitive agents is necessarily according to finality, and chance on the noncognitive level seems impossible. For example, baking soda stirred into the batter will inevitably leaven the cake. The atmospheric conditions here today will necessarily bring about rain tomorrow. As far as the noncognitive agents within it are concerned, then, our universe is one of finality, of tendency to definite results, of determinism, of necessity.[76]

* But there are examples which make us pause. Suppose rain falls immediately after an earthquake which somehow started a number of fires. Because the rain is falling now and here, it quenches fires—an effect it does not have always or elsewhere. Is not that effect a chance event? I would say no, but several points must be clarified. A noncognitive agent such as rain has what might be called an essential effect (providing moisture) and various side effects (here it is beneficial to growing crops, there it cleanses dusty

---

they be, are useful in view of the three possible combinations of agents: two creatures, more than two creatures, creatures and God.

[76] Although predictability is not at the heart of finality, in some areas it is its sequel. Take, for example, weather forecasting. Because noncognitive agents act according to what they are, they act in a determined, necessary way. Hence, by studying what atmospheric conditions are today, meteorologists can tell with reasonable accuracy what the weather will be tomorrow, everything else being equal (see n. 71). In fact, Dr. Irving P. Krick, head of a commercial meteorological laboratory in Denver, makes forecasts months or even years in advance. How does he go about it? "His forecasts are based on past performances the weather has given throughout history. He believes that the whole solar system is orderly and can be relied on, given the same atmospheric causes, to produce the same atmospheric effects. Today the Krick laboratory knows what the weather was like for every day back to 1899" (*This Week Magazine*, April 8, 1962, p. 5).

buildings, here it quenches fires). The essential effect it procures directly of itself, and hence always; the others it procures in conjunction with other noncognitive agents, which vary, so that these effects vary also. But not even the second sort of effect is chance, because the space-time relations in which noncognitive agents find themselves also help constitute what they are. This rainstorm, by acting in compliance with what it is here and now, puts out fires, whereas that one soaks vineyards and acts in compliance with what it is there and then.

* Apparently, the only way chance can enter the arena of noncognitive agents is through the interference of cognitive agents. Rain can be produced "artificially" by airplanes seeding clouds with pellets of Dry Ice. In such a case rain could perhaps be called "chance" insofar as its falling in this place and at this time (with varying side effects) is not the result of natural atmospheric processes. Nevertheless, in their chemical reactions Dry Ice and clouds both act according to what they are, and thus according to finality. The element of "chance" (that the condensation should be here and now, with its own attendant side effects) is directly due to the cognitive agents.[77] Perhaps a clearer example would occur if someone by mistake filled the sugar containers in the obstetric section of a hospital with salt. Suppose a nurse adds this to milk and gives bottles filled with this mixture to the babies, so that several of them die from this "chance" event. It is chance, though, only as far as the nurse is concerned, for she does not intend their deaths. It is not chance as far as the salt is concerned, for it acted in compliance with finality in acting precisely according to its nature as sodium chloride when mixed with milk and taken internally by infants. This event is another illustration of the third point made earlier: that which is not chance with reference to noncognitive agents may be so with respect to cognitive ones.[78]

---

[77] Explosions of nuclear weapons by various nations may have so disturbed the natural meteorological conditions that our weather will never again be entirely "natural."

[78] Because evils frequently occur through chance, a brief word can be appropriately added here on the causes of evils. Take the case of a man with poor eyesight. What are the efficient and final causes of the lack of 20/20 vision? Obviously, the efficient cause is the man himself through his visual organs and powers insofar as he efficiently causes an act of seeing which suffers from a lack of full vision. In efficiently causing the seeing, he also and inevitably causes the lack (to the extent that it can have a cause: it is, one must remember, a privation, an absence, a nothingness—see Ch. 6, Sec. 4).

5. Summary and Conclusions

Because of the two previous summaries (see Secs. 2c and 3c of this chapter), this section can be brief. It will center around the question which finality entails above all: "*Why*?"

(a) *Why* do cognitive agents act? For the sake of goals which are goods-as-known. These actuate their appetitive powers and the resultant actuation is their operations of love, which are caused telically by the goods and efficiently by those powers and which are determinate tendencies to make or obtain those goods.

(b) *Why* do noncognitive agents act? Because of what they are. By reason of their very entity, by reason of the operative powers and active qualities stemming naturally from them, they are determinate structures for and tendencies to activities. These latter are the telic causes, whereas the agents themselves in their entity and structure are the telic effects. By acting in compliance with what they are, then, they automatically act in accordance with finality and for a goal (those activities).[79]

Such finality is naturalistic in the sense that it *is* the natures of things; it is deterministic, programmed, teleonomic, since it is nothing more than their very entitative structure. But such is not the whole story, because finality here necessarily points to God. If noncognitive existents are the telic effects of operations which do not yet exist, if they are already structured now to produce future operations, Someone must have made them with those operations

---

But what about the final cause of that privation? The man directly desires to see, but inasmuch as his seeing is imperfect, he cannot help but desire (at least, permit) the imperfection along with the seeing: if he is going to see at all, he must see imperfectly. Evil, then, can be desired only insofar as it is connected somehow with good (see Ch. VI, Sec. 4, and Sec. 2a of this chapter). Hence, evil as evil has no final cause; it is never directly desired.

Does an evil entail intrinsic causes (that is, receiving and actuating causes—see Ch. VIII, introductory section)? Obviously, it has an intrinsic receiving cause—the subject of which it is predicated and which it affects (in the case of poor vision, that subject is the man, and, more proximately, his visual powers and operations—see Ch. VI, Sec. 4 and n. 68). Just as obviously it has no intrinsic actuating cause, for evil is the very absence of a perfection.

See M. Vaske, *Introduction to Metaphysics*, pp. 195–96.

[79] With reference to a noncognitive agent, then, a final cause may be described as "a good to which an agent tends because of its very being"; with reference to cognitives, "a good to which an agent tends through love." In the light of those two definitions, the heart of both noncognitive and cognitive finality is that agents determinately tend to a good.

in mind. Thus, finality on the noncognitive level requires God as its ultimate complement. Does this requirement merit the charges of superstition and supernaturalism?[80] Hardly, since God is demanded by the agents' very natures, entities and structures as their ultimate explanation.

(c) *Why* did this or that chance event happen? To the extent that they are chance, no answer is possible, for they are outside the realm of finality. The cognitive agents responsible for them did not intend them, although they did efficiently cause them. Of course, one can understand how they can happen—cognitive agents are limited in knowledge and in power, their freedom of choice makes them capable of multiple and disparate decisions, their proximity to one another in space and time makes them mutually vulnerable. But as far as the agents directly involved in an accident themselves are concerned, it has no reason, no motive, no telic explanation, because it was beyond or even against their intention. It escapes finality.

(d) In view of the finality to be found in cognitive and noncognitive agents alike, our universe is a dynamic one, shot through with tendencies and consequent activities. But in view of the factors which make chance events (both relative and absolute) possible and almost inevitable, it is a precarious and challenging one. On how delicate a point is our well-being balanced. How precious does actual existence become.

> To grasp what it means to exist, one needs to grasp the fact that he might not exist, that he treads at every moment on the sharp edge of possible annihilation and can never escape the fact that death will arrive at some unknown moment in the future. Existence, never automatic, not only can be sloughed off and forfeited but is indeed at every instant threatened by non-being. Without this awareness of non-being—that is, awareness of the threats to one's being in death— . . . existence is vapid, unreal, and characterized by lack of concrete self-awareness. But with the confronting of non-being existence takes on vitality and immediacy, and the individual experiences a heightened consciousness of himself, his world, and others around him.[81]

---

[80] As examples of those charges, see the texts of Simpson and Mayr cited in n. 12 and n. 14. For an accurate meaning of "supernatural," see n. 53.

[81] Rollo May *et al.* (eds.), *Existence: A New Dimension in Psychiatry and Psychology* (New York: Touchstone Books, 1967), pp. 47–48. Also see p. 42:

* 6. Exemplary Causality

Since exemplarity is closely linked with finality,[82] we shall add a brief consideration of exemplary causes. Let us begin by recounting how exemplarity worked in one concrete case. As told in the *New Yorker*, Richard Lippold was asked to construct two mobile sculptures for the foyer in the Lincoln Center, New York, according to these plans:

> "From the street level two escalators carry the public up to an area two hundred feet long, thirty feet wide, and fifty feet high. All the levels of auditorium and balcony open to this promenade. It is suggested that two vertical Lippolds be suspended at some point above or just in front of the escalators, brilliantly lighted and visible from all eye levels from the balconies. Seen from the balconies, they will hang surrounded by glass and the city as a background. Does this perchance set your imagination to work?"[83]

Lippold realized that this commission presented special problems because

> ". . . the space was so long and narrow, and because there would be very strong competition from the balconies and the vertical columns of the building. The sculpture would have to be pretty strong to hold its own against that kind of architecture."

How did the finished artifact come about? In retrospect, Lippold feels that two unrelated incidents of that summer went a long way toward shaping his ultimate concept.

> The first was a warm, spontaneous friendship that had sprung up on board the *Queen Frederica* between the Lippolds [on

---

"[Man] is that particular being who knows that at some future moment he will not be; he is the being who is always in a dialectical relation with non-being, death"; F. Wilhelmsen, *Metaphysics of Love* (New York: Sheed & Ward, 1962), pp. 97–145, especially 124–45.

[82] See M. Vaske, *Introduction to Metaphysics*, p. 150; R. Kreyche, *First Philosophy*, p. 262; H. Renard, *Philosophy of Being*, pp. 161–64.

[83] Calvin Tomkins, "A Thing Among Things," *New Yorker*, March 30, 1963, p. 49, col. 2. The plans are a quotation from a letter to Lippold.

> their way to Europe for the summer] and two young Italians, a girl of seventeen and her nineteen-year-old brother. "It was a vitalizing experience to be with them, and the friendship did a lot for me," Lippold recalls. "There was something about it, the idea of strangers reaching out to one another across a generation, that touched me deeply, and I think now it may have influenced the form of my sculpture, with its two forms reaching out and its father-son connotation in my mind." The other incident occurred at the end of the summer, in Denmark. . . . By this time, Lippold had become anxious and depressed; it was nearly time to go home, and he had nothing to show to Abramovitz [who had given him the commission]. "I was waiting and waiting for something to happen," he says. One morning, walking in the formal garden of a neighboring castle, with its clipped borders and elaborately shaped shrubs, he wandered off across the lawn toward a great tree, whose lower branches swept the ground. He made his way through the branches and stood there looking up into the inverted green bowl of the tree, and it struck him that there was something in that shape—that "open yet closed form," as he has called it—that should be his sculpture. All at once, "a roundness with forms reaching across it like the limbs of a tree" seemed to him the only concept that could hold its own against the strong vertical columns of Abramovitz's building without violating the space. "From then on the form of the sculpture determined itself in my mind," Lippold says. "Of course, it was transformed, like all my artistic ideas, into concepts of space and of form in space, and the inverted-bowl thing was reversed, so that it opened upward, but the essential idea stuck."[84]

Once he had his basic concept, idea, exemplar for the mobiles, what remained was to implement it, first in a series of sketches and finally in whatever material he would choose.

> His first renderings [of sketches] consisted merely of a generalized impression of two mases stretching out toward one another. . . . [Later] he began in his drawings to fragment the forms, breaking them up into smaller elements that would hang every which way and would glitter and sparkle like the

[84] *Ibid.*, p. 49, col. 3–p. 50, col. 1.

> leaves of a tree in sunlight. This led him naturally to the idea of using milled metal sheets of various lengths, suspended from the ceiling by fine cables. . . . By deciding to use solid metal sheets, he virtually ruled out the kind of geometrical symmetry that had characterized many of his previous large constructions, and he also found himself moving in a direction that rather surprised him. "Although I did not intend these forms to be figurative . . . they seem to be acting like people. By their gestures . . . these two figures seem to me like friendly gods (atomically conceived like all of us), reflecting in their splendor the splendor of man."[85]

After the sketches came a scale model and, finally, the artifact itself.

We have quoted from this article at length because it gives an artist's own account of how he acquired his exemplar (which he calls "concept" or "idea"), as well as an indication of how it exercises its causality upon the artist and the artifact. It was acquired from actual existents (his friendship with the two Italian youths, the inverted green bowl of the enormous tree). But one must note that it came from them in a special way: insofar as the data they provided were worked upon by the artist's imagination, were fused together into a whole, were "transformed . . . into concepts of space and of form in space," which in turn became figurative and symbolical. The result was a dynamic, compelling pregnant idea which directed his activity from drawing preliminary sketches to suspending the final metal sheet. Through his activity it also directed, specified, and determined what the artifact itself is.[86]

This instance includes all the main elements of exemplarity. The exemplary cause is the idea directing the artist in his making. The causality it exercises is that very direction or specification of his activity and, through it, of the artifact.[87] The exemplary-effect is that

---

[85] *Ibid.*, p. 50, col. 2–p. 52, col. 2.

[86] In Lippold's own words, "The idea of strangers reaching out to one another . . . influenced the form of my sculpture, with its two forms reaching out." Again, his awareness of "a great tree, whose lower branches swept the ground . . . the inverted green bowl of the tree" produced "a roundness with forms reaching across it like the limbs of a tree . . . smaller elements that would hang every which way and would glitter and sparkle like the leaves of a tree in sunlight."

[87] Because of the close and necessary liaison between activity and artifact, whenever in subsequent sentences of this section we say "activity," we should be interpreted as saying, "activity and artifact."

activity as so directed and specified. The efficient cause of that activity is the artist through his operative powers and habits (these last are various arts, together with the artistic talents and technique they demand and arise from). Let us very briefly comment on each of those factors.[88]

(a) The exemplary cause is, then, the concept or idea directing the artist in his artistic activity. It is the "beautiful-as-known," in which phrase each term is important. As seen earlier, the beautiful is "an actually existing item as splendent, and thus in relationship to contemplation and joy."[89] Since the beautiful is an actually existing item, the exemplar arises too from actual existents (and frequently not from just one, but from many). The beauty of those existents consists precisely in their objective splendor—the wealth of their perfections (among which are surely to be counted brilliant colors, comely shapes, and other sensible qualities), harmoniously ordered to one another and flashing forth in attention-catching radiance.

Nonetheless, the exemplary cause is precisely what is beautiful-*as-known*. The addition explains why not one but several actual existents generally form the basis of an exemplar: the creative imagination of the artist automatically and instinctively welds them together, bringing into sharp relief some factors and downplaying others. It also explains how the exemplar can grow and develop, especially during the initial stages of the artistic process: the artist's fertile mind is always at work.

(b) In what does exemplary causality of the beautiful-as-known consist? What does it do? It does not strictly *do* anything, since it is not an efficient cause. It is a cause, though, because it produces an effect—the agent's activity by which he endeavors to project that exemplar into matter. But how does it produce that activity? By the direction it exerts upon the agent. This is not, however, to be understood in a physical sense (in which, for example, a jockey directs a race horse): it is not an efficient cause. The beautiful-as-known sets the artist into a state of absorbing and ecstatic[90] con-

---

[88] We can be brief because what we shall say will closely parallel the earlier section on the causal factors in cognitive finality (see Sec. 2a of this chapter).

[89] On the beautiful, see Ch. VI, prgrs. corresponding and subsequent to n. 55.

[90] "Ecstatic" in the sense that he transcends himself, his usual surroundings, and the petty routine and concerns of his day-by-day life. The term is not used in any religious or mystical sense.

templation, so that the ensuing efficiency by which he tries to externalize the contents of that contemplation is itself colored, influenced, specified, and directed by that very contemplation. This state in which the artist finds himself is the exemplar.

One and the same set of activities is, then, simultaneously caused in a twofold way: exemplarily by the beautiful-as-contemplated, efficiently by the agent through his operative powers and art habits. Just as a single operation of love within a final-cause situation is both the attraction which the good exerts upon the lover and at the same time the response of the lover to the good, so too a single line of efficiency is both the direction which the beautiful-as-known exerts upon the artist and simultaneously the response of the artist to the beautiful.

The beautiful as contemplated is a genuine cause because it helps produce the efficiency of an artist. Its causality is the nonphysical direction which the artist experiences within himself and which is, in fact, also his very artistic activity as produced not efficiently, but exemplarily, by the beautiful. The direction or specification is that activity in reference not to himself, but to the beautiful.[91]

(c) Because the factors of exemplary-effect and efficient cause have been given rather full treatment in connection with exemplary-cause and its causality, we shall mention them without discussion. The artistic activity of the artist is the exemplary effect.[92]

---

[91] Is an exemplar a final cause as well? One and the same object can be both an exemplary cause and a final cause (in the sense of the initial *finis operis*—see n. 34), since it can be both beautiful and good. Even so, it exerts a different causality as an exemplar than it does as a goal. As the former it directs the artistic activity of the artist, and that direction *is* that efficiency as exemplarily caused (see Sec. 6b of this chapter). As the latter it attracts and actuates his appetitive powers, and that attraction is that operation of love as telically caused by the good (see Sec. 2a2). On exemplarity, see C. Hart, *Thomistic Metaphysics* (Englewood Cliffs, N.J.: Prentice-Hall, Inc., 1959), pp. 386–403.

[92] Described from the side of the effect, the situation is one of participation: the artifact produced by the artistic activity shares a perfection with the exemplar which makes it similar to the latter but which is less fully present in the product (thereby they are dissimilar). Thus, participation arises from analogous and not univocal causes—that is, from agents which produce through cognition rather than through biological powers (see Ch. VIII above, Sec. 2b). On participation see Leo Sweeney, S.J., "Participation in Plato's Dialogues: *Phaedo, Parmenides, Sophist* and *Timaeus*," *Divine Infinity in Greek and Medieval Thought* (New York/Bern: Peter Lang Publishing, Inc., 1992), ch. 4; *idem*, "Participation and Structure of Being in Proclus' *Elements of Theology*," *ibid.*, ch. 12.

Its efficient cause is the artist through his operative powers and art habits. One and the same activity is midway between two sets of causes, exemplary and efficient.

[beautiful as contemplated]	. . . .	[activity of artist]	. . . .	[artist's operative powers and art habits]
exemplary cause	⟶	*effect*	⟵	*efficient cause*

(d) Such, then, are the causal factors in exemplarity:

Exemplary cause:	beautiful-as-contemplated.
Its causality:	the direction it exerts on the agent (which is rooted in its objective splendor but which is the agent's artistic activity as exemplarily caused).
Exemplary effect:	the agent's artistic activity, together with the artifact it produces.
Efficient cause:	the agent himself, through his operative powers and art habits.

Suggested Readings

De Finance, Joseph, *Connaissance de l'être: Traité d'Ontologie.* Paris: Desclée de Brouwer, 1966. Pp. 407–46 *re* final and exemplary causes.

De Raeymaeker, Louis, *The Philosophy of Being,* trans. E. H. Ziegelmeyer, S.J., pp. 270–81. St. Louis: B. Herder Book Co., 1954. On final and exemplary causality.

Gerrity, Brother Benignus, *Nature, Knowledge, and God,* pp. 83–101. Milwaukee: Bruce Publishing Co., 1947. On finality.

Hart, Charles A., *Thomistic Metaphysics,* pp. 297–324. Englewood Cliffs, N.J.: Prentice-Hall, Inc., 1959. On finality.

Jaki, Stanley L., *The Purpose of It All.* Washington, D.C.: Regnery Gateway, 1990.

Janet, Paul, *Final Causes,* trans. Robert Flint. New York: Charles Scribner's Sons, 1892. An interesting testimony to a nineteenth-century approach to finality.

Klubertanz, S.J., G. P., "St. Thomas' Treatment of the Axiom, *Omne Agens Agit Propter Finem,*" in *An Etienne Gilson Tribute,* ed. Charles O'Neil, pp. 101–17. Milwaukee: Marquette University Press, 1959. Contains a collection of Thomas' texts on the Final Cause Proposition.

Russell, John L., "The Principle of Finality in the Philosophy of Aristotle and Teilhard de Chardin," *Heythrop Journal*, 3 (1962), 547–57, and 4 (1963), 32–41.

Smith, S.J., Gerard, and Lottie H. Kendzierski, *The Philosophy of Being*, pp. 96–148. New York: The Macmillan Company, 1961. On exemplary cause; on finality.

Sweeney, S.J., Leo, *Divine Infinity in Greek and Medieval Thought* (New York/Bern: Peter Lang Publishing, Inc., 1992), ch. 4: "Participation in Plato's Dialogues: *Phaedo, Parmenides, Sophist* and *Timaeus*," pp. 47–68; ch. 12: "Participation and Structure of Being in Proclus' *Elements of Theology*," pp. 257–88.

———, *Infinity in Plato's "Philebus": A Historical, Bibliographical and Philosophical Study* (forthcoming), ch. 4 sqq. on finality, participation, dialectics.

Van Melsen, Andrew Gerard, *The Philosophy of Nature*, pp. 217–34. Pittsburgh: Duquesne University Press, 1953. On determinism, scientific causality, predictability, probability, random events.

Ward, Leo R., *God and the World Order*. St. Louis: B. Herder Book Co., 1961.

Wild, John, "Tendency: The Ontological Ground of Ethics," *Journal of Philosophy*, 49 (1952), 468–72. On tendency in relationship to finality.

Part IV

Metaphysics as a Science

X

Separation and Knowledge of the Real

"The science of pure being cannot be called a science," we heard R. G. Collingwood exclaim at the beginning of this book, "in the sense in which an ordinary science is so called. . . . This is only a roundabout way of saying that there can be no such science. There is not even a quasi-science of pure being."[1] Why does he, as well as other contemporary authors, take this attitude toward metaphysics? Fundamentally because for them a genuine science can be based only on the measurable, the quantitative. Metaphysics, however, is not built upon such evidence and consequently cannot be a valid science. In their opinion only physics, chemistry, experimental psychology, and other empiriological knowledges are genuine and valid sciences.

Against this view we contended that perhaps material existents give out evidence not only as they are viewed under laboratory conditions but also as they are directly perceived in their actual, day-by-day conditions and that, consequently, a genuine science of metaphysics is possible. Our contention has proved true. Material existents in their very status of actuality have provided evidence for a science which is valid, because that evidence cannot be gainsaid. Since sensible things not only involve change/stability but also actually exist, we came to conclude that they consist not only

---

[1] R. G. Collingwood, *An Essay on Metaphysics*, pp. 15–16, quoted above in Ch. I, n. 9. For other pessimistic statements on metaphysics, see those collected by Robert Miller, C.S.B., "The Empiricist's Dilemma: Either Metaphysics or Nonsense," *Proceedings of American Catholic Philosophical Association*, 29 (1955), pp. 151 sqq.

of substance/accidents and prime matter/substantial form[2] but also of another component, the act of existing.[3] Because the fact that they actually exist is what contributes perfection and objective worth to them, we realized that to be real is to be actual, with the result that the act of existing is the source of an existent's reality[4] (and, we might add, of its unity, truth, goodness, beauty, and individuality as well).[5] Since nothing acts unless it actually is, the act of existing is also the root of efficient causality in an existent. In fact, the *rapport* between an existent and its actuality determines what it can do in efficiently causing existence. Only subsistent actuality can properly cause things to exist and, accordingly, material existents cause existents solely by co-operating with God as instruments with a principal cause.[6] Finality too rests on actuality insofar as a final cause is a good to which an agent tends (either through love or under the impetus of its very entity) and insofar as goodness or perfection stems ultimately from existence.[7] Even the very peril to which chance makes us heirs sharpens our appreciation of existence. "With the confronting of non-being [through death], existence takes on vitality and immediacy, and the individual experiences a heightened consciousness of himself, his work and others around him."[8]

These conclusions coalesce into a body of organized knowledge and thus are the science we call "metaphysics." Because they are grounded in objective data gained through direct perception of existents and are carefully worked out through reflection and reasoning, metaphysics is a valid science. Because they have to do with existents precisely as existent (the formal object of no other science), metaphysics is a distinct science.[9] It is not a radical essentialism, since there essence (with attendant immutability, and other such properties) is the heart of reality, but here actuality has primacy.[10] It is, then, an existentialism, but not of the radical sort, where to exist is to be a subject.[11] But here to exist is actually to be,

---

[2] See Ch. III.

[3] See Ch. IV.

[4] See Ch. V.

[5] Ch. VI, Secs. 3–5.

[6] Ch. VIII, especially Sec. 3.

[7] Ch. IX.

[8] R. May, *Existence: A New Dimension*, p. 48. On chance, see Ch. IX, Sec. 4.

[9] See Ch. I, especially Sec. 5 and n. 17.

[10] On essentialism, see Ch. II, Sec. 3. On the primacy of actual existence see Chs. V and VI.

[11] See Ch. II, Sec. 2; also Ch. V, Sec. 1, and Ch. VI, n. 86.

whether the existent be changing or stable, subject or object, human or subhuman, subsistent or participant, infinite or finite. Actuality is the common denominator of them all, the heart of every reality. The science which recognizes that primacy of actuality is a metaphysics of authentic existentialism.[12]

* 1. Metaphysics and Separation

But is it possible to understand more exactly the nature of metaphysics as a science? Can we more keenly appreciate the unique sort of knowledge it is?

Contemporary Thomists reply by pointing to the fact that metaphysics alone involves *separation* and therein differs from all other sciences. But what is separation? On this they hold widely differing views. For some separation is not to be classified as an abstraction, and this for several reasons.[13] The former is a negative judgment, whereas the latter is a simple apprehension. The former concerns existence, the latter involves only essences. The former deals with items which actually are not the same and merely expresses that ontological nonidentity; the latter deals with items which are associated in the real order and simply does not consider the one while

---

[12] See Ch. V, especially Sec. 1. For a different interpretation of authentic existentialism, see John Wild, "Christian Rationalism (Aquinas, Gilson, Maritain)," in *Christianity and Existentialism* (Chicago: Northwestern University Press, 1963), pp. 40–65.

[13] For example, Louis Geiger, O.P., *La participation dans la philosophie de s. Thomas d'Aquin*" (Paris: J. Vrin, 1942), pp. 315 sqq.; *idem,* "Abstraction et séparation d'après S. Thomas," *Revue des sciences philosophique et théologique,* 31 (1947), 3–40; Louis Marie Regis, O.P., "Quelques apories," *Études et recherches,* 1 (1936), 127–156; *idem,* "Analyse et synthèse dans l'oeuvre de S. Thomas," *Studia Mediaevalia* (Bruges: de Tempel, 1948), pp. 301–30; Philip Merlan, "Abstraction and Metaphysics in St. Thomas' *Summa,*" *Journal of History of Ideas,* 14 (1953), 284–91; Jean Dominique Robert, O.P., "La métaphysique, science distincte de toute autre discipline philosophique selon s. Thomas d'Aquin," *Divus Thomas* (Piacenza), 50 (1947), 206–22; G. P. Klubertanz, S.J., *Introduction to Philosophy of Being,* pp. 45–52; Robert W. Schmidt, S.J., "The Use of Separation in Metaphysics," *Proceedings of the Twentieth Annual Convention of the Jesuit Philosophical Association* (Woodstock, Md.: Woodstock College Press, 1958), pp. 10–33. For a competent survey of the authors listed here and in notes 14–16, see Sr. Mary Roberta McMahon, O.P., "Separation: Its Development in Recent Thomism" (Doctoral Dissertation, St. Louis University, St. Louis, Mo., 1963).

concentrating on the other.[14] According to others, though, abstraction may occur either through simple apprehension or through judgment. That abstraction which one makes through judgment is called separation, and, accordingly, separation is one sort of abstraction.[15]

A third and original position has been outlined by Henri J. Renard, S.J.[16] All abstraction involves judgments. Total abstraction terminates in a judgment of *unity*—namely, "That the subject of the philosophy of nature is concerned with things which must exist in matter."[17] Formal abstraction concludes also with a judgment of *unity*—that quantitative forms can exist only in matter.[18] But the sort of abstraction proper to metaphysics ends in a judgment of *separation*—that the concept of substance (and, in general, of being) shows it need *not* exist in matter, "that matter does not enter into the definition of substance, that it does not belong to its *ratio* to exist in matter."[19]

---

[14] Members of this same group rather commonly maintain that the doctrine on abstraction and separation of Aquinas (whom they claim to be following) is not identical with that of Cajetan, an important Renaissance Thomist commentator. They maintain that Cajetan's three degrees of abstraction distort Aquinas' position. See Jean Dominique Robert, *art. cit.;* G. P. Klubertanz, *op. cit.*

[15] Matthias Thiel, "De abstractione," *Studia Anselmiana,* 7 (1938), 99–119; F. A. Blanche, O.P., "La théorie de l'abstraction chez S. Thomas Aquin," *Mélanges thomistes* (Paris: Vrin, 1934), pp. 237–51; J.-M. Ramirez, O.P., "De Ipsa Philosophia in Universum secundum Doctrinam Aristotelico-thomisticam," *Ciencia tomista,* 27 (1922), 325–64, and 29 (1924), 48–52; Jacques Maritain, *Existence and the Existent,* pp. 26–32 and notes 13 and 14; Marie Vincent Leroy, O.P., "Le savoir speculatif," *Revue thomiste,* 48 (1948), 328–39.

These same scholars tend to view Cajetan's degrees of abstraction as basically harmonizing with those of Aquinas. (For example, see M. V. Leroy, *ibid;* J. Maritain, *op. cit.,* p. 30, n. 14). Separation is the third degree of abstraction, or, in Maritain's language, eidetic visualization (see *ibid.,* p. 30: "The abstraction proper to metaphysics . . . proceeds from the eidetic visualization of a transcendental which permeates everything").

[16] "What Is St. Thomas' Approach to Metaphysics?" *New Scholasticism,* 30 (1956), 64–83.

[17] *Ibid.,* p. 71.

[18] *Ibid.*: "From a consideration of the *rationes abstractae* studied in mathematics such as quantities and geometric figures, we are able to judge likewise in a judgment of unity, that quantitative forms cannot exist without matter, because quantity . . . cannot be understood without its relation to intelligible matter."

[19] *Ibid.,* p. 72. Why the emphasis on substance? Because "substance is the principal, the most important of the *rationes* which are connected with the subject of metaphysics" (p. 73).

Such, then, are at least three divergent interpretations of the nature of separation in metaphysical knowledge—it is judgmental but not an abstraction, it is judgmental and an abstraction, it is judgmental but so too are the other two abstractions. However different these interpretations may be, though, they all agree in this—separation is a mental operation, it is an intellectual activity, it is fundamentally a negative judgment.

The position which I think accurate differs from all three. If described strictly and directly, separation (and, more generally, abstraction) is itself not an intellectual operation at all. Rather, it is a property, condition, status (call it what you will) of our intellectual awareness. Truth is one such property or condition—namely, the conformity existing between the content of an intellection and the thing known. Certitude, together with probability and doubt, is another such. Abstraction is a third, although a negative one but also concerned with the content of our awarenesses. It is the absence of matter within their very content. As one sort of abstraction, separation is the absence of matter within the content of the intellection proper to metaphysics. The unique factor in separation is that the absence within our metaphysical awarenesses arises because the things known somehow are themselves actually nonmaterial.

Let us now endeavor to explain and defend this position, thereby coming also to understand the unusual nature of metaphysics better.

2. Twofold Description of Knowledge

First of all, we must note that human knowledge arises from at least two causes, one of which is the intellect itself (together with the senses, of course), which efficiently produces the knowledge. The other is the thing known, which determines the content of the knowledge, and thus is its (for want of a better word) content-determining-cause.[20] That the *cognitum* is a genuine cause of cogni-

However, one should note that all three abstractions or judgments arise from an analysis of *rationes*, concepts, definitions (*ibid.*, p. 71).

[20] This is one more example of the enlargement which the notion and nomenclature of cause must undergo (see Ch. VII, notes 9 and 53, and Ch. VIII, n. 5). The *cognitum* is like an exemplary cause (see Ch. IX, Sec. 6) in that it specifies what the content of the conception will be. But it also differs from the exemplar. The latter is an idea influencing the thing made; the former is a thing influencing an idea. For the time being at least, the best description of the *cognitum* seems "content-determining cause."

tion can be easily seen in one's spontaneous knowledge of "dog." The reason why I am aware of "dog" is that a dog and not a giraffe is present before me and determining what I am thinking about.

Since, then, human knowledge has two sources, it can and must be described in a twofold way—from the point of view of the mind itself and from that of the *cognitum*. When a philosopher undertakes the first sort of description, he speaks in terms of the intellectual operations involved. He asks whether the process consists of simple or complex apprehensions, of perceptual or intellectual judgments, of affirmative or negative judgments, of reasoning or mere reflection. He investigates whether the process as a whole is inductive or deductive (see Sec. 3 below).

But in the second description his concern is quite different. He considers whether the conclusion to which the process in question leads is actually in conformity with reality, and this consideration involves the truth of the proposition and of the process. He also inquires whether the firmness of his assent to the proposition is justified by objective evidence; this inquiry concerns certitude. He can also reflect more directly upon the content of the awarenesses in which the process culminates, thereby realizing that by his intellection he has to some degree transcended the singular, the restrictive, the limiting—in a word, matter. By this reflection abstraction lies disclosed. It is a property of those awarenesses: the absence of matter within the very content of the intelligibilities in which our mental operations terminate.

Let us now endeavor to describe various philosophic processes from the point of view of those two causes, first with reference to their efficient cause (the intellect). Such descriptions will disclose where one is to locate the difference between metaphysics and other sciences.

* 3. First Description: Intellectual Operations Involved

When we undertake the first description, we speak in terms of the intellectual operations which knowledge involves. What are those operations? Through knowledge the knower becomes the known.[21] This becoming or be-ing another does not occur physi-

---

[21] This aspect of knowledge will be more readily understood if we recall what we experience in reading a novel or seeing a movie: we enter into its

cally, as happens when the food we eat is assimilated and becomes part of us, since what is known is not changed or destroyed in being known. It must, then, occur in a nonphysical or "intentional" way. Let us take the cause of my knowing the red rosebush I have just planted. By affecting (through light waves, etc.) the organs of my external and internal senses, the bush actuates my visual, olfactory and other powers of sensation and, ultimately, my intellect.[22] This series of noncognitive actuations entitatively unites the sensible object to me since they are actuations at once of what will be known (the rosebush) and of the knower (me) but they are in the knower solely.

> The actuation of what is known and of the faculty knowing is one and the same but it is present in the faculty and not in the known. It is an actuation of the known and is caused by the known, while simultaneously it is also an actuation of the knower too and, in fact, is solely in the knower. This is truly remarkable. The very same actuation which precognitively conditions, determines, forms the faculty by being present in it is also the actuation of that which is known (precisely as known, though, and not as it is outside the cognitive process, where its actuations are its substantial and accidental forms and its act of existing) and which is causing it in the knower. Through its actuation, which is *in* and *of* the knower and *of* and *from* the known, the object known is the content-determining-cause of my knowledge.[23]

---

characters, suffer and rejoice with them. In short, we somehow become what we read and see.

[22] On sense faculties and the brain in relation to the intellect and will, see Robert M. Augros and George N. Stanciu, *The New Story of Science* (Lake Bluff, Ill.: Regnery Gateway, 1984, ch. 2: "Mind," pp. 9–35.

[23] Leo Sweeney, "Can St. Thomas Speak to the Modern Mind?" in Victor B. Brezik (ed.), *One Hundred Years of Thomism* (Houston: Center For Thomistic Studies, 1981), pp. 137–38 (forthcoming as ch. 19 in *Christian Philosophy: Nature, Origin, Developments* [New York/Bern: Peter Lang Publishing, Inc., 1994]). See Aristotle, *On the Soul,* III, 425b26 and 426a10 (where *energeia* is almost universally mistranslated as "activity": the correct translation is "actuation"). Aristotle's and my epistemology is not a representationalism because the noncognitive actuations which sensible objects produce in the cognitive faculties are not images or representations but are formal determinants of the faculties receiving them. They perform the same function *mutatis mutandis* that a substantial form does *re* prime matter: just as a canine soul is the

Consequent upon this union of knower and of known, cognition occurs: I come to be *aware* of what I had already become entitatively through those actuations—namely, I am aware of "this blooming, perfumed, swaying, green bush." Such an awareness is followed by the additional cognitive operations I efficiently cause of judging ("Yes, this is indeed the red rosebush which the nursery company sent by mistake") and of thinking ("In view of my unemployment can I afford to keep it? Where will I obtain the money to purchase it?").

Awareness, judgment, thinking—such are the operations in which we are currently interested with reference to the various philosophical processes. But before attending to them there, we must view them more generally and in themselves: how many there are, what the nature of each is, how they differ from one another. Prior to this, however, two points should be mentioned. First, we know the sort of operations an intellect has not in an *a priori* way but rather by reflecting on the multiple and varied cognitive activities we actually experience in ourselves and observe in others. Second, only the results of this reflection can be given here because of the limits space and time impose.[24]

A human intellect shows itself, then, to have at least three main operations, each of which has its own subdivisions, as the following table shows:

1. Awareness of what an item is	1. *apprehension*
(a) which arises spontaneously, nontechnically	(a) simple
(b) which arises technically and which summarizes some such previous operation as reflection, reasoning, judgment	(b) complex

---

actuation which makes matter be canine, so the actuations caused in my faculties by a sensible object makes them first be (say) this red rosebush and thus enables me to know "this-red-rose-bush." See Joseph Owens, "Form and Cognition in Aristotle," *Ancient Philosophy*, 1 (1980), 17–28; Robert J. Henle, *A Theory of Knowledge* (Chicago: Loyola University Press, 1983), pp. 379–83.

[24] On the cognitive operations of the human knower, see the books on the philosophy of man listed in Ch. I, n. 18. Also see the following: L. M. Regis, O.P., *Epistemology* (The Macmillan Company, 1959), pp. 151–74, 253–306; Frederick D. Wilhelmsen, *Man's Knowledge of Reality* (Edgewood Cliffs, N.J.: Prentice-Hall, Inc., 1956), pp. 75–133; also see "Suggested Readings" below, especially the publications of Eccles, Jaki, Penrose, Searle, Sweeney and Wallace.

2. Assent that an item is such or is not such, is or is not	2. *judgment*
(a) directly based upon sense perception	(a) perceptual
(b) directly based upon intellection (which may itself, however, be working upon data furnished by perception)	(b) intellectual
3. Activities by which we prepare ourselves for #2—for example, inference, analysis, synthesis, and so on	3. *thinking*

The last type of operation (#3) is so complex that we should pause briefly to describe it in more detail. When sufficient evidence is not at hand to enable the mind to make a judgment, it must first analyze, synthesize, compare, consider, infer—in fact, use any sort of intellectual activity which helps. All of these activities constitute a sort of operation which is other than apprehension (#1) and judgment (#2) and which traditionally has been described as *cogitatio* and in English can be called "thinking." Of those various activities, inference seems most important and frequent.

Inference is a process by which our mind proceeds from one item to another which is somehow seen to be linked with the former. This process reveals itself to be one of two general kinds inasmuch as the human mind arrives at truths in two rather obviously different ways. Either it proceeds from the singular to the universal, from the perceptible to the nonperceptible, or it proceeds from the universal to the singular, from the more general to the less general. The first process let us call "induction"; the second, "deduction." Note that a process is inductive or deductive because of its starting point and general direction. If it starts with sensibles and moves upward, it is induction. If it starts with general knowledge and moves downward, it is deduction. Induction and deduction, then, are used to describe mental processes in which the mind is actually proceeding in a unified, organically developing manner.

Let us explain induction a bit more in detail because of its main role in authentic metaphysics. At the beginning of the previous paragraph inference is described as the process by which our mind proceeds from one item to another which is somehow seen to be linked with the former. For example, that seeing may be my sensibly observing a flock of birds in these bushes and could result in my affirming that "all the birds in this thicket except two are sparrows." Such an affirmation (which we might call "induction by enumeration") can be certain but it fits only a definite situation and that at a particular time. It does not rest upon any intrinsic necessity: there is no necessary, universally operative reason why sparrows should be here rather than blackbirds. Obviously, such an assent is nonscientific, and if "induction by enumeration" were the only inductive process of which the human knower is capable, metaphysics or any science seems impossible.

But we human knowers formulate other affirmative propositions when we are confronted with concrete cases in which the intrinsic necessity underlying such affirmations is clear and which thus issue into what can be called "intellective inductions."[25] These show themselves to be of three sorts. For instance, my knowledge that a nonmathematical whole is greater than any of its parts issues spontaneously and directly from data present within the concrete case represented by this diagram:

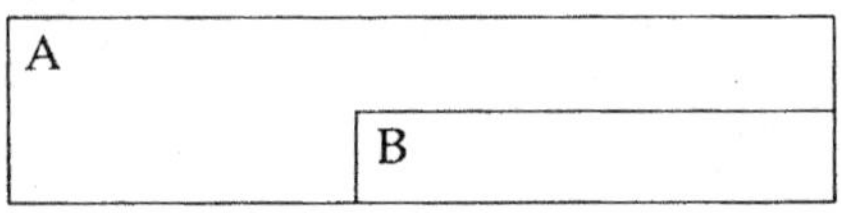

There we immediately become aware not only that this *A* is bigger than this *B* but also that every *A* is bigger than every *B*, and this because of the very natures of *A* and *B*. This awareness issues into our affirming "Every [nonmathematical] whole is larger than any of its parts"—a psychological process describable as "intellective induction *through immediate insight*" because a single concrete case can furnish all the data needed for such an affirmation.[26]

---

[25] "Intellective" as here interpreted comes from the Latin phrase "intus legere" and means literally "to read within"—that is, to understand the inner meaning of the data of a situation.

[26] Other examples are the affirmation, "Diverse evidences indicate the actual presence within of distinct constitutive parts"—see Ch. III above, Sec. 1; the efficient-cause proposition, "Every new item comes about because of some agent"—see Ch. VIII above, prgrs. corresponding to notes 47–49; the final-cause proposition *re* cognitive agents, "Every new item comes about through an agent acting because of a goal"—see Ch. IX above, prgrs. corresponding to notes 40–46; the final-cause proposition *re* noncognitive agents, "On the noncognitive level a change in activity comes about through a change in the thing acting, which in turn comes about because of the goal the cognitive agent making the change had in mind"—see *ibid.*, prgrs. corresponding to notes 65–67.

A second sort of intellective induction occurs when more than one concrete case may be required to see the intrinsic necessity they entail and this through technical reflection. Let us take as an example our experience of realizing that "whatever changes does so because of the influence of an agent": (1) in change that which is potential becomes actual; (2) the potential is not of itself actual; (3) still the potential becomes actual through the change; (4) consequently, the potential becomes actual not of itself but from that which is actual—an agent.[27] This realization can be designated as "intellective induction *through reflection*."

Still a third sort of intellective induction occurs when we need one or more middle terms to formulate a proposition. Consider the example of the "Final Cause Proposition" when achieved through reasoning by bringing God into the scene. This process can be represented simply in this fashion. God has produced cognitive agents with goals in mind; but a product is its maker's goal as concretized; therefore, a cognitive agent when acting according to its cognitive nature acts for a goal which is a good-as-known and which simultaneously is also the goal intended by God; hence, every cognitive agent acts because of a goal (both its own and God's).[28] That psychological process enables us to understand the intrinsic necessities embedded in the final-cause situation of cognitive agents and thus is an *intellective* induction. But technical reflection needs to be complemented by strict reasoning and thus a third kind of such induction has revealed itself—namely, "intellective induction *through reasoning*."

In contrast to this third sort of intellective induction is the psychological process which occurs in the physical sciences and which can be called "rational induction"—*induction* because it starts with data from concrete cases, *rational* because of the mathematical equations with which laboratory experimentation is formulated. It also can originate outside the laboratory. Take as an instance the general proposition, "Unsupported bodies fall to the earth." As R. J. Henle observes, "the passage from the individual cases [of leaves,

---

[27] For more ample discussion see Ch. VIII above, prgrs. corresponding to notes 50–54. On the final-cause proposition *re* cognitive agents as known by intellective induction through reflection, see Ch. IX above, prgrs. corresponding to notes 47–49; on the final-cause proposition *re* noncognitive agents see *ibid.*, prgrs. adjacent to note 68.

[28] See Ch. IX above, prgrs. corresponding to notes 50–55. On the efficient-cause proposition as known by intellective induction through reasoning, see Ch. VIII above, prgrs. corresponding to notes 42–46.

rain, rocks, hail, people, roof tiles falling down] to the generalization does not take place by way of an intellective insight into the true connection (the 'why' bodies fall), but through the mediation of [such] a general principle" as "Determined happenings require a determined intelligible cause."[29] Hence, although the process is

---

[29] *Theory of Knowledge*, p. 183. For Henle's definition of what we call "rational induction" and he "reasoned induction," see *ibid.*, p. 184. He adds: "One of the most prestigious examples of reasoned induction is the development of the principle of universal gravitation. The principle is formulated as follows: 'The gravitational force between two objects is directly proportional to the product of their masses and inversely proportional to the square of the distance separating their centers.' It is recognized that this principle . . . is an accurate description and measurement of the way nature acts, but the intelligible necessity underlying this way of acting remains unknown. The latest explanatory theory is the idea of gravitational field, but this is only a theoretical model" utilizing mathematics.

For a different position on induction see Harry Gensler, *Logic: Analyzing and Appraising Arguments* (Englewood Cliffs, N.J.: Prentice-Hall, 1989), ch. 8: "Inductive Reasoning," pp. 248–97, where he apparently restricts induction to what I call "induction by enumeration" and "rational induction" (on the latter see especially *ibid.*, pp. 280–89). See *ibid.*, p. 250, for his contrast between deduction and induction: "A *deductive argument* is one in which the truth of the premises is supposed to necessitate the truth of the conclusion. An *inductive argument* is one in which the truth of the premises is only supposed to make the conclusion probably true." In his subsequent book, *Symbolic Logic: Classical and Advanced Systems* (Englewood Cliffs, N.J.: Prentice-Hall, 1990), he comments: "Inductive reasoning is a reasoned form of guessing."

Although Paul K. Moser, *Knowledge and Evidence* (Cambridge University Press, 1989), has no section on induction as such, he does speak of "experience," pp. 83–88—see p. 83: "A perceptual experience is an event or state of awareness essentially having as an object a sensory item or feature such as a shape, color, sound, odor, taste, or some combination thereof. . . . A conceptual perceptual experience is an event of awareness that essentially has [as] an object not only a sensory item or feature, but also a concept, i.e., a classificatory item that can be a constituent of a proposition" and illustrated by one's conceptual taste experience of a lemon. On whether his "book's epistemic principles are analytic as opposed to synthetic, and *a priori* as opposed to *a posteriori*," he answers that those principles are "analytic truths justified *a priori* via my strategy of metajustification called 'explanatory particularism' " (p. 266). For him knowledge is "justified true belief" (see pp. 3–4, 13–23, 47–48). Also see *idem*, "Realism and Agnosticism," *American Philosophical Quarterly*, 29 (1992), 1–17.

In my approach "belief" is an assent I give because I trust the one who tells me something is true. Thereby belief is in contrast with knowledge, in which I assent because of evidence given (say) by actual existents in the concrete cases which are the content-determining-causes of my knowledge through the two-

inductive by starting with our perception of physical things falling, it is not intellective because we do not understand the link (established by referring to that general principle) between those bodies and their falling. Hence, let us call it "rational induction."

Here, then, are the three sorts of induction:

1. by enumeration
2. intellective:
   (a) through immediate insight
   (b) through reflection
   (c) through reasoning
3. rational

Since they all proceed from the singular to the universal, from the perceptible to the nonperceptible, all of them are in contrast with deduction, which proceeds from the universal to the singular, from the more general to the less general. Of those inductions only the second (intellective) with its three subdivisions is directly relevant to metaphysics. It helps exemplify "thinking," the third of the main operations which the human intellect reveals itself to have (see the paragraph and table immediately subsequent to note 24 above). And having attended to those operations of apprehension, judgment and thinking, let us now investigate various philosophical processes to see which operations each entails.

Let us begin with the process by which we came to assent to substance and accidents as actual components of a material existent (see Ch. III above, Sec. 3).

1. [Directly perceived fact:] In accidental changes one and the same thing
   (a) remains specifically and generically what it is (stability)
   (b) and yet acquires new individual perfections (change);
2. But evidence #a is other than evidence #b;
3. But diverse evidences indicate the actual presence within of diverse constitutive parts;
4. Therefore, such evidences indicate that the thing is actually made up of diverse constitutive parts:

---

fold actuation it entails. See prgrs. corresponding to notes 21–24 above and, especially, my "Preller and Aquinas: Second Thoughts," referred to in "Suggested Readings" below.

(a) that by which the thing specifically and generically remains what it is and yet receives various individual perfections—"substance";
(b) that by which the thing, while remaining specifically and generically what it is, is actually modified through a new individual perfection—"an accident."

Through this process, then, we come to realize that a material thing is composed of at least two different components, substance and accidents. The question now is how to describe the mental operations which underlie that process. Obviously it involves judgments, since it consists of four propositions which have arisen because the mind has assented (for example) that in accidental changes one and the same thing does remain specifically what it is while acquiring new individual perfections, and so forth. Some of those judgments are perceptual (for example, Proposition #1), others are intellectual (for example, #3 and #4). Some are negative (#2 and the judgment implied in #4 that substance is really other than the accidents it receives), others are affirmative (#3 and the affirmation in #4 that substance and accidents actually are constitutive parts of a sensible existent). That process also involves apprehensions, since in and through it we become aware of what various items are. Some of these apprehensions are simple—for example, in Proposition #1 the spontaneous awarenesses of various existents which are accidentally changing (this man, this dog, this flower). Others are complex: our technical cumulative awareness of what substance is and what accidents are (#4). Also, the process is an induction, because the intellect starts with sensible existents, together with the twofold evidence of change/stability they furnish, and terminates by assenting to the imperceptible components which compose them. It is an intellective induction, since we see why we assent: change/stability are nothing more than accidents/substance manifesting themselves.[30] It is an intellective induction which involves reflection rather than reasoning because, however complex the process may be, we can find within concrete cases of change/stability all the intelligible data needed for the process, and hence do not use a middle term.[31]

Next let us diagnose the process by which we came to realize that a material existent involves an additional composition—that

[30] On intellective induction, see n. 25.

[31] See the prgr. corresponding to note 27 above.

of prime matter and substantial form. The structure of the process is similar to the preceding one.

1. [Directly perceived fact:] A substantial change in a thing involves
   (a) the loss and acquirement of specific perfection (change)
   (b) together with corporeal continuity (stability);
2. But evidence #a is other than evidence #b;
3. But diverse evidences indicate the actual presence within of diverse components;
4. Therefore, such evidences indicate that on the substantial level a material thing is actually made up of two real and diverse components:
   (a) that by which a thing is such-and-such a specific nature and hence has its own distinctive characteristics—"substantial form";
   (b) that by which a material thing receives a substantial form and yet which is capable, through subsequent substantial change, of receiving other substantial forms—"prime matter."

As the process itself is similarly structured to that by which we know substance and accidents, so too the intellectual operations it entails are similar to those of the earlier operations. Accordingly, it will suffice if we list them with little or no explanation. It involves judgments (#1 and #4), some of which are perceptual (#1), others intellectual (#3, #4). Some are negative (#2 and the assent implicated in #4 that prime matter is not the same as the substantial form it receives and limits), some are affirmative (#3 and the affirmation in #4 that prime matter and substantial form actually are components of the substance within a sensible existent). Also the process involves apprehensions, some of which are simple (in #1 our spontaneous awareness of various material things capable of substantial change or actually undergoing such a change), others are complex (our technical and dynamic awareness of what matter and form are in #4). Finally, because it moves from sensible existents to a new set of imperceptible components, the process is an induction. It is an intellective induction because we see why we assent: corporeal continuity and the newly acquired specific perfection are nothing else than prime matter and substantial form manifesting themselves. It involves reflection rather than reasoning because we do not use a middle term but rather find within concrete cases of such change all the intelligible data needed.

Now, how did we as metaphysicians acquire the knowledge that, over and above the components so far discovered, a material existent also involves an act of existing? The process can be outlined as follows:

1. [Directly perceived fact:] An actual material existent
   (a) not only is what it is (Paul is this man)
   (b) but also actually exists (Paul *is*);
2. But evidence #a is other than evidence #b;
3. But diverse evidences indicate the actual presence within of diverse components;
4. Therefore, such evidences indicate that an existent is actually made up of two real and distinct components:
   (a) that by which it is what it is—"essence" (that is, the composite of substance [prime matter/substantial form] and accidents);
   (b) that by which it actually exists—the "act of existing."

Obviously, the structure here is again similar to that found in the two previous processes, but it contains great diversity in content. Here, the directly perceived facts are no longer merely change and stability within one or other order. They involve the contrast between *what* a material existent is and the fact *that* it does actually exist. In the last analysis this contrast is rooted in the fact that to be real is to be actual. Actual existence perfects and literally realifies that which does exist. A consequence is that the act of existing, the component which actualizes the thing and manifests itself through this evidence, is perfection *par excellence,* is the ultimate source of all other perfections within the existent, has primacy over essence, and so on. Another consequence is that "being" ("any actually existing item") expresses both *what* a thing is and *that* it is, both essence and existence, and yet emphasizes existence. That which makes a being be *being* is its actual existence.[32] Metaphysics, then, is a science other than the philosophy of nature because the metaphysician no longer studies beings-as-mobile but beings-as-being, or existents *precisely as existing*.

Despite those important differences, though, the fact still remains that this third process is similar in structure to its two prede-

[32] On "being" see Ch. VI, Sec. 1, and Appendix B.

cessors. Consequently, the intellectual operations which underlie it are similar to those found in the previous ones, and we shall catalogue them with little or no comment.

This process, then, involves judgments (#1-#4) some of which are perceptual (#1 includes both attributive ["Paul is this man"] and existential ones ["Paul actually is"]),[33] others are intellectual (#3, #4). Some are negative (#2 itself, the judgment implied in #4 that the act of existing is not identical with the essence which it actualizes, the realization permeating the entire procedure that "To be real is not to be material or to be any other kind of being, is not to be this or that"); others are affirmative (#3, the affirmation in #4 that the act of existing actually is a component within the existent, the realization operative throughout that "to be real is to be actual"). The process also involves apprehensions, some of which are simple (in #1, our spontaneous awareness of this or that existent), others complex (in #4, our technical and dynamic awareness of what the act of existence is, of its nature and of its relationship to essence). Finally, the process is an induction because the intellect moves from sensible existents to the component which intrinsically accounts for their existential status. It is an intellective induction because we understand why we assent: the fact that something actually exists is the perceived result of the act of existing functioning within. It involves reflection rather than reasoning because we do not use a middle term but rather find within actual existents themselves all the intelligible data we need.

Such, then, are three basic philosophic processes, together with a description of them in reference to their efficient cause, the intellect. However complex and tedious, that description illustrates the fact that isolating the intellectual operations which underlie them can and should be done if one's account of his philosophic knowledge is to be adequate. But it performs a function even more relevant to our present discussion by revealing that negative judgments are not restricted to metaphysics. A philosopher of nature also uses them, as when he concludes that substance is not identical with accidents and that prime matter is not the same as substan-

---

[33] Existential judgments are of extreme importance in metaphysics, for they are a cognitive means through which the human knower achieves contact with actual existence. For helpful studies, see Ch. IV, n. 45; John Wild, *Challenge of Existentialism* (Bloomington: University of Indiana Press, 1959), pp. 223–26; Joseph Owens, "Aquinas on Knowing Existence," *Review of Metaphysics*, 29 (1975–76), 670–90.

tial form.[34] Moreover, it discloses that the distinction between philosophic disciplines is not grounded in intellectual operations as such. All such disciplines are judgmental. They all terminate in awarenesses which arise within complex apprehensions, gathering together into a dynamic, psychological unity all the cognitive treasure amassed in immediately preceding reflection and judgments.

In what, then, is the distinction between the various philosophic sciences rooted? Not in the intellectual operations as such, but in the content of the insights gained through those operations.

Manifestly, our next step is to consider our philosophic cognition in the light of its content and, ultimately, of the *cognita* causing it. This consideration will illuminate what abstraction and separation are.

* 4. Second Description of Philosophic Knowledge: Abstraction

When a philosopher attempts an inventory of the various sorts of knowledge he possesses, certainly one sort he finds is his spontaneous, nontechnical and therefore nonphilosophic awareness of other material existents—trees, plants, other humans, rocks, and so forth. Even that knowledge is twofold: he knows this dog both as "this" and as "dog." If we suppose that he could only know the dog as "this," then his knowledge of dogs would be confined merely to sensation of now this [dog], now that [dog]. But, actually, his cognitive powers are such that he also knows this dog as "dog." Thereby he cognitively transcends signate matter, which would restrict and limit his cognition to this or that individual. Within the very content of his awareness of "dog," then, there occurs an absence of signate matter. An absence of matter within the very content of an awareness is what we mean by abstraction and, to some degree, is the property of every intellection.

Two additional facts must be noted. The absence of matter in such an awareness as "dog" does not arise because actual dogs are themselves without signate matter, but rather because the human knower, in concentrating on a dog as "dog," simply leaves the "thisness" out of consideration. Yet that absence is grounded in reality, in the *cognita*: if what makes a dog be *dog* would also make

---

[34] In the first two processes we were working as philosophers of nature, since we were studying existents precisely as mobile.

him be *this*, it would be impossible even intentionally to separate "this" and "dog." That is, this first sort of abstraction[35] ultimately rests upon the real composition within a dog of prime matter (that, ultimately, by which he is *this*) and of substantial form (that by which he is *dog*). In addition, although our awareness of "dog" does not contain signate matter, matter is not entirely absent from its content, since a dog even as *dog* does involve matter: it is his very nature to be a material, living, sentient, canine substance. Accordingly, abstraction here involves only a partial absence of matter, and this again because of the *cognitum*, whose very nature includes matter as a constitutive part.

Another kind of knowledge a philosopher discovers within himself is a spontaneous and nontechnical awareness of the external characteristics of various material things—the softness of human flesh, feathers, sponges, foam rubber; the durability of oaken floorboards, mahogany panels, steel plates, granite slabs; the roundness of water tumblers, basketballs, wedding rings, automobile wheels; the whiteness of swans, newly fallen snow, cirrus clouds, bed linen. This knowledge also is in its own way twofold, for a human knower not only knows the various kinds of things[36] which are, say, white but is also aware of "whiteness," the characteristic they have in common. Suppose that he could only know whiteness as inherent in swans. Then his knowledge of it would be restricted to that sort of existent. But, actually, he also is aware that fresh snow, cirrus clouds and so on also are white, and he is cognizant of "whiteness" itself as a common attribute. Thus he

---

[35] How shall we name this abstraction? The Latin term given it has been *abstractio totius*. The force of the second word is that the relation of a common nature to the individuals sharing it is like that of a *whole* to its parts.

What English expression seems best suited? Perhaps "abstraction of whatness" will do, the last word pointing to what the human knower is concentrating upon: he is aware of *what* sort of thing a dog is. The whole phrase, then, can be spelled out as follows: "The absence of matter within the content of an awareness through nonconsideration (abstraction) because of concentration upon what sort of thing the existent is (whatness)." On the meaning of "whatness," "quiddity," "essence," see Ch. IV, prgrs. corresponding to notes 51–54. We are here using "whatness" in its spontaneous, nontechnical, nonphilosophical meaning.

In expressions for subsequent kinds of abstraction, the last words in the phrase will have the similar function of indicating what the human knower is concentrating upon in his nonconsideration of matter.

[36] This knowledge would, of course, be another example of "abstraction of whatness."

cognitively transcends the various kinds of things which would confine and limit his cognition to this or that sort of existent. Within the very content of his awareness of "whiteness," then, there occurs an absence of the restrictive, confining, limiting—factors which we can call "matter." Here, then, is another absence of matter within the very content of an awareness and, consequently, a second sort of abstraction.[37]

As with the first sort, so too here additional facts are to be mentioned. The absence of matter in the content of such an awareness as "whiteness" does not arise because whiteness as actually found in white things has no connection with matter, but rather because the human knower, in concentrating on this or that sort of white thing precisely as *white*, simply does not consider what the sort of thing is which is white. Yet that absence is rooted in the actual *cognita*: if what makes a swan be *white* would also make him a *swan*, then it would be impossible even intentionally to distinguish validly between swan and whiteness. In other words, this kind of abstraction basically is grounded upon the fact that (for instance) a white swan is composed of really distinct components of substance (that by which he is a swan) and the accidental perfection by which he is white. And, although our awareness of "whiteness" does not contain "swan" or any other definite sort of thing which is white, matter is not entirely absent from its content, since whiteness itself does involve matter: by its very nature whiteness demands there be extended surfaces which reflect light of all wave lengths. Accordingly, abstraction here involves only a partial absence of matter, and this, again, because the *cognitum* is such as actually to be intrinsically linked with extension and matter.

Still a third kind of knowledge a philosopher can possess is a technical grasp of logic, mathematics, physics, and other constructural sciences. For instance, he is aware of what genus, species, and other logical conceptions are. He may be conversant with Euclidean geometry, with current theories on the atomic and subatomic structure of matter or with biological classification of plants and animals. Such knowledge is twofold, although it differs from the two previous kinds because it is constructural. Perhaps we might preferably say that such knowledge involves two stages—the "stuff" as it exists (a) originally and then (b) as worked upon by

---

[37] Let us call it "abstraction of external characteristics," where the last words point to what the mind concentrates upon (see n. 35).

the human knower.[38] Instances of those stages with reference to logic are: (a) "dog" as a direct universal and (b) as a reflex universal; or with reference to mathematics: (a) "roundness" as an external characteristic of various material things and (b) "circularity" as a strictly mathematical conception; with reference to physics: (a) hydrogen before and (b) after entering a cyclotron, with results expressed in mathematical formulae.

Suppose that the human knower could know only stage #a. Then the sciences of logic, mathematics, and physics would be nonexistent, and, in fact, impossible. But his cognitional power and ingenuity are so great that he actually transcends stage #a, together with the restriction and confinement it connotes. Within the very content of his awareness of "dog" as a reflex universal, of "circle," and so forth, there occurs an absence of what would restrict, confine and limit and which can be again designated as "matter."[39] Here, then, is another absence of matter within the very content of awarenesses, and accordingly a third type of abstraction.[40]

Once again, two facts are to be stressed. The absence of matter, in the sense just indicated, within the content of constructural intelligibilities does not occur because they have no connection with the first stage (#a), which has the important function of providing a basis for the subsequent process. Rather, that absence arises because the mind concentrates upon the contributions it itself makes to those intelligibilities and upon the various changes it has effected in the original data (#a), so that the latter no longer holds its attention. Also, the absence of matter (again, in the sense explained) in our constructural intelligibilities is not complete. True, such intelligibilities are a significant advance over stage #a. Still they are not entirely independent of it, they are not divorced from it. In fashioning those awarenesses the intellect cannot proceed arbitrarily. The original data still exercise an influence.

A fourth knowledge which a philosopher can have acquired is a philosophy of nature—a study of material, mobile beings precisely

---

38 Although "stuff" is an inelegant term, it is useful as applicable to items which are both intramental (our awareness of "dog" and of "round") and extramental (hydrogen).

39 By this time it should be clear that matter is an extremely analogous term. In general, it is that which, if present, would restrict, confine, and limit the content of an intellection.

40 Let us designate it as "abstraction of addition," however paradoxical that may sound. The final word expresses what the mind fixes its attention upon while ignoring the original "stuff"—it attends to its own contribution.

as mobile. Reflecting upon the evidences of change/stability which such existents show in both the accidental and substantial order, he concludes that they are composed of substance/accidents and prime matter/substantial form. This judgmental process culminates in his technical awareness, within complex apprehensions, of what those two sets of imperceptible but actual components are.[41] Obviously, such knowledge involves two levels, the first of which is occupied by mobile things as we directly perceive them undergoing various kinds of accidental changes (that is, quantitative, qualitative, local) and of substantial changes (generation, corruption). The second is occupied by those same things, but now understood as constituted by transsensible but real components: substance/accidents and matter/form. We now know the intrinsic causes of such existents in their very mobility. On the first level change/stability are mere facts; on the second they are evidences pointing to components within, and the thing lies transparent before our intellectual gaze.

Suppose, though, that the human knower could not rise above the first level. He might achieve a phenomenological, day-by-day description of material things (a history, a biography), but any philosophic science of nature would escape him. His intellectual powers are such, though, that he actually can and does ascend to the second level, thereby transcending the first, as well as the cognitional restriction and limitation it implies. Within the very content of his awareness of mobile beings *precisely as mobile* and of the components which intrinsically cause them, then, there is to be found an absence of the restrictive, limiting, confining—that is to say, of matter. Here, accordingly, is another absence of matter within the content of awarenesses and thus another type of abstraction.[42]

Again, several additional facts must be listed. First, the absence of matter in the sense indicated (that is, directly perceived data of this or that definite kind of accidental or substantial change) in the content of such awarenesses as "substance," "accident," "prime matter" and "substantial form" does not occur because the material thing they constitute is to be found without various and perceptible accidental or substantial modifications, or because the com-

---

[41] See prgrs. prior, corresponding and directly subsequent to notes 30–31 above.

[42] This let us term "abstraction of natural components," where the final words indicate that to which the knower attends as a philosopher of nature: the components of substance, and so forth.

ponents exist independently of it, or because the sensible evidences of change and stability have no bearing upon them (in fact, change/stability are nothing more than the components, so to speak, externalizing themselves). Rather, that absence arises because the philosopher of nature, having been guided by various actual manifestations of change/stability to the components, now concentrates upon the latter with inattention to the former. This absence, though, is fundamentally grounded in the components themselves, none of which can itself be perceived but is known through intellectual judgments (albeit formulated by a mind working upon perceived data), and each of which has no extended parts outside of parts, and thus is itself somehow immaterial.[43] Second, although our awareness of such components is free in content from directly perceived data of this or that definite kind of accidental and substantial changes, matter is not entirely absent from such awarenesses, because the components, however imperceptible and immaterial each may be in itself, do constitute a thing which is perceptible, material and changing, and they are dependent upon it. A general reference to change/stability enters into the definition of them all.[44] Consequently, abstraction here involves only a partial absence of matter, and this because the *cognita* (the components) are such as actually to be linked with matter.

---

[43] Although the components studied by a philosopher of nature are intrinsically dependent upon matter, they can still be described as immaterial because none of them is itself extended or has parts outside of parts. To contrast them with the act of existing and the human soul, we have previously called them "barely immaterial" (see Ch. V, Sec. 4)—that is, components within a material essence which are immaterial in such a way as to be intrinsically dependent upon matter. The act of existing is *amaterial* because it is a component which is within a material existent (although not within the material essence) and yet which is immaterial to such a degree as to be both extrinsically and intrinsically independent of matter. The human soul (together with its operative powers of intellect and will and their operations and operative habits) is *spiritual* because it is a component within a material essence and yet it is immaterial to such a degree that it is intrinsically independent of matter. One should note that the human soul lies within the range of a philosophy of nature when considered precisely as the substantial form of the body (as spiritual and subsistent, it belongs to metaphysics).

[44] For example, "Substance is that by which the thing specifically and generically remains what it is and yet receives various individual perfections"; "prime matter is that by which a material thing receives a substantial form and yet which is capable, through subsequent substantial change, of receiving other substantial forms."

Another sort of knowledge which a philosopher must include in his inventory is metaphysics—the science of beings precisely as being, of existents precisely as existing. By reflecting upon the existential status of material things which confront him and which are known through existential judgments, by realizing that actual existence is an important factor in them—in fact, even more important than what they are—and by granting that actuality is the font of reality, he is led to acknowledge the actual presence of the act of existing in these material things. This is a component over and beyond those discovered through the evidence of change/stability, and its disclosure lifts the philosopher from the science of beings-as-mobile to the science of beings-as-being, since what makes a being *be* being is the fact that it does actually exist, that it is actualized by the act of existing.[45]

Obviously, such cognition occurs in two stages. The first is that of perceptual judgments, by which we spontaneously realize not only that this man, that woman, this horse, this mimosa tree, and so on are indeed this man, woman and so on, but also that they actually are. The second is the moment of intellection and insight when we realize that each actual existent involves a component which is other than those accounting for what it is and which ultimately accounts even for what they are—namely, the act of existing. Here we know actual existents in the light of the intrinsic cause of their very actuality, reality and being. In the first stage actual existence is a mere fact; in the second it is an evidence indicating the act of existence within, and an actual existent in its reality and being lies unfolded before us.

But let us suppose that the human knower could not go beyond the first stage. He might achieve a census of actual existents, a catalogue, a chronicle. But metaphysics in the sense of a philosophy of beings qua being would be out of the question. However, the human knower can and does attain the second stage, and thus transcends the first with its limitation and confinement. Within the very content of his awareness of the act of existing and of his consequent understanding of "beings-as-being," then, an absence of the restrictive and limiting is to be found and, accordingly, another instance of abstraction appears. This time, though, the abstraction is quite unique, for here the mind has come upon a component with no inherent link to any matter whatsoever. Even when actualizing a material existent, the act of existing is both

[45] See prgrs. corresponding to notes 32–33 above.

intrinsically and extrinsically independent of matter: unlike the other components, the reason it is present is that the material existent is *existent* and not that it is material.[46] This ontic absence of matter simply transfers itself to the intentional order, and our awareness of "act of existing," of "being" and of the other transcendents contains no matter because there actually is no matter in the *cognita*.[47] Unlike all four previous abstractions, then, the abstraction proper to a metaphysician tends to be a complete and not merely a partial absence of matter within the content of his awarenesses: it occurs because of the absolute freedom of matter in the *cognita* themselves and not because the mind simply does not consider the matter which nonetheless actually is there.

In view of its special status, then, a metaphysician's abstraction is given the special name of "separation," signifying an absence of matter within the very content of awarenesses caused by *cognita* which themselves are actually independent of matter and, in that sense, separated from it.[48]

---

46 See n. 43. Not only does the act of existing have no necessary or intrinsic link with physical matter, but also it is itself free from any sort of potency or limitation. As far as it itself is concerned, it is *pure* act because *nothing but* act, since its sole function is to actuate and the sole relationship it has to any other component is that of the perfective to the perfected.

Accordingly, the freedom from restriction and limitation which the act of existing as such enjoys is freedom both from physical matter and from any sort of potency.

47 The content of what "being" and the other transcendents express is somewhat different from what the "act of existing" expresses. The former refer to more than actual existence: "being," for example, signifies "an actually existing item," where the last word points to essence, which in all existents save God is potency and in some even includes physical matter. Accordingly, the absence of matter in what "being," "good" and the other transcendents signify also differs to some degree from that entailed by the "act of existence." Nonetheless, it continues to be an ontic abstraction inasmuch as the transcendents have to do with essence not in itself but only in reference to existence, not as material or potential but only as actualized and realified. Thus they share in all the characteristics which "act of existing" itself has, one of which is ontic abstraction.

48 Such seems to be the derivation of "separation." Aquinas seems to have been one of the first to apply it to knowledge. He used it to describe actual things free from matter and motion ("separated substances"—see *De Ente et Essentia*, Ch. 4 [Maurer translation, p. 43—the translation referred to here and in subsequent quotes is that listed in the "Suggested Readings" at the end of this chapter]): "It remains for us to see in what way essence is in separated substances, namely, in the soul, in the intelligences, and in the First Cause"

Such, then, are several kinds of knowledge which a philosopher can find within himself. No attempt has been made to ask whether his appreciation of literature and other fine arts directly involves abstraction, or what sort a philosophy of art, ethics, epistemology, psychology and sacred theology entail. But the other kinds of knowledge investigated provide enough information, I hope, to clarify what abstraction is, why it is manifold, and what separation (the abstraction peculiar to metaphysics) entails. In separation the unique nature of metaphysics lies exposed: a knowledge whose content is caused by *cognita* which themselves are unique—items genuinely independent of matter, actuals qua actual, beings precisely in their be-ing.

* 5. Summary and Conclusions

(a) Intellectual knowledge can be adequately described only if both its causes are taken into account—its efficient cause, which is the intellect itself, and its content-determining-cause, which is the *cognitum*. A description made with respect to the former will investigate the various sorts of mental operations involved. In the case of the basic processes by which a philosopher learns of the act of existing and of the other components, these would include both simple and complex apprehensions, perceptual and intellectual judgments (both affirmative and negative), and intellective induction through reflection and reasoning. Note that the presence of judgmental knowledge (even of a negative sort) is not what distinguishes one philosophic science from another; they all are judgmental.

(b) A description made with respect to the content-determining-cause of knowledge (the *cognita*) will include a discussion of abstraction: the absence of matter within the very content of

---

(Latin text in Roland-Gosselin Ed., p. 29, ll. 1–3; *De Potentia*, 5, 8, resp.; *S.T.*, I, 7, 2 ad 2; *In Meta.*, Proemium). But he also transferred it to the knowledge they cause in us (*In Boet. de Trin.*, 5, 3, resp. [Decker Ed., pp. 183, 186]).

In its remote origins the words as applied to *cognita* free from matter reaches back to Aristotle (for example, *Metaphysics*, XII, Ch. 7, 1073a2: "It is clear . . . that there is an entity which is eternal and unmovable and separate from sensible things") and, even earlier, to Plato (see F. Astius, *Lexicon Platonicum* [Bonn: Rudolf Habelt Verlag, 1956], III, 564–66). Whether other medieval authors besides Aquinas applied it also to the knowledge proper to a metaphysician has not yet been investigated.

knowledges.[49] Manifestly, abstraction itself is not an intellectual operation. It is, rather, the negative property or condition of the content of an intellectual awareness as omitting matter (in some sense and to some degree) from its ken. It can be predicated of mental operations only through extrinsic denomination—they are that which produce knowledges the content of which is characterized by an absence of matter. But abstraction itself is directly and intrinsically predicable only of their contents. In line with this, negative judgments can be termed separation, but only in the sense that they are among the operations through which a metaphysician attains awarenesses which contain no matter whatsoever inasmuch as the act of existence and other *cognita* actually are genuinely immaterial. Separation as such is an immediate attribute only of the content of those awarenesses; it is predicable of negative judgments merely through extrinsic denomination.

(c) A partial inventory of various kinds of knowledge which a philosopher can possess discloses five instances of abstraction. These in turn fit into two general categories, inasmuch as matter is absent from the content of the awarenesses involved for two reasons: either the mind simply does not consider the matter (in some sense or other) which the *cognita* actually involve or the *cognita* themselves are actually without matter. The following table locates these five abstractions with respect to that twofold category:

"Absence of Matter within the Content of Intellection"	=	**Abstraction**
1. Because of the nonconsideration of matter, which nonconsideration arises because of one's concentration upon		through nonconsideration
(a) the sort of thing an existent is ("dog" *vs*. signate matter)		abstraction of whatness

[49] Obviously, abstraction does not involve merely the actual exclusion of physical matter, an exclusion which even sense knowledge entails, because the sense faculty, as well as its sensible actuation and operation, is immaterial (see n. 22 above). It is rather an exclusion within the content of knowledge, within what-is-represented-and-known. In this sense it is found only within intellection and not within sense cognition, which is an awareness of something as here-and-now-and-this and, accordingly, within whose content matter is present.

(b) external characteristics ("white" *vs.* various definite kinds of white things [swans, snow, and so on])	abstraction of external characteristics
(c) the contribution which the mind itself imposes upon the original data in the elaboration of constructs ("dog" as reflex universal *vs.* "dog" as direct universal; "circle" *vs.* "roundness")	abstraction of addition
(d) components within a mobile being studied as mobile ("substance," "accidents," "prime matter," "substantial form" *vs.* various definite kinds of directly perceived accidental and substantial changes)	abstraction of natural components
2. Because of the actual absence of matter in the *cognita,* which either are amaterial (act of existing) or spiritual (God, the human soul as subsistent, and so forth)	through actual absence = SEPARATION

(d) This table makes several points clear. First, "matter" has an extremely analogous meaning. In general, it is any factor which would restrict, confine or limit the content of an awareness. That factor can be signate sensible matter (see #1a), various kinds of existents with reference to an external characteristic shared in common (#1b), the original "stuff" (whether intramental or extramental) in contrast to its intelligible status after the human knower has worked upon it (#1c), definite kinds of directly perceived accidental and substantial changes (#1d) and, finally, any matter whatsoever (whether sensible or intelligible, whether signate or common) and, in some cases, any potency whatsoever (#2).

Second, separation is one sort of abstraction because it is an absence of matter within the content of what a metaphysician knows. In fact, it is abstraction *par excellence* inasmuch at it involves a complete absence of matter within the content of such knowledge.

Third, "abstraction" itself is obviously an extremely analogous concept. A genuine similarity exists between abstraction through actual absence (#2: separation) and that through nonconsideration

(#1): each is an absence of matter within awarenesses. But they also differ greatly, and for reasons now too evident to need comment. The various abstractions listed as arising through nonconsideration (#1) also differ widely from one another. They are not, for instance, mere degrees of one and the same univocal sort, but rather differ greatly in nature and kind from each other. Nor is the list of abstractions necessarily complete, because no account has been taken of such knowledges as philosophy of art, moral philosophy and moral theology, sacred theology, or epistemology.[50]

(e) Finally, why is metaphysics distinct from all other sciences? Why is it an unusual sort of knowledge? There are two answers: because it studies beings precisely as being and because it is marked by separation. Those replies seem different, because the former is concerned with the formal object of metaphysics, the latter with its special mode of abstraction. The former expresses what is present in the content of such intellection, whereas the latter signifies what is absent. Nevertheless, the two amount to the same. That by which a being is being is the act of existence. But this is amaterial: even within a material existent it is a component which is immaterial to such a degree as to be both extrinsically and intrinsically independent of matter.[51] But by reason of this independence the act of existing, when known, causes the content of a metaphysician's awareness of being to be free from matter. But this cognitive free-

---

[50] This much seems clear with regard to moral philosophy or ethics, which is the science of what man ought to do. A philosopher knows what man *is*, and thereafter comes to know what he *ought to do*. But suppose that he could not rise above the first sort of knowledge. It would confine and restrict him. Actually, however, he does transcend it, together with its relative confinement and restriction, and he comes to know what man ought to do. In the content of the intelligibilities on this second level of knowledge, there is an absence of the restrictive and limiting (= matter, which here is equivalent to a mere knowledge of what man is), and this is the abstraction proper to ethics.

So too with sacred theology, which can be described as the science derived from divine revelation. If someone is unaware of that revelation or refuses to accept it, he is restricted to purely natural knowledges achieved from data given by sensible existents through perception and elaborated by human reason alone. But by accepting and elaborating divine revelation, a sacred theologian transcends merely natural knowledges with the restriction and confinement they would embody in this context. In the content of what a theologian knows, then, there is an absence of the restrictive and limiting (here, merely natural knowledge) and hence an abstraction peculiar to sacred theology.

[51] See n. 43.

dom from matter is separation. Therefore, affirming that the subject of metaphysics is actuals qua actual is equivalent to stating that metaphysics is characterized by separation. They are two sides of the same coin. Since no other science has identically the same inscriptions, metaphysics is indeed a rare coin, quite unlike any other. It is a coin of great price.[52]

Suggested Readings

Anderson, James F., "On Demonstration in Thomistic Metaphysics," *New Scholasticism,* 32 (1958), 476–94.

———, "Some Disputed Questions on Our Knowledge of Being," *Review of Metaphysics,* 11 (1958), 550–60. An important article on metaphysical knowledge.

Augros, Robert M., and George N. Stanciu, *The New Story of Science,* ch. 2: "Mind." Lake Bluff, Ill.: Regnery Gateway, 1984.

Copleston, S.J., F. C., "Man and Metaphysics," *The Heythrop Journal,* 1 (1960), 3–17.

Eccles, John, and Daniel N. Robinson, *The Wonder of Being Human: Our Brain and Our Mind.* New York: The Free Press, 1984.

Eslick, Leonard, "What Is the Starting Point of Metaphysics?" *Modern Schoolman,* 34 (May, 1957), 247–63. On metaphysics as grounded in sensible existents.

D'Espagnat, Bernard, *Reality and the Physicist: Knowledge, Duration and the Quantum World.* Cambridge University Press, 1990.

Gilson, Etienne, *The Spirit of Mediaeval Philosophy,* trans. A. H. C. Downes, pp. 1–41 and 403–26. New York: Charles Scribner's Sons, 1940. On thomistic metaphysics in relationship to divine revelation and sacred theology.

Griesbach, M. F., "Judgment and Existence," *Proceedings of the American Catholic Philosophical Association,* 30 (1956), 205–11.

Henle, S.J., Robert J., "Existentialism and the Judgment," *Proceedings of the American Catholic Philosophical Association,* 21 (1946), 40–53.

———, *Method in Metaphysics,* Aquinas Lecture, 1950. Milwaukee: Marquette University Press, 1951.

———, "A Phenomenological Approach to Realism," in *An Etienne Gilson Tribute,* ed. Charles J. O'Neil, pp. 68–85. Milwaukee: Marquette University Press, 1959. On the necessity of induction in metaphysics.

———, *A Theory of Knowledge: A Textbook and Substantive Theory of Epistemology.* Chicago: Loyola University Press, 1983.

---

[52] Because Thomas was among the first to transfer the term "separation" from existents to knowledge, it would be interesting to check our interpretation with his texts. For this check, see Appendix C.

Jaki, Stanley L., *Brain, Mind and Computers*. Washington, D.C.: Gateway Editions, 1989.

Kane, O.P., William H., "The Subject of Metaphysics," *Thomist*, 18 (1955), 503–21.

Maritain, Jacques, *The Degrees of Knowledge*, trans. G. B. Phelan. New York: Charles Scribner's Sons, 1959.

Maurer, Armand, *On the Division and Method of the Sciences.* Toronto: Pontifical Institute of Mediaeval Studies, 1953. A translation of Aquinas' *In Librum Boethii de Trinitate*, questions 5 and 6.

Owens, Joseph, *St. Thomas and the Future of Metaphysics*, Aquinas Lecture, 1957. Milwaukee: Marquette University Press, 1957.

———, *An Elementary Christian Metaphysics*, pp. 213–308. Milwaukee: Bruce Publishing Co., 1963. On knowledge (its operations of apprehension, judgment, demonstration, and so forth; intentional being; truth); on sciences (their division, nature).

———, "Metaphysical Separation in Aquinas," *Mediaeval Studies*, 34 (1972), 287–306.

———, "Aquinas on Cognition as Existence," *Proceedings of the American Catholic Philosophical Association*, 48 (1974), 74–85.

———," Aristotle—Cognition a Way of Being," *Canadian Journal of Philosophy*, 6 (1976) 1–11.

Penrose, Roger, *The Emperor's New Mind: Concerning Computers, Minds and the Laws of Physics.* Oxford University Press, 1989.

Schmidt, Kenneth, "Toward a Metaphysical Restoration of Natural Things," in *An Etienne Gilson Tribute*, ed. Charles J. O'Neil, pp. 245–62.

Schmidt, S.J., Robert W., "The Evidence Grounding Judgments of Existence," in *An Etienne Gilson Tribute*, ed Charles J. O'Neil, pp. 228–44.

Searle, John R., *The Rediscovery of the Mind*. Cambridge, Mass.: The MIT Press, 1992. A convincing rebuttal of those who believe the mind is essentially a computer program. See A. Gottlieb's review in *The New York Times Book Review* for Oct. 11, 1992, pp. 15–16.

Simmons, Edward D., "The Thomistic Doctrine of the Three Degrees of Formal Abstraction," *The Thomist*, 22 (1959), 37–67. See references to other authors in notes 13–15.

Sweeney, S.J., Leo, "Preller and Aquinas: Second Thoughts," in *Christian Philosophy: Nature, Origin, Developments*, ch. 22, especially the sections "Aristotle's Theory of Knowledge" (with diagram) and "Aquinas: Existence and Actuation 'A.'" New York/Bern: Peter Lang Publishing, Inc., 1994.

Tyrrell, Francis M., "Concerning the Nature and Functions of Judgment," *New Scholasticism*, 26 (1952), 393–423.

Wallace, William A., *From a Realist Point of View: Essays on the Philosophy of Science.* Washington, D.C.: University Press of America, 1979. Excellent on Thomas' philosophy *re* empiriological sciences.

Wippel, John F., "Metaphysics and *Separatio* According to Thomas Aquinas," *Review of Metaphysics*, 31 (1978), 431–70.

XI

Recent Developments in Metaphysics

by John J. Furlong

> Upon their surface, the reports of the world which form our different philosophies are various to the point of stark contrariness. They range from spiritualism to materialism, from absolutism to relativistic phenomenalism, from transcendentalism to positivism, from rationalism to sensationalism, from idealism to realism, from subjectivism to bald objectivism, from Platonic realism to nominalism. The array of contradictions is so imposing as to suggest to sceptics that the mind of man has tackled an impossible job, or that philosophers have abandoned themselves to vagary.[1]

During the twenty years or more since this metaphysics book was published, contemporary philosophy has evolved in an interesting—and an unpredictable—way. Also, the distance of time has bestowed a more mature perspective on the metaphysical battles of two decades ago. It is fitting, then, in this last chapter, to attempt a brief history of these developments in order to put into historical context Professor Sweeney's discussions of positivism and existentialism. Our account will not attempt a refutation of any meta-

---

[1] John Dewey, *Experience and Nature* (New York: Dover Books, 1958), p. 46. I owe a debt of thanks to Professors Suzanne Cunningham and Kenneth Thompson for helpful criticisms of a draft of this chapter.

physical positions but rather will describe as clearly as possible the evolving scene and point out the major points of contention.

Recent work in metaphysics has been so diverse that our first task will be to limit our scope; we shall paint our picture with large brush strokes, necessarily ignoring certain details for the sake of illuminating the whole. We limit our discussion in four ways. First, as we shall be canvasing only large "mainstream" movements, individual metaphysicians and less influential metaphysical positions will be mentioned only insofar as they exemplify features of a major trend. Second, we will discuss only *metaphysical* movements—we will not attempt to map out related terrain, such as Marxism, Freudian metapsychology, and the various versions of "structuralism," although relevant to recent metaphysical developments and raising metaphysical questions all their own.

Third, we will be interested only in systematic metaphysical movements or in those that attempt a *systematic* revision of traditional metaphysics. As we shall see, metaphysical thinking over the last twenty years or more has been occupied with the very value of the enterprise of metaphysics itself. Most of this reflection has been self-critical, questioning, even self-doubting. A good bit of it has been fruitful, promising a transformation of the subject. Some of the attacks on metaphysics, however, have been less straightforward challenges than declarations of victory before any battle is enjoined. This strategy, often called "deconstructionism," will not be treated as a separate movement in this chapter because of its lack of rigor and its "willingness to settle issues by theoretical decree."[2] Nonetheless, individual deconstructionists, like Michel Foucault, Gilles Deleuze, Roland Barthes, Jean-François Lyotard, and Jacques Derrida, are worth reading for their insights about specific metaphysical issues, and Derrida will be mentioned when we discuss the later Heidegger.

Fourth, our "big picture" will not include all systematic metaphysical movements—"process philosophy," championed by Alfred North Whitehead and his followers, has made very little impact upon mainstream philosophy. Dorothy Emmett, author of the article on Whitehead in the *Encyclopedia of Philosophy*,[3] suggests as a

---

[2] Frederick Crews, *Skeptical Engagements* (New York: Oxford University Press, 1986), p. 164. See also John Searle's critique of Jonathan Culler's exposition of deconstructionism in the *New York Review of Books*, January 21, 1984.

[3] Dorothy Emmett, "Whitehead," in P. Edwards, ed., *The Encyclopedia of Philosophy*, VII (New York: Macmillan, 1967), 290–96.

reason the fact that Whitehead's followers are preoccupied with clarifying "Whitehead's system in its own terms"[4] and not in terms of contemporary discussion. No significant impact will be made by process philosophy until "philosophers working independently of direct exegesis find that some of its ideas can be developed, perhaps in different terminology, and put to use in particular philosophical problems."[5]

1. Whitehead's Cosmology

Nonetheless, though his influence on mainstream thought is not great and his most lucid followers are theologians,[6] Whitehead is the only major figure in contemporary metaphysics to advocate practicing metaphysics in the grand "revisionary"[7] style of Leibniz, Spinoza and Hegel. Unlike his contemporaries, Whitehead repudiates the prevailing "distrust of speculative philosophy."[8] "The study

---

[4] *Ibid.*, p. 294.

[5] *Ibid.*

[6] See the works of Charles Hartshorne, *The Logic of Perfection and Other Essays in Neoclassical Metaphysics* (New York: Open Court, 1962); *Anselm's Discovery: A Re-Examination of the Ontological Proof for God's Existence* (New York: Open Court, 1965); *The Divine Relativity: A Social Conception of God* (New Haven: Yale University Press, 1982); *Creative Synthesis and Philosophic Method* (New York: University Press of America, 1983); *Omnipotence and Other Theological Mistakes* (Albany, N.Y.: SUNY Press, 1983). See also the work of Schubert M. Ogden, *The Reality of God* (New York: Harper and Row, 1977), and Lewis S. Ford, *The Emergence of Whitehead's Metaphysics* (Albany, N.Y.: SUNY Press, 1984); Hartshorne with George Kline (eds.), *Explorations in Whitehead's Philosophy* (New York: Fordham University Press, 1983). Hartshorne has introduced the term "neoclassical metaphysics" to describe the activities of process theologians, but the term is not coextensive with "process philosophy." Our concern in this chapter is largely with the latter. See Eugene H. Peters, *Hartshorne and Neoclassical Metaphysics* (Lincoln, Nebr.: University of Nebraska Press, 1970).

[7] Peter Strawson in *Individuals* (New York: Anchor Books, 1959), p. xiii, distinguishes between "descriptive" and "revisionary" metaphysics: "Descriptive metaphysics is content to describe the actual structure of our thought about the world, revisionary metaphysics is concerned to produce a better structure." Whitehead is clearly a revisionist: although he claims merely to describe the way things are, he only begins to do so *after* he has presented his "revisionary" terminology.

[8] Alfred North Whitehead, *Process and Reality: An Essay in Cosmology* (for publishing data see "Suggested Readings" below), p. viii.

of philosophy," he urges, "is a voyage toward the larger generalities."[9] It must attempt to recover and describe the totality, to fashion a "coherent, logical, necessary system of general ideas in which every element of our experience can be interpreted."[10] Our language at this level, however, cannot be precise. In fact, we must "delve below the apparent clarity of common speech,"[11] making metaphysical discourse "elliptical, requiring a leap of the imagination to understand its meaning in its relevance to immediate experience."[12] Even the term "metaphysics" needs to be revised a bit. This term he reserves for study of the ultimate formal principles of any possible world; a study of the application of these formal principles to our particular world he terms "cosmology." And it is his cosmology that we will very briefly discuss.

Whitehead seems to begin his "cosmological" speculations with the assumption that whatever entity is being studied—a rock, a quark, a person, or even God—will exhibit the same general characteristics. This means, to take the most striking example, that if a rock has a "physical pole" as part of its ontological make-up, then so must God. God is "not to be treated as an exception to all metaphysical principles," for he is "their chief exemplification."[13] What are these general characteristics for our world, including God? They are conceived on analogy to the coming-to-be of human feelings:

> I find myself as essentially a unity of emotions, enjoyments, hopes, fears, regrets, valuations of alternatives, decisions—all of them subjective reactions to the environment as active in my nature. My unity . . . is my process of shaping this welter of material into a consistent pattern of feelings. The individual enjoyment is what I am in my role of a natural activity, as I shape the activities of the environment into a new creation, which is myself at this moment; and yet, as being myself, it is a continuation of the antecedent world.[14]

---

[9] *Ibid.*, p. 10.

[10] Alfred North Whitehead, *Adventures of Ideas* (New York: The Free Press, 1961), p. 222.

[11] *Ibid.*

[12] *Process and Reality*, p. 13.

[13] *Ibid.*, p. 343.

[14] Alfred North Whitehead, *The Modes of Thought* (Cambridge University Press, 1938), p. 228.

The basic realities of the universe will exhibit just this same structure and content—subconscious feelings welling up to become unities of feeling and subsequently radiating into the world. These elements are what Whitehead calls actual entities. Actual entities are the final real things making up the world.[15] God is an actual entity; yet rocks, quarks, and persons are societies or nexus of actual occasions.[16] Every actual entity is a synthesis of "prehensions," which are negative and positive (feelings)—the negative inhibiting and the positive stimulating the current vector aiming at unity of feeling in an actual occasion. Any actual occasion comes to be as a result of the coming-to-be and perishing of antecedent actual occasions which function as data for the present occasion:[17]

> The process of concrescence is divisible into an initial stage of many feelings, and of subsequent phases of more complex feelings integrating the earlier simpler feelings, up to a satisfaction which is one complex unity of feeling.[18]

This unified feeling is the "subjective aim" of the evolution and is, hence, the subject (or "superject") and final cause:

> The feelings are inseparable from the end at which they aim; and this end is the feeler. The feelings aim at the feeler, as their final cause. The feelings are what they are in order that their subject may be what it is.[19]

The way this entity feels is its essence, but its essence points outward toward more fullness, and its own subsumption in a new unity. Yet in attaining its end, no actual occasion ever ceases altogether to be; for it enjoys an objective immortality in the world that transcends its own immediacy of becoming.

---

[15] *Process and Reality*, p. 19.

[16] See *Adventures of Ideas*: "The real actual things that endure (such as stones or animal organisms) are all societies. They are not actual occasions" (p. 211).

[17] Professor Kenneth Thompson aided immensely in the proper formulation of Whitehead's position as described in this paragraph.

[18] *Process and Reality*, p. 220.

[19] *Ibid.*, p. 222.

> The attainment of a peculiar definiteness is the final cause which animates a particular process; and its attainment halts its process, so that by transcendence it passes into its objective immortality as a new objective condition added to the riches of definiteness attainable, the "real potentiality" of the universe.[20]

In this manner, the potential becomes actual and the many become one. The principle of this expanding process is creativity, "that ultimate principle by which the many, which are the universe disjunctively, become the one actual occasion, which is the universe conjunctively."[21] But, we may ask, what is the purpose of this creativity? Into what is this converging universe growing? Whitehead's answer, in short, is God.[22]

God is not the traditional Creator or *Primum Movens* for Whitehead, since God is "not *before* all creation, but *with* all creation."[23] However, by a "distinction of reason," we may imagine God in His "primordial nature" before the immense potential of the universe began to actualize. God is this immense potential, but He is "deficiently actual," for His feelings are only "conceptual and so lack the fullness of actuality" or consciousness.[24] God's primordial nature, however, provides the possibility for all actuality and is the prime exemplification of creativity:

> He is the unconditioned actuality of conceptual feeling at the base of things; so that, by reason of this primordial actuality, there is an order in the relevance of eternal objects to the process of creation. His unity of conceptual operations is a

---

[20] *Ibid.*, p. 223.

[21] *Ibid.*, p. 21.

[22] The relation between God and creativity is unclear in Whitehead's writing and has generated the most intense discussions among process philosophers and "neoclassical" theologians. See Robert Neville, *Creativity and God* (New York: Seabury Press, 1980); Norris W. Clarke, "Theism and Whiteheadian Process Philosophy: Are They Compatible?" *Logos*, 1 (1980), 9–44; Lewis Ford, "The Search for the Source of Creativity," *Logos*, 1 (1980), 45–52, and "A Response to Neville's *Creativity and God*," *Process Studies*, 10 (1980), 105–9. In our brief analysis, we attempt to stay neutral as to the question of the *degree* of independence of creativity from God.

[23] *Op. cit.*, p. 343.

[24] *Ibid.*

> free creative act, untrammelled by reference to any particular course of things. It is deflected neither by love, nor by hatred, for what in fact comes to pass. The *particularities* of the actual world presuppose it; while it merely presupposes the *general* metaphysical character of creative advance, of which it is the primordial exemplification. The primordial nature of God is the acquirement by creativity of a primordial character.[25]

Finally, God's nature is also "consequent." Each creature is a "prehension into God."[26] Each novelty is a specification of God's primordial nature. Hence, "it is as true to say that God creates the World, as that the World creates God."[27] Indeed, the only difference between the World and God seems to be one of emphasis: "For God the conceptual is prior to the physical, for the World the physical poles are prior to the conceptual poles."[28]

It is regrettable that more has not been done to weave some of Whitehead's central concepts into current metaphysical controversies. Some attempts have been made, of course,[29] but none has survived the problem of translating Whitehead's imaginative language into standard philosophical argot and from there to traditional discussions of philosophical problems.[30] In a way, then, process philosophy forces its own omission from the mainstream of philosophy by dint of its very exuberance.

---

[25] *Ibid.*, p. 344.

[26] *Ibid.*, p. 345.

[27] *Ibid.*, p. 348.

[28] *Ibid.*

[29] Paul Weiss's work, for instance, attempts to form a rapprochement between the metaphysical tradition and process philosophy. See especially his ongoing *Philosophy in Process*, Vols. 1–6 (Carbondale, Ill.: Southern Illinois University Press, 1966–1974); Vol. 7 (Albany, N.Y.: SUNY Press, 1977). Charles Hartshorne has also entered the dialogue to some extent. See his *The Logic Of Perfection and Other Essays in Neoclassical Metaphysics.* For other attempts see G. Kline and L. Ford (eds.), *Explorations in Whitehead's Philosophy*, especially Richard Rorty's "Matter and Event." Also see Victor Lowe *et al.*, *Whitehead and the Modern World: Science, Metaphysics and Civilization* (Salem, N.H.: Ayer Company, 1985; repr. of 1950 ed.); Dorothy M. Emmet, *Whitehead's Philosophy of Organism* (Westport, Conn.: Greenwood Press, 1981).

[30] See Robert Hanna, "The Nature of Creativity in Whitehead's Metaphysics," *Philosophy Research Archives* 9 (1983), 109–76.

2. Empiricism, Positivism and Beyond

We have now defined our field of inquiry narrowly enough to be able to paint a clear picture. In the first chapter of this book Professor Sweeney discusses positivism and in the second introduces existentialism. These movements are good compass points in the lush forest of contemporary metaphysics because they represent the two dominant styles of metaphysical thinking that have reigned in this century. Positivism characterizes the spare and wiry Anglo-American style of philosophy, existentialism the aphoristic and dramatic European. From these two points of purchase we will look both backward and forward in time. As we go forward from our chosen points, we will see the heretofore parallel paths miraculously merging the closer we approach our own time.

Like most British philosophical movements since the late Middle Ages, positivism is a sort of minimalism. To the fourteenth-century British Franciscan William of Ockham is often attributed the motto: "Entities should not be multiplied without necessity."[31] From that time on, philosophy in the English-speaking world seems to take Ockhamist minimalism ("Ockham's Razor," as the tradition has it) as the criterion of acceptability. The Anglo-American metaphysical style is economical: the fewer entities to posit the better.

This metaphysical minimalism fits neatly the growth of experimental science in the ensuing centuries. It engendered in early scientists the desire to make their explanations of phenomena increasingly more simple and to favor a single hypothesis explaining a number of phenomena over multiple hypotheses. However, as the British empiricists were the first to attempt to demonstrate, scientific discoveries under the compression of minimalist theory challenge metaphysical speculation. John Locke (1632–1704) and David Hume (1711–1776) argued that since experimental methods were the only reliable methods of discovering what is true, their results would give us our metaphysical commitments. If, for instance, phlogiston is shown to be unnecessary in explaining combustion, then we may assume it does not exist; if oxygen is a

---

[31] This phrase is usually assumed to come from the Latin "entia non sunt multiplicanda sine necessitate," which is not found in Ockham's work, although the very similar "pluralitas non est ponenda sine necessitate" appears often. See *De Sacramento Altaris*, cap. 28; *Ordinatio*, d. 30, qu. Ie; *Reportatio* II, qu. 150.

proven ingredient in combustion, then oxygen must exist.[32] In other words, says the empiricist, show me experimentally that x exists and I will make it part of my metaphysics; if you cannot, then I will assume it does not exist until it is so demonstrated. What one takes to be real, then, is not to be discovered by reflection on experience or on obvious truths, but is to be wrested from nature by the scientific method. Hume expresses this point somewhat brutally in his *Enquiry Concerning Human Understanding,* where he offers a "litmus test" for the worth of a book.

> *Does it contain any abstract reasoning concerning quantity or number?* No. *Does it contain any experimental reasoning concerning matters of fact and existence?* No. Commit it then to the flames: for it can contain nothing but sophistry and illusion.[33]

(a) Early Linguistic Analysis: Antecedents to Positivism

British empiricism persisted with relatively little change in style from Locke in the seventeenth century, to Hume in the eighteenth, through John Stuart Mill in the nineteenth. In the early decades of the twentieth century, Bertrand Russell (1872–1972), G. E. Moore (1873–1958), and Ludwig Wittgenstein (1889–1951) began to develop new techniques for determining metaphysical commitments.[34] Though there are significant differences among these three, they all brought to the preoccupations of empiricism a concern with language. Richard Rorty calls this new emphasis the "linguistic turn," but Willard van Ormond Quine's vertical metaphor, "semantic ascent," more vividly suggests the shift in empiricist metaphysics from reflection on objects to reflection on object-talk:

---

[32] For the classic account of the discovery of oxygen see A. N. Meldrum, *The Eighteenth Century Revolution in Science—The First Phase,* and other works cited in Thomas S. Kuhn, *The Structure of Scientific Revolutions* (Chicago: University of Chicago Press, 1970), Ch. VI.

[33] David Hume, *Enquiry Concerning Human Understanding,* ed. L. A. Selby-Bigge (Oxford: Clarendon Press, 1951), p. 165.

[34] Recent revisions of Wittgenstein's and Moore's motives for inaugurating these new methods notwithstanding, their actual use of them is undisputed. See Allan Janik and Stephen Toulmin, *Wittgenstein's Vienna* (New York: Simon and Schuster, 1973); Tom Regan, *Bloomsbury's Prophet: G. E. Moore and the Development of His Moral Philosophy* (Philadelphia: Temple University Press, 1987).

> Semantic ascent, as I speak of it, applies anywhere. "There are wombats in Tasmania" might be paraphrased as "'Wombat' is true of some creatures in Tasmania," if there were any point in it. But it does happen that semantic ascent is more useful in philosophical connections than in most, and I think I can explain why. . . . The strategy of semantic ascent is that it carries the discussion into a domain where both parties are better agreed on the objects (viz., words) and on the main terms concerning them. Words, or their inscriptions, unlike points, miles, classes, and the rest, are tangible objects of the size so popular in the marketplace, where men of unlike conceptual schemes communicate at their best.[35]

Moore, for instance, in his proof of an external world is concerned with what philosophers have said about the external world and not about the features of the world itself. His quarrel is with the eighteenth-century philosopher Immanuel Kant who, in the *Critique of Pure Reason*, asserted that "it still remains a scandal to philosophy . . . that the existence of things outside us . . . must be accepted merely on faith."[36] Moore takes umbrage with the uses of the words Kant employs, arguing that such phrases as "to be met with in space" are used in inappropriate ways and such linguistic confusions lead Kant away from what, to Moore, is the correct, Common Sense, view.[37] In fact, Moore was to say later that "I do not think that the world or the sciences would ever have suggested to me any philosophical problems. What has suggested philosophical problems to me is things which other philosophers have said about the world or the sciences."[38]

Bertrand Russell is just as sweeping as Moore in his complaints about the linguistic conflations of philosophers—even empiricist philosophers: "I think that practically all traditional metaphysics is

---

[35] W. v. O. Quine, *Word and Object* (Cambridge, Mass.: M.I.T. Press, 1960), p. 272.

[36] Immanuel Kant, *Critique of Pure Reason*, Norman Kemp Smith, trans. (New York: St. Martin's Press, 1965), p. 34.

[37] See G. E. Moore, "Proof of an External World," in Robert R. Ammerman (ed.), *Classics of Analytic Philosophy* (New York: McGraw-Hill, 1965), pp. 68–84. See also Moore's later discussion of the external world in *Some Main Problems of Philosophy* (New York: Collier Books, 1966), Chs. 8 and 9.

[38] G. E. Moore in Paul Schilpp (ed.), *The Philosophy of G. E. Moore* (Evanston, Ill.: Northwestern University Press, 1942), p. 14.

filled with mistakes due to bad grammar."[39] His solution to the problem, however, is much more specific and more self-conscious in its debt to his minimalist forebear. Citing Ockham's Razor as an historical embodiment of his position, Russell sets out his method for metaphysics.

> What is the smallest number of simple undefined things at the start, and the smallest number of undemonstrated premises, out of which you can define the things that need to be defined and prove the things that need to be proved? . . . You cannot possibly get at the solution of such a problem as I am talking about if you go at it in a straightforward fashion with just the ordinary acumen that one accumulates in the course of reading or in the study of traditional philosophy. You do need this apparatus of symbolical logic that I have been talking about.[40]

This phase of Russell's philosophical development[41] is often called Logical Atomism and was inspired, in part, by the young Ludwig Wittgenstein's *Tractatus Logico-Philosophicus.* Although their metaphysical commitments are quite different, both philosophers aimed at resolving all philosophical problems by regimenting ordinary language according to the rules of mathematical logic. It would be this symbolic logic, they averred, that would eventually make philosophical language scientific and would eliminate metaphysical confusions.

(b) Logical Positivism

Russell, Moore and Wittgenstein were immensely influential in turning empiricism away from traditional metaphysical concerns and "upward" in semantic ascent toward the analysis of language. They begat an empiricist-minimalist style of philosophizing that is often called "Linguistic Analysis." Wittgenstein attracted an especially wide audience, extending to Germany, where his *Tractatus* was essential reading for a group of empiricist philosophers known

---

[39] Bertrand Russell, *Logic and Knowledge,* ed. R. C. Marsh (London: Allen and Unwin, Ltd., 1956), p. 269.

[40] *Ibid.,* p. 271.

[41] See, among other competent treatments, David F. Pears, *Bertrand Russell and the British Tradition in Philosophy* (New York: Random House, 1967); George W. Roberts, *Bertrand Russell: The Memorial Volume* (Atlantic Highlands, N.J.: Humanities Press, Inc., 1979).

as the Vienna Circle.[42] Through their founder Moritz Schlick (1882–1938) and especially through Rudolph Carnap (1891–1954), logical positivism began to catch on in England and in the United States. In the late 1930s, the golden age of positivism, A. J. Ayer wrote the most vivid and incendiary positivist tract to date: *Language, Truth and Logic.* In it he upheld the linguistic minimalism of his predecessors:

> The propositions of philosophy are not factual, but linguistic in character—that is, they do not describe the behavior of physical, or even mental, objects; they express definitions, or the formal consequences of definitions. Accordingly, we may say that philosophy is a department of logic.[43]

He also refined the Verification Principle, a criterion of meaningfullness introduced earlier by Carnap. Professor Sweeney's first chapter (Section 1) cites one formulation of the Principle. In effect, positivism enriched by the Verification Principle requires of a metaphysician (1) to make the semantic ascent; (2) to relegate discussions of the truth or falsity of propositions to scientists; (3) to concern themselves solely with the meaning of terms and propositions; and (4) to use the Verification Principle as the sole criterion of meaningfulness. The bulk of the literature on or by logical positivists involves the defense and clarification of this last point. It is not surprising, then, that philosophers began to abandon logical positivism as it gradually became clear that the verificationist constraint was too strict and, to some, illusory.

(c) Analysis Pragmatized: Sellars and Quine

Beginning in the 1950s in both England and the United States new directions began to be taken. The early years of that decade saw the publication of Willard van Ormond Quine's "Two Dogmas of Empiricism,"[44] Wilfred Sellars' "Empiricism and the Philosophy

---

[42] For a firsthand account of Vienna Circle discussions, especially as they involved Wittgenstein, see Brian McGuiness (ed.), *Ludwig Wittgenstein and the Vienna Circle: Conversations Recorded by Friedrich Waissmann* (New York: Barnes and Noble, 1979).

[43] A. J. Ayer, *Language, Truth and Logic* (London: Victor Gollancz, Ltd.; New York: Dover Publications, 1946), p. 35. On logical positivism in general see Ayer's *Logical Positivism* (Westport, Conn.: Greenwood Press, 1978).

[44] Willard van Ormond Quine, "Two Dogmas of Empiricism," *Philosophical Review*, 60 (1950), 20–43. This much-discussed paper is first anthologized by

of Mind,"[45] and Ludwig Wittgenstein's *Philosophical Investigations*.[46] Two types of analysts converge here to oppose positivism: the pragmatist-influenced Americans, whose foremost spokesmen have been Quine and Sellars, and the contingent of American and British followers of the later Wittgenstein, practitioners of what has often been called Ordinary Language Philosophy.[47] The key difference between the two lies in their stance on the metaphysical importance of science. For the pragmatized Americans, Sellars provides the motto: "Science is the measure of all things, of what is that it is, and of what is not that it is not."[48] Wittgenstein counters with his famous comment in *The Blue and Brown Books*, "Ordinary language is all right,"[49] implying that whatever "metaphysics" we may need is to be found in the analysis of everyday language. Sellars, Quine and the scientific analysts equate science and metaphysics, reducing the one to the other; Wittgenstein and followers show that metaphysical questions are the diseases for which a careful analysis of ordinary language is the therapy.[50]

First to the analysts influenced by pragmatism. The founders of pragmatism, Charles Sanders Peirce (1839–1914), William James (1842–1910), and John Dewey (1859–1952), were all well within the British tradition of minimalism and respect for science, though not affected by the "linguistic turn" of their British counterparts. Russell's criticism to the contrary,[51] pragmatists were as interested

---

Quine himself in *From a Logical Point of View* (Cambridge, Mass.: Harvard University Press, 1953), Ch. II.

[45] Wilfred Sellars, "Empiricism and the Philosophy of Mind," in H. Feigl and M. Scriven (eds.), *Minnesota Studies in the Philosophy of Science* (Minneapolis: University of Minnesota Press, 1956), I, 253–329.

[46] Ludwig Wittgenstein, *Philosophical Investigations* (Oxford: Basil Blackwell, 1953).

[47] One qualification: not all so-called Ordinary Language philosophers are followers of Wittgenstein. Gilbert Ryle and J. L. Austin have their own followings and are thought to consider themselves distant admirers of Wittgenstein. See Ryle's various comments in "Autobiographical," in O. P. Wood and G. Pitcher (eds.), *Ryle: A Collection of Critical Essays* (New York: Anchor Books, 1970), pp. 1–17.

[48] Wilfred Sellars, *Science, Perception and Reality* (London: Routledge and Kegan Paul, 1963), p. 173.

[49] Ludwig Wittgenstein, *The Blue and Brown Books* (New York: Harper Torchbooks, 1958), p. 28.

[50] See Wittgenstein, *Philosophical Investigations*, paragraphs 109–33.

[51] Bertrand Russell, *Philosophical Essays* (New York: Longmans, Green and Co., 1910), "Pragmatism," pp. 109–14.

as the analysts in conceptual clarity,[52] but their purpose was different. Peirce urges that the "rational purport of a word or other expression, lies exclusively on its conceivable bearing upon the conduct of life."[53] Glossing on this position, John Dewey observes, "In order to be able to attribute a meaning to concepts, one must be able to apply them to existence."[54] Conceptual clarity, then, is not an end in itself, nor, by the way, is science or philosophy. To quote James: ". . . the effective meaning of any philosophic proposition can always be brought down to some particular consequence, in our future practical experience. . . ."[55]

Quine is the first major philosopher trained in the school of linguistic analysis to criticize its positivist foundations with the aid of pragmatism. In "Two Dogmas of Empiricism," he argues for the abandonment of two key empiricist/positivist doctrines. "One effect of abandoning them," he contends, "is . . . a blurring of the supposed boundary between speculative metaphysics and natural science. Another effect is a shift toward pragmatism."[56] One "dogma," held by empiricists at least since Locke, is the distinction between matters of fact and truths of reason—Hume's "matters of fact and existence" and "abstract reasoning." Positivists especially spent much of their work attempting to distinguish analytic statements (statements which were true in virtue of their definitions—truths of reason) from synthetic statements (statements true in virtue of representing facts). What Quine shows, to the satisfaction of many analytic philosophers, is that this distinction is "an unempirical dogma of empiricists, a metaphysical article of faith."[57] Granted that positivists held the work of philosophy to be largely analytical and the work of science largely synthetic, but if that distinction is bogus, then the distinction between philosophy—especially metaphysics—and science is bogus also, leaving the metaphysician unemployed, so to speak.

---

[52] See Peirce's "How to Make Our Ideas Clear," in A. Rorty (ed.), *Pragmatic Philosophy* (New York: Anchor Books, 1966), pp. 12–18.

[53] *Ibid.,* p. 17.

[54] John Dewey, "The Development of American Pragmatism" in A. Rorty, *op. cit.*, p. 205.

[55] William James, "What Pragmatism Means," in Ralph Perry (ed.), *Collected Essays and Reviews* (New York: Russell and Russell, 1969), p. 412.

[56] Willard van Ormond Quine, "Two Dogmas of Empiricism," in Robert R. Ammerman, *op. cit.*, p. 197.

[57] *Ibid.*, p. 207.

The disfranchisement of the philosopher may seem a heavy price to pay for the unseating of positivism. But more is to come in Quine's destruction of the second "dogma." In this he is aided and abetted by Sellars, and Quine himself dedicates a great deal of subsequent work to its complete demolishment. It will be important, then, to go more slowly over this point. For virtually all philosophers from the sixteenth century onward their theory of knowledge has driven their metaphysics. For the empiricists in particular, the proper scientific method yields the correct metaphysical truths and not *vice-versa.* Hence, the positivist's verifiability principle could be seen as a tool for discovering certain metaphysical foundations for science. If all meaningful statements were reducible to observational/experiential statements, it was because these latter corresponded to fact, opened on to reality, and anchored all other statements. From certain foundations come true metaphysical commitments.

But what if we cannot make a distinction of kind between observation statements and other more theoretical statements? What if it could be shown that observations, too, are always filtered through a particular theory or set of concepts? What if we cannot get at nonlinguistic reality? This line of questioning is precisely what Sellars and Quine suggest we pursue. "All awareness of sorts, resemblances, facts, etc., in short, all awareness of abstract entities—indeed, all awareness even of particulars—is a linguistic affair," states Sellars.[58] And how does this count against traditional empiricism?

> For the point is specifically that observational knowledge of any particular fact, e.g., that this is green, presupposes that one knows general facts of the form X is a reliable symptom of Y. And to admit this requires an abandonment of the traditional empiricist idea that observational knowledge "stands on its own feet."[59]

The vaunted Principle of Verifiability, Quine argues in a similar vein, suffers from the fatal assumption that there can be sense-data or "raw feels" that give us discrete pieces of knowledge without the aid of everything else we know.

---

[58] Sellars, *op. cit.*, p. 289.

[59] *Ibid.*, p. 298.

> The totality of our so-called knowledge or beliefs, from the most casual matters of geography and history to the profoundest laws of atomic physics . . . is a man-made fabric which impinges on experience only along the edges. Or, to change the figure, total science is like a field of force whose boundary conditions are experience. A conflict with experience at the periphery occasions readjustments in the interior of the field. . . . No particular experiences are linked with any particular statements in the interior of the field, except indirectly through considerations of equilibrium affecting the field as a whole.[60]

This is the first formulation of Quine's "web of belief," which is the framework for his metaphysical position. At the periphery of the web are our sensory registers, and these give us information about the outside world.[61] But our observations are modulated by our belief system, and our more entrenched, better-warranted beliefs—analytic truths, say—are closer to the center. Only physical objects are really real,[62] but how do we know what they are if they have to be filtered through our whole belief system?[63] Science is our only hope of getting reality right (if even science can), for it alone has a method for revising our system of beliefs systematically. Hence, to quote Sellars, who is at one with Quine on this point, "Empirical knowledge, like its sophisticated extension, science, is rational, not because it has a foundation but because it is a

---

[60] Quine, *op. cit.*, p. 211.

[61] Quine, *The Web of Belief* (New York: Random House, 1970), p. 22: "The world with its quarks and chromosomes, its distant lands and spiral nebulae, is like a vast computer in a black box, forever sealed except for its input and output registers. These we directly observe, and in the light of them we speculate on the structure of the machine, the universe."

[62] Quine, *Word and Object*, Chs. I, IV and VII.

[63] If one is skeptical that observations have to be so filtered, Quine contends that if we ran into a tribe of non-English speakers and "if we are wondering whether to translate a native expression 'gavagai' as 'rabbit' or as 'undetached rabbit part' or as 'rabbit stage,' we could never settle the matter simply by ostention—that is, simply by repeatedly querying the expression 'gavagai' for the native's assent or dissent in the presence of assorted stimulations." *Ontological Relativity and Other Essays* (New York: Columbia University Press, 1969), pp. 30–31. The "gavagai" example first appeared in *Word and Object*, section 12, pp. 51–57.

self-correcting enterprise, which can put any claim in jeopardy, though not all at once."[64]

Physical objects, claims Quine, "and the gods differ only in degree and not in kind. Both sorts of entities enter our conception only as cultural deposits. The myth of physical objects is . . . superior to most in that it has proved more efficacious than other myths as a device for working a manageable structure into the flux of experience."[65] This is how pragmatism alters positivism: whereas positivism could claim that what is really real is the big picture of the physical universe that all observation statements will give us, Quine's and Sellars' pragmatized empiricism proposes that, while science is the measure, it is an imperfect one at best, modulated as it is through our whole system of beliefs. This particular type of pragmatism-cum-empiricism is sometimes called "holism." Before we explore its implications (see below, paragraphs adjacent to notes 85 and 123), however, let us pick up the other strand of post-positivist linguistic analysis, that practiced by Wittgenstein.

(d) Wittgenstein

Wittgenstein's *Philosophical Investigations* is, in a significant way, an attack upon his own *Tractatus*, out of which developed positivism. "This development," comments Norman Malcolm,

> is probably unique in the history of philosophy—a thinker producing, at different periods of his life, two highly original systems of thought, each system the result of many years of intensive labors, each expressed in an elegant and powerful style, each greatly influencing contemporary philosophy, and the second being a criticism and rejection of the first."[66]

Indeed, there seems to be something for everyone in Wittgenstein. His early work inspired positivism; even Quine and Sellars and

---

[64] Sellars, *op. cit.*, p. 300.

[65] Quine, "Two Dogmas of Empiricism," p. 212.

[66] Norman Malcolm, "Wittgenstein," in P. Edwards (ed.), *The Encyclopedia of Philosophy* (New York: Macmillan, 1967), VIII, 327. There are, needless to say, equally significant continuities between the two works. See Garth Hallett, *A Companion to Wittgenstein's "Philosophical Investigations"* (Ithaca, N.Y.: Cornell University Press, 1977). As Wittgenstein himself said, "To every thinker there cling bits of the shell from which he hatched. People can tell *what* you fought

other like-thinking analysts often proclaim their debt to him.[67] Ordinary Language Philosophy would not have existed without Wittgenstein, Ryle and Austin. There are even similarities between Wittgenstein's *Philosophical Investigations* and the work of such contemporary Continental philosophers as Husserl, Heidegger, and Gadamer.[68] "Academic philosophy in our day stands to Wittgenstein," Rorty declares, "as intellectual life in Germany in the first decades of the last century stood to Kant. Kant had changed everything, but no one was sure what Kant had said."[69] In keeping with his universal significance and the current uncertainty about his philosophical position, we will approach the later Wittgenstein by way of his relation to other philosophical positions:

1. Against the early analysts—and his earlier self—Wittgenstein eschews the project of discovering a pure, formal language for metaphysical statements, accenting actual, ordinary use of words.[70] Yet he preserves his early conviction that metaphysical positions cannot be arrived at or formulated but rather lived and shown.[71]

2. With the pragmatic analysts, Wittgenstein holds that the positivist search for ultimate observations which open up reality to us is illusory, but his reasons for rejecting positivism are quite different. It is not science that should weave the web of belief; it is our form of life (*Lebensform*) which shapes our ordinary language. Or-

---

against as you grew up." ("Manuscripts" 229. 1791, available in microfilm or xerox form from Cornell University Library, Ithaca, N.Y.)

[67] Richard Rorty memorializes this debt in *Philosophy and the Mirror of Nature* (Princeton, N.J.: Princeton University Press, 1979), Chs. III, IV and VI.

[68] See Joseph Simons, "Leben" in *Handbuch Philosophischer Grundbegriffen* (Munich: Verlag, 1973), III, 857, and Nicholas Gier, *Wittgenstein and Phenomenology* (Albany, N.Y.: SUNY Press, 1981).

[69] Richard Rorty, "Keeping Philosophy Pure: An Essay on Wittgenstein," *Consequences of Pragmatism* (Minneapolis: University of Minnesota Press, 1982), p. 20.

[70] "If I had to say what is the main mistake made by philosophers of the present generation, including Moore, I would say that, when language is looked at, what is looked at is a form of words and not the use made of the form of words," *Lectures and Conversations on Aesthetics, Psychology, and Religious Belief*, C. Barrett (ed.) (Oxford: Oxford University Press, 1966), p. 2.

[71] "Positivism holds—and this is its essence—that what we can speak about is all that matters in life. *Whereas Wittgenstein passionately believes that all that really matters in human life is precisely what, in his view, we must be silent about*," in Paul Englemann, *Letters from Ludwig Wittgenstein, With a Memoir*, L. Furtmuller (trans.), B. McGuinness (ed.) (Oxford: Oxford University Press, 1967), p. 97.

dinary language is "all right" in the same way that our bodies are "all right"—both are "all we have."[72]

How does Wittgenstein's early insight about truths being lived and his later one about forms of life fit together? This is what we must now attempt to show.

The subject matter of philosophy, Wittgenstein urges, is neither reality, nor formal logic, nor science but rather our ordinary expressions. Why? Because they encompass all we can say: no other language system or other method of discovery (science) will unearth new metaphysical truths because "the limits of our language mean the limits of our world" (*Tractatus*, 5.6). But our subject matter is not clear and neat; it is a labyrinth,[73] an ancient city laid out in no particular order.[74] And this disarray determines the nature of philosophy (and, hence, metaphysics):

> Consider the geography of a country for which we have no map, or else a map in tiny bits. The difficulty about this is the difficulty with philosophy; there is no synoptic view. Here the country we talk about is language and the geography grammar. We can walk about a country quite well but when forced to make a map we go wrong.[75]

Philosophy, then, does not produce theory,[76] and contains "no universal pronouncements about the world and language."[77] Philosophical problems "are not empirical problems; they are solved, rather, by looking into the workings of our language"; they are elaborated "not by giving new information, but by arranging what we have always known."[78] To put it another way, the philosopher studies "language games," different practices in language use,[79] rather than Language itself.

---

[72] See a similar analogy by David Pears, *Ludwig Wittgenstein* (New York: Viking, 1969), p. 179.

[73] Wittgenstein, *Philosophical Investigations*, #203.

[74] *Ibid.*, #18.

[75] Reported by Alice Ambrose in "Wittgenstein on Universals," in K. T. Fann (ed.), *Ludwig Wittgenstein: The Man and His Philosophy* (New York: Dell Publishing Co., 1967), p. 336.

[76] Wittgenstein, *op. cit.*, #109.

[77] Wittgenstein, Manuscript #110.

[78] Wittgenstein, *Philosophical Investigations*, #109.

[79] *Ibid.*, #7.

What are the implications of viewing philosophy this way? Let us look at two passages about forms of life:

> "So you are saying that human agreement declares what is true or false?"—It is what human beings *say* that is true or false; and they agree in the *language* they use. That is not an agreement in opinions but in forms of life.[80]

> Now, I would like to regard this certainty, not as something akin to hastiness or superficiality, but as a form of life. . . . But that means I want to conceive it as something beyond being justified or unjustified; as it were, something animal.[81]

What makes a statement true or false or certain? Not science, not correspondence with reality, but deep agreement among humans in forms of life:

> Giving grounds, however, justifying the evidence, comes to an end;—but the end is not certain propositions striking us immediately as true, i.e., it is not a kind of seeing on our part; it is our acting, which lies at the bottom of the language-game.[82]

Philosophy studies language games, but such study merely cures us from misunderstanding;[83] it does not show us the way things are. The way things are is filtered through our human forms of life, our traditional actions, practices, and customs as well as the structure of our bodies and brains.[84] This position is similar, of course, to what we are calling pragmatic analysis, except that for Wittgenstein, science would be just another complex language-game developing from a form of life. Both positions recently have been termed "holism,"[85] and they seem to have more points of agreement than dispute. We will say more about what this amalgamated

---

[80] *Ibid.*, #241.

[81] Wittgenstein, *On Certainty*, G. E. M. Anscombe and G. von Wright (trans.) (New York: Harper Torchbooks, 1969), #358–59.

[82] *Ibid.*, #204.

[83] *Philosophical Investigations*, #109 and #383.

[84] *Ibid.*, #241.

[85] Hubert L. Dreyfus, "Holism and Hermeneutics," *Review of Metaphysics*, 34 (September, 1980), 3–25.

position amounts to (see below, paragraph adjacent to note 123) after we discuss Continental developments.

3. Existentialism and Beyond

We traced the historical roots of contemporary Anglo-American philosophy to Ockham and the empiricists and found the transition to the present easy to make. It was easy, we must now admit, because the contemporary analysts have been uninterested in their own genealogy or, for that matter, in the history of ideas. The same cannot be said of Continental philosophers, who, as a rule, have worked out their positions in constant dialogue with philosophy's past and, often, have made historicity (the thesis that ideas are determined by their historical origins) a major premise in their arguments. Moreover, perhaps because of their deep historical sensibilities, most Continental thinkers see themselves quite consciously opposed to the philosophical tradition, seeking to "overcome" it in some way. In this process, few major philosophers—Plato, Aristotle, Descartes, Hume, Kant, Hegel—escape radical criticism or revision. In fact, it is arguable that only through criticism of the great philosophers of the past have Continental philosophers arrived at their current positions. Just as science motivates contemporary Anglo-American criticisms of metaphysics, so too history impels the Continental critique.

The catalyst in almost all Continental thinking of the last forty years has been Martin Heidegger (1889–1975). Even setting aside his influence in disciplines as different as psychology and theology, Heidegger rivals Wittgenstein in his involvement with a number of schools of thought. Nietzsche before him and Derrida after him are bolder; but Heidegger is by far the most influential—and, arguably, the most astute—reader of the philosophical tradition. Specifically, Heidegger has made original contributions to, or founded, the following schools of thought:

(a) *Phenomenology*. In the early years of this century, Heidegger studied the work of Edmund Husserl, the founder of the school of phenomenology, and, after World War I, was Husserl's assistant.[86]

[86] See Herbert Spiegelberg, *The Phenomenological Movement*, 3rd ed. (The Hague: Martinus Nijhoff, 1971), pp. 339–49. See also Heidegger's own very brief account of his early exposure to Husserl in "My Way to Phenomenology," *On Time and Being*, J. Stambaugh (trans.) (New York: Harper and Row, 1972).

The First Division of his monumental work, *Being and Time*[87] is a rethinking of phenomenology with the specific aim of understanding the "question of the meaning of Being."[88]

(b) *Existentialism*. Throughout *Being and Time*, as a result of his pursuit of the question of Being, Heidegger deepens the conceptual base of existentialism, working out ideas—care, angst, death, call, *existentialia*, nothingness, thrownness—that became an integral part of existentialist literature.[89]

(c) *Hermeneutics*. Beginning the Second Division of *Being and Time* and continuing through the latter works, Heidegger provides the philosophical basis of contemporary hermeneutics (theory of interpretation).

(d) *Deconstruction*. Although Heidegger's final position is very likely not a deconstructionist one, his latter works provide inspiration for the analyses of Jacques Derrida, Gilles Deleuze and others of this school.

Clearly, then, whatever else these movements have in common, they have Heidegger prominently placed. Let us take each transformation in turn, showing how each has evolved in the context of Heidegger's thought.

(a–b) From Phenomenology to Existentialism

The development of young Heidegger's thought makes him a prime candidate for entering the disciplines both of existentialism and phenomenology. Early in his career he moves from religious faith to hope in theology, from complete loss of faith to philosophy—pursued by Nietzsche's proclamation of the death of God.[90]

---

[87] Martin Heidegger, *Being and Time*, J. Macquarrie and E. Robinson (trans.) (New York: Harper and Row, 1962).

[88] *Ibid.*, p. 1.

[89] Heidegger is often counted as an existentialist and has certainly enriched existentialist themes. See, for instance, William Barrett, *Irrational Man* (New York: Doubleday, 1962); H. J. Blackham, *Six Existentialist Thinkers* (London: Routledge and Kegan Paul, 1965); W. Kaufman, *From Shakespeare to Existentialism* (Princeton, N.J.: Princeton University Press, 1980). He is, however, no more *only* an existentialist than he is *only* a phenomenologist. See Martin Heidegger, "Letter on 'Humanism,'" E. Lohner (trans.) in W. Barrett and H. D. Aiken (eds.), *Philosophy in the Twentieth Century* (New York: Random House, 1962), vol. 3, and below, paragraphs corresponding to notes 109–10.

[90] See Karsten Harries, "Fundamental Ontology and the Search for Man's Place," in Michael Murray (ed.), *Heidegger and Modern Philosophy* (New Haven, Conn.: Yale University Press, 1978), p. 65.

He was driven to philosophy especially by the struggle to bring some meaning to his life after the disintegration of the tradition in which he had served.

Phenomenology held much promise for Heidegger, since Edmund Husserl (1859–1938), its founder, is the one prominent Continental thinker who consciously attempts to carry forward a traditional philosophical project in the midst of prevailing deterioration. Philosophy to Husserl is an all-embracing, absolutely certain knowledge of all that is.[91] Trained as a mathematician, Husserl inherited the problems and goals of philosophy since Descartes, for his demand is that all philosophical knowledge be founded on an absolutely certain foundation, one about which it would be impossible to have a single doubt. Philosophy should be, as Husserl put it early in his career, "a rigorous science."[92] Any similarity between Husserl and the early analysts, however, ends at this point,[93] for he goes on to argue that a scientific philosophy is quite different in concept from the physical and biological sciences:

> Philosophy lies in an entirely different dimension. It needs entirely new starting points and an entirely new method, which is in principle different from those of any "natural science."[94]

Philosophy explores what science presupposes—the experience of the experimenter and theorist. Science is pursued, as are all human activities, in the "natural attitude," the world in which all is pre-given. To quote Eugen Fink, a principal defender of phenomenology after Husserl's death, "The world which we know and

[91] Edmund Husserl, *Ideen zu einer reinen Phänomenologie und phänomenologischen Philosophie* (The Hague: Martinus Nijhoff, 1950–52), "Nachwort" vol. 3, pp. 138–39. Also see *The Crisis of European Sciences*, David Carr, trans. (Evanston, Ill.: Northwestern University Press, 1970), section 12, pp. 65–67.

[92] Edmund Husserl, "Philosophie als strenge Wissenschaft," *Logos*, 1 (1910–11), 289–341.

[93] It must be remarked here, however, that the most striking similarities between Husserl and such thinkers as Bertrand Russell occur in their common cause against psychologism in logic. See the articles by Dagfinn Follesdal and J. N. Mohanty in Hubert Dreyfus and Harrison Hall (eds.), *Husserl, Intentionality, and Cognitive Science* (Cambridge, Mass.: M.I.T. Press, 1982), and also Ernst Tugendhat, "Phenomenology and Linguistic Analysis," in P. McCormick and F. Elliston (eds.), *Husserl: Expositions and Appraisals* (University of Notre Dame Press, 1977), pp. 325–37.

[94] Edmund Husserl, *The Idea of Phenomenology*, W. Alston and G. Nakhnikian, trans. (The Hague: Martinus Nijhoff, 1964), p. 24.

within which we know ourselves is given to us as a universe of acceptances, is given to us in terms of a universal belief in the world in which all particular positings of being in experience come together. . . ."[95] This gloss extends Husserl's own words on the natural attitude: "Through sight, touch, hearing, etc., in the different ways of sensory perception, corporeal things somehow spatially distributed are *for me simply there* . . . whether or not I pay them special attention by busying myself with them, considering, thinking, willing."[96]

Husserl's phenomenology describes this same world from another "attitude." In language that is purposely Kantian, Husserl posits a "transcendental" attitude by which we "bracket" all the things, thoughts, and feelings that come before our minds as to whether they actually exist; we focus on the conditions of their appearance. We take what passes as "phenomena," things that appear whether they exist or not.[97] Every movement of our minds and senses—every conscious act—requires an object we are conscious of. It is through these "intentional" acts of consciousness that meaning is constituted. In this world the phenomenologist, by means of various "reductions," must seek the "essences" of things by pealing away culturally-accrued layers of meaning to get to those original lived-experiences *(Erlebnisse)* in which any being appears as itself-given.[98] In short, reflective inquiry leads Husserl from pre-scientific understanding of things in the "natural attitude" to pre-scientific "transcendental subjectivity," which is that original region in which things appear for us in their most primordial association with our consciousness. Besides the general title "phenomenology," Husserl also calls this enterprise of seeking essences First Philosophy.[99]

---

[95] Eugen Fink, "Husserl's Philosophy and Contemporary Criticism," in R. O. Elveton (ed.), *The Phenomenology of Husserl* (Chicago: Quadrangle Books, 1970), p. 108.

[96] Edmund Husserl, *Ideas,* trans. W. R. Boyce-Gibson (New York: Collier Books, 1962), p. 91.

[97] *Ibid.,* Chs. 5 and 6.

[98] These formulations are found in Husserl's *Ideas,* Chs. 8 and 12, and in *Experience and Judgment,* trans. J. Churchill and K. Ameriks (Evanston, Ill.: Northwestern University Press, 1973), *passim.* See also H. Boelaars, "Husserls reducties en haar betekenis voor het thomisme," *Tijdschrift voor Philosophie,* 6 (1944), 345–62, and Fink, *art. cit.,* pp. 110 ff.

[99] Edmund Husserl, *Erste Philosophie: Erster Teil* (The Hague: Martinus Nijhoff, 1956). Also Ludwig Landgrebe, "Husserl's Departure from Cartesianism," in R. O. Elveton, *op. cit.,* pp. 259–303.

(1) Heidegger's own style and reputation. Husserl's move from a "natural" to a "transcendental" attitude captivated Heidegger and kept him a loyal student of phenomenology for years. We find him at the writing of *Being and Time,* however, thinking himself beyond phenomenology (yet with the help of Husserlian concepts) into the domain of what he chose to call "fundamental ontology." Especially in the First Part of this work, this project has many features that endeared it to existentialists from Sartre to Merleau-Ponty. Three features in particular are noteworthy: Heidegger's own personal style and reputation at the time of the publication of *Being and Time,* his criticisms of the metaphysical tradition, and his analysis of human existence.

Heidegger's personality imprinted a special urgency and freshness to his insights that stunned his contemporaries. Hannah Arendt speaks of a "rumor" finding its way about the German universities regarding the great teacher.

> The rumor about Heidegger put it quite simply: Thinking has come to life again; the cultural treasures of the past, believed to be dead, are being made to speak, in the course of which it turns out that they propose things altogether different from the familiar, worn-out trivialities they had been presumed to say. There exists a teacher; one can perhaps learn to think.[100]

And what should one think about? Again, the rumor held it that

> there was someone who was actually attaining "the things" that Husserl had proclaimed, someone who knew that these things were not academic matters but the concerns of thinking men—concerns not just of yesterday and today, but from time immemorial—and who, precisely because he knew that the thread of tradition was broken, was discovering the past anew.[101]

Heidegger heeds Husserl's "return to things themselves" but with a unique energy—and a care for the tradition he must overthrow.

(2) Heidegger's criticism of the metaphysical tradition. From Husserl Heidegger takes certain tools to help him investigate a question supposedly addressed by the whole metaphysical tradi-

---

[100] Hannah Arendt, "Heidegger at Eighty," in M. Murray, *op. cit.*, p. 295.
[101] *Ibid.*

tion—the question of the meaning of Being. In fact, Heidegger contends, the tradition has "forgotten" even how to ask this question. Husserl is some help to Heidegger in rekindling the question of the meaning of Being. But Husserl's discovery of the natural standpoint led him to investigations of the transcendental realm grounding it; Heidegger is led to the very shape and nature of the natural standpoint itself, what Heidegger calls "average everydayness." For it is here, in everydayness, that Being manifests itself. This regard for everydayness is the guiding insight that the metaphysical tradition and even Husserl himself missed. The meaning of Being is "always already" available to us, although vaguely. "But this vague average understanding of Being is still a Fact."[102] Far from helping understand the meaning of Being, our tradition has completely overshot it:

> This vague average understanding of Being may be so infiltrated with traditional theories and opinions about Being that these remain hidden as sources of the way in which it is prevalently understood.[103]

Investigations into particular regions of Being or into particular classes of beings have yielded theories that add to the concealment of Being. Individual sciences are immensely productive of theories about how beings behave and how we may devise methods of controlling them. The question of what makes all these beings *be,* however, is missed. The metaphysical tradition covers up the proper question no less surely. Take the very influential school begun by Descartes. He distinguishes *res cogitans,* thinking things such as ourselves, from *res extensa,* the other things in the world. All other nonthinking things in the world are extended in space and time, have length, breadth, thickness, etc. The way we experience these things, however, may not be the way they actually are. In the famous ball of wax thought-experiment of his second *Meditations on First Philosophy* Descartes shows that through the transformation of the wax from cold and hard substance to hot and pliable, it still remains wax; its extension remains constant. Hence, what things really are *escapes* our human experience of them.

Heidegger argues that what *escapes* Descartes in this analysis is precisely the Being of things that Descartes seeks. According to

---

[102] Martin Heidegger, *Being and Time,* p. 25.

[103] *Ibid.*

Heidegger, things do not appear to us "primordially" as Cartesian objects, as things that are there to be inspected or interpreted, as "present-at-hand." Things in everyday existence appear to us as "equipment." We encounter them "holistically" as implements for doing something, because they are not detached from our purposeful concern.[104] This "kind of Being which equipment possesses . . . we call "readiness-to-hand." A hammer, for instance, is ready-to-hand for us as we make a fence. When hammering, we do not gaze at the hammer as a thing; it is not an object, but a part of our concernful activity of hammering something. Our theoretical interest in the hammer detaches it from this "referential totality" and thereby extracts it from its potential to manifest Being.

> And here again, when the equipmental characters of the ready-to-hand are still circumspectively undiscovered, they are not to be interpreted as bare Thinghood presented for an apprehension of what is just present-at-hand and no more.[105]

We don't inhabit an environment of things in our everyday, concernful activity, nor do we inspect or interpret except when something is out of place or needs taking care of.[106] But how would one study such a thing if studying is precisely what would make it

---

104 *Ibid.*, p. 97. Compare similar comments by John Dewey in *Experience and Nature* (New York: Dover Books, 1958), Ch. IV.

105 Heidegger, *op. cit.*, p. 112.

106 Karsten Harries, *op. cit.*, p. 71, provides a remarkably fitting example of the relation of care to equipment and of these to Heidegger's criticism that traditional metaphysicians have missed this way of being. " 'Proximally and for the most part' things are given to us as meaningful. For the peasant the tree is not simply one tree among others, just one more thing in his world; it is irreplaceable. Perhaps he does not even notice its quiet presence in the backyard; perhaps it is taken too much for granted that it is noticed only on certain occasions when it seems to demand attention. Such attention will not be detached contemplating, but a caring for the tree; it requires pruning; the apples have to be picked. . . . In such care the tree reveals itself. At the same time this care binds the peasant and the tree into a larger order which includes fields and village, home and church, family and neighbors. Caught up in that order he knows his place and what is to be done. He understands the meaning of life. But what is it that he understands? What could he answer if someone were to ask him? No doubt, such an itinerant philosopher would be disappointed. What would he say? The meaning of our place in the world does not disclose itself in clear and distinct ideas. There is only a feeling, a mood."

go away? Heidegger's answer to this question lies in his analysis of the human.

(3) Heidegger's account of the human condition. This brings us to the third feature of *Being and Time* that animates existentialism. Heidegger's "fundamental ontology," from which alone all other ontologies can take their rise, must be sought in the *existential analytic of Dasein*. *Dasein* is Heidegger's term for the sort of beings we are, the *loci* of thinking and questioning. But thinking and questioning are always attended by states of mind, ways of being, that must be explored, which are called *existentialia*. An examination of these uncovers *Dasein*'s being-in-the-world. Instead of discovering universal categories of entities, then, the fundamental ontologist seeks to discover the different pre-theoretical ways in which *Dasein* encounters those things that pass by, whether they be "inauthentic" ways which aid in forgetting the call to Being (engaging in idle talk, being fearful, and other modes of fallenness and being-alongside)[107] or "authentic" ways which heed the call (care, resoluteness, and the authentic ways of being-in-angst and being-toward-death). *Dasein*, then, or

> Being-what-it-is *(essentia)* must, so far as we can speak of it at all, be conceived in terms of its Being *(existentia)*. . . . The 'essence' of *Dasein* lies in its existence.[108]

The demand that philosophy should emphasize actual human existence as opposed to the essence of things, and the preference for such themes as care, *angst*, authenticity certainly show that Heidegger read deeply in Nietzsche and Kierkegaard, the forerunners of existentialism, and in Karl Jaspers' *Existenzphilosophie*. There is also little doubt that he was taken to be an existentialist by many commentators and by major figures such as Sartre.[109] But as existentialism began to wane in Europe after World War II, a new interpretation of *Being and Time* began to emerge along with a new philosophical movement.

---

[107] See *Being and Time*, Ch. IV of Division II, "Temporality and Everydayness."

[108] *Ibid.*, p. 67.

[109] The very title (*Being and Nothingness*) and subtitle (*An Essay on Phenomenological Ontology*) of Sartre's major existentialist work show the influence of Heidegger. See Joseph S. Catalano, *A Commentary on Jean-Paul Sartre's "Being and Nothingness"* (New York: Harper Torchbooks, 1974), p. 15.

(c) Hermeneutics

While it may be granted that the three features of Heidegger's work seem to warrant an existentialist reading of *Being and Time,* his own later work and the pronouncements of his most thoughtful students have forced a different reading. Hans-Georg Gadamer (1900–), one of these, has argued that the existentialist influence "was more a concealment of Heidegger's real aims than an actual apprehension of the intentions of this thought."[110] Although Gadamer admits that the "existential seriousness" of Heidegger's teaching style might give a different impression, nonetheless,

> it is not difficult today, on the basis of Heidegger's later work, to recognize that even *Being and Time* did not represent a philosophy of existence, but only used its vocabulary to deal with the question that both bound Heidegger to the great line of classical philosophical thinkers stretching from Plato to Nietzsche and at the same time made it necessary to inquire behind this tradition.[111]

Heidegger's larger purpose, if we accept Gadamer's interpretation, is to point out certain limits that traditional metaphysicians had largely ignored. Terms such as "care," "guilt," "angst" and other *existentialia* must not be taken "morally" or "psychologically." They are meant to be constraints upon how we can talk about traditional themes such as Being, Reality, and Truth by signaling that everything we say about them is "always already" interpreted. But how does this get us to hermeneutics and what does the term mean in this context?

"Hermeneutics" originally referred to the attempt to formulate principles of biblical interpretation.[112] In the modern tradition of

---

[110] Hans-Georg Gadamer, "The Philosophical Foundations of the Twentieth Century," in *Philosophical Hermeneutics*, trans. and ed. D. E. Linge (Berkeley: University of California Press, 1976), p. 125.

[111] Hans-Georg Gadamer, "The Phenomenological Movement," *op. cit.*, p. 141. Heidegger may have abetted the impression of existentialist sympathies, however. According to Gadamer, he would describe the world of "idle chatter" with scathing acrimony and then assert that "this is intended without any negative meaning." In the light of practices such as these, it is difficult to embrace wholeheartedly Gadamer's judgment that "against his will, then, he became a kind of philosopher of existence" (p. 141).

[112] See Richard E. Palmer, *Hermeneutics* (Evanston, Ill.: Northwestern University Press, 1969), Ch. 2.

hermeneutics begun by Schleiermacher, the principle that "misunderstanding [of a text] arises naturally"[113] and that true understanding must be wrested from difficult passages became the guiding assumption. Heidegger energizes and generalizes the discipline of hermeneutics by making it a synonym for his own fundamental ontology. "Phenomenology of *Dasein* is hermeneutics in the original sense of the word, which designated the business of interpretation."[114]

To take an example of how fundamental ontology is hermeneutics: there is no pure meaning of Being, for it is already embedded in our concernful human activities. In other words, our understanding of Being, Truth, and Reality will always be encapsulated in a "hermeneutic circle." *Dasein* is radically temporal. We don't encounter primordially a world external to us; we don't know ourselves as "thinking things" apart from a world. *Dasein* and the external world arise together. The mistake of traditional metaphysicians is that they attempted to begin either with a *Dasein*-less world or a "worldless" subject, neither of which exists. What exists can only be considered in the context of *Dasein*; what a subject is can only be explored in-the-world. Thus, "even the Real can be discovered only on the basis of a world which has already been disclosed. And only on this basis can anything Real still remain hidden."[115]

We cannot aspire to a viewpoint outside ourselves, to a God's-eye view of Reality; nor can we imagine a pure subjectivity apart from our personalities and worldly concerns. But if the Being of entities "is equiprimordial with the Being of *Dasein*,"[116] won't we be moving in a circle if we attempt to explore the Being of *Dasein* itself? Heidegger's answer is *Yes;* the circle is unavoidable and "hermeneutic." Instead of trying to bypass the inconsistency "we must rather endeavour to leap into the 'circle,' primordially and wholly, so that even at the start of the analysis of *Dasein* we make sure that we have a full vision of *Dasein*'s circular Being."[117]

Hermeneutics, then, is not just a method of interpretation. It indicates our mode of Being; we always understand things as "fore-

---

[113] F. Schleiermacher, *Hermeneutik*, trans. H. Kimmerle (Heidelberg: Karl Winter, 1959), p. 85.

[114] *Being and Time*, p. 37.

[115] *Ibid.*, p. 247.

[116] *Ibid.*, p. 264.

[117] *Ibid.*, p. 363.

understood": even before we attempt to know, we anticipate our knowledge. Every understanding is a "fore-having"—we already move out in front of our understanding with presuppositions. We will never be able to attain a "presuppositionless" beginning to our ontological inquiries.[118] If we want to understand, say, a hammer, we must see it as ready-to-hand, in its total, "holistic" equipmental context and as used. This is hermeneutical understanding and the only method for fundamental ontology. If we take the hammer out of its context, describe it as an object scientifically, judging its size, weight, etc., we are seeing it as an object present-at-hand, apart from its natural context. This 'apophantic' method of understanding does violence to the whole of *Dasein*/world. Hermeneutic inquiry, then, does not search for the final interpretation but rather the widest and richest interpretation that can be found.

This is Heidegger's development of hermeneutics. Hans-Georg Gadamer, the leading hermeneuticist today, is critical of Heidegger and develops his thought in a way different from the master. Yet he clearly closes ranks with him against realists and idealists alike. Gadamer particularly takes up hints by his teacher about the nature of understanding. The Enlightenment philosophers inaugurated a presuppositionless search for foundations, and Gadamer finds them guilty of "a prejudice against prejudice."[119]

> It is not so much our judgments as it is our prejudices that constitute our being. This is a provocative formulation, for I am using it to restore it to its rightful place as a positive concept of prejudice that was driven out of our linguistic usage. . . . Prejudices are not necessarily unjustified and erroneous, so that they inevitably distort the truth. In fact the historicity of our existence entails that prejudices . . . constitute the initial directedness of our whole ability to experience. Prejudices are biases of our openness to the world.[120]

Our temporal natures ensure that we cannot outrun or undercut our pre-knowledge, nor should we want to. But how, then, do we know when we are holding "justified" or "enabling" prejudices as opposed to "blind" ones? Only through constant and ever-wider

---

[118] *Ibid.*, p. 150.

[119] Hans-Georg Gadamer, *Truth and Method* (New York: Seabury Press, 1975), p. 240.

[120] *Ibid.*

dialogue with the philosophical tradition, with our contemporaries, and with the text, fact, or problem we are trying to understand. But even the product of this dialogue will only be provisional and temporary, always needing to be open to future revision. This constant reference to our circumstances as we think about universal things makes hermeneutics a "practical" philosophy,[121] whose aim is precisely a form of self-understanding in which

> a placement between strangeness and familiarity exists between the historically intended, distanced objectivity of the heritage and our belongingness to a tradition. In this "between" is the true place of hermeneutics.[122]

To summarize, then: the hermeneuticist is interested in self-understanding as much as any other philosopher. However, "self-understanding is always on-the-way; it is on a path whose completion is a clear impossibility." And, hence, we must presume our knowledge "to be no more than an approximation: only an attempt, plausible and fruitful, but clearly never definitive."[123] The similarities between this way of thinking and the "holism" of Wittgenstein, Quine and Sellars is striking. In all of these systems, knowledge is systematically provisional, but even this partial knowledge "does some work." It is fruitful in that it increases our never completable self-understanding (hermeneutics), or it keeps our options open for better scientific theories (Quine and Sellars), or it enriches the complexity of our language-games (Wittgenstein). Heidegger, however, is not content to rest his thinking even partially on knowledge. He takes a further step.

(d) Beyond Hermeneutics . . . Deconstruction?

We come to the famous "turn" *(Kehre)* in Heidegger's thought which characterizes his later work. *Being and Time* is not a complete work. The Third Division of the First Part, "Time and Being," never appeared. Heidegger indicates the reason for this incompleteness: "The Division in question was held back because thinking failed in adequately articulating this turn *(Kehre)*, and did not achieve its

---

121 See Hans-Georg Gadamer, *Reason in the Age of Science*, F. G. Lawrence, trans. (Cambridge, Mass.: M.I.T. Press, 1984), pp. 69–113: "What Is Practice? The Conditions of Social Reason," and "Hermeneutics as Practical Philosophy."

122 Gadamer, *Truth and Method*, p. 279.

123 Gadamer, *Reason in the Age of Science*, pp. 104–5.

goal by means of the language of metaphysics."[124] Even Heidegger's hermeneutic approach is too confined to hold the inevitable progress of his thought. In *Being and Time* Heidegger proposed to show the history of metaphysics mistaken because it missed the question of the meaning of Being. He then goes on to give an account of Being from the viewpoint of *Dasein*. But *Dasein* proves to be radically temporal, historical, and its understanding always "prejudiced." But if all of this is true, then two questions confront Heidegger: why go on doing philosophy? And if philosophy is at an end, what shall we replace it with?

It seems that the inner dynamism of Heidegger's thought must lead him to these troubling questions, and he does in fact call for the end of philosophy[125] and even proclaims its death.[126] Where does that leave us on the second question, then? What shall we do now? Heidegger himself asks:

> Does the name of the task of thinking read instead of *Being and Time:* Opening and Presence? But where does the opening come from and how is it given? What speaks in the "It gives"?[127]

It is difficult to understand even what Heidegger means by this question much less to attempt an answer to it. His later work is allusive and poetical, and he has foresworn the possibility of giving a straightforward answer to such questions. In fact, what seems to be left after philosophy is another type of thinking, poetry.

> To stand in the presence of the gods and to be involved in the proximity of the essence of things. Existence is 'poetical' in its fundamental aspect—which means at the same time: insofar as it is established (founded), it is not a recompense, but a gift.[128]

---

[124] Martin Heidegger, *Brief Über den Humanismus* (Frankfurt a. M.: Klostermann, 1949), p. 178; also see Martin Heidegger, *Discourse on Thinking,* trans. John Anderson (New York: Harper Torchbooks, 1966), "Introduction," p. 18.

[125] Martin Heidegger, "The End of Philosophy," in *On Time and Being,* trans. J. Stambaugh (New York: Harper and Row, 1972), pp. 55–74.

[126] Martin Heidegger, *Nietzsche,* Vol. II: "The Eternal Recurrence of the Same" (New York: Harper and Row, 1979), pp. 200–204.

[127] Martin Heidegger, "The End of Philosophy," p. 73.

[128] Martin Heidegger, *Erlaüterungen zu Holderlins Dichtung* (Frankfurt a. M.: Klostermann, 1963), p. 39; see also ". . . Poetically Man Dwells . . ." in *Poetry,*

So far, "man has acted too much and thought too little."[129] We are still not truly thinking. We can only truly think within "this owning in which man and Being are delivered over to each other, that is, we must enter into what we call the Event of appropriation *(Ereignis).*"[130] Mindful of earth and gods, we must experience a "releasement toward things and openness to the mystery"[131] which is beyond our willing and doing. Our thinking should be a constant "thanking," a "commemoration" of the Event.

An excellent summary of Heidegger's path to this form of "poetical" thinking is provided by Otto Pogeller:

> The later Heidegger, of course, rejects any attempt at constructing "methods" in order then to reflect upon them. He does not even wish explicitly to propose that manner in which the event of appropriation needs thought as the hermeneutic circle itself. Instead, he wished in his thought to turn more primordially back to and dwell in the hermeneutical relationship itself, in which the meaning of Being is "announced" to *Dasein* which already has an understanding of Being.[132]

There have been few philosophers who have wanted to follow Heidegger into this later stage. Some, of course, reject the idea that philosophy has come to an end. Others, however, such as Jacques Derrida, contend that Heidegger did not take his declaration of the end of philosophy seriously enough. Heidegger, contends Derrida, holds on to one small piece of the metaphysical tradition: he thinks there is an Event, a primordial, original contact of *Dasein* with Being. There are no origins, claims Derrida, and there is nothing to commemorate. Making the later Heidegger more consistent with his earlier self, Derrida points out that for us humans there can be nothing ever newly thought or even felt or perceived: everything is a re-origination, a re-thinking, even a re-perceiving.[133] Our words

---

Language, Thought, A. Hofstadter, trans. (New York: Harper Torchbooks, 1971), pp. 213–29.

[129] Martin Heidegger, *What Is Called Thinking?* F. D. Wieck and J. G. Gray, trans. (New York: Harper Torchbooks, 1968), p. 25.

[130] Martin Heidegger, *Identity and Difference,* J. Stambaugh, trans. (New York: Harper Torchbooks, 1969), p. 36.

[131] Heidegger, *Discourse on Thinking,* p. 55.

[132] Otto Pogeller, "Being as Appropriation," in M. Murray, *op. cit.,* p. 112.

[133] "There never was any 'perception.'" Jacques Derrida, *Speech and Phenomena,* D. Allison, trans. (Evanston, Ill.: Northwestern University Press, 1973),

(signifiers) do not refer to things (the signified) because those things, the signified, are "always already in the position of the signifier."[134] Thus, in this very real sense, we are always "reading" texts whose reference can only be other texts—and there is never an Origin or an Outside that gives the text its significance.

Derrida criticizes Heidegger's implication that Being and *Dasein* constitute a unity or a "gathering." For if there are no origins, there cannot very well be any unities.[135] There are no "gatherings" at all; there are only "differences." Hence, the task left a thinker after philosophy has ended is not poetry but "deconstruction"—showing that those things we take to be unities are really "differences." Texts and theories are not destroyed but shown to cover over inner tensions, to be differences masquerading as unities. And the discovery of these tensions is a form of play, without commitment or constraint; it is a

> Nietzschean *affirmation*, that is, the joyous affirmation of the play of the world and of the innocence of becoming, the affirmation of a world of signs without fault, without truth, and without origin which is offered to an active interpretation. *This affirmation then determines the noncenter otherwise than as loss of the center*. And it plays without security.[136]

4. Summary

What may we conclude from this very brief history of contemporary metaphysics? Whitehead's process philosophy aside, one conclusion is unavoidable: both Continental and Anglo-American phi-

---

p. 103. Also, in a sarcastic attack on Heidegger's attempt to find "origins" in early Greek fragments, Derrida suggests that what Heidegger finds is really the "absolute erasure" of such origins. See "*Ousia* and *Grammê*: Note on a Note from *Being and Time*," in A. Bass (trans.), *Margins of Philosophy* (Chicago: University of Chicago Press, 1972), p. 66.

[134] Jacques Derrida, *Of Grammatology*, trans. G. Spivak (Baltimore: Johns Hopkins University Press, 1974), p. 73.

[135] See Edward Casey, "Origin(s) in (of) Heidegger/Derrida," *The Journal of Philosophy*, 81 (October, 1984), 601–10; John D. Caputo, "Telling Left from Right: Hermeneutics, Deconstruction, and the Work of Art," *The Journal of Philosophy*, 83 (November, 1986), 678–85.

[136] Jacques Derrida, "Structure, Sign, and Play," in A. Bass (trans.), *Writing and Difference* (Chicago: University of Chicago Press, 1978), p. 292.

losophy, despite very different starting points, seem to have ended up with strikingly similar insights about the nature of metaphysics. Quine, Wittgenstein, Heidegger, and Derrida, for instance, all declare the project of Western metaphysics, the search for eternal truths, abiding Reality, and certain foundations to be either dead or moribund. They all seem to share a similar diagnosis: our "form of life," or our "hermeneutic situation," is inarticulable; we can never speak about our own "prejudices," or our primordial contact with the world. Our own situation is "concealed" from us. There is even some consensus regarding the prognosis: Quine, Wittgenstein, Gadamer, Heidegger, and Derrida all point to attention to language, not to Reality or Truth, as our main pursuit. Whether it is scientific language, poetic language, or merely the play of signifiers, we cannot press beyond linguistic forms to a Reality. Though Richard Rorty is surely wrong in making the following claim of all of these thinkers, the dominant tone, or mood, is true enough.

> In this attitude, getting the facts right . . . is merely propaedeutic to finding a new and more interesting way of expressing ourselves, and thus of coping with the world. From the educational, as opposed to the epistemological or the technological, point of view, the way things are said is more important than the possession of truths.[137]

No doubt there are deep insights to be plumbed from study of the contemporary crisis of metaphysics. One such may be that metaphysics has lost its way, arrived at a dead end. A return to origins may be contemplated, but this very call has resulted in giving up searching for eternal truths and reality, in restricting philosophy to science, to language or to a mere form of life or social practice. Perhaps, then, an alternative thinking-through of metaphysical themes should be attempted, one that is sensitive to contemporary human concerns, to the concrete situations in which humans and other existents give evidence directly of themselves, to the objective and eternal truths issuing therefrom. For it is difficult for many of us to accept the idea that the philosophical tradition is only making up words when it speaks of truth, reality, God, essence, existence, and other metaphysical topics. If that is your feeling, then, in this age of unreality, the authentic metaphysics explored in this book may provide an attractive alternative.

---

[137] Richard Rorty, *Philosophy and the Mirror of Nature*, p. 359.

Suggested Readings

Derrida, Jacques, *Writing and Difference,* trans. A. Bass. Chicago: University of Chicago Press, 1978. Essays exhibiting the deconstructive method.

Gadamer, Hans-Georg, *Truth and Method.* New York: Seabury Press, 1975. On the hermeneutic method.

Heidegger, Martin, *Being and Time,* trans. J. Macquarrie and E. Robinson. New York: Harper and Row, 1962. On the meaning of the question of Being.

Husserl, Edmund, *Ideas,* trans. W. R. Boyce-Gibson. New York: Collier Books, 1962. On the "natural attitude," transcendental ego, and other Husserlian themes.

Murray, Michael, ed., *Heidegger and Modern Philosophy.* New Haven, Conn.: Yale University Press, 1978. Articles by analysts, hermeneuticists, and others on Heidegger's influence.

Quine, W. v. O., *Word and Object.* Cambridge, Mass.: M.I.T. Press, 1960. An influential "pragmatic analysis" treatment of metaphysical themes.

Rorty, Richard, *Philosophy and the Mirror of Nature.* Princeton, N.J.: Princeton University Press, 1979. On the recent history of metaphysics and epistemology from a philosopher sympathetic to Derrida and other deconstructionists.

Russell, Bertrand, "The Philosophy of Logical Atomism," pp. 175–281, in *Logic and Knowledge,* ed. R. C. March. London: George Allen and Unwin, 1971.

Sellars, Wilfred, *Science, Perception and Reality.* London: Routledge and Kegan Paul, 1963. A "pragmatic analyst's" view of the relation of science to traditional metaphysical themes.

Spiegelberg, Herbert, *The Phenomenological Movement,* 3rd ed. The Hague: Martinus Nijhoff, 1984. The standard history of phenomenology.

Whitehead, Alfred North, *Process and Reality: An Essay in Cosmology: Corrected Edition,* ed. D. R. Griffin and D. W. Sherburne. New York: The Free Press, 1978. The classic text in process philosophy.

Wittgenstein, Ludwig, *Philosophical Investigations.* Oxford: Basil Blackwell, 1953. On meaning, words, names, rules, and other topics relating language to the world.

Appendices

Appendix A

Jacques Maritain On Existence/Essence

In view of the fact that Jacques Maritain is prominent among twentieth-century Thomists and has had widespread influence, it will be profitable to review what he says concerning the real distinction between existence and essence. He has explained his view in some detail in at least two treatises—*Preface to Metaphysics: Seven Lectures on Being*, the English translation of which first appeared in 1939, and *Existence and the Existent*, translated in 1948.

One's awareness of essence and existence arises, Maritain informs us in the *Preface to Metaphysics*, as a result of a metaphysical intuition of being.

> I will attempt to bring out more clearly the intelligible subsistence contained in . . . [being], the first object grasped by the metaphysician's first intuition. We are immediately aware of this characteristic of it, that when we consider different things there is in each alike a typical relationship between *what is*, that which philosophers term essence or nature, and its *esse*, or existence. That is to say, this notion of being involves a species of polarity, essence-existence.[1]

Accordingly, we must briefly consider what our French author states concerning this intuition.

---

[1] Jacques Maritain, *Preface to Metaphysics* (New York: Sheed & Ward, 1948), p. 64.

First of all, it is not the "primitive"[2] or "obscure"[3] intuition by which someone first apprehends being vaguely, blindly,[4] infra-scientifically,[5] as the general class into which all diverse sensible things can be placed.[6] But what, positively, is it? In answering, let us first quote the two actual examples Maritain gives, which can be kept in mind when we then recount his own description of it. The first instance given is that of his wife Raïssa, who describes it thus:

> I have often experienced in a sudden intuition the reality of my being, the profound first principle which makes me exist outside nonentity. It is a powerful intuition whose violence has sometimes frightened me and which first revealed to me a metaphysical absolute.

The second instance he takes from the autobiography of Jean-Paul Richter:

> One morning when I was still a child, I was standing on the threshold of the house and looking to my left in the direction of the woodpile when suddenly there came to me from heaven like a lightning flash the thought: *I am a self*, a thought which has never since left me. I perceived my self for the first time and for good.[7]

Now, how does Maritain describe this intuition?

> We are confronted here with a genuine intuition, a perception direct and immediate, an intuition not in the technical sense which the ancients attached to the term, but in the sense we may accept from modern philosophy. It is a very simple sight, superior to any discursive reasoning or demonstration, because it is the source of demonstration. It is a sight whose

---

[2] *Ibid.*, p. 63. Maritain also calls this a concrete (*vs.* abstract) intuition, "like that of an external sense or of introspection, of an intuition centered upon a reality grasped concretely in its singular existence" (p. 58).

[3] *Ibid.*, p. 60.

[4] *Ibid.*, p. 29.

[5] *Ibid.*

[6] *Ibid.*, p. 31 sq.

[7] *Ibid.*, p. 47.

> content and implications no words of human speech can exhaust or adequately express and in which in a moment of decisive emotion, as it were, of spiritual conflagration, the soul is in contact, a living, penetrating, and illuminating contact, with a reality which it touches and which takes hold of it. Now what I want to emphasize is that it is being more than anything else which produces such an intuition. . . . Thus we are confronted with objects and as we confront them, the diverse realities made known by our senses or by the several sciences, we receive at a given moment, as it were, the revelation of an intelligible mystery concealed in them.[8]

One final quotation, which occurs immediately after Maritain had given the two examples already referred to:

> There are, therefore, metaphysical intuitions which are a natural revelation to the soul, invested with the decisive, imperious, and dominant character of a "substantial word" uttered by reality. They reveal the intelligible treasure, the unforgettable transobjective fact, which is either her own subsistence, the "Self" that she is, or being either her own or the being apprehended in objects. . . . [This intuition] is always, so to speak, a gift bestowed upon the intellect, and beyond question it is in one form or another indispensable to every metaphysician. . . . Moreover, it is as true to say that this intuition produces itself through the medium of the vital action of our intellect, I mean as vitally receptive and contemplative, as to say that we produce it. It is difficult . . . inasmuch as it is difficult to arrive at the degree of intellectual purification at which this act is produced in us, at which we become sufficiently disengaged, sufficiently empty to *hear* what all things whisper and to *listen* instead of composing answers.[9]

In the light of the preceding quotations, then, what is this metaphysical intuition of being? Replying to that question is difficult, among other reasons, because of Maritain's somewhat lyrical language, but this attempt seems accurate. The intuition he describes is a perception which has these characteristics.

---

8 *Ibid.*, p. 45 sq.

9 *Ibid.*, p. 48.

1. It is relatively spectacular and sudden.
2. It is direct and immediate, "a very simple sight," superior and prior to reasoning and demonstration.
3. It is intellectual and abstractive.[10]
4. It is absolutely necessary for every metaphysician.[11]
5. It is passive rather than active insofar as it can occur only when the mind is sufficiently purified and empty so as to listen to reality rather than to dictate to it; then actual existents can reveal their intelligible mystery—namely, that being is "that which exists or can exist."[12]
6. Its object is being precisely as the subject matter of metaphysics,[13] being-as-being, being "beheld in itself and in its essential properties . . . in its essentially analogous value."[14]

In short, the intuition of a metaphysician is the immediate, unique, sudden awareness by which he knows being precisely as being.

What is to be said of Maritain's contention? Some have rejected it because such an intuition can find no place in Thomistic psychology.[15] Such rejection seems a bit hasty. If actual cases of such intuition have occurred (they seemingly have—see Ch. IV, Sec. 3b), then one's psychological theory must be enlarged to include them. Still others may hesitate to accept his stand because an intuition is commonly regarded as an intensely individual, personal, private affair. How then can it ground a science, which has connotations of universality and certitude? Granted that an intuition is personal and individual with reference to its efficient cause (as in any act of knowledge)—it is *I* or *you* who is knowing. Still, if what is known is universal and common, if I intuit the nature of being and of existence themselves, if I realize what "to exist" means not just for myself but for any existent, then the hesitation is needless.

---

[10] *Ibid.*, pp. 58–61.

[11] Also see *Degrees of Knowledge* (London: Geoffrey Bles, 1959), p. 215: "[This intellectual perception of being] constitutes our primordial philosophical intuition without which we can no more acquire the science of metaphysical realities than a man born blind acquires the science of colors."

[12] *Preface to Metaphysics*, p. 63.

[13] *Ibid.*, p. 62.

[14] *Ibid.*, p. 63.

[15] See Etienne Gilson, *Elements of Christian Philosophy* (Garden City, N.Y.: Doubleday & Company, Inc., 1960), p. 130: "[The recognition of the notion of the act-of-being] cannot possibly be an intellectual intuition, because there is no such thing in Thomism."

A much more serious reservation can be lodged against Maritain's position, and this directly concerns existence/essence. As we have already seen, he talks as though the notions of essence and existence are handed over in one's intuition simultaneously with the notion of being. This latter contains, involves, implies, includes them:

> In virtue of its essential structure the concept of being also includes in itself indissolubly . . . these two linked and associated members of the pair essence-existence, which the mind cannot *isolate* in separate concepts. Whatever being I may think of, its concept implies this double aspect.

According to such statements, one's knowledge of essence/existence is as immediate as that of being itself. But he continues:

> Metaphysics teaches us that in God the distinction between essence and existence is a *distinctio rationis,* a purely ideal distinction, but that in all created objects there is a real distinction between them.[16]

What are we to conclude from that sentence? Although we know from intuition that being somehow involves essence/existence, yet we can decide whether their relationship is one of identity (as in God) or of real diversity (as in creatures) only from other sources—"metaphysics teaches. . . ." But the difficult question which every metaphysician must face is precisely how he can conclusively establish that real distinction. On this point Maritain is not very informative.

In *Existence and the Existent* he does furnish a bit more information. On the topic of intuition this second book differs somewhat from the *Preface,* although mainly by explicating what remains implicit in the earlier treatise. For instance, he devotes more attention to how judgment functions in the intuition[17] and to the fact that the senses play a primordial and indispensable part in attaining such intuitions.[18] He more frequently stresses the role of existence—for example, the intuition terminates above all in awareness

---

[16] *Preface to Metaphysics,* p. 65.

[17] *Existence and the Existent* (New York: Pantheon Books, Inc., 1948), pp. 15 sq.

[18] *Ibid.,* p. 20.

of the act of existing.[19] What he says on the distinction between essence/existence is another case in point, since his comments can be looked upon as developing what he left largely unstated in the *Preface*.

After sections devoted to "The Intuition of Being"[20] and to "The Concepts of Existence . . . and That of Being,"[21] he discusses "The Implications of the Intuition of Being,"[22] where he shows how all the major Thomist theses are rooted in the act of existing, the insight into which is gained through intuition. The real distinction is the first of those theses:[23]

> The most fundamental and most characteristic metaphysical thesis of Aristotelianism as re-thought by Thomas Aquinas, the thesis of the real distinction between essence and existence in all that is not God—in other words, the extension of the doctrine of potency and act to the relation between essence and existence, is directly connected with this intuition. This is, in truth, a thesis of extreme boldness, for in it potency (essence) . . . is completed or actuated by an act *of another order* which adds absolutely nothing to essence as essence, intelligible structure, or quiddity, yet adds everything to it in as much as it posits it *extra causas* or *extra nihil*. . . . Made real by the act of existing—that is to say, placed outside the state of simple possibility—they [essences] are really distinct from it

[19] *Ibid.*, p. 19: "At the root of metaphysical knowledge, St. Thomas placed the intellectual intuition of that mysterious reality disguised under the most commonplace and commonly used word in the language, the word *to be;* a reality revealed to us . . . when we release . . . the act of existing. . . ." *Ibid.*, p. 20: "[This intuition of being] owes its purity and power of illumination only to the fact that the intellect, one day, was stirred to its depths and trans-illuminated by the impact of the act of existing apprehended in things, and because it was quickened to the point of receiving this act. . . ." *Ibid.*, p. 26: "When . . . the intellect . . . conceptualizes the metaphysical intuition of being . . . what the intellect releases into that same light is, here again, first and foremost, the act of existing."

[20] *Ibid.*, pp. 19–22.

[21] *Ibid.*, pp. 22–34.

[22] *Ibid.*, pp. 35–46.

[23] The other theses pertain to universals and virtual distinction, potency and prime matter, the human composite, evil, immanent acts of knowing and loving, liberty and the *rapport* divine motion has to liberty, efficient and final causality, and the superabundance of being.

> as potency is really distinct from the act that actuates it; for if they were their own existence they would be Existence and Intelligibility in pure act, and would no longer be created essences.[24]

The doctrine of the real distinction is, then, an application of act/potency to existence/essence. Because act is really distinct from potency and because existence is act and essence is potency, existence is really distinct from essence. Moreover, if an essence were not really other than existence, it would be pure, subsistent act, and thus it would be God rather than a creature.

But doubts can be raised against each of Maritain's arguments. How do I know that existence *is* act, that essence *is* potency? Does not this knowledge presuppose I already am aware that existence is actually present in an existent as a component? Is not my knowledge of existence/essence as act/potency a sequel to that prior awareness? Also, if existence means simply (as an essentialist asserts) that an essence has been efficiently caused by God, then the identity of essence and existence does not destroy creaturehood but rather establishes it by setting up the relationship of effect-to-cause between that essence and God.

As a final comment: actual intuitional experiences (see Ch. IV, Sec. 3b) seem each to be an awareness not of the act of existing itself (as Maritain would have them) but of actual existence as a fact. In such an intuition one realizes vividly and enduringly that he actually exists and that this fact is of prime importance, affecting him profoundly.

Suggested Readings

Fraga de Almeida Sampara, Laura, *L'intuition dans la philosophie de Jacques Maritain.* Paris: J. Vrin, 1963.

Maritain, Jacques, *Frontières de la poésie.* Paris: Rouart, 1935.

———, *Preface to Metaphysics.* New York: Sheed & Ward, 1948.

———, *Existence and the Existent.* New York: Pantheon Books, 1948.

———, *La philosophie bergsonienne* (Paris: Tequi, 1948), pp. 125–28, 143–57.

———, *Degrees of Knowledge.* London: Geoffrey Bles, 1959.

———, *Situation de la poésie.* Paris: Desclée, 1964.

———, *Peasant of the Garonne.* New York: Holt, Rinehart and Winston, 1968.

---

[24] *Existence and the Existent,* pp. 35–36.

———, "Réflexions sur la nature blessée et sur l'intuition de l'être," *Revue thomiste,* 68 (1968), 17–34. Reprinted in his *Approches sans entraves* (Paris: Payard, 1973), pp. 249–91.

Sweeney, S.J., Leo, "The Christian Existentialism of Jacques Maritain," in *Jacques Maritain: A Philosopher in the World,* Jean-Louis Allard (ed.), pp. 31–42, especially "Appendix Two: The Intuition of Being." Ottawa: University of Ottawa Press, 1986 (forthcoming as ch. 20 in my *Christian Philosophy: Nature, Origin, Developments* [hereafter: *Christian Philosophy*] [New York/Bern: Peter Lang Publishing, Inc., 1994]).

Van Riet, Georges, *L'épistémologie thomiste* (Louvain: Institut Superieur de Philosophie, 1946), pp. 349–76.

Appendix B

How the Meaning of "Being" Is Worked Out

The deliberate elaboration of the metaphysical meaning given "being" entails reflection upon at least the following steps.

(a) If this man, that plant and other such intrinsic unities were the only subjects of which the term is predicated, then its meaning could be formulated as "an actually existing thing," with "thing" referring to essence and "actually existing" to act of existence, which is really distinct from the former.

(b) But once components are known to exist, and thus to be real, the formulation becomes "an actually existing item." "Item" is general enough to express what a component is, as well as what an intrinsic unity is (#a). The other words in the formula point to actual existence, which is really other than what each component is, with the exception of the act of existing itself, which exists by being what it is (although only within some existent).

(c) When one is confronted with the peculiar nature of such extrinsic unities as a family, a machine, or a painting (they are and, hence, are real, but what they are is a mere complex of real relations [see Ch. VI, Sec. 1, *ad finem*, and Ch. VII]), then one realizes that "item" signifies this relational complex, whereas "actually existing" points to the acts of existing actualizing the various subjects in which the relations inhere and through which they exist.

(d) Once God is known to exist, then "item" is made to refer to an essence which is identical with the actuality expressed by "actually existing," because it is God's very nature to exist (Ch. V, Sec. 6).

(e) As predicable of such extremely divergent actual items, then, "being" is shown to be a very general awareness. It expresses both *what* an actual is (whether God, this man, a component, a family) and *that* it is. Despite its generalness, though, "being" is also most rich in content—in fact, it is as rich in content as is possible for a concept with maximal extension. Why so? Because it also expresses everything in each actual of which it is predicated: "item" has to do with what each is, the other words to the fact that it is. Insofar as it signifies each *as actual*, it points to each in its very uniqueness and determinateness, for everything is actual in a determinate, unique, individual way. (See Ch. VI, Sec. 2, third last paragraph.)

(f) There is this difference between "being" (as well as the concepts of other transcendents and of any pure perfection) and such a concept as "man" or "animal." The common perfection which the latter signifies is never found actually existing precisely as such, of and in itself. There is no Man or Animal: there is this or that human, this or that dog, none of which exhausts the intelligibility. But Being (as well as Truth, Goodness, Wisdom, and so forth) does exist as such, of and in itself. This *is* God, in Whom all other existents participate and thereby are beings. In summary, "man" or "animal" is, as such, only the content of an awareness and never extramental. "Being" is both the content of an intellection and an extramental subsistent.

(g) There is this similarity, however, between "being" and "man." One who understand truly and deeply what to be human means thereby also knows all humans, whoever and wherever they may be, precisely as human. So too, one who finally understands what to be actual means also grasps all beings (whether they be God, creatures, components or accidental unities) precisely as being, all existents qua existent, whatever is real precisely as real. And this is a much greater victory, for this has extended the mind to a much greater degree than in the previous example or in almost any other kind of knowledge. In attaining this understanding, then, the human knower has performed a tremendous intellectual feat and has achieved what is certainly one of the aims of metaphysics as a science.

Suggested Readings

Anderson, James F., "Some Disputed Questions on Our Knowledge of Being," *Review of Metaphysics*, 11 (June, 1958), pp. 553 sq. and pp. 566 sq.

Owens, J., *Elementary Christian Metaphysics* (Milwaukee: Bruce Publishing Co., 1963), pp. 115–17.

Sweeney, S.J., Leo, "Analogy and Being," *Modern Schoolman*, 39 (March, 1962), 261–62.

———, "Existence/Essence in Early Writings of Aquinas," *Proceedings of the American Catholic Philosophical Association*, 37 (1963), 124, n. 43 (forthcoming as ch. 20 of my *Christian Philosophy*).

Appendix C

Aquinas on Separation

How does our interpretation of separation and abstraction (see Ch. X, Secs. 4 and 5) square with Thomas' texts? Considerably better than might appear at first sight, although our aim has not been textual exegesis but rather presentation of our own position. True, in both key passages (*In Boethii de Trinitate*, 5, 3, resp. and *S.T.*, I, 85, 1 ad 1 and ad 2) Thomas speaks of abstraction in terms of the intellectual operations involved, and thus seems to combine the description of knowledge in reference to its efficient cause with that in reference to the *cognita* or even seems to be oblivious of the latter as cause. But according to him knowledge does flow from those two causes,[1] and his apparent identification of abstraction with simple apprehension and judgment[2] perhaps might more accurately be understood as predication through extrinsic denomination: apprehension and judgment are the operations by which we produce knowledges marked by various abstractions. Moreover, the various abstractions involved in diverse kinds of knowledge are determined by the objective status of the *cognita*. When one item actually is not the other,[3] we have that abstraction called

---

[1] For example, see *De Veritate*, 10, 6, resp.

[2] *S.T.*, I, 85, 1 ad 1: "Abstraction comes about in two ways. First, through composition and division [Thomas' language for "judgment"]. . . . Second, through simple and absolute consideration." Also see *In Boet. de Trin.*, 5, 3, resp., especially *ad finem* (Decker Ed., p. 186, l. 13 sq.; Maurer translation, pp. 31–32).

[3] *Ibid.* (Maurer's translation, p. 31): "In the case of things which can exist separately, separation rather than abstraction obtains" (Latin text in Decker Ed., p. 185, l. 31). *S.T.*, I, 85, 1 ad 1: "[The first way in which abstraction occurs

separation.[4] When one is linked with the other but is somehow independent, we have a nonseparative abstraction.[5] When the one is dependent upon the other, even such nonseparative abstraction is impossible.[6] Thus, the *cognita* themselves decide whether or not abstraction is possible, and if so, which kind it will be and whether matter is to be partially or totally absent from the awareness.

Accordingly, Thomas would seem to agree with our theory of abstraction as a description of knowledge in the light of the *cognita*. It is a negative property of the content of intellections: the absence of matter within their very content. Separation too is an abstraction, and thus is the negative property of intellection arising within the study of beings-as-being: the absence of matter within the content of awarenesses caused by *cognita* which are intrinsically independent of matter.

---

is] through composition and division, as happens when we realize that something is not in another but is separated from it."

4 In the *S.T.* passage (I, 85, 1 ad 1), separation is an abstraction: "*Abstraction* comes about in two ways. First, through composition and division, as happens when we realize that something . . . is *separated* from another" (emphasis mine). Also *ibid.*, ad 2 *ad finem*.

5 *Ibid.* (Maurer's translation, p. 28): "If one thing does not depend on another with regard to what constitutes the intelligibility of the nature, then the intellect can abstract it from that other thing so as to know it without that other" (Latin text in Decker Ed., p. 183, lines 14–16). Among the examples Thomas gives of items having that independence are animal *re* feet, hands, and so on; letter of alphabet *re* syllables of words; quantity *re* quality; nose *re* pug-shaped; man *re* whiteness, whiteness *re* man; elements *re* mixtures; circle *re* semicircle.

6 *Ibid.* (Maurer's translation, pp. 27–28): "When that through which the intelligibility of a nature is constituted and through which the nature itself is understood has a relation to, and a dependence on, something else, clearly we cannot know the nature without that other thing" (Latin text in Decker Ed., p. 183, lines 3–6). Among the instances Aquinas gives of items which are thus dependent: feet, hands, and so on *re* animal; syllables *re* letters of the alphabet; pug-shape *re* nose; father *re* son; quantity *re* intelligible matter; accidents *re* substance; mixtures *re* elements; triangle *re* lines; man *re* soul/body; this soul/body *re* Socrates.

Suggested Readings

Owens, Joseph, "Metaphysical Separation in Aquinas," *Mediaeval Studies*, 34 (1972), 287–306.

Wippel, John, "Metaphysics and Separation in Thomas Aquinas," *Metaphysical Themes in Thomas Aquinas* (Washington, D.C.: Catholic University of America Press, 1984), pp. 69–104.

Indices

Index of Names

Page number accompanied by letter *n* indicates entry found only within footnotes.

A

Abelard, 113n
Adams, 237n
Adenauer, 284n
à Kempis, 23, 26
Albertson, 95n, 241n, 264
Albert the Great, 213n
Anderson, 106, 158n, 198, 264, 350, 403
Antisthenes, 207n
Aquinas, 55n, 67–68, 73–81, 106, 115n,119n, 139, 147n, 164n, 179n, 208–9, 210n, 220, 222n, 228n, 250n, 256–57, 261n, 290n, 303n, 324n, 345n, 346n, 350n, 398, 405–6
Arendt, 377
Aristotle, 19, 41–69, 103, 186n, 221n, 226n, 232, 236n, 268, 271–73, 279n, 299n, 327n, 346n, 373
Armstrong, 20n, 30n, 38
Arnou, 278n
Astius, 346n
Athanasian Creed, 182
Augros, 15, 139, 350
Augustine, 30n, 31n, 38, 83, 175n
Avicenna, 163n
Ayer, 5, 15, 364

B

Bachhuber, 55n
Bahm, 4n, 7n
Baldwin, 203n
Barth, 157n
Barthes, 354
Beethoven, 149, 152
Benedetto, 136n
Berdyaev, 180n
Bergson, 38
Berkeley, 145n
Bernard of Chartres, 17
Berry, 232
Blackham, 26n, 38
Blackwell, 232
Blanche, 324n
Bobik, 198, 236n
Born, 15, 238n
Bourke, 30n, 106, 198
Boyle, 155n
Brady, 139
Brenner, 261n
Brightman, 7n
Brooks, 202n
Brown, 237
Bunge, 264, 298n

C

Cajetan, 183, 184n, 198, 324n
Caldin, 15
Camus, 27n
Carnap, 5, 364
Charlesworth, 38
Chesterton, 19n, 109n
Chroust, 4, 15
Clarke, G., 202n
Clarke, N., 106, 139n, 147n, 358n
Clarkson, 182n

Coffey, 213n, 214–18, 220, 224, 255n, 278n
Collingwood, F., 42n
Collingwood, R., 5n, 321n
Collins, 24n, 26n, 38, 112n, 137n, 238n
Conant, 42n
Copernicus, 268
Copleston, 20n, 38, 54n, 350
Council of Chalcedon, 182n

D

Darwin, 267, 272–73, 275
De Chardin, 202n, 279n
De Finance, 202n, 238n, 251n, 317
De Gaulle, 45
De la Taille, 183n–85n, 198
Deleuze, 354, 374
De Raeymaeker, 6n, 15, 68, 106, 183n, 198, 239n, 264, 317
Derrida, 354, 373, 374, 386–89
Desan, 26n
Descartes, 84, 113n, 207n, 252–56, 276, 279n, 286–87, 300, 373, 375, 378–79
Dewey, 353, 365–66
Diemert, 188n
Dostoievsky, 92n, 180n
Dougherty, 49n
Drennen, 15, 38
Ducasse, 7n
DuNoüy, 276n

E

Echarri, 49n
Eckhart, 158n
Eco, 198
Einstein, 89n
Emmett, 354–55
Eschmann, 74n
Eslick, 106, 350
Exodus, 74, 80

F

Faulkner, 145
Fink, 375–76
Fisher, 6n
Foucault, 354
Frank, 42n, 239n
Frick, 35n, 147n, 219n, 255n

G

Gadamer, 370, 381, 383–84, 388, 389
Galileo, 268
Gallagher, 106
Garrigou-Lagrange, 276–77, 286–87
Geiger, 323n
Genesis, 18
Gensler, 332n
Gerrity, 68, 317
Gilson, 15, 30n, 33n, 35n, 38, 68, 73n, 80n, 95n, 119n, 123n, 139, 148n, 149n, 151n, 172n, 185n, 190n, 198, 202n, 252n, 257n, 264, 350, 396n
Gracia, 198
Greene, 145, 156, 246n
Grenet, 210n
Griesbach, 350
Gurr, 252n, 255n, 264
Guthrie, 21n, 29n, 38, 68

H

Hagspiel, 5n
Hamlet, 145, 149
Hanson, 15
Harper, 186n
Hart, 210n, 317
Hartshorne, 355n, 359n
Hawking, 21n
Hawkins, D., 42n
Hawkins, D. J. B., 68, 139, 213–14, 238n, 265
Hegel, 355, 373
Heidegger, 15, 354, 370, 373–75, 377–89
Heisenberg, 42n
Henle, 95n, 331–32, 350
Heraclitus, 21–29, 31, 37, 41, 64, 86
Hitler, 186n
Hocking, 16, 180n
Hoenen, 49n
Holloway, 14n, 116n, 128n, 136n, 139, 148n, 210n

Hopkins, 19n
Hume, 207n, 237–39, 256, 360–61, 366, 373
Husserl, 35n, 38, 370, 373, 375–78, 389
Huxley, A., 4
Huxley, J., 275

J

Jaki, 16, 21n, 139, 317, 351
Janet, 317
James, 365–66
Jaspers, 380
Jastrow, 21n, 68
Johann, 198, 202n, 251n, 265
John of St. Thomas, 213n
Johnson-Laird, 259n
Journet, 199

K

Kahn, 21n
Kane, W. H., 351
Kane, W. J., 209n, 232
Kant, 164n, 362, 370, 373
Kaplan, 265
Karmiloff-Smith, 259n
Kattsoff, 206n
Keller, 19n
Kemeny, 239n
Keyser, 204n
Kierkegaard, 380
Kirk, 20n, 21n, 54n
Kleutgen, 35n, 214
Klubertanz, 6n, 14n, 47n, 58n, 98n, 123n, 199, 213n, 214n, 217n, 220n, 223n, 224–25, 260n, 280n, 298n, 317, 323n, 324n
Koren, 164n, 210n, 218n, 241n
Kosman, 232
Kossel, 207n, 209n, 222n, 232
Kovach, 106, 140
Krempel, 209n, 213n, 230n
Kreyche, 164n, 281n, 297n, 304n, 312n
Krick, 308n

L

Lateran Council, 182n
Lauer, 158n
Leibniz, 252n, 256, 355
Lenzen, 239n
Leo, St., 182n
Lerner, 265
Leroy, 324n
Lippold, 312–314
Locke, 360, 361, 366
Loewenberg, 237n
Lowrie, 157n
Lutherans, 158n
Lyotard, 354
Lyttkens, 199

M

Macbeth, 156
McCormick, 252–55
McDougall, 271
McInerny, 199
MacLeod, 269–75
McMahon, 323n
McMullin, 69
Manicheans, 176n
Marcel, 26n, 211n
Maritain, J., 3n, 6n, 19n, 23n, 39, 90–93, 112n, 115n, 136n, 140, 172n, 174, 184n, 199, 278n, 324n, 351, 393–400
Maritain, R., 180n
Martin, 16
Marx, 186n
Matczak, 157n
Maurer, 107, 351
Mauriac, 92n, 203n
May, 85n, 311n, 322n
Mayr, 273–75, 290–91, 297n, 311n
Meehan, 265
Mencken, 4
Merlan, 323n
Merleau-Ponty, 377
Michelmore, 19n
Mill, 361
Miller, A., 246n
Miller, R., 16, 321n
Montague, 124n

Moore, 361, 362, 363
Morrison, 10n
Moser, 332n
Mounier, 39

N

Nagel, 42n, 239n
Newton, 268, 269n
Nicolaus of Autrecourt, 207n
Nielsen, 157n
Nietzsche, 373, 374, 380, 387
Nozick, 138n
Nys, 49n

O

O'Brien, J., 155n
O'Brien, K., 278n
O'Brien, R., 10n
Ockham, 113n, 158, 193, 207n, 213n, 360, 373
O'Connor, 201n
Oedipus Rex, 246n
O'Neill, 199
Owens, 4n, 16, 20n, 21n, 29n, 42n, 54n, 68n, 69, 77n, 107, 140, 199, 210n, 223n, 226n, 227n, 232n, 242n, 252n, 257n, 265, 328n, 337n, 351, 403, 407

P

Parmenides, 54n
Pasternak, 240n
Pattin, 230n
Pegis, 199
Peirce, 86n, 365–66
Pendergast, 19n
Penrose, 351
Pesch, 219n
Peters, E., 355n
Peters, J., 210n
Phelan, 107, 140, 199
Piaget, 259n
Pieper, 107, 142n
Plato, 19n, 29–37, 41, 64, 113, 145, 268, 193, 346n, 373
Plotinus, 30–35, 246n
Poe, 92n
Pogeller, 386
Psalms, 22–23

Q

Quine, 5n, 364–69, 384, 388, 389

R

Ramirez, 324n
Reany, 241n
Régis, 323n, 328n
Reith, 164n
Renard, 14n, 102–103, 124n, 136n, 148n, 183n, 255n, 280n, 312n, 324
Reichmann, 199
Richards, 238n
Ricoeur, 200
Robert, 323n, 324n
Roland-Gosselin, 190n
Ross, A., 56–58
Ross, D., 29n
Rossner, 165n
Rorty, A., 366n
Rorty, R., 5n, 7n, 361, 370, 388, 389
Royce, 14n, 48n
Russell, B., 6n, 256, 361, 362–63, 365–66, 389
Russell, J., 279n, 298n, 304n

S

Saintonge, 49n
Salinger, 156n
Salmon, 200
Sambursky, 20n
Saroyan, 204n
Sartre, 23–28, 41n, 87, 111–12, 113, 133, 176n, 193, 377
Scheu, 232
Schlick, 364
Schmidt, K., 351
Schmidt, R., 206n, 323n, 351
Sciacca, 200
Scotus, 113n, 183
Searle, 354n
Sellars, 364–69, 384, 389
Selvaggi, 49n
Shakespeare, 23, 89n

Simmons, 351
Simon, 265
Simpson, 272–73, 275, 311n
Sinnott, 276n
Siwek, 200
Smart, 138
Smith, G., 136n, 172n, 200, 217n, 265, 318
Smith, V., 49n
Spinoza, 355
Stace, 267–70
Stanciu, 15, 139, 350
Stevens, 69
Suarez, 35, 77–78, 183–84, 213
Sullivan, 16
Sweeney, 32n, 34n, 39, 74n, 75n, 76n, 77n, 78n, 80n, 90n, 107, 136n, 140, 154n, 155n, 167n, 188n, 193n, 200, 246n, 257n, 318, 327n, 353, 360, 400, 403
Symposium: *The Principle of Individuation*, 200

T

Tertullianists, 14n
TeSelle, 30n
Teske, 186n
Thales, 20, 37
Thiel, 324n
Thomas (*see* Aquinas)
Tillich, 17
Tomkins, 312n
Tournier, 200
Tyrrell, 351

U

Urraburu, 214

V

Van Melsen, 16, 42n, 69, 239n, 318
Vann, 19n
Van Roo, 69, 107
van Steenberghen, 213n, 214
Vaske, 14n, 164n, 172n, 297n, 304n, 310n, 312n
Veatch, 69
von Mises, 6

W

Wahl, 39
Wallace, 351
Walton, 107
Ward, 318
Weiss, 239n
Wells, 78n
Whitehead, 269, 354–59, 387, 389
Wild, 69, 115n, 140, 207–8, 232, 239n, 265, 318, 323n, 337n
Wilhelmsen, 140, 200, 202n, 312n, 328n
Williams, 280n
Wippel, 107, 351
Wittgenstein, 361, 363–65, 369–73, 384, 388, 389
Woolf, 201n
Wolff, 252n

Z

Zeller, 20n
Zeno, 54n

Index of Topics

Page number accompanied by letter *n* indicates entry found only within footnotes.

A

Abilities:
  intellectual, 8–9
  physical, 8
Absence of matter:
  re abstraction/separation, 325–26, 346–50
Absolute chance (*see* Chance)
Abstractio totius, 339n
Abstraction:
  absence of matter in content of intellection, 325–26, 346–50
    "of addition": *re* constructs, 340–42
  analogous notion, 348
  Aquinas' texts on, 405–7 (*see also* Separation)
  Cajetan's three degrees of, 324n
  re cognita actually immaterial: separation, 325, 343–50
  "of external characteristics," 339–40
  five kinds (*table*), 347–48
  formal/total, 324
  in moral philosophy, 349
  "of natural components," 341–43
  not found in sense cognition, 346–47
  in sacred theology, 349
  Thomists' opinions, 323–25
  "of whatness," 338–39
Accident, 50–55, 65–66, 123–26 (*see also* Substance)
  an act, 53–54
  caused by substance, 125–26
  definition, 51, 66
  etymology, 53n
  four classes of, 230
  known through intellection, 52, 66
  for logician, 55–56
  metaphysical definition, 142
  not autodetermining, 125–26
  property/nonproperty, 124–25
  "that by which," 52
  transcends perception, 52, 66
  various meanings, 55
Accidental change, 50–51, 58
Accidental level, 42
Act (*see also* Perfection):
  of existing (*see* Existing, act of)
  pure, 104n
Act/potency, 53–54, 102–6
  re accidents/substance, 54–55
  defined, 54n
  esse/essence, 95–97
  historical origin (Aristotle), 54–55
  inductive approach, 103–6
    general propositions concerning, 103–6
    "in the same order," 104
    a sequel, not a beginning, 103, 106
    Renard, 102–3
  re specific/individual essence, 77

Action/passion, 226n, 227, 242n, 283
Active qualities, 297, 299, 305, 310
Activity, 280
  immanent/transient, 240n, 241, 245, 283
  is thing's change, 242, 244
Actual existence:
  re chance, 311
  contributes reality, 86–88
  description:
    C. S. Peirce, 86n
    imaginative, 84–85
    literal, 85
  and evil, 175–80
  as fact, evidence, 344
  intrinsic to existent, 88–89
  meaning, 83–86
  not efficiency, 86–89
  other than quiddity, 89–93, 100–101
    because common factor, 89–90, 101
    because realifies, 89, 94
Agent:
  as agent, 242, 283
    not changed, 244
  cognitive:
    finality, 279–96 (*see also* Finality)
  cognitive/noncognitive, 280n
  as finite, material, 242, 244
  noncognitive:
    finality, 296–305 (*see also* Finality)
  principal/instrumental (*see* Efficient cause; Instrumental agent; Principal agent)
  product similar to agent, 244–47
Amaterial, 343n, 349
Amateriality, 129–33 (*see also* Amaterial; Immaterial; Material; Spiritual)
  re act of existing, 132–33, 343n, 349
  re God, angels, 133n
Analogous cause, 245–46
Analogy:
  in abstractions, 348–49
  based on act of existing, 195–96
  of being, 151–60, 194–96
    in actual existents, 151–53, 194, 195n (*see also* Similarity/diversity)
    in metaphysical knowledge and predication, 152–53, 195
  corollary of one's metaphysics, 158–60
  crucial difference between Catholicism and Protestantism, 157n
  kinds, 154–58, 195
    denomination, 156–57
    eminence, 154
    proportionality, 154–55
    reference, 155–56
  lacking in monists and nominalists, 158
  linked with autodetermination, 159n
  none for Neo-Platonists, Lutherans, Christian Scientists, 158–59
  re perception, 152n
Angel, spiritual or amaterial, 133
Appearances:
  same after death, 58
  Sartre: material thing consists only of, 24–26 (*see also* Material universe)
Appetitive powers, 280
  efficient cause of love, 285, 291–94
  object: good-as-known, 291–94
Apprehension, simple/complex, 328, 334, 335, 337
Artifacts:
  and "being," 149–51
  how individuated, 189–90
Artist, analogous cause, 246
Atomism, *re* real relations, 207–8
Attraction, 298n
  causality of good-as-known, 283–84
Autodetermination, 119–29
  re analogy, 159n
  Aquinas' texts, 119n

re existence/essence, 126–29
meaning, 119–20
re prime matter/substantial form, 121–23
self-individuation of form, 123n
re substance/accidents, 123–26
of substantial form, 193
two senses of "determine," 119–20
Awareness:
restrictive, 161–62
transcendent, 162–65 (*see also* Transcendents)
Awe at actual existence:
Smart, 138

B

"Barely immaterial," 131–32, 343n
"Beautiful," 164, 165, 171–72
transcendent (*see also* Transcendents):
defined, 171n, 172, 173
known metaphysically, 172–73
known spontaneously, 164, 165
Beautiful-as-known, exemplary cause, 314–16
Beauty, 172–73, 315n
"Being":
re accidental unities, 149–51
"actually existing" expresses similarity and diversity, 159–60, 194–95
analogy, 144n, 151–60, 194–96
re artifacts, 149–51
Avicenna: first known, 163n
general yet rich awareness, 160, 402
content of intellection and a subsistent, 402
meaning ("an actually existing item"), 100, 143–44, 152, 166, 173, 175, 194–95
meaning deliberately elaborated, 143–44, 401–2
re possibles, 147–49
predicated (*table*), 147
of intentional universe, 144–46
primacy of existence in, 143–51, 194
and separation, 345
transcendent (*see also* Transcendents):
known metaphysically, 166
known spontaneously, 162–64
Being:
as being, 3, 68, 344–46, 349
aim of metaphysics, 402
intuition of (*see* Intuition)
as mobile, 341–42, 344

C

Cartesian atmosphere, 252–57, 276
Cartesian philosopher, 279n
Categories (*see* Predicaments)
Causality other than efficient, 205–6
Cause:
of accidents:
efficient, 124
emanative (or active), 124
analogous, equivocal, univocal, 245–46
efficient (*see* Efficient cause)
emanative, 221
in empiriological sciences, 238n
exemplary, 312–17 (*see also* Exemplary cause)
extrinsic, 88n, 235n (*see also* Efficient cause; Final cause; Exemplary cause)
final (*see* Final cause)
intrinsic, 235–36
actuating/limiting, 236, 243
Aristotle: formal/material, 236n
of knowledge:
content-determining: *cognitum*, 325–26, 346–47
efficient: cognitive powers, 325, 326, 346
presential, *re* relations, 221–22
primary/secondary, 251n, 264
proper: *re* God/creatures, 135n, 247–51
Certain (probable, doubtful) conclusions, 169n
Certitude, formal (*vs.* material), 260–61, 289, 302–3

Chance, 306–9, 311
on noncognitive level, 308–9
relative/absolute, 306–8
total, 307–8
Change:
center of unreality for Platonist, 29 (*see also* Radical essentialism)
claimed impossible, 54
factor in reality, 28–29, 36–37
heart of reality (Heraclitus; Sartre), 21–22, 26–27
material/immaterial, 11–12
shown possible through act/potency, 54–55
Changes in activity:
variously caused, 300n
Change/stability, 11 (*see also* Stability)
on accidental level, 42–43, 45, 50–55
as evidences, 50–51
as facts, evidences, 342–43
make-up of individuals, 41
on substantial level, 42–43, 56–64
Chemicals, 47n
"pure," 58n
virtual, 48n, 58
Christ, 181–85, 187n (*see also* Supposit; Nature)
Circularity, 341
Cognitive agent:
final situation, 279–96 (*see especially* 280)
Cognitum:
content-determining cause, 325–26, 338–48, 405–6 (*see also* Knowledge)
Complex apprehension, 328, 334, 335, 338, 342, 346 (*see also* Apprehension)
Component:
re abstraction on natural components, 342–43
Aristotle: only four, 67
defined, 53, 65
on inanimate level, 67n
Comprehension (*vs.* Extension), 160, 163, 173
Concrete case, 43
re inductive knowledge, 260–61, 288–90, 294, 302–3
Constancy, 297–98
Constitutive part (*see* Part)
Construct:
re evil, 179n
re predicaments, 228–29
re relation, 212–13
in teleology, 270
Constructural sciences, 6n, 146 (*see also* Construct; Knowledge)
involve "abstraction of addition," 340–41
Contemplation:
re beautiful, 171–73
means of possessing God, 291–92
"Corporeal" continuity, 58–59, 113n
Corporeity, 191
Cosmic influences, 202n
Creation, 250n
Creature:
defined, 136n
not instrumental cause in creation, 250n
not proper cause of existence, 136n
proper cause of existence as determined, 248–51, 263
posterior in being and efficiency, 251, 263–64

D

Dasein, 380–87
Death, 311–12
as evidence, 56–58
not annihilation, 58, 113n
Deconstruction, 354, 374, 387
Deduction, 329, 333 (*see also* Inference)
place of in human knowledge, 260n
re "Principle of "Causality," 252–55
Definition:
metaphysical *vs.* cosmological, 141–43 (*see also* Metaphysical knowledge)
Denomination, analogy of, 156–57, 195

Denomination:
  extrinsic:
    "abstraction" *re* intellectual operations, 347
    "being" *re* intentional universe, 144, 146–47, 151
    definition, 88n
    effect's perfection *re* cause, 246n
    "good" *re* free choice, 164n, 171n
    "good" *re* nonexistents, 281n
    material, 130, 131
    material *re* components, 62n
    prime matter, 67
    "real" *re* possibles, 88n
    "separation" *re* negative judgment, 347
    "substantial/accidental" *re esse*, 95n
    "true" *re* actuals, 157n, 165n, 168–70
    "true" *re* components, 170n
  intrinsic:
    "being" *re* actuals, 147, 150, 157
    "good" *re* actuals, 171n
    "true" *re* God, 170n
    "true" *re* knowledge, 157n, 169–70
Dependence on matter:
  extrinsic, 131
  intrinsic, 131–32, 135
Determinate tendencies, 293, 295, 301, 304–5
Determination:
  love *re* cognitive agent, 284
  re noncognitive agent, 285n, 290–91, 297–98, 301 (*see also* Determinate tendencies)
  twofold, 63n, 119–20
Direction, causality of exemplar, 315, 316–17
Distinction (*see* Real distinction; Mental distinction)
Diversity (*see* Similarity)
Divine revelation:
  and Greek philosophers, 13, 18
  and sacred theology, 14
  re supposit/nature, 181–87
Dream experiments, 10

E

Ecology, 201n
Ecstatic contemplation, 315–16
Efficiency:
  as involving direction/response, 316
Efficient cause, 235–65
  contemporary opinions, 236–37, 256–57
  co-operation with God, 248–51, 264
    as instrument with principal cause, 248–51, 264
    further problem, 250
  corollaries, 244–47, 263
    agent as agent not changed, 244
    every agent has proper effect, 247
    product similar to agent, 244–47
  factors, 240–44, 243–44, 263
    activity (transient/immanent), 240, 241–42
    preexisting matter, 241
    principal/instrumental agents, 240–41
    product, 243
    real relation of effect to cause, 242
  human parents: "furnishing" causes *re* soul, 241n
  Hume: position and critique, 237–38
Efficient Cause Proposition, 251–62, 261–62, 287, 288
  Cartesian approach, a deductive principle, 252–55
    McCormick, 253–55
    rejection of, 256
  known through induction, 256–62
    Aquinas, 256
    by child, 258–59
    a conclusion, 256–58, 263
    Owens, 256–57

premise in reasoning process, 261
self-evident through immediate insight, 258–60, 262
self-evident through reflection, 260–61, 262
Eminence (*see* Analogy)
Empiricism, 360–69
Empiriological sciences, *re* "cause," 239n
"End of agent" (*finis operantis*), 282n
"End of work" (*finis operis*) 283n
Entitative cohesion, 49
Environment, 201n
Epistemologist, 99n
Equivocal cause, 246
Equivocal meaning, 153n, 159
Esse ad of relation, 217n
Essence:
vs. act of existing:
defined, 94
a potency, 95–97
for authentic existentialist, 112–15
for essentialists, possible more real than actual, 34–35
grounded in God, 112–13
how called material, 130n
immediate source of diversity, 159n
metaphysical definition of, 143
not autodetermining, 126–27
not mere negation, 115n
for Sartre, 112
specific/individual, 77
various meanings, 97–99
to epistemologist, 99n
to logician, 99n
to metaphysician, 99, 101
nonphilosophical meaning, 98–99
in philosophy of nature, 99
Essence-argument (*see* Real distinction)
Essence/*esse:* potency/act, 95–97
Essences (*see* Forms)
Essential components:
"barely immaterial" 132, 135, 343n
how called material, 130
Essentialism (*see* Radical Essentialism)
Ethics, 3 (*see also* Philosophy of morality)
Evidence:
"different sort," 9–12
"Diverse evidences indicate . . .":
re existence/essence, 93–95
re matter/form, 59, 60
origin of proposition, 43–45
re substance/accidents, 51–52
material things:
as actual, 10–11, 13–14, 37, 321
within laboratory, 9–10
for opponents of metaphysics, 4–7, 321
Evil, 175–80, 196–97
absence of good, 177–79, 196
causes of, 309n
a challenge, 180n
re finality, 281
known through construct, 179
moral/physical, 178
positions:
Christian Scientist, 176n, 180
intermediate, 177–80
Manichean, 176n, 180
three factors of, 178–79, 196
Exemplar, 313
Exemplarity and efficient cause, 240–41, 250n
Exemplary causality, not final causality, 316n
Exemplary cause, 312–17
factors, 315–17
beautiful-as-known, 315
causality: direction, 315–16
efficient cause, 316–17
exemplary effect, 316–17
Lippold, 312–14
"Exercises act of existing," 142n
Existence (*see also* Actual existence):
Aquinas' interpretation of *Exodus*, 74–75, 80–81
an evidence for Aquinas, 67–68
for Sartre, 111–12

Existence/essence:
act/potency, 95–97 (*see also* Existing, act of)
in Aquinas' early writings, 74–78
in Aquinas' subsequent writings, 78–80
knowledge-process described, 336–37
"that by which," 94
"Existence precedes essence" 110–15
for authentic existentialist, 112–15, 133
for Sartre, 111–12
Existentialia, 374, 380, 381
Existentialism
apocryphal, 23n
authentic, 23n, 115, 322–23
re form, 219
on predicaments, 226–30
valid science of metaphysics, 112–15, 322–23
radical, 21–29, 374, 380, 381
consequences of, 26–28
devaluates individuals, 41n
re God, 26–27
re moral conduct, 27
resultant psychological state, 27 (*see also* Nausea)
re Self, 26n
various groups in, 23–24
Existents:
as effects of efficient causality, 251–62
as efficient causes, 240–51, 262–63 (*see also* Efficient cause)
Existing, act of:
absolutely necessary, 90n, 96n, 110, 114, 128, 129, 133
Aristotle unaware of, 67, 68n
described, 94, 100, 101
re evil, 180, 196–97
"exercises . . . ," 142n
existential judgments, 95n, 101, 337
how called material, 130–31
an intrinsic cause, 235–36
knowledge of, marked by separation, 344–45
known through intellection, 95
necessary for efficient, intrinsic emanative causalities, 257n
no *esse accidentale*, 94n, 142n
not form, 219
one to an existent, 94n
re possibles, 147–49
primacy, 109–40 (*see also* "Existence precedes essence")
because absolutely necessary, 110, 114–15, 133
because amaterial, 129–33, 134–35
in analogy, 195–96
because autodetermining, 119–29, 134 (*see also* Autodetermination)
basis to prove God, 135–39
re individual (supposit/nature), 181–94, 197
in metaphysical knowledge, 141–97, *especially* 141–43, 194 (*see also* Metaphysical knowledge; "Being"; Transcendents)
because pure act, 110, 133
because source of all perfections, 115–19, 133–34 (*see also* Perfection)
in supposit, 183–88, 197
in transcendents, 161–75, 196
pure act, 96–97, 101–2, 345
pure perfection as a component, 117
root of efficient causality, 251, 264
transcends mere perception, 95, 101
wholly independent of matter, 132–33, 134–35, 343n, 344–45
Extension (*vs.* Comprehension) (*see* Comprehension)
Extrinsic dependence (*see* Dependence)
Extrinsic cause (*see* Intrinsic/extrinsic)

F

Filiation, 210n
"Final" as adjective, meaning, 280n

Final cause, 267–311
  Aristotle, 268, 269n, 270–71, 279n
  current opinions:
    Garrigou-Lagrange: self-evident, *a priori*, 276–77
    MacLeod: insert into social sciences, 269–73
    Mayr: reduce teleology to teleonomy, 273–75
    Simpson: no evidence for finalism, 272–73
    Stace: rejected by contemporaries, 267–70
Final Cause Proposition *re* cognitives, 286–96
  immediately known:
    Cartesian approach, 286–87
    by child, 288–89
    through induction, immediate insight, 288–90
    through induction, premise in reasoning process, 289, 331
    through induction, reflection, 289–90, 331
  known inductively through reasoning, 290–94, 331–33
    basis: product *is* producer's goal, 290
    cognitive agents *re* God, 291–96
Final Cause Proposition *re* noncognitives, 300–305
  immediately known:
    by child, 302
    through induction, immediate insight, 300–302
    through induction, from new activity, 303n
    through induction, premise in reasoning process, 302–3, 331
    through induction, reflection, 302–3
  known inductively through reasoning, 303–4
Finalism, 273 (*see also* Final cause)
Finality *re* brute animals, 280n
Finality *re* cognitive agents, 279–96, 310 (*see also* Cognitive agents)
  factors, 281–85
    causality: attraction, 283–84
    effect: love, 284–85
    efficient cause: appetitive powers, 285
    good-as-known, 281–82, 283
Finality and efficient cause, 240, 250
Finality *re* noncognitive agents, 296–305, 310 (*see also* Noncognitive agents)
  factors, 297–99, 299 (*table*)
  manifested by determination/tendency, 297–99
  viewed *re* God: their operations His goals, 296, 299n, 304
Finis cui, 282
Finis operantis, 282n
Finis operis, 283n, 316n
Finis qui or *cuius*, 282
Finis quo, 282
Flux (*see* Change)
Form:
  in authentic existentialism, 219
  as determinant, 63
  identified with reality: essentialism, 218–19
  ponit aliquid, 220
  re predicaments, 229 (*see also* Predicaments)
  re relation, 217–19 (*see also* Relation)
  substantial, 59–64, 66–67, 121–23, 128, 143
Formal/material causes, Aristotle, 236n
Formally certain proposition, 260, 289, 302
Forma totius, 228n
Forms or essences:
  in radical essentialism, 29–30
  and God, 32–33
  human soul's contact with, 29–30
Fundamental ontology, 380–87

G

Generic perfection (*see* Perfection)
Genus argument (*see* Real distinction)
Goal, 271–72, 279, 284 (*see also* Final cause)
God:
  all perfect, 137–38
  Aquinas, 74–75
  attributes, 136–37
  Augustine, 30n, 31n
  cause without cause, 135
  Collins, 137n
  esse at heart of His reality, 133n
  goal for human existent, 291–92
  re goodness of creatures, 171
  grounds essences, 112–13
  "He Who Is," 74
  infinitely perfect, 138
  is Actuality, 136–38
  is Beauty, 172
  is Knowledge, 169
  is Love, 170–71
  is Truth, 170n
  Plato, 33n
  Plotinus, 34–35
    not efficient cause, 246n
    contains no perfection of effects, 246n
  proper cause of existence, 248–51
  proved from evils, 180n
  proved to exist, 135–39
  proved by finality in non-cognitives, 299n, 305, 310–11
  in radical essentialism, 32–33
    proper cause of immutability, 249n
  in radical existentialism, 26–27
  Smart, 138–39
  sole cause in creation, 250–51
  spiritual or amaterial, 133n
  subsistent unity, 49n, 167n
  re transcendent truth, 169–70
Good (*see also* Transcendents)
  analogous, 171n
  Augustine, 175n
  contrasted with evil, 177–78
  extrinsic denomination *re* nonexistents, 281n
  known metaphysically, 171
  known spontaneously, 164
  moral, 171n
Good-as-known, 281, 283, 285, 294 (*see also* Finality *re* cognitive agents)
  cause without changing, 283
  object of appetitive powers, 292–94
Grammatical predications, 226–29 (*see also* Predicaments)
Gravity, 298n

H

Habit, operative, 14n
Habitus (*see* State)
Harmony:
  re co-operation between creatures/God, 251
Hermeneutics, 374, 381–84
History of philosophy:
  aid to philosophizing, 20n, 37
  as methodology in metaphysics, 12–13, 17–18
Humanity, a construct, 228n
Human parents:
  causes of body, 243n
  efficient "furnishing" causes *re* soul, 241n, 243n
Human soul:
  efficient causes of, 241n
  individuation of, 190
  mutable for Platonist, 32
  Plotinus, 34–35
  spiritual, 131, 135, 343n, 348
Hylomorphism, 42n

I

Ideal, 284n (*see also* Goal)
Imagination of artist, 314
Immanent activity (*see* Activity; Operation)
Immaterial, 131–33, 135 (*see also* Amateriality; Material; Spiritual)
  amaterial, 132–33, 135, 343n, 349

"barely" *vs.* "spiritual," 62n, 131–33, 343n
blanket description, 131
re natural components, 342–43 (*see also* Abstraction of natural components)
re sense cognition, 347n
spiritual, 62n, 131, 343n
Immediate insight, 330
Immutability (*see* Stability)
Indeterminacy in biology, 297n
Indeterminate/determinate:
re awarenesses (restrictive, transcendent), 161–63
re essence-argument, 76–77
Individual, 181–93, 197 (*see also* Supposit; Nature)
analogous, 188–89
contemporary thinkers, 186
re extramentals, 181
re intramentals, 181
meaning prior to divine revelation, 185n
modern education, 186n
re nature: "individuation," 188–93, 197
supposit, 181–87, 197
Cajetan/Maritain, 183–84
divinely revealed, 181–83, 185
primacy of existence, 187
Scotus, 183
Suarez, 183–85
De la Taille, 183–84
Individual existents:
combinations of change/stability, 36–37, 41
devaluated:
by radical essentialists, 34–35 (*see also* Radical essentialism)
by radical existentialists, 41
show themselves knowable, 36, 37
show themselves real, 36
starting point of metaphysics, 37
Individuality:
two sorts (supposit/nature), 186, 188, 197
Individuation:
in artifacts, 189–90
vs. individuality, 123n
none for Plato/Ockham, 193
principle of, 188–93, 197
from quantified (signate) matter, 190–91
radically from prime matter, 122–23, 188–93
four questions/answers, 190–93
of soul, 190
from substantial form, 191–93
Induction:
re Efficient Cause Proposition, 256–62 (*see also* Efficient Cause Proposition)
re Final Cause Proposition, 286–96, 300–305 (*see also* Final Cause Proposition)
through immediate insight, reflection, reasoning, 329–31
intellective, 51n, 330–31
through insight, 44n
kinds: intellective/rational/by enumeration, 329–33
for scholastic rationalists, 260n
Inference:
deduction/induction, 329
Infinite series, 136n
Innate ideas:
re "Principle of Causality," 252–55 (*see also* Efficient Cause Proposition)
re "Principle of Finality," 286–87 (*see also* Final Cause Proposition)
Instrumental agent, 240–41, 243, 247n, 248–50 (*see also* Efficient Cause)
Integral parts:
inadequate real distinction between, 181n
Intellection:
re existence/essence, 95
re matter/form, 60
re substance/accidents, 52
Intention, 277 (*see also* Tendency)

Intentional becoming, 326–27 (*see also* Knowledge)
Intentional being, 143–47
Intrinsic dependence (*see* Dependence)
Intrinsic/extrinsic, 88n, 235n
Intuition of being, 90–93, 393–99 (*see also* Real distinction)
  Maritain's *Existence and the Existent*, 397–99
    critique, 399
    explication of *Preface*, 397–98
  Maritain's *Preface to Metaphysics*, 393–97
    critique, 396–97
    negative/positive characteristics of, 394–96
"I-Thou" dialogue, 187n

J

Joy/contemplation: *re* beauty, 171–73
Judgment:
  existential, 95, 337, 344 (*see also* Existing, act of)
  negative, 323–25, 334, 335, 337
    not restricted to metaphysics, 337
    separation through extrinsic denomination, 347
  perceptual/intellectual, 329

K

Knowledge:
  abstraction in, 338–50 (*see also* Abstraction)
  cause of human openness, 201–2
  causes of:
    content-determining: *cognitum*, 325–26, 346–50
    efficient: cognitive powers, 325–26, 346–50
  of child *re* Efficient Cause Proposition, 259
  constructural/nonconstructural, 6n, 146n
  empiriological, 6n
  intentional becoming, 144–47, 326–27
  metaphysical *re* transcendents, 166–75
  nonconstructural, 238n
  operation *vs.* content, 144n
  operations of: apprehension, judgment, thinking, 326–33
    re existence/essence process, 336–37
    re matter/form process, 334–35
    re substance/accidents process, 333–34
  spontaneous *re* restrictive awarenesses, 161–62
  spontaneous *re* transcendents, 162–65
  twofold description, 325–50

L

Linguistic analysis, 363–73
Literature, 145
Logic, 206n
  involves "abstraction of addition," 340–41 (*see also* Abstraction)
Logical accident (*see* Accident)
Logical property (*see* Property)
Logician *re* predicaments, 99n, 229
Love:
  attraction/response, 283–84
  cause of human openness, 201–2
  determination of cognitive agent, 284
  efficiently caused by agent, 283–84, 285, 293 (*table*)
  re good, 164n, 171
  means of possessing God, 291–92
  not applied to noncognitive agents, 304n
  "outside of numbers," 10–11, 50, 56
  synonymous with desire, etc., 280n
  telic cause and effect, 293 (*table*)
  telically caused by good-as-known, 283–84
  tendency to goal, 284
  unlike other operations, 293

M

Material (*vs.* formal), 62–64
Material (*vs.* immaterial):
defined, 61–62
how predicated, 129–31
of act of existing, 131
of essence, 130
of essential components, 130
of quantity, 130n
of "that which," "that by which," 61–62, 130n
Material universe:
aggregation of appearances (Sartre), 24–26
mirrors Forms, 30
Plato, 29
Materialistic monism, 20
Mathematics, 206n
involves "abstraction of addition," 340–41 (*see also* Abstraction)
Matter:
re abstraction: a restricting factor in content of intellection, 348
factor in efficient-cause situation, 241
prime, 59–64, 66–67
cause of individuation, 122–23
defined, 59, 66
for essentialist, 218–19
how called "material," 130
known through intellection, 60, 66
metaphysical definition, 142–43
more direct cause of quantity, 122
not form, 219
a perfection, 116 (*see also* Perfection)
Pesch, 219n
principle of individuation, 174, 188–93, 197
pure potency, 61, 66, 105n, 219
as "that by which," 60
transcends perception, 60, 66
why so named, 61–64
second, 64, 243
signate, 347, 348 (*see also* Quantified matter)
re "abstraction of whatness," 338–39
"signed by quantity," 190n
Matter/form:
basis for "abstraction of whatness," 338–39
knowledge process described, 334–36
knowledge of, marked by "abstraction of natural components," 341–43 (*see also* Abstraction)
not synonymous with potency/act, 63n
Matter *vs.* form, 62–63
Mental distinction, 82 (*see also* Real distinction)
between essential perfections, 123n, 191–92
major, 123n, 192n
between predicaments, 227–28
between restrictive awarenesses, 161n
between transcendents, 163n
Mental relation, 206, 231
of cause to effect, 242n
Metaphysical knowledge:
primacy of existence in, 141–97, *especially* 141–43, 194
exemplified in definitions, 142–43
because re-presents act of existing, 141
re transcendents, 166–75
Metaphysics, 3–15, 321–51
Aristotle, *re* First Movers, 68n
current opponents, 4–7, 9, 13, 362–63, 366, 377–80, 384–85, 387–88
Collingwood, 5n, 321
definitions in antiquity, 3–4
distinct science, 9, 14, 349–50
formal object of, 13–14, 349
four classes of accidents, 142n, 230
Frick, 35
negative judgments not restricted to, 337
recognition of change, 37

science of beings as being, 336, 344, 349, 402
science of existents as existing, 14, 336, 344
unique because of separation, 323–25 (*see also* Separation)
valid science, 8–9, 321–51
conclusions summarized, 322–23
authentic existentialism, 323
Methodology:
Aquinas' *re* relations, 208–9
re efficient cause: inductive, 238–40
re final cause: inductive, 278–79
history of philosophy, 12–13, 17–18, 20n, 37
for kinds of analogy, 153, 156n
for metaphysics: observe actuals, 18–19, 37, 80–81
mistake in: from predicaments to existents, 224–26, 229n
of radical essentialism, 30
re real relations, 208–9
Middle Ages, 73
Mind: tendency to knowledge, 295
Mixed perfections (*see* Perfection[s])
Mode:
re relation (Coffey), 217–18, 223
re supposit (Cajetan, Suarez), 183–84
Modifications (*see* Change/stability)
specific, 56
substantial, 58–59
Monism (*see* Materialistic monism)
Moral evil, 178n
Motion, local:
Aristotle's definition, 54n, 244

N

Nature, 181–93 (*see also* Individual; Supposit)
philosophy of, 12, 29, 68, 99 (*see also* Philosophy)
Nausea, 27, 87n
Nonbeing, 85, 101
Nonentitative cohesion, 49n
Non-Thomists: on real relations, 207–8
Nuclear war, 307 (*see also* Chance)

O

Object:
formal/material, 14n
Objective value (*see* Value)
"One":
analogous, 167n
transcendent:
known metaphysically, 167
known spontaneously, 162–64
The One of Plotinus, 32, 33, 34–35
Ontic: synonym for "entitative," 49n
re abstraction: separation, 345
Openness:
actually experienced between ourselves, 210–11
in humans, through knowledge and love, 202
in subhumans, 201–2
Operation:
not a form, 219
one class of accidents, 230
synonymous with activity/act, 280n
transient/immanent, 240n, 245
Operations:
intellectual:
called abstraction through extrinsic denomination, 347
three kinds: apprehension, judgment, thinking, 328–33
Operative powers:
re noncognitives, 299, 310
in supernatural order, 292n
telic effects, because determinate tendencies, 291–93
Otherness, 181–94, 197 (*see also* Individual)
"Other than" (*see also* Individual):
transcendent:
known metaphysically, 167–68
known spontaneously, 162–63

P

Participation, 75n, 154n, 292n, 316n, 402

Parts:
constitutive, 45–46, 51–52, 59, 65
of accidental unity, 45, 53
called "principles," 53
indicated by diverse evidences, 43–44, 65
integral (physical), 46–47, 53, 181
intrinsic causes, 44, 51, 59, 120, 235
Passion (*see* Action)
Perception:
analogous, 152n
re existence/essence, 94–95, 101, 337 (*see also* Judgment, perceptual)
re matter/form, 60, 66, 335
re substance/accidents, 52, 66, 334
"Perfect," linked with good, 164n, 171
Perfection(s), 115–19 (*see also* Value)
re act of existing (source of all perfections), 117–19, 134
defined, 115–16
essential, 190–93
how distinct, 122–23, 192
not identical with act, 116–17
re prime matter, 116
pure, 116
re God, 136–38
specific:
from substantial form, 121
specific/generic, 122
three classes of (mixed, pure, transcendent), 116
Person: one kind of supposit, 187n (*see also* Supposit)
Personalism, 187n
Phenomenology, 373–76
Philosopher (*see* Thomistic philosopher)
Philosophy:
Christian, 185n
of morality:
abstraction in, 349 (*see also* Abstraction)
of nature, 29, 68, 99, 338n, 341–43
Aristotle's: inadequate, inaccurate, 42n
Frick, 35n
re predicaments, 229 (*see also* Predicaments)
uses "abstraction of natural components," 341–43 (*see also* Abstraction)
of subjectivity, 187n
Physical evil, 178n
Physics:
involves "abstraction of addition," 340–41 (*see also* Abstraction)
Place, 226n, 227
Positivism, 360–71
Possibles:
in authentic existentialism:
are nonbeing, 147–48
[essence/existence]-as-known, 148–49
real through extrinsic denomination, 88n
in natural theology, 148n
in radical essentialism, real because of immutability, 87n, 147–49
Possible/actual, 87
in radical essentialism, 87n
Posture (*situs*), 226n
Potency (*see also* Act/potency):
pure, 61, 66, 105n, 219
Pragmatism, 365–69
Predicaments, 224–30
Aristotle, 226n
in authentic existentialism, 226–30
based on grammatical predications, 226–29
defined, 226
grammatical "forms," 229
grammatical, not metaphysical, accidents, 228–29
have no function, 229–30
not constructs, 228
re relations:
Coffey, 224
Klubertanz, 224–26
Predictability, 238n
sequel of finality, 308n

Presence: virtual/formal, 47n, 58, 243
Primacy (*see* Existing, act of)
Principal agent, 240–41, 243, 247 (*see also* Efficient cause)
Principal/instrumental agents:
  re proper effect, 247, 248–50
  two sets of, 251n
Principle, 53 (*see also* Part, constitutive)
  of Causality, 251–55, 277 (*see also* Efficient Cause Proposition)
    self-evident through deduction, analysis of concepts, 251–54
  of Finality:
    Garrigou-Lagrange, 276–77
  of Identity, Contradiction, Sufficient Reason, 253–55
  of Indeterminacy, 297n
Probable (certain, doubtful) conclusions, 169n
Product: producer's goal realized, 290–91, 300–301
Programming:
  linked with purposeful activity, 274–75, 305, 310 (*see also* Teleonomy; Final cause)
Proper effect, definition of, 247 (*see also* Efficient cause)
Properties, really distinct from one another, 191–92
Property:
  logical, 55n
  not autodetermining, 125–26
  one kind of accident, 125
  really distinct from nature, 122n
Proportionality, analogy of:
  re God/creature, 155n
  re individuals of same species, 154
  proper *vs.* metaphorical, 155n
Proposition:
  re act/potency, 103–6
  re efficient cause, 251–62 (*see also* Efficient Cause Proposition)
  re intrinsic causes, 43–45
  principle or conclusion, 257n
  whole-part, 44n
Psychoanalysis, uses Efficient Cause Proposition, 261n
Psychology:
  Aquinas: based on actuals, 80n
Pure position in philosophy, 255n
Purpose, 268–70, 272, 275 (*see also* Final cause)
Purposeful activity, 274–75
Purposive striving, 271–72

Q

Quantified Matter, 174, 183 (*see also* Matter, signate)
Quantity:
  causes only three relations (bigger, smaller, equal), 222–23
  emanative causes of relations, 221
  how called "material," 130n
  in individuation, 190–93, 230
  more directly from prime matter, 122, 191–93
  not specific property, 122n
Quiddity (*see* Essence)

R

Radical essentialism, 29–37, 322
  "being" *re* intelligible universe, 145–46
  Coffey, 255n (*see also* Predicaments)
  consequences of, 31–34
  devaluates individuals, 34–35, 41
  re God, 31–33
    proper cause of immutability, 248n
  re law, 33
  McCormick, 254n (*see also* Efficient Cause Proposition)
  methodology of, 30–31
  re possibles, 145, 147–48
  reality *is* intelligibility, 218–19, 223
  re real relations, 207–8, 213, 214–15, 216–17, 218–19, 223
  resultant psychological state, 33
  signs of, 35n
Radical existentialism (*see* Existentialism)

"Real":
  caused by actual existence, 87, 89
  meaning, 86
  radical essentialists' view, 87n
    identified with form, 218
  various positions, 86–87
Real distinction:
  defined, 82–83
  between existence/essence, 73–102
    Aquinas' argument from essence, 76–79
    Aquinas' argument from genus, 75
    Maritain: intuition of being, 90–93, 393–400 (*see also* Intuition)
    two initial points, 81–86
    valid arguments, 86–94
  re integral parts, 181n
  kinds: major/minor, 82–83
  between properties, 191–92
  between relation and its *S, F, T*, 207–12, 227n
"Really real," 32
Real relation:
  accident, not accidental form, 219, 231
  distinct from *S, F, T*, 207–12, 231
    Aquinas, 208–9, 220
    how established, 210–12
  of effect to cause, 242
  identified with *S, F, T*, 212–24
    an abstraction, construct, 213
    Coffey, 214–16
    essentialism, 218–19
    imagination, use of, 218
    otherwise, absurdity and impossibility, 216–20
    otherwise, infinite relations, 221
    otherwise, *R* a form, 217–19
    otherwise, *R* dominated by *T*, 220–23
  multiple "respects," 222–23, 232
  not abstract, 223
  ponit ad aliquid, 220
  predicamental *vs.* transcendental, 229n
  quantitative: only three, 222–23
  quantity as emanative cause of, 221
  term as "presential cause," 221–22
  two positions, 204, 207, 242n
  unilateral/bilateral, 231n
    unilateral between effect/cause, 242n
Reasoning, 328, 331
  re Efficient Cause Proposition, 256–57, 261–63
  re Final Cause Proposition, 290–94, 296, 303–4
Reference, analogy of, 155–56
Reflection (*vs.* reasoning), 331
  re components, 335, 336, 337
  re Efficient Cause Proposition, 260, 261, 262
  re Final Cause Proposition, 289–90, 302–3, 331
Relation(s), 201–23 (*see also* Real relation)
  countless, 204
  foundation of, 205–6
  mental, 206, 213n, 231
  predicamental:
    Coffey, 224
  re predicaments, 224–30 (*see also* Predicaments)
  problem concerning, 205–7
  quantitative, 211n, 222n
  rationate, 206n, 213n (*see also* Mental relation)
  scholastic positions on, 209n
  subject of, 206
  term of, 206, 220–22
  transcendental, 229n
Relational situations, 205–6, 226–27
Relative chance (*see* Chance)
"Respects" of relations, 222–23
Revelation (*see* Divine revelation)

S

Sacred theology, 14
  abstraction in, 349n
Skepticism, 295

Science:
broadly defined, 8–9, 13–14
empiriological, 6, 9, 12 (*see also* Knowledge)
as operative habit, 13–14 (*see also* Object, formal and material)
rejection of finality, 267–70
restricted to quantitative, 6–7, 9 (*see also* Knowledge, empiriological)
as transcending the quantitative, 7–9, 10–12
Scientia, 13n
Self-evident (*see* Principle of Causality; Efficient Cause Proposition)
Sense appetites, 280n
Sense cognition:
immaterial, 347n
Separation:
Aquinas, 345n, 350n, 405–7
authentic view: absence of matter in content of metaphysical intellections caused by *cognita* actually without matter, 325, 344–45, 347–50 (*table*)
re "being" and other transcendents, 344–45
etymology of, 345n
inaccurate view: a negative judgment, 325
ontic abstraction:
caused by *cognita* actually immaterial, 344–45, 348 (*table*)
Thomists' opinions, 323–25
Similarity/diversity, 151–60, 194–95 (*see also* Analogy)
in actual existents, 151–53
Similarity of product to agent, 244–47
Situs (*see* Posture)
Specific ends, 296n
Specific modifications, 56, 58–59
Specific perfection, 58 (*see also* Perfection[s])
from substantial form, 61, 191, 192, 193
Specifying-individuating-individualizing, 115n, 127, 128, 134
Sperm/ovum, 243
instrumental, intrinsic causes of body, 243n, 246n
Spiritual, 62n, 131, 343n
re God, angels, 133n
Splendent, *re* beautiful, 171–73
Spontaneity (*see* Tendency)
Stability (*see also* Change):
factor in reality, 28, 36–37
heart of reality for Platonist, 29, 33–34
State (*habitus*), 226n, 227
Student:
Aquinas' function for, 81
"Stuff," 340–41
Suarezian essentialists (*see also* Suarez):
esse as mere efficiency, 77–78
re relations, 213, 214
Coffey, 214–18 (*see also* Relation[s])
Subject/object, 187n
Substance, 50–55, 65
autodetermining, 123–24
cause of accidents:
efficient and emanative, 124
definition, 51, 55, 66
etymology of, 52n
Hume: collection of ideas, 237n
known through intellection, 52, 66
re matter/form, 122n
metaphysical definition of, 142
a potency, 53–55
"that by which," 52, 53n
transcends perception, 52, 66
various meanings, 55
Substance/accidents:
basis for "abstraction of external characteristics," 339–40
knowledge of, marked by "abstractions of natural components," 342–43, 348 (*see also* Abstraction)
knowledge-process described, 333–34

Substantial change, 58–59
Substantial form, 59–64, 66–67
  an act, 60–61
  as cause of individuation, 191–93
  defined, 59, 66
  metaphysical definition of, 143
  self-individuating, 122–23, 174n, 193
  as "that by which," 60
Substantial level, 42, 55, 58
Sufficient reason (*see* Principle of)
Suicide, 56n
"Supernatural," 273
Supernaturalism, 278, 311
Supernaturalistic conclusion, 274
Supernatural order, 292n
Superstition, 273, 278, 311
Supposit, 181–87, 197 (*see also* Individual)
Syllogism, 51n

T

Teleology, 270–72, 273, 305 (*see also* Final cause)
  reduced to teleonomy, 275
Teleonomy, 275, 305, 310
Telic cause, 280n (*see also* Final cause)
Tendency, 276–77 (*see also* Final cause)
  applied to cognitive/noncognitive agents, 284–85, 304n
  in noncognitive agents, 297–99
  noncognitive agent's very entity, 290–91
  operative powers, 291–92
Term:
  presential cause of relation, 221–22
"That by which" (*id quo*), 53, 65 (*see also* Accident; Substance; Substantial form; Prime matter; Existence/essence)
"That which" (*id quod*), 65
  re existence/essence, 94
  re matter/form, 60
  re substance/accidents, 52
Thinking, 329–33
Thomistic philosopher, 81n
Thomistic psychology, 80n
  no place for intuition, 396
Thomists:
  on relations, 207, 213–14 (*see also* Relation[s])
  re separation/abstraction, 323–25
Time, 22, 226n, 227
  Augustine's remarks, 83
Total chance (*see* Chance)
Transcendental relation, 229n
Transcendents:
  known metaphysically, 166–75, 196
    "beautiful," 171–73
    "being," "one," "other than," 166–68 (*see also* Individual)
    "good," 171
    "true," 169–70
  known spontaneously, 161–65
    "good," "beautiful," "true," 164–65
    "real," "one," "other than," 162–64
    two causes, 165
  summary of, 173–75
Transcendents *vs.* transcendentals, 164n
Transient activity, 240n, 283
Transient operation:
  in agent and patient, 241–42
Trinity, 181–82 (*see also* Supposit)
"True" (*see also* Transcendent):
  known metaphysically, 168–70
  known spontaneously, 164–65
Truth:
  conformity, 168n
  viewed with/without God, 169–70

U

Unilateral relation (*see* Real relation)
Unity, 45–50, 65
  accidental:
    definition, 49
    evidences for, 46–48
  Aristotle's position, 45–50

re constitutive parts as real, 45
intrinsic (*per se*, essential):
definition, 49
evidences for, 46–48
re existence/essence as real, 94
on inanimate level, 49n
re matter/form as real, 59–60
re pure potency, 61n (*see also* Matter, prime)
re substance/accident as real, 51–52
togetherness *vs.* aggregation, 46
Universal: direct/reflex, 341
Universe:
actual/intentional, 144–47
dynamic, precarious, 311
extramental/intramental:
analogy of denomination, 156–57
Univocal cause, 245
Univocal meaning, 152n, 153n, 158–59

V

Value:
three sorts (arbitrary, subjective, objective), 86n
Virtues: theological/moral, 292n
Vulnerability, 201–4 (*see also* Openness)

W

Water, 20 (*see also* Thales)
Weather forecasting, 308n
Will, 280n
tendency to good, 295
Wonder, 18–19
Worth (*see* Value)